Also by Michael S Lief and
H. Mitchell Caldwell

The Devil's Advocates:
Greatest Closing Arguments in Criminal Law

Ladies and Gentlemen of the Jury:
Greatest Closing Arguments in Modern Law
(with Ben Bycel)

AND THE WALLS CAME TUMBLING DOWN

Greatest Closing Arguments
Protecting Civil Liberties

Michael S Lief
H. Mitchell Caldwell

A LISA DREW BOOK
SCRIBNER
New York London Toronto Sydney

A LISA DREW BOOK/SCRIBNER
1230 Avenue of the Americas
New York, NY 10020

First LISA DREW/SCRIBNER trade paperback edition 2006

SCRIBNER and design are trademarks of
Macmillan Library Reference USA, Inc., used under license
by Simon & Schuster, the publisher of this work.

A LISA DREW BOOK is a trademark of Simon & Schuster, Inc.

For information about special discounts for bulk purchases,
please contact Simon & Schuster Special Sales:
1-800-456-6798 or business@simonandschuster.com.

Text set in Bembo

Manufactured in the United States of America

1   3   5   7   9   10   8   6   4   2

Library of Congress Cataloging-in-Publication Data

Lief, Michael S
And the walls came tumbling down: greatest closing arguments protecting civil
liberties/Michael S Lief, H. Mitchell Caldwell.
p. cm.
"A Lisa Drew book."
Includes index.
1. Civil rights—United States—Cases—Popular works.
I. Caldwell, Harry M. II. Title.
KF4750.L54 2004
342.7308'5—dc22   2004045431

ISBN-13: 978-0-7432-4666-8
ISBN-10:   0-7432-4666-7
ISBN-13: 978-0-7432-4667-5 (Pbk)
ISBN-10:   0-7432-4667-5 (Pbk)

This book is dedicated to the memory of
Jack Harry Caldwell, 1922–2003, and
Marjorie Kay Caldwell, 1929–2004. Lives well lived.

And Corporal Harry (Weiner) Lief, U.S. Army, Troop E,
Third Cavalry, 1916–1923.
You're going to eat those eggs or wear them.

Acknowledgments

First thanks must go to our mentors and agents supreme, Maureen and Eric Lasher, and to our brilliant editor, Lisa Drew. We are pleased to note the contributions of the law students whose industry and creativity were the lifeblood of this work: Michael Blinde, Josh Stambaugh, William Bollard, Jason Barsanti, Charles Kenyon, Michael Cernovich, Kjirstin Graham, Susan Hill, and especially Charity Hansen.

We are also indebted to Mary Cosgrove of Phillips Nizer LLP, for providing the transcripts from the Faulk case; and to Mrs. Paul Conrad and the *Los Angeles Times* for graciously granting permission for us to include Paul's drawing of Karen Ann Quinlan.

Last—but by no means least—we must acknowledge our word processors and sounding boards: Lisa Schmidt, Candace Warren, Sheila McDonald, and Arlene Jakes.

Thank you all.

Contents

AND THE
WALLS CAME
TUMBLING
DOWN

Introduction

September 11, 2001. November 22, 1963. December 7, 1941. Americans of all ages remember where they were, what they were doing, when they first became aware of monstrous acts of murder and war. In an instant, everything changed. With a thunderclap—the whine of jet engines, a rifle shot, and the screams of the doomed—the nation loses its innocence yet again.

But not every momentous paradigm shift is announced by the thundering hoofbeats of the Four Horsemen of the Apocalypse.

Other events, more subtle, have changed the way we live. Profound, tectonic shifts in America's cultural, social, and legal landscape have taken place far removed in time and space from the glare of the media, experienced by a relative few who witnessed history being made. And, like a pebble tossed in a pond, these seemingly insignificant events—writ small upon a canvas larger than any could then imagine—send ripples out in ever-increasing circles, affecting us in ways impossible to foretell.

A woman walks into a voting booth, casts her ballot, and is arrested by the police for the crime of voting. An anguished family asks a doctor to let their daughter die with dignity, only to be told the law won't allow it, the patient's wishes be damned. State doctors decide a young woman they deem of below-average intelligence must not be allowed to pass her defective intellect on to her children and order her forcibly sterilized.

Years later, another woman casts her ballot without giving it a second thought and a man sits with his wife and signs a Do Not Resuscitate order before his operation. Every day millions of Americans enjoy the freedom to decide what they shall do with their property, their body, their speech, their vote, as a result of hard-fought battles won or lost over the last 150 years in courtrooms from Maine to California.

When our society has attempted to untangle the Gordian knots of slavery or the right to die, the political process has often proved unable or unwilling to address these complex issues. Stepping into the breech were the men and women of the bar. When legislators will not or cannot legislate, Americans have turned to the judicial system. And so lawyers and judges have often been the first to tackle some of the most vexatious dilemmas to confront this nation. With twenty-twenty hindsight, we can say that sometimes they got it right (freeing the *Amistad* slaves), and sometimes they got it wrong (sterilizing Carrie Buck). But, again with hindsight, we know that these trials have helped bring us closer to resolving profound and complex problems that have faced the American people.

The process has not changed over time. In the courtroom, the fundamentals of our democratic heritage and our future come together. It begins like this: The testimony is done; the witnesses have left. While the jurors sit waiting, an expectant hush falls over the room. The trial lawyer strides into the well and stands before them, pauses, then begins speaking. The jurors listen to the skillful interweaving of testimony, facts, storytelling, and analogy, some swept up in the words and rhythms of the advocate's argument, some taking notes, others just watching.

The argument reaches a climax as the attorney asks, sometimes demands, that the jurors do the right thing. Then they retire to mull over all that they've seen and heard. And when they return to the courtroom, the judge asks, "Have you reached a verdict?" The foreperson stands and answers, "We have, Your Honor."

Tension mounts. "What say you in the matter before this court?" As the answer echoes throughout the courtroom, the lives of all Americans are affected.

We have collected summations from trials that have, without overstating the case, changed the way we live our lives. The arguments we have chosen for this book deal with issues that have defined our civil rights. Selected for the impact they have had upon American society, these represent the finest work of lawyers still famous and others now little known to the modern reader.

We've edited many of the arguments for length. Our experiences in the courtroom have shown us that lawyers often go into fact-specific detail—necessary perhaps for the jurors, but adding nothing to the reader's understanding and enjoyment. Wielding as delicate a knife as possible, we've excised those portions, leaving behind these marvelous summations. And, of course, nothing has been added.

Until now, only the twelve jurors sitting in the box or the nine justices of the Supreme Court sitting on the bench have felt the full power of those words aimed at their hearts and minds. But now *you* can be in the courtroom, listen to some of the most important battles of all time, and ask, "What would *I* have done? How would *I* have voted?"

CHAPTER ONE

To Be or Not to Be

Karen Ann Quinlan and the Right to Die

Can anything be more degrading, than to be offered up as a living sacrifice to the materialistic and misguided belief that death can somehow be cheated, if only we find the right combination of wires and gauges, transistors and tubes?

—*Paul W. Armstrong, attorney for Karen Ann Quinlan*

If Karen Ann Quinlan has one chance in a thousand, if she has one chance in ten thousand, if she has one chance in a million, who are we and by what right do we kill that chance? Who are we and by what right do we kill that life?

—*Ralph Porzio, attorney for Karen Ann Quinlan's doctors*

Living wills. DNR orders. Extraordinary measures. Americans hear the terms every week, courtesy of TV shows like *ER,* yet their very familiarity serves to hide the tragedy behind their origin. Joseph and Julia Quinlan lost a daughter, and in the process Americans gained the right to control, if not always the time, then the manner of their own passing.

The Quinlans were a young, middle-class couple when they moved from western New York to Landing, New Jersey, in 1953. Devout Catholics, they hoped for a home filled with the sounds of many children, but Julia suffered several miscarriages and a stillbirth. Adoption seemed the answer to their prayers, and in 1954 they decided to bring a baby girl, Karen Ann, into their home. When the nun from Catholic Charities handed the baby to Julia, she said, "Although this baby comes to you through us, she is a gift from God." The Quinlans loved their daughter, and although Julia was able to give birth to two children after the adoption, Karen Ann would serve as the focal point of the family for the remainder of her life.

On April 15, 1975, Karen Ann, then twenty-one, was out with her roommates for a birthday celebration. They went to a roadside tavern, where Karen Ann had several drinks and soon began acting strangely—as if she were about to pass out. Her friends would later note at the hospital that they didn't think Karen Ann had had enough alcohol to get so drunk. What they didn't know was that Karen Ann, for some unknown reason, had consumed a lethal mix of barbiturates and alcohol.

They loaded their staggering friend into the car and set off for home, Karen Ann continually nodding off in the backseat. When they arrived, her roommates carried her upstairs and put her to bed, then went downstairs to talk. Later, when they went to check on her, they found her on the bed, not breathing. The sedatives and liquor had induced cardiac arrest.

Her frantic roommates began trying to save Karen Ann's life, one giving her mouth-to-mouth resuscitation, while another called the paramedics. Karen Ann began to turn blue, and not until a policeman arrived and administered mouth-to-mouth did she begin breathing on her own; however, she did not regain consciousness and would never awaken.

When the doctors in the emergency room at Newton Memorial Hospital examined Karen Ann, her temperature was one hundred degrees, her pupils did not react to light, and she did not respond to pain. Joseph and Julia Quinlan rushed to the hospital to be by Karen Ann's side. When Julia kissed her daughter on the forehead, she hoped Karen Ann was only in a deep sleep and would awaken the next morning.

Three days later, Dr. Robert Morse examined Karen at the request of the admitting physician. He found her comatose, suffering from damage to the cortex of the brain, causing her to lie with her arms flexed and her legs extended, breathing with the assistance of a respirator. Dr. Morse was unable to obtain what he considered an adequate account of the circumstances leading up to Karen Ann's admission to the hospital—he would later testify that this knowledge is crucial in neurological diagnosis. Forced to rely upon scant hospital records and his own examination, he concluded that her condition was most likely due to a prolonged lack of oxygen in the bloodstream.

When Karen Ann was transferred to St. Clare's Hospital in Denville, New Jersey, she was still unconscious and still on a respirator, and a tracheotomy had been performed. Dr. Morse conducted an electroencephalogram (EEG) to measure the electrical activity of the brain; the results were "abnormal but it showed some activity and was consistent with her clinical state." Other significant neurological tests, including a brain scan, an angiogram, and a lumbar puncture, were normal.

Morse explained that there are basically two types of coma, sleeplike unresponsiveness and awake unresponsiveness. Karen Ann was originally in a sleeplike unresponsive condition but soon developed "sleep-wake" cycles, apparently a normal improvement for comatose patients occurring within three to four weeks. In the awake cycle, she blinked and cried out but was still totally unaware of anyone or anything around her.

Karen Ann's condition was characterized as a "persistent vegetative state." Her body was able to maintain the simple, "mechanical" parts of neurological functioning, but her brain was not functioning on a higher, intellectual level. Patients in a vegetative state are unconscious and unaware, but the primitive portions of the brain that control body temperature, blood pressure, chewing, swallowing, sleeping and waking, still function. Essentially, the part of Karen Ann's brain that controlled that which made her human—talking, feeling, singing, and thinking—had died.

Karen Ann was fed through a nasogastric tube inserted through the nose and down into her stomach. She was living at a primitive reflex level, and the little brain-stem functioning that she retained was inadequate to control her breathing. Therefore, she required a respirator.

Unlike the stereotypical notion of a comatose person lying still like Sleeping Beauty, Karen Ann was often in motion, although unaware of her surroundings. Patients—like Karen Ann—in a chronic vegetative state may react to certain stimuli, change their facial expressions, even move their limbs, but these actions are linked to a state of "wakefulness without awareness." Although her eyes could move, they could not fix on a stationary object, let alone follow a moving target.

Karen Ann's skin was pale and she was almost constantly sweating, often profusely. She would sometimes respond with a grimace to painful stimuli, followed by an increased stiffness in her arms and legs. Further stimulation would result in blinking, eye-opening, and random eye movements. Karen Ann would experience periodic contractions and spasms, and sometimes she would yawn widely. Rashes erupted on her body, and nurses constantly moved, positioned, and bathed her.

When first confronted with Karen Ann's condition, Julia prayed to God to return her daughter to her and her husband, regardless of the risk of irreversible brain damage. But, as time went on, Julia began accepting the inevitable. By late May, six weeks after Karen Ann had been admitted to the hospital, Julia came to believe that it was the will of God to summon Karen Ann at this early age to heaven. Julia recalled ominously prophetic remarks Karen Ann had made to her—incongruous remarks for a young, healthy girl to make. Karen had asked her mother to be sure to donate her eyes to an eye bank if she died, and she had said on more than one occasion to both her mother and an assortment of friends that she would die young and go down in history.

Julia, struggling with her faith, consulted her parish priest—and friend—the Reverend Tom Trapasso. Julia told him of her increasing sense that perhaps sustaining Karen Ann's life through the use of a respirator was inconsistent with God's will.

Trapasso believed this was "a classic case of a hopeless life being prolonged unnecessarily through the use of extraordinary means." He explained that the Catholic faith does not morally obligate the faithful to prolong life by extraordinary means. This belief finds its roots in the sixteenth century, and the advent of medicine as a science. The question arose as one of medical ethics in an era when anesthesia did not yet exist.

Suppose a person's arm or leg became fatally diseased and required amputation to save the life of the patient. Was the patient obligated to submit to the unendurable pain of this surgery to sustain life? The Catholic Church reasoned no. A person without benefit of anesthesia might choose to die as opposed to subjecting himself to a painful procedure that itself might cause death. Amputation without anesthesia was considered "extraordinary means," and a patient might refuse it, even if refusing the procedure would cost the patient his life.

Julia Quinlan had never heard of this concept of extraordinary means before, and she asked the priest if he believed that the respirator sustaining Karen's breathing constituted such extraordinary means. Trapasso replied that he had no doubt that it did. His opinion was based on an address given by Pope Pius XII to a group of anesthesiologists in 1957. The pope said that when there is no hope of recovery, there is no moral obligation to prolong life by using technological medical devices. Trapasso presented Julia with the following analogy:

> Often a terminally ill patient, in pain or blessedly unconscious, has a disease that is being held back by a technologically designed dam. Nature is demanding death, and the dam is preventing it from happening. If you make the decision that there is no need to keep the dam in place and it is taken away, then the process of nature just takes place.
>
> Now this decision is not without its moral implications. You have to ask if, by keeping the dam in place, you are allowing this person to continue to live a human life. Or is the dam retained simply because of some kind of obligation to keep the purely biological organism functioning? If that is the case, then there is no longer respect for life, for the dignity of human life.

While Julia had come to accept that Karen Ann's death was inevitable, it took longer for Karen Ann's father, Joe, and younger siblings, John and

Mary Ellen, to come to terms with her condition. Joe was a World War II veteran who worked in accounting at Warner-Lambert in Morris Plains, New Jersey. He would eventually become the final holdout. Joe desperately clung to signs that Karen Ann might emerge from her coma. One day it might be reflexive blinking of her eyes when he held his hand close to her face, the next an idea that if she could be slowly weaned from the respirator and the family took her to Arizona, the fresh air might restore her.

But even Joe couldn't ignore what was happening to Karen Ann's body. A reporter who was allowed to visit Karen Ann described her:

> Her [seventy-pound] body was a small, rounded mound concealed under a sheet [at the time of the accident and upon admission to the hospital she had weighed 115 pounds]. All that was exposed were her head and hands. The hands were drawn tight over her chest, the wrists sharply cocked so that the long, white fingers pointed straight downward, stiff and thin as pencils. Karen's head was in constant movement, straining back and forth in an erratic and swiveling motion—as though seeking relief from her rigid body. The eyes, still intensely blue, roved wildly, never quite focusing, and her mouth closed and opened in a series of grimaces that gave the impression she was soundlessly crying out in anguish. Her once tawny, sun-streaked hair was short and curled in damp wisps around her cheeks and forehead. Her jaw had receded . . . causing Karen's upper teeth to bite into her lower lip; as a result, the teeth had been encased in a protective plastic mold. She was attached to a series of machines and hanging bottles by a variety of tubes: two thin ones into her nostrils fed her; another delivered antibiotics directly into her kidneys; a transparent, hoselike tube was attached to her upper chest, sputtering and gurgling as it pumped air from a respirator into Karen's lungs. Occasionally, she would emit a low moaning sound.

Joe Quinlan met with the Reverend Tom Trapasso in mid-July, when the priest assured him the Catholic Church did not require that Karen Ann be kept on the respirator. In late July 1975, two weeks after his meeting with the priest, and two months after his wife had come to the same decision, Joe Quinlan made up his mind:

> She has permanent brain damage and she is going to die. I didn't know why this could happen, but I thought again—it is God's will. He has a plan for everything, so there had to be a reason. You can fight doctors, and you can fight nature and even fate, and you can say

all of them, every one of them, is dead wrong. But you can't fight God's will, and as I tried to sleep, I knew what I was meant to do.

From now on, a united Quinlan family would fight a theological, medical, and legal battle to end the "extraordinary means" keeping their Karen Ann alive. In her case, this meant unhooking her from a respirator.

The MA-1 respirator was a gray box, three feet deep, two feet wide, and about two and a half feet high. A plastic tube connected to the box was siphoned through a pumping container and then connected into a plastic cuff taped to a surgical opening just above the patient's breastbone. Mary Ellen, Karen's sister, remarked, "It just seems like such a cold machine, and it seems to be more alive than Karen."

The Doctor's Refusal

On July 31, 1975, three and a half months after their daughter had lost consciousness, the Quinlans met with Karen Ann's treating doctors and hospital officials to discuss removing the respirator. Joe and Julia Quinlan said they wanted their daughter restored to a natural state, and the hospital drafted an authorization form to that effect; it directed Dr. Morse to discontinue all extraordinary measures, including the use of a respirator, and it released the hospital and any physicians involved from any liability. Julia would testify at trial that she remembered the doctors signing the authorization, but when the document itself was examined, no doctors' signatures were found.

The Quinlans believed that the respirator would be disconnected, their wishes honored. But Dr. Morse faced moral dilemmas of his own. The thirty-six-year-old neurologist was—like the Quinlans—a Catholic, and he also had a daughter named Karen Ann. While his personal sympathies lay with the Quinlans, his professional obligation to Karen Ann was that he honor the Hippocratic oath: "If any shall ask of me a drug to produce death, I will not give it," and therefore do no harm to his patient.

Morse understood the Quinlans had come to view the use of the respirator as extraordinary means, sustaining Karen Ann's life and preventing the natural process of dying. However, he believed that, as a physician, he must view it as a life-sustaining instrument, even though the life it was sustaining was a hopelessly, irreversibly vegetative life. Morse knew Karen Ann might well be liberated from the machine only to gasp for air and thrash her arms and legs as she suffocated over several long minutes. Could he, as a doctor sworn to do no harm, permit this? Morse refused to disconnect the respirator.

The stage was thus set for *In re Quinlan,* a trial that would make Karen Ann Quinlan a macabre Sleeping Beauty celebrity and answer a question that had confounded lawyers, theologians, and philosophers over the centuries: Does each of us possess an inalienable right to die?

In the fall of 1975, Americans joined the debate.

Euthanasia through the Ages

The "right to die" debate was hardly new, but the concept had metamorphosed over time, garnering support and popularity as a means of ending suffering, but also viewed by some as homicide, manslaughter, and even murder.

While euthanasia is today commonly defined as mercy killing by a physician, in the nineteenth century it referred more to the experience of the patient. It was a "good death" for a patient: "good death" was the literal translation from the Greek of *euthanasia,* a term coined by the English philosopher Francis Bacon in the seventeenth century. Indeed, if there was any dilemma surrounding euthanasia as it was perceived in the nineteenth century, it was merely how best to provide the means for that "good death."

One Philadelphia surgeon in 1894 said, "Where there is no hope . . . it should be a grateful and sacred duty, nay, it should be the highest triumph of the physician to minister unto the wants of a dying fellow creature by effecting the Euthanasia."

Yet by the twentieth century, the focus was no longer on the patient's state of mind, but on the doctor's decision whether it would be appropriate to hasten death. As medical technology became more sophisticated, so too did the physician's ability to prolong life—and suffering.

In 1906, when an Ohio legislator unsuccessfully attempted to introduce a bill legalizing euthanasia, it was clear that the concept was no longer viewed as a "good death." "Shall we legalize homicide?" one newspaper editorial asked. Another decried "the awful frank cruelty and crudity" of euthanasia. Similar voluntary euthanasia bills were introduced in Florida and Idaho in 1967 and 1969 respectively, both ultimately failing to become law.

Historical developments of the late 1930s and the early 1940s did little to help euthanasia's cause. While the Euthanasia Society of America (ESA) campaigned vigorously for mercy killing, the onset of World War II undermined the group's efforts, as rumors filtered out of occupied Europe that the Nazi regime had instituted a program to kill off the unfit. The Nazis were practicing eugenics, as opposed to euthanasia. While euthanasia is a form of mercy killing, eugenics is an attempt to strengthen the gene pool by weeding out persons deemed mentally, physically, or genetically inferior.

The Euthanasia Society tried to dissociate itself from the taint of eugenics; however, many of the ESA's members were ardent believers in the practice. As the atrocities of the Holocaust came to light, eugenics became associated with euthanasia and the two became taboo.

Between the 1930s and 1960s, trials involving mercy killings arrived at differing verdicts and conclusions. It seemed that euthanasia born of passion and emotion might be tolerated while, ironically, the objective and methodical decision of a trained medic would be punished as murder.

John Stephens, thirty-two, was allegedly so devoted to his terminally ill aunt, Allie Stephens, a former mission-board worker, that he sat by her bed during much of her illness. In 1933, overcome at the sight of the pain she suffered as a result of her bone cancer, he crushed her skull with a flowerpot. He confessed that he wanted to "hasten her death from the torture she was undergoing." Stephens was acquitted of "mercy slaying" by a coroner's jury. The jury found that his aunt had died of natural causes created by her hopeless illness, that the blow to the head was superficial, and that she would have survived only a few more hours due to the cancer. The victim's brother-in-law and sister both testified they had heard the woman say she hoped someone would kill her if her illness became hopeless, and Stephens testified that his aunt had pleaded with him to kill her.

In 1939, Louis Greenfield chloroformed his seventeen-year-old retarded son, whom he had been nursing for seventeen years. He was acquitted of manslaughter charges.

And then there was Carol Paight, whom the February 13, 1950, edition of *Newsweek* dubbed the Father Killer. Paight, a tall, blond twenty-one-year-old from Stamford, Connecticut, had learned that her father, a police sergeant, would die of cancer within the next three months. She got in her father's car, took his revolver from the glove compartment, picked up her mother, and drove to the hospital to visit her dying father. Paight ran ahead of her mother to her father's room, where he was sleeping after exploratory surgery. Paight fired one fatal shot into her father's head, then calmly walked into the hallway and asked a nurse to look at her father.

Paight did not become histrionic until the police arrived, when she declared that she "had to do it," that she couldn't "bear to see him suffering." Paight was then herself hospitalized for shock. When she awakened, she asked in a calm voice, "Is Daddy dead yet? I can't ever sleep until he is dead." Paight's mother said her daughter had "the old Paight guts" and that Carol had only done what she herself would have done if she had had the courage. On October 1, eight days after the shooting,

Paight was arraigned on a charge of second-degree murder. At her trial forty-seven witnesses were called by the defense, thirty of them character witnesses. Mrs. Paight spoke of her daughter's happy home life and of the abiding love between father and daughter. She also pointed out that many in the Paight family had succumbed to cancer and that her daughter suffered from a "cancer phobia" of sorts.

When Paight herself took the stand, she clutched a small crucifix and a white handkerchief. She testified that she remembered being told that her father had cancer, waking up the next day, and nothing else. She was found not guilty. The jury of nine mothers and three fathers deliberated for less than five hours.

By contrast, Dr. Hermann Sanders's trial in 1949 generated more controversy. Sanders injected oxygen into the vein of his terminally ill patient Abbie Burroto, who had been bedridden with cancer for many months. Sanders did not argue that his actions were justified; his defense simply took the position that Sanders's injection of 40 cc of oxygen was not the proximate cause of Burroto's death. While Sanders was acquitted, his trial was long and highly publicized, generating substantial debate on the editorial pages of newspapers.

By the mid-1950s, public opinion was shifting toward an individual's right to die, including a subtle semantic change. Euthanasia was no longer perceived as the nineteenth-century "good death"; now, the question of euthanasia had become more complex, not primarily concerned with the doctor's choice of which remedies to implement, but focused on the patient's experience. Moreover, euthanasia was no longer viewed as merely some beatific, heavenly "good death." It was now being perceived by some as a right to die, and people wished to fight, to their own death if necessary, to protect this right.

But what exactly was this right to die? Karen Ann Quinlan would provide the answer.

Legal Recourse—the Only Option

When Joe Quinlan initially sought help at the Legal Aid office, he was refused assistance because he made too much money, but Joe said it was for his daughter who was unemployed, and more importantly unconscious. He was ushered into the office of Legal Aid lawyer Paul Armstrong and spent the remainder of the evening explaining to the young attorney what he wanted. Armstrong was thirty years old and, to Joe, "looked like an elongated schoolboy from a rich Ivy League preparatory school."

Joe Quinlan wanted Armstrong's legal help to have Karen Ann disconnected from life support, but to make such a decision on her behalf Joe Quinlan had to become Karen Ann's guardian.

Armstrong took two weeks to make his decision. He, like the Quinlans, was a devout Catholic and felt, by his own admission, "a compelling desire to take the case." But there were other considerations. How would Armstrong argue for the Quinlans' right to disconnect Karen Ann from the respirator? There was the First Amendment, which guarantees the free exercise of religion. Karen Ann and her parents were staunch Catholics. Shouldn't they, reasoned Armstrong, be allowed to honor their religious beliefs, free of government intervention, and allow their daughter to die a natural death unimpeded by extraordinary means?

Armstrong then considered the constitutional right of privacy—the right of people to make decisions affecting themselves, in circumstances where there is no danger to society at large. That might be his second argument. But before Armstrong could consider how he would proceed, he had to decide if he was up to the challenge; he was only two years out of Notre Dame Law School. Moreover, Armstrong realized that this case would take all of his time and energy.

The young attorney, a newlywed, working toward a postlaw degree in constitutional rights at New York University night school, realized that he would not only have to drop out of his academic program but also leave his job for perhaps the next year and a half, devoting himself solely to the Quinlans' plight. He also knew immediately that despite the Quinlans' protestations to the contrary, he would not under any circumstances accept money from his prospective clients.

After consulting with his wife and poring over their meager finances, the Armstrongs decided together that Paul should take the case. His wife would keep her job as a librarian—and act as her husband's secretary too—and they would sell off a small cache of stock as the need arose. Finally, Armstrong withdrew from his graduate classes. As the Quinlans put it succinctly in their book *Karen Ann,* "There would no longer be time [for Armstrong] to study constitutional law. His goal, instead, was to change it."

Joe Quinlan remembered Armstrong's words when the attorney called to say he'd take the case without a fee, adding, "Just the privilege of helping in a noble cause . . . is enough."

Armstrong filed his first documents on September 12, 1975, and the media immediately moved in. Karen Ann Quinlan seemed an improbable celebrity.

Who knew that Karen Ann Quinlan from Landing, New Jersey, would be sharing headlines that September with a crowd as disparate as Patricia

Hearst (recently arrested after her nineteen-month captivity with the Symbionese Liberation Army) and Squeaky Fromme (her Charles Manson murder days behind her, she had moved on to presidential assassination attempts, setting her sights on President Gerald Ford)?

Basically, the Karen Ann Quinlan case posed three fundamental questions. Should a person such as Karen Ann, languishing in a "persistent vegetative state," be considered alive? Where was the line drawn between the state's responsibility to protect life and an incompetent patient's right to end life-prolonging treatment? And finally, who should make these decisions—parents, doctors, or judges? During the five weeks between Armstrong's filing of the Quinlans' petition to have Joe appointed as Karen Ann's guardian and the actual start of the trial—at which one judge without assistance of a jury would decide Karen Ann's fate—the national debate began.

The Quinlans received thousands of letters during these weeks. So well-known was the case that some communications that the family received were simply addressed "To Karen Ann Quinlan's Family— USA." Most people who wrote to the Quinlans sympathized with their plight. These people also had terminally ill relatives and hoped the Quinlans would be able to end their child's suffering. However, those who wrote to Karen Ann's hospital seemed for the most part to propound the agenda that "where there's life, there's hope."

The Trial

When the trial began, the Morris County Courthouse was packed. In a pretrial order, Judge Robert Muir, Jr., instructed that no cameras, television, radio, or sound equipment would be permitted in the courthouse. He also ruled that attendance during the hearings would be limited to the courtroom's seating accommodations, and that news media would not be permitted inside the bar railing. The first row was reserved for parties to the lawsuit, witnesses, and assistants to attorneys participating in the proceedings for whom there was no place at counsel table. The second, third, and fourth rows were reserved for accredited representatives of the news media, who would be admitted to the courtroom upon presentation of credentials, and all other seats behind the bar railing were available to members of the public in the order of their appearance.

Inside, the two sides appeared unevenly matched. While the Quinlans were represented by one attorney, Armstrong, the defense boasted an array of lawyers, each representing a different party interested in sustaining Karen Ann's life. There was New Jersey attorney general William Hyland, present on behalf of the state to prevent the "execution" of

Karen Ann Quinlan. Morris County prosecutor Donald Collester said in his opening statement that sympathy for the Quinlans had to be outweighed by the duty to preserve life. The medical community was represented as well, Ralph Porzio appearing on behalf of Karen Ann's doctors, Morse and Arshed Javed. Theodore Einhorn, the attorney for St. Clare's Hospital, hoped the court would give the medical community some indication that they might use their more advanced medical criteria to determine if a person is dead without fear of criminal or civil prosecution. Finally, the court-appointed guardian for Karen Ann, Daniel Coburn, was present to argue that she be kept alive. Pursuant to New Jersey statutory procedure, Coburn had been appointed by the court to be Karen's guardian ad litem, or her guardian "for purposes of the suit." During his appointment, he was to be available for consultation with Drs. Morse and Javed as to the care and treatment of Karen Ann.

The courtroom reminded Julia Quinlan of a church, with its high ceilings and "red cushions like pews" as she took her seat. Next to her sat Joe, the Reverend Tom Trapasso, Karen's sister, Mary Ellen, and several close friends, also members of the clergy. Behind them sat twenty rows of reporters, the rest of the benches filled with curiosity seekers who had waited four hours in the rain to get in. Along the sides of the courtroom were artists who would make sketches for television and newspapers.

Armstrong had to overcome two large stumbling blocks if he was to win. One would be based in historical precedent. The atrocities of the Nazis were still fresh. Would a decision in favor of the Quinlans create a "slippery slope" effect? If Karen Ann was allowed to die, where would society draw the line against the extermination of others who were judged not to be enjoying sufficient quality of life? Ralph Porzio, the attorney representing Karen Ann's doctors, finished his opening statement with "And so . . . once you make a decision [for the Quinlans], I think it is like turning on the gas chamber."

The other problem for Armstrong was based in legal precedent, namely the case of *Kennedy Memorial Hospital v. Heston*. In that case, a twenty-two-year-old girl (Heston) had suffered a ruptured spleen in a car accident. When she was brought to the hospital, she was in shock. Doctors determined she would die unless they operated immediately. Both Heston and her mother were Jehovah's Witnesses, and their religion prohibited the blood transfusion necessary for the operation. Heston's mother, upholding the tenets of her faith, refused the transfusion on her daughter's behalf. The hospital then arranged for a court-appointed guardian to authorize the transfusion. Heston survived and later sued the hospital, claiming it had violated her rights of self-determination and religious freedom. The New Jersey Supreme Court, in a unanimous decision, disagreed, saying that Heston's personal rights were outweighed by the state's interest in preserving life. Clearly the *Heston* decision undercut Armstrong and the Quinlans.

Armstrong decided not to attack the defense on the eugenics issue; if his opponents wanted to analogize Karen Ann to a Holocaust victim, he'd agree with them. Karen Ann wasn't a victim of genocide, however; rather, she was a victim of medical technology. Armstrong told the court during his opening statement, "The time of life is over [for Karen Ann], and . . . further treatments merely hold her back from the realization and enjoyment of a better, more perfect life." Karen Ann's First Amendment rights were being violated. She had a right to free exercise of religion, and Joe Quinlan should be appointed her guardian so that she might exercise this freedom and be disconnected from the respirator.

But Armstrong did not stop there. Karen Ann was also being deprived of her Eighth Amendment right not to suffer cruel and unusual punishment. Armstrong sought to extend this proscription, which had traditionally been reserved to prohibitions against criminal sanctions, to a medical and physiological setting. Although her pain was not inflicted by the state, Armstrong asserted if the state decided to keep her in that situation, it would constitute cruel and unusual punishment.

In addition, Armstrong argued that Karen Ann's right of privacy was being violated. This was a particularly astute—and possibly controversial—argument for Armstrong to present because the U.S. Supreme Court in *Roe v. Wade* (1973) had recently found a right of privacy for women in cases involving contraception and abortion.

Following opening statements, Armstrong called both doctors to the witness stand. First was Dr. Morse, Karen Ann's principal physician. While Armstrong used Morse to prove that the prognosis for Karen Ann was hopeless and the respirator should thus be unplugged, the attorneys on the other side used him to establish that sometimes miracles happen, but even if they don't, treatment is appropriate so long as a patient remains alive. The defense was successful in creating the vivid impression that Morse and his colleagues, consummate professionals, were performing these life-sustaining practices for the benefit of Karen Ann, because they cared for her and her family, as they did for all of their patients.

Armstrong, in an effort to reinforce the idea that Karen Ann's life was effectively over, called Dr. Julius Korein to the stand. Korein, ten years older than Morse and far more self-assured, was a New York University professor, chief of the EEG laboratories at Bellevue Hospital, and author of countless medical articles. Armstrong hoped Korein would bring the compelling voice of medical experience to the fore. Unfortunately, for all his credentials and accomplishments, Korein was a terrible witness. He was aloof, dispassionate, and insufferably addicted to professional jargon. Korein's efforts to convince Judge Muir that Karen Ann should be disconnected were unpersuasive.

The case for the Quinlans was off to a poor start; it was time for Armstrong to call his strongest witnesses, Joe and Julia Quinlan. First, Joe was called to the stand, speaking so quietly that his voice was often barely audible.

"It was most difficult . . . and it took almost six months for me to personally arrive at a decision," he explained to Judge Muir. Joe said that when he realized that Karen Ann's situation was irreversible, he wanted only to disconnect the respirator and leave the rest to God. "This is what I want to do," concluded Joe Quinlan, ". . . physically take her off the machine, remove all the tubes from her body, since she's going to die anyway, and place her completely in the hands of the Lord."

Joe Quinlan's heartfelt testimony—an articulate, broken man speaking simply and from the depths of profound sadness—was powerful and effective. When one of the opposing lawyers asked Joe to define his understanding of "extraordinary means," he answered, "The only [extraordinary means] I know of is the machine, but I understand there's a lot of other gadgets."

Julia followed her husband, and she too spoke from the heart for herself, as well as Karen Ann. Julia described two incidents when Karen Ann had made her position on life-sustaining measures clear, the first when an aunt was dying of breast cancer, the second when her friend's father was dying of a brain tumor: "[Karen Ann] was very full of life, a very active young girl, and she had always said that if she was dying, 'Mommy, please don't ever let them keep me alive by extraordinary means,' or in any way that she could not really enjoy her life to the fullest."

Both Quinlans testified that when they had first presented their desire to have Karen Ann disconnected from the respirator, they had thought Dr. Javed agreed with them. They both stated that they thought he had, in a sense, advised them to do just that. Although Dr. Javed vehemently denied that he had ever given the Quinlans this advice, it made the parties opposed to Karen Ann's natural death appear untrustworthy.

The press portrayed the Quinlans as "shocked," "saddened," and "breaking down frequently." Julia was the "slender, red-haired homemaker . . . wobbly legged . . . [making her way] . . . from the courtroom with tears welling in her eyes." With Joe and Julia's heart-wrenching testimony, Karen Ann was now front-page national news.

"Dad: Put Karen in Lord's Hands," read the *Daily News* on October 22, 1975, and a forty-point banner topped the *Los Angeles Times:* "Mommy Don't Keep Me Alive."

On the third day of the trial, the Reverend Tom Trapasso took the stand and stressed the importance of the afterlife, how this life's significance was dwarfed when viewed in the more panoramic perspective of the hereafter. In such a context, death "with dignity" became a more important consideration, the priest said, going on to tell the court of Pope Pius XII's views on euthanasia.

The defense team found themselves in a quandary. Trial attorneys must be extremely cautious when cross-examining a priest and questioning the papal authority that he represented and upon which he expounded. Ralph Porzio, the doctors' attorney, tried. He reasoned that because Pope Pius XII's dicta specifically said that the Church was not in a position to decide whether a person in a persistent vegetative state was dead, it could not be considered a venial or mortal sin to continue Karen Ann's life-sustaining treatments. Trapasso had to agree that this seemed logical.

Donald Collester, the county prosecutor, went a step further. If Karen was still alive, for all intents and purposes, wasn't her soul still inside her body? Trapasso agreed that, yes, "the source of life . . . the thing that, theologically anyway, distinguishe[d] a corpse from a living human being" was still within her.

Both Porzio and Collester questioned the priest about the authoritative nature of the pope's 1957 address. Without specifically inquiring into the pope's infallibility, the attorneys tried to explore the nature of a papal bull, an *allocutio,* an encyclical, or any general statement by the pope. They attempted to elicit testimony from Trapasso that this particular address, given on a particular occasion, to a particular group of people, was rather inconsequential to the Catholic world at large in outlining the Church's theological framework. In other words, they wanted testimony to the effect that in this address, the pope was not speaking *ex cathedra,* or from the throne, and therefore this statement was not infallible. As a consequence, his address would be subject to interpretation. This matter of interpretation, of course, would center on the words *ordinary* and *extraordinary.*

Armstrong also called the Reverend Pat Caccavalle, the chaplain of St. Claire's Hospital, to the stand. He testified that in a meeting with the Quinlans in mid-July he had advised them of the pope's address, just as Trapasso had done. He informed them that there was no moral obligation to continue use of the respirator.

Armstrong then called Mary Ellen Quinlan, Karen Ann's sister, to testify about Karen Ann's conversations with her about what she'd want if she was ever in a comatose state. Just as her mother had done, Mary Ellen told the court Karen Ann had said she wouldn't want to be kept alive under hopeless circumstances.

Armstrong's last witness was Lori Gaffney, Karen Ann's friend who had been present during two of the conversations between Karen Ann and her mother regarding the use of extraordinary means, and she reiterated what Karen Ann had said. Karen Ann's brother was scheduled to testify on this subject, but Judge Muir ruled the testimony unnecessarily repetitive and refused to hear it. With that, Armstrong rested.

Daniel Coburn, the guardian ad litem, called three doctors to the stand, all neurologists. All three testified that Karen Ann was not brain-dead according to modern accepted medical standards, concluding that Karen Ann was in a persistent vegetative state.

Despite the consistent testimony of six previous doctors, David Baime, the deputy attorney general working under William Hyland (the New Jersey attorney general), also felt the need to call a doctor of his own. This particular neurologist also testified that Karen Ann was not brain-dead. In a blow to the Quinlans' case, he also provided a bold additional statement. He said that keeping the respirator on and functioning in Karen Ann Quinlan's situation conformed with *all* standard medical canons of the day. This presumably meant that it would be fruitless for the Quinlans to attempt to find another physician to treat Karen Ann who would comply with their wishes.

Following this fourth day of testimony by doctors describing in graphic and clinical detail Karen Ann's moribund state, the trial ended with the attorneys' closing arguments the following Monday, October 27, 1975.

Argument by Ralph Porzio
on Behalf of Drs. Morse and Javed

Your Honor, we have now reached an end of the evidence, and the disposition of the momentous issues in this case now rests in your hands. I am sure that I reflect the thoughts of all counsel in expressing our appreciation to you for your unfailing courtesies and for your patience throughout these proceedings.

Now, there are some conclusions in this case that you must accept because they are beyond dispute, and once having done that, these conclusions must form a major premise or a base for the consideration of other evidence in the case.

Number one and the obvious one, that Karen Ann Quinlan is legally and medically alive under the laws of New Jersey and under standard medical practice.

Number two, that Karen Ann Quinlan is alive under the older criteria of death: namely, cardiac respiratory function. And she is alive under the newer criteria of death involving cerebral function, and every physician who took the witness stand was unanimous and certain in the statement that she has not sustained brain death under any of the existing criteria, whether it be the Harvard Ad Hoc Committee, whether it be the Sydney Declaration, whether it be the Duquesne Declaration, or whether it be the statement of the Council of International Organizations of Medical Science.

Number three, it is undisputed that this girl, because of irreversible brain damage, is in a persistent vegetative state.

Number four, it is undisputed that the Quinlan family has undergone and is undergoing great anguish because of Karen's condition, and that they are deserving of our compassion and our sympathy and our understanding.

Now, does all of this, Your Honor, justify this Court's intervention to mandate the steps to terminate her life? And here there are seemingly great complexities that involve ethics and morality and theology and law and medicine and psychology and economics and sociology and many other fields. But what can the law do?

There has not been too much stress during this trial, or even in the briefs, on the subject that there are some limitations as to what the law can do to resolve some human problems. As far as Karen Quinlan is concerned, we have undisputed medical testimony that she is in a comatose condition and the probabilities are that, because of her condition, she is not aware of great pain. But at the same time, Your Honor, I do not feel that that should be, in any way, the basis of your decision.

Now, there is also the anguish and pain and the sorrow of the Quinlan family, which is real. It's demonstrable, it's ascertainable, and with justification, I think we may say that this is one of the motivations that has brought about this extraordinary application before this Court.

Admittedly, medical science, according to the testimony of all the doctors, has limitations as to what can be done in the way of alleviation, and the question that I put to Your Honor is this: Can the law do better than medicine for the plight of the Quinlan family? I respectfully submit, Your Honor, that there are episodes of pain and anguish and sorrow and grief in this life that neither the law nor any legal system can cure, and I say this not only about the Quinlan family, who have impressed us with their sincerity and their devotion and their inspiring religious beliefs, but I say it about hundreds of thousands of other families who are similarly situated.

In a general way, Your Honor, we are born in pain and we live in pain, and unless we're very fortunate, we die in pain. A small child is told by its mother to go out to play. The child falls, sustains a hematoma, comes back to the mother, is crying. We feel sorry. Can the law do anything about that? A family lives through the death of a loved one. Unfortunately, we can't go to court and ask for a declaratory judgment to wipe out that pain, to wipe out that grief, to wipe out that anguish. The law cannot do anything about that. The member of a family has a serious accident, an affliction, an incurable state, let us say. Can the law wipe that out? Can the law turn back the clock? And the answer is that the law cannot do anything about that, and yet, that is not to say for one single moment that any of us—and I mean any of us—do not have empathy with the Quinlan family. I think that we must recognize as a fact of life, Your Honor, that all of us believe that we can live in a painless society. Well, we can't. And how can that be, at least in this world, as long as we have death and illness and disability and the cruelties of human nature, and even the eruptions of nature itself all around us? So, Your Honor, we do live in a vale of tears and that is why we point to judicial restraint rather than to judicial intervention.

Now, I'd like to make some comments about the evidence. On page two of the complaint the relief sought is "the express power of authorizing the discontinuance of all extraordinary means of sustaining the life processes" of Karen Ann Quinlan.

I call to your attention the following: Number one, not one single doctor stated that what is being done here at the hospital and by these treating physicians represents departure or deviation from accepted medical practices.

Number two, not one single doctor stated that Karen Ann Quinlan should be left to die. On the contrary, they have admitted that she has received excellent care and that that is standard medical practice.

Number three, even Dr. Korein spoke hypothetically about "judicious neglect" in some very extreme cases, and yet, Your Honor, he did not put Karen Ann Quinlan in that category.

Number four, according to Dr. Stuart Cook, an eminently qualified neurologist, there is hope in this case, even though remote, that a chance for recovery would not be ruled out; and what were his reasons? First, this may be so because one may not say anything with absolute certainty about medicine. Two, that there is confusion as to the precipitating events or causes in this particular case. Three, that there have been patients in a comatose state for a period longer than a year who have returned to a useful recovery. Number four, although the chances are remote, there is—and I'm quoting now from Dr. Cook—"always a possibility of a medical breakthrough and new research advances."

Now, Your Honor, before I leave this question of chances, and I've said this before, and I stress it again, if Karen Ann Quinlan has one chance in a thousand, if she has one chance in ten thousand, if she has one chance in a million, who are we and by what right do we kill that chance? Who are we and by what right do we kill that life? And that is the point that I think that we must always bear in mind, and that brings us to the next point.

If you decide in favor of the plaintiff, there are further questions that this Court must resolve. First, it seems that you must determine a definition of "all extraordinary means." You can't do otherwise, Your Honor, because even the applicant [Joe Quinlan] has his own ideas as to what extraordinary means are, and, moreover, there is even medical disagreement as to what extraordinary means are. For example, Dr. Diamond testified that if you took her off the respirator, that would be an extraordinary means, and if you left her on the respirator, that would not be an extraordinary means.

Number two, you cannot make your judgment, if you are going to decide it that way, in terms of the generalities of the language in the complaint for the guidance of the physicians and the nurses and the technicians and the administrators and the personnel at the hospital, everyone who may be directly or indirectly concerned with the treatment of this girl. Your Honor would have to establish the mechanics of the acts or omissions that would have to be followed. You are going to have to practice medicine.

You would have to establish the who, and the when, and the where, and the how. And if you don't, then you are going to have all of these people going around and saying, "What can I do? What can't I do in order to avoid being held in contempt of court?" And so you may even need expert assistance in the enforcement of your decree. And at least the treating physicians in this case have declared under oath that they would not perform any such acts or omissions.

Now I don't think that that is too horrendous, particularly when we understand that all that the complaint asks of them is "no interference." But I might add, parenthetically, that if the medical profession in Nazi Germany had shown more independence—if they had refused to partake in human experimentations—perhaps the Holocaust would not have been so great in terms of human lives and deformities.

Now, I would like to discuss next what I call the erosion of medical standards. I could not talk about this in the beginning of the trial because I didn't know what the evidence would disclose. The medical experts demonstrated that their efforts with respect to death follow universally recognized criteria. And they are firm in the conclusion that the medical profession feels bound by those criteria. And all of the medical experts have testified that there are medical standards that bind them; and they have said that there were proper medical standards followed in this case by Dr. Morse and by Dr. Javed.

Now, each one of the medical experts, after assessing the condition of Karen Ann Quinlan, declared that she did not meet the various medical criteria of brain death that have been established and accepted throughout the world. Now, for this Court to come along and determine that it will approve of the measures to terminate this life, even where it is unanimously agreed that the attending physicians have followed medical tradition, they have given her total care, they have followed medical standards, they have followed medical ethics, they followed the universally accepted criteria, and then to have this Court come along with the attending physicians deciding in the aura of all of these ethics and traditions and criteria, that she is supposed to get total care, and that what Mr. Armstrong wants you to do is to step in and to say, "No, I want to give her something less than total care. I want to give her the kind of care that will instantaneously terminate her life or, in the alternative, that will shorten it drastically."

So you see, Your Honor, if your decision goes that way, if it goes that way wittingly or unwittingly, you would be undermining and eroding all of the accepted standards and ethics and traditions and criteria of the medical profession, and think of the consequences that that would mean, not only to the practicing physicians, but also to the patients and their relationships to those ethics and those standards and those traditions and those criteria. This Court in effect would be eroding the very integrity of the medical profession, upon which the patients have come to rely.

Now, a word about the constitutional issues about which Mr. Armstrong places much stress, and with all due respect to him—and I mean no offense—I think the constitutional argument is riddled with flaws, and I believe I have dealt adequately with this in my brief. Let me simply add that we have got to recognize as basic in this case the crucial difference between belief and practice. Beliefs, under the First Amendment of the Constitution relating to religious freedom, are absolute, Your Honor, sacrosanct. The government cannot interfere. Practices under those beliefs are not immune from governmental immunity—immune from governmental restraint. Supposing we had a religious cult in the United States, even let's assume a million people belonged to it, and they believed in human sacrifice. Now, if Your Honor please, they would have every right in the world to believe in it. But if they practiced it, it comes in conflict with the law of the land, and the law of the land would prevail.

Now, if Your Honor please, in my opening statements I presented to the Court two major questions. The evidence is now all in and put to you in the hope that they would help us to resolve the real major issue in this case. And the first question was: Isn't the applicant asking this Court to put an end to the life of a person who is medically and legally alive; that is, to predicate a death sentence based upon the low quality of that life?

Now, Your Honor, with all that evidence in, that question still has validity and vitality, and I have said at the outset that there are many degrees or gradations of quality of life, and once that becomes the determining factor, then I have to say this: You make a godlike decision. Then you swing open the gates to the potential deaths of hundreds of thousands of people in the United States who are doomed to die because of a low quality of life under somebody's definition. And I raise with you again the question of the dangerous potential, not only for the present, but also for the future; and the widespread human experimentations—and I return to them because, Your Honor, they were real—the widespread human experimentations that resulted in death and horrible deformities carried on in the name of a superrace by the Nazis are still very much real among the living; and I implore you not to open the door to a culture or to a society that can go mad.

To use as a measuring rod the quality of life in determining life or death calls for titanic decision-making, and it's within the context of a civil suit. We are not dealing with this girl's life in terms of criminality at all. And even if you made that decision, Your Honor, even if you made that decision, you have another much more serious decision to make. And that is, by what standard or standards are you now going to determine that one person alive medically and legally shall continue to live, and another person alive medically and legally shall die? And it seems to me that that is absolutely essential to your decision, if you are going to find in favor of the applicant.

I call Your Honor's attention to one more fact: Anglo-Saxon jurisprudence is rooted in many parts of the world, in the British Isles, in Australia, in New Zealand, in the Far East, in Canada, in the United States, and even in some parts of Africa and South America. If you decide, by judicial declaration, to end the life of Karen Quinlan, it will be the first time in the long history of Anglo-Saxon jurisprudence that a human being, universally recognized as being alive medically and legally, will be put to death in a civil suit outside of the context of criminality and through the guise of what we have called the doctrine of substituted judgment.

Now some observers have called this case an unprecedented one. If Your Honor makes that decision of inevitable death for Karen Quinlan, this will truly be an unprecedented case. And I dread to think of the Pandora's box of medical, legal, ethical, and moral implications that will be born from such a determination. And I say, most respectfully, Your Honor, even though you have already determined that your decision will be confined to the facts in this case, that to try to stop the precedential effect of your decision will be like trying to stop the waters of Niagara.

Now Your Honor may recall that I put to you in my opening statement a second major question; namely, does not Mr. Armstrong and his client want you to put judicial sanction to an act of euthanasia? And again, let us not be bound by the tyranny of labels. If we do something or fail to do something intentionally that will bring a life to an end, what difference does it make if you describe the act one way or the other in terms of commission or omission? If a person is legally and medically alive, and an individual deliberately and intentionally deprives that person of a life-sustaining drug or life-sustaining equipment, or injects a lethal drug or gives an overdose of lethal pills, in every one of those cases, Your Honor, the effect is the same: the life is being terminated.

Now, I care not for euphemisms. I care not for semantics, and I care not for the niceties of language. I look to the substance and I ask Your Honor to look to the substance, and I ask Your Honor sitting here as a court of equity to look to the substance in accordance with the great maxim of the court of equity which has come down to us from British law, and that is that equity will look to the substance and not to the form.

In conclusion, Your Honor, dare we defy the undisputed premise—

the granite foundation of this case—that Karen Ann Quinlan is legally and medically alive? Dare we deny nature's immutable command to survive? And dare we deny the divine command "Thou shall not kill"? And out of the darkness of the night, as in the book of Revelations, there comes the rider on the pale horse crying, "Despair, despair," and humbly ask you to listen to the same soft answer from the dawn of time. I humbly ask you to cast your lot with the whisper on the wind: hope, humanity, and the preciousness of human life.

Argument by Morris County District Attorney Donald Collester

There is one word used by petitioner in his initial papers that I think appropriate to this case, and that word is *awe,* because we do sit here—stand here—in awe of some of the questions which are presented to this Court. My role in this case comes from my position and my duty, my duty to protect life and to uphold the integrity of the criminal law and to enforce the criminal law within the County of Morris.

Homicide, Your Honor, is defined traditionally, and under the laws of this state, as the unlawful taking of human life. A good motive is no excuse. A merciful motive is not a justification. Euthanasia is a homicide; and a homicide is a crime. I'm not here in this case to wave the fist of prosecution at a family which is aggrieved by the spectacle of their daughter. I'm here, at this point, to ask the Court's assistance. I'm asking for a declaratory judgment as to the legal implications of the relief that's sought by this family. I'm asking for a declaratory judgment. In particular, if the Court grants this relief and opens the way to termination of the respirator, I am asking for a declaratory judgment as to the parameters of my obligation then of enforcement of the criminal laws, as prosecutor of this county.

The law, I believe, is clear here, and the relief sought is to change it. There's an old legal maxim—that hard cases make bad law; and what is meant by that is, of course, the more sympathetic the cause, the more natural instinct to grant relief out of compassion to go for a particular result, and sometimes the law suffers as a result of this. Certainly we have an example of that here, as Mr. Porzio [counsel for the doctors] so eloquently points out. What is being requested here, if Your Honor please, goes even beyond the common understanding, or my common understanding, of euthanasia. It goes a little further because euthanasia is usually thought of in terms of putting someone out of their misery, their pain. Here, for all we know, Karen Ann Quinlan does not suffer pain. This poor family suffers pain. And the request is being made to end their pain by terminating a respirator supporting their daughter.

Mr. Porzio mentions a phrase called "quality of life," and he mentions it with trepidation. I too have trepidation about that. First of all, there's a bootstrap argument, which I don't think should come into this case, and that is, that terminating the respirator doesn't really terminate the life of Karen Quinlan because the quality of her life now is such that she should not be considered to be alive at all.

Certainly that's understandable—that feeling—just as the feeling of the mother who testified here that she would not—that Karen would not—want to live life if she could not live life to its fullest. That is a statement of "quality of life." It's fraught with peril, when we say the "quality of life" should be a factor; it should outweigh what we consider to be the biological life of a human being.

How do we define these "qualities"? What is "quality of life"? To see? To hear? To love? To understand? To communicate? The greater peril lies in forgetting the sanctity of life, and substituting for it the quality of life, because once we open this door, the precedential value of this decision will be great.

I recognize that the Court has only before it this one case, but there will be other cases brought before Your Honor, or before other courts. And if quality of life is the basis of its decision, then we will have parents of other stricken children who will also say she wouldn't want to live this way; she would want to live life to its fullest. We'll have sons and daughters saying this about their parents who are stricken by paralysis due to a stroke. We'll have others saying it about the aged who are senile. We'll have it said about other persons who have never known quality of life—those poor unfortunates of our society, the brain damaged, the mentally retarded, the Mongoloid. Evil has a very small beginning. And when "quality of life" replaces "sanctity of life," I fear a beginning may have commenced.

Preservation of life is paramount; and that sanctity of life is so well respected in this state that to carve out an exception might somehow lessen its importance. In our society, our collective humanity is defined by how we could, in effect, treat our unfortunates, even such an unfortunate as Karen Quinlan, as she lies in a nearby hospital today.

Karen Quinlan will die, as we all must. She will suffer, and her poor family will suffer. The sorrow that we have for them will not abate. But that sorrow may be the price we have to pay here for upholding the sanctity of life and the law as we presently have it.

Argument by New Jersey Attorney General William Hyland

I am here because, like the prosecutor of this county, I have no private client but I have some eight million clients, the people of this state, who have a very deep stake in the outcome of the case.

I think it's quite possible that this trial is the most important thing that's been happening in the state of New Jersey during the past several weeks. The trial has greater potential for affecting the lives of people on into the future than almost anything else that could be happening.

I have read in the paper that I have equated the pulling of the plug—and I hate that term, but I have to use it—with murder; which simply is not the case. I have said that there is a grave risk of criminality presented if conduct of this kind is engaged in, and of course we're talking about homicide, not necessarily murder.

What I am concerned about, in the criminal aspects of the matter, is that the application in effect would seek to carve out of the homicide statute some exception for medical practitioners; perhaps for practitioners of other disciplines, as well, possibly. I don't think that's the function of the Court. I don't see how the tragedy of one family, and the beliefs of one faith—of which I happen to be a serious practitioner myself—the circumstances of a very narrow case can do full justice to the many profound questions that are involved in asking that under given circumstances the life can be shortened.

All of us would agree that the discontinuance of the respirator would be humane, but with the first critical step taken toward the development of a society which might well go mad, I think that we have produced the possibility of stepping into a darkness instead of into light. Because, for the first time, a court in this country in a civil matter would have issued a judgment of execution.

I don't think this Court has a right to do that. I don't think the plaintiff has carried the burden, which I think is a burden, beyond a reasonable doubt of demonstrating that he has a right to the relief as requested, and I ask that the complaint be dismissed.

Closing Argument by Daniel Coburn, Karen Ann Quinlan's Court-Appointed Guardian ad Litem

When I was chosen as guardian in this particular case, I felt like the little Dutch boy with ten fingers and twenty holes in the dike. I had no idea where this case was going, much less what position I should take, or whether I would be right. I can state a couple of things that, as a result of this case, I have come to definite conclusions on.

One is that for whatever the criteria will ever be for a father, Mr. Quinlan should be that criteria. Mr. Quinlan has subjected himself to something that I can't imagine any father or person would want to subject himself to. There are always lingering doubts. What are the motives? There is no doubt, in my opinion. There is nothing I am more certain of in life than Mr. Quinlan's motives. They are on the highest level, both from the religious point of view and the point of view of a father, which is probably at least in my opinion more important.

We have had references in this case to euthanasia. What we are asking for is religious euthanasia. It is as simple as that. It is not medical euthanasia; it is religious euthanasia. Putting a religious label on it doesn't change it. There are no exceptions in the law, and there can't be any exceptions, no matter how valid the motives are. Whether it is in a religious framework, or any other framework, it can't be allowed.

The significance of this case, as I see it, will not be in a legal sense. I think the decision will probably—despite requests that Your Honor define brain death, or say what procedures should be employed should another case arise, or even in this case, I don't think anything of that sort should be done. It should be resolved strictly on the issues before us. Karen Quinlan is not brain-dead. She is alive—absolutely.

I use the word *hope.* Obviously no one is going to come in here and say there is a means of recovery. I doubt that anyone will suggest that if Karen makes any recovery in this case at all that it would be to a twenty-one-year-old woman. Certainly physically she can never recover. I think it was Dr. Plum who stated that her atrophied condition, her joints are arthritic, that she will always be, in the sense of physical appearance, grotesque; but that is not the criteria. You can't use a quality of life argument based on what someone looks like, any more than you can go back into Karen's background.

I am saying this in all respect to the family, but it is a point that has to be made. There have been all sorts of discussions as to what caused this. It makes no difference at all whether this was caused from lead poisoning, from her job, from falling in her home, from a drug overdose; Karen is in this condition today. Medically, it might have some significance, but legally it has none.

As to her lifestyle before this, it makes no difference whether she was the Virgin Mary, or Mary Magdalene. It is of no consequence at all. She is in that position. The case has to be decided on that basis. You can't talk about whether this has an effect on the family, in a financial sense, or it hasn't, because that is an artificial criteria.

Karen is entitled to the same treatment as the wealthiest person in the world, or as the poorest person in the world. Everyone is entitled to that. As to the mass hysteria that may flow from this case, one thing we can say for the case of *In re Karen Quinlan* is that in the highest traditions of both the medical and legal proofs, we have had a hearing to determine this case. There aren't any quack doctors. We haven't a family that has an insurance policy with something to gain. There is no personal motive at all on the part of anyone here. None of the lawyers are going to profit from this case. They may profit in a financial sense; they may not. But certainly the price that has been paid by all of us is not worth whatever the rewards may be.

I would just like to state that the hope exists. No one is a miracle worker, but hope exists; and she is entitled to that right. As Mr. Porzio said, one out of a thousand, or one out of a million, at least that is hope. As it stands now, if nothing else is done for Karen Quinlan, the chances are none out of the million. She is going to die. There is no doubt about it. She is going to die, whether on or off the respirator, unless something is done. She is entitled to that chance. If she dies on an operating table during surgery, at least she had gone out fighting. She hasn't just died. That is why we are sitting here.

As to Dr. Korein, with his request, I am sure he said it in good faith. I hate to take it out of context. Dr. Korein has a request that clarification of the unwritten law be stated. I say there is a message to Dr. Korein, to Mr. Armstrong, to Mr. Crowley, and even to Mr. Quinlan with his religious beliefs, and that is, that in the Ten Commandments, the most important commandment is "Thou shalt not kill." That is the message that should be given to all of them.

Closing Argument of Paul W. Armstrong, on Behalf of Joe Quinlan

Dean Roscoe Pound, in the preface to his monumental work on jurisprudence, points out that "justice is the great interest of man on earth. Of the three instrumentalities of social control by which that interest is made effective, namely, religion, morals, and law, the brunt of the labor in the world of today has fallen upon the law."

Accepting that their daughter and sister, Karen Ann, now lies in a gradually deteriorating chronic vegetative state in the intensive care unit of St. Clare's Hospital; that there is a hopeless prospect of her cure through the art of medicine; counseled by their shared belief and the teachings of the Roman Catholic faith and supported by the love, faith, and courage unique to a father and mother, sister and brother, the Quinlan family now turns for guidance to the law personified in this Honorable Court.

Uncontroverted and expert medical testimony adduced during the course of this trial has revealed that Karen Ann Quinlan has sustained massive and irreparable brain damage, and that she now lies in a persistent or chronic vegetative state in the intensive care unit of St. Clare's Hospital, where, through the use of a mechanical respirator, her deteriorating bodily functions are maintained.

Let no one falsely state that the Quinlans' plea is based solely upon human compassion. Indeed, it is grounded under the most fundamental principles of common law and the United States Constitution. This Court clearly has the power to grant relief in this case, and at the same time to frame its decision in a manner that will protect the legitimate interests of all who appear before you today. The Chancery Court is the supreme guardian of all incompetents, and by an exercise of that venerable doctrine known as the doctrine of substituted judgment, it may exercise on behalf of an incompetent any right which that unfortunate person could himself, if competent, exercise.

It is submitted that Karen Ann Quinlan could lawfully take the action which is proposed to this Honorable Court, and that the Court may therefore in appropriate circumstances authorize such action on her behalf. Indeed, no competent adult is required by law to submit to medical treatment which offers no reasonable hope for relief or cure. Illustrative of this principle is the case of *J.F.K. Memorial v. Heston,* which is, unfortunately, often relied upon for the opposite proposition. There, a blood transfusion was administered to an injured girl over the objection of her parents. It was in this case that the New Jersey Supreme Court had occasion to pen the dictum "That it seems correct to say there is no constitutional right to choose to die." While granting the existence of such dicta, it must be pointed out that the relevant facts in *Heston* were quite different from those in the case at bar.

In *Heston* the important fact to be borne in mind was that Miss Heston's ailment was completely curable, and curable by means of a technique which is practiced thousands of times every day in hospitals all over the world. On the other hand, uncontroverted evidence has shown that Karen's condition is medically hopeless.

In the light of such evidence, another statement in *Heston* would provide sure guidance to this court. While stating that refusal of treatment in Miss Heston's case would be tantamount to suicide, the Court realized that the situation would be, and I quote, "arguably different when an individual, overtaken by illness, decides to let it run a fatal course."

Indeed the cases whose facts most closely parallel those before this Court all indicate that the refusal of treatment in medically hopeless situations is lawful and permissible. When it is realized that Karen could lawfully consent to the discontinuance of treatment, the Court must then consider whether such withdrawal would be appropriate. That is, as supreme guardian, the Court must ask itself whether the discontinuance of the treatment would serve Karen's best interests. In rendering this decision, the Court must address itself to Karen's physical, moral, spiritual, and material welfare. The testimony offered at this trial leads us to the conclusion that medicine must be the servant of man; and that technology must be the servant of medicine. The proper role of a physician is to promote the unified function of an organism. The testimony has also shown that both the treating physicians and the consulted medical experts know of no treatment which can offer any hope of improvement, or even arrest the deterioration of her body. Indeed, it has been testified that were she to have a sudden hemorrhage, or require major surgical procedures, no doctor would take such measures. From such testimony, the use of the terms *physical best interests* assumes a new meaning. In such cases, further treatment can provide no medical benefit to the patient, and thus commanding its continuance will in no way further Karen's physical best interests. Surely the Court, charged with determining the best interests of Karen, cannot advance that her maintenance in this chronic vegetative state in any way serves her interests, let alone her best interest.

Next, in determining Karen's moral best interests we ask the Court to take into account that complex of values and attitudes which recognize and give meaning to the term *dignity of man*. At present, Karen lies in St. Clare's Hospital, no more than sixty or seventy pounds of flesh and bone; a poor and tragic creature whose life is no more than a patterned series of the most primitive nervous reflexes, while in this courtroom it is seriously proposed, in the face of the most compelling contrary medical testimony, that her now disunified and unperceiving body be constrained to function against all its natural impulses.

Could anything be more degrading to a human being—a human being who has come on this earth full of love and promise, who has known peace and joy, who has been the daughter of Joseph and Julia Quinlan? Can anything be more degrading, than to be offered up as a living sacrifice to the materialistic and misguided belief that death can somehow be cheated, if only we find the right combination of wires and gauges, transistors and tubes?

Let her own prior expressions guide the way for those whom fate has charged with the decision. In conversation with those whom she held most dear, mother, sister, and brother, confidante and friend, Karen's own words emerge to light the way. Evidence has shown that from a medical and religious point of view the use of the respirator and intensive care facilities in Karen's case is extraordinary, by reason of the unprecedented commitment of medical resources and personnel and the hopeless nature of Karen's condition.

In addition the Court, acting as guardian, cannot fail to consider the tenets of the faith to which Karen belongs. That faith, which holds that life is good but not an absolute good, and that death is an evil but not an absolute evil, wisely teaches that man need not make use of extraordinary means to preserve earthly life. And, lastly, the Court as guardian must realize expenditures and liabilities incurred on behalf of an incompetent should carry with them some reasonable hope of benefit. All the evidence indicates that Karen will receive no benefit from continuation of treatment and, therefore, neither she nor her estate nor indeed society should be charged with the burden that continued treatment would entail.

For the foregoing reasons, then, it is clear that the Court would be acting properly as supreme guardian if it consented to the withdrawal of the extraordinary life support measures currently being administered to Karen Quinlan.

It will be recalled, Your Honor, that Joseph Quinlan has made this unusual request within the framework of a guardianship petition. Within such a framework it is submitted that, should the Court not authorize the proposed withdrawal of treatment, Joseph Quinlan is nonetheless a fit person. Indeed, he is the fittest of persons to serve as guardian for his daughter. Testimony has shown him to be a loving father, interested only in the welfare of his family and children. Testimony, as well as his appearance before you today, has shown him to be a man of sound judgment and abundant good faith. Before taking any action, he has sought medical guidance, moral guidance, and guidance from this Court. He has stated that he would abide by whatever judgment the law should render and would never take it upon himself to act in opposition to that judgment.

Taking into account the good faith of Joseph Quinlan, and the natural bond existing between him and Karen Ann, this Court, we feel, cannot deny him at least this small comfort: that he be recognized before the law as, what he is and always will be, the father and guardian of Karen Ann Quinlan.

We now turn the Court's attention to the constitutional arguments advanced in support of the plaintiff's petition. Plaintiff contends that, while the determination of the constitutional issue is not necessary for the granting of the instant petition, failure to grant such would violate the constitutional rights of both Karen Ann Quinlan and her family.

Plaintiff submits the state cannot, without demonstrating a contrary interest both compelling and secular, interfere with the free exercise of the Quinlans' religious beliefs, with their personal decisions, or with their sovereignty over their own bodies. The right to privacy includes individual and familial decisions to terminate the futile use of extraordinary medical measures.

The evidence has shown that Karen has expressed a desire not to be subjected to extraordinary medical treatment, and that the family has decided that her wishes should be honored. The right of individuals to be sovereign over their own person received its fullest exposition in the case of *Griswold v. Connecticut,* which found support for the right to privacy in all the specific guarantees enumerated in the Bill of Rights as well as in the Ninth Amendment protection granted to unenumerated rights. This right has grown to include individual and familial life-influencing decisions, and it cannot be denied that a family is legally competent to make the decisions implicit in the plaintiff's request.

Further, the plaintiff sets forth that the free exercise clause of the First Amendment, as applied to the state's Fourteenth Amendment, protects the right of Karen Ann Quinlan and her family to discontinue the futile use of extraordinary medical measures. Plaintiff contends that this request is the product of a religiously based decision, made in accordance with the tenets of the religion to which he and his family belong.

The evidence has shown that the Quinlan family, including Karen Ann Quinlan, are members and believe in the Roman Catholic faith, which teaches that, as stated in the discourse of Pius XII admitted into evidence, natural reason and Christian morals say that man, and whoever is entrusted with the task of taking care of his fellow man, has the right and the duty in case of serious illness to take the necessary treatment for the preservation of life and health. This duty that one has toward himself, toward God, toward the human community, and in most cases toward certain determined persons, derives from well-ordered charity, from submission to the Creator, from social justice, and even from strict justice, as well as from devotion toward one's family. But normally one is held to use only ordinary means, according to circumstances of persons, places, times, and culture. That is to say, means that do not involve any grave burden for oneself or another.

A more strict obligation would be too burdensome for most men and would render the attainment of the higher, more important good too difficult. Life, health, and temporal activities are in fact subordinated to spiritual ends. On the other hand, one is not forbidden to take more than the strictly necessary steps to preserve life and health, as long as he does not fail in some more serious duty. Given this total subordination, it makes no difference that a given action is obligatory, or merely optional, so long as it is done or chosen within the framework of man's quest for spiritual good. If it is done within such a framework, it is, we submit, entitled to the protection offered by the free exercise clause of the First Amendment.

Moreover, the Quinlan family believes that in the quest of the highest spiritual good, familial decisions can have equal weight with individual decisions, especially with regard to an incompetent; and that medical advice can influence, but not determine, individual and familial decisions.

The rights and duties of the family depend in general upon the presumed will of the unconscious patient if he is of full age and capacity. Where the proper and independent duty of the family is concerned, they are usually bound only to the use of ordinary means.

Consequently, if it appears that the attempt at resuscitation constitutes in reality such a burden for the family that one cannot in all conscience impose it upon them, they can lawfully insist that the doctor should discontinue these attempts, and the doctor can lawfully comply. There is not involved here a case of direct disposal of the life of the patient, nor of euthanasia in any way: this would never be licit. Even when it causes the arrest of circulation, the interruption of attempts at resuscitation is never more than an indirect cause of the cessation of life.

Here the state, in its case, has demonstrated no compelling interest in overcoming either the Quinlans' right of privacy, or their right to the free exercise of their religion. They have stated that such rights may, in some circumstances, be overcome. And we agree with this, as a general proposition of law. But they have cited us to no law which requires that state interest prevail in the instant circumstances; nor have they cited us to any case whose relevant facts are similar to those before this court.

In addition, medical testimony presented in this case bears out plaintiff's contention that continuation of the treatment currently being administered to Karen would, if mandated by the Court, constitute cruel and unusual punishment of the type proscribed by the Eighth Amendment of the United States Constitution.

We support the requests of defense counsel that guidance be given to the Prosecutor's Office and to St. Clare's Hospital, and we think that the guidance should be given to the physicians as well, with regard to the effect on all of them of the granting of plaintiff's request.

The fact that the withdrawal of treatment is in the best interests of Karen leads to the conclusion that the Court should authorize consent to such withdrawal. The fact that such consent may be lawfully given is based on the determination that the doctors and the hospital have exercised sound medical judgment. That is, in the face of hopeless and irreversible coma, where life processes are sustained only by extraordinary means, continued treatment serves no valid medical purpose; and that withdrawal of such extraordinary means would not constitute homicide since the causality implicit in such withdrawal is not predicated upon a breach of duty to Karen and is, therefore, not culpable.

Such determinations of the rights of parties are the proper subject of a declaratory judgment and may properly serve as a basis for enjoining both criminal prosecution and civil or administrative suits or proceedings.

Thus it is, Your Honor, that we conclude our review of the sad and weighty issues that have brought us here before you in rare unanimity of spirit. The plea of all of us through this trial has been "Help us resolve these issues."

The Quinlans' request, which initiated these proceedings, is clear: "We love Karen Ann, but we know that hope is gone. Let her return to her God, but let none who suffer by her illness suffer yet the more by her departure."

This Court, moved not by compassion but by thirst for justice, can grant that request to the full. It can say not only, "Karen, pass on in peace"; it can say as well, "Mr. Hyland, Mr. Collester, there is no murder here. Mr. Einhorn, your clients may accede to the request. They have done all the law can ask, and more. Dr. Morse and Dr. Javed, you have come to us for guidance. We give it to you now. Six long months of vigils over Karen's bed, six long months of loving conversation with Joe and Julia in their anguish, six long months of searching and of doubt, these will be counted nothing by us. Take counsel, once again among yourselves, far from crowded court-rooms. We have seen enough to know that your decision will be true. You're your sister Karen, and if in your heart of hearts, coun-seled by your brother physicians and unfettered by fears that uncomprehending law will stay your hand, you determine that fur-ther ministrations would be no more than useless punishment, return her with our blessing to that state where her own body can heed, if it will, the gentle call that beckons her to lasting peace."

Paul Armstrong's brilliant summation on behalf of Karen Ann and her family was in the finest tradition of a skilled and dedicated trial lawyer delivering a great closing argument. His argument was impassioned, per-sonal, perfectly organized, and provided a firm legal footing for the posi-tion that the Court should intervene and allow Karen Ann's family to order the cessation of all extraordinary measures.

The Judge's Decision

When the trial concluded, all attention was focused on the chambers of Judge Muir. At the end of the closing arguments the judge took the 745-page transcript, his twelve legal pads full of notes, the legal and med-ical texts he had amassed during the hearing, and sequestered himself, promising a decision in two weeks.

Two thousand letters arrived at the Quinlan home during those two post-trial weeks, mostly supporting the family's wishes. Packages con-taining crucifixes and holy water arrived at the courthouse. Psychics and faith healers prowled the halls at Karen Ann's hospital, begging to be granted admission to the comatose woman's room.

Meanwhile, Judge Muir refused Armstrong's suggestion that he visit Karen Ann's bedside. Emotion, Judge Muir explained, was not an element he could allow to cloud his decision, a decision that was to be made on evi-dence alone. At forty-three, the Newark-born Muir was a balding, athletic man, the father of three, an elder in the Presbyterian Church, and a Republican.

On November 10, Judge Muir had his decision ready. He alluded to his emotions: "The compassion, empathy, [and] sympathy [Muir felt] for Mr. and Mrs. Quinlan and their two other children . . . [was] . . . unparalleled." However, personal feelings must defer to judicial conscience and objectivity. Karen was not to be removed from the respirator, as long as even an iota of hope existed that she might recover. A duty existed to continue the life-sustaining activity. Furthermore, the judge was reluctant to let his judicial authority spill into the medical profession. After explaining in detail a physician's responsibility in treating a patient, he asked rhetorically, "What justification is there to remove it from the control of the medical profession and place it in the hands of the courts?"

Judge Muir then went on to dismiss Armstrong's arguments. Neither the right to privacy or religion, nor the protection against cruel and unusual punishment, overrode Karen Ann's physicians' authority, and even if any of these rights could be invoked, Mr. Quinlan's emotional bias disqualified him as a viable candidate for the position of guardian of his daughter, a post that would require him to make objective, logic-driven decisions while she was unable to make them for herself.

Outside the courthouse, more than two hundred members of the media had gathered to see the Quinlans' reactions. All three TV networks were prepared to air a live news conference when the family emerged. When the family appeared, they expressed their disappointment, but also relief that the trial was finally over. During the press conference, a reporter yelled to them, "What are you going to do now?" The Quinlans replied that they didn't really know. During a second press conference in the basement of St. Margaret's Catholic Church in Morristown, Joe admitted his frustration with the ruling, but he also mentioned that Judge Muir "showed courage in saying that the matter belonged with the physicians."

Conservative columnist George Will applauded the judge: "A decision for the Quinlans would have authorized a killing." The *Los Angeles Times* complained that while the decision may have been legally correct, "the iron words of the law" did not resolve the "human tragedy."

To Appeal or Not to Appeal

The decision to appeal Judge Muir's decision did not take the Quinlans and Armstrong long to make, once the young lawyer assured the family that the New Jersey Supreme Court was likely to be more receptive than Judge Muir had been to their arguments.

After being assured they would not again be forced to testify, the Quinlans agreed to the appeal.

On November 17, 1975, Armstrong drove to Trenton, New Jersey, and filed his appeal. The Supreme Court reacted immediately, announcing on the same day that it would review the case. The hearing was set for January 26, 1976, just two and a half months after Judge Muir's decision.

Letters poured in at Karen Ann's hospital and the Quinlans' home. And now Father Tom Trapasso found himself writing a letter of his own to his twelve hundred parishioners. "How was it possible," he mused in his missive, "that 892,000 lives were exterminated by abortion in 1974 in the United States and yet the law would not allow Karen Ann to die a peaceful death?"

But then the odyssey of Karen Ann Quinlan took an unexpected turn. On December 16, 1975, the *New York Post* hit the streets with the headline "Probe Beating of Coma Girl." According to the article, William Zywot, twenty-two, one of the young men out with Karen the night she fell into a coma, was under suspicion for beating her and causing the coma. Attorney General Hyland issued a public statement explaining that the purpose of Zywot's interrogation was to determine if he was responsible for an egg-shaped bump on Quinlan's head, and if it had anything to do with her condition.

The day after the article appeared, Zywot was flown to Trenton, New Jersey, by state investigators acting under orders of Attorney General Hyland. He was questioned for several hours before being released. Nothing came of the investigation, but Joe Quinlan was shaken by the sensationalistic turn of events. He later said this new development left him prostrate, unable to eat or speak coherently. How could the media and the attorney general begin dragging his daughter's name through the mud at this late date? The earliest examinations of Karen Ann had found definitively that the coma had nothing to do with any trauma she had sustained, but now her lifestyle was subjected to public rumors.

Father Trapasso again felt compelled to put pen to paper:

> Should [my anger] be toward the Attorney General, who was quoted as [initially] saying he had no reason to believe there was criminality involved? Yet he has not to date questioned or even contacted the doctors who were most intimately involved in Karen's treatment. These same doctors at no time seriously considered that Karen's treatment was due to a trauma.

Should my anger be directed toward those unnamed police officers who stated to the press they were investigating a "possible connection" of Karen Ann with an unsavory local character? Why were they talking to the press at all? My concept of an investigation always meant the utmost secrecy and discretion. Do they want to prosecute this seventy-pound comatose girl for some crime?

But Trapasso and Joe Quinlan were not the only ones affected. On December 20, Julia Quinlan woke up with sharp pains knifing through her chest, the victim of a severe anxiety attack. That same night, Karen Ann's brother called home from a police station, where he had been detained for brawling in a bar. It would be a long wait until January 26.

When that day finally arrived, the seven justices of the New Jersey Supreme Court filed into the courtroom promptly at 9 A.M. At their center sat Chief Justice Richard J. Hughes, the former governor of New Jersey, a Catholic, and father of eleven children. The hearing that followed would last an arduous four hours.

The oral argument began with Paul Armstrong. Selected portions of the questions and answers from the participants follow:

Oral Argument of Paul W. Armstrong on Behalf of Appellant Joseph Quinlan

THE COURT: Specifically, Mr. Armstrong, what do you ask this Court to do?

MR. ARMSTRONG: We ask this Court on behalf of the Quinlan family that an individual who is terminally ill in a persistent vegetative state, that they can request the suspension of futile medical measures in order to allow the natural processes of the body to take place. That's what we're advancing.

THE COURT: Are you asking this Court to direct something?

MR. ARMSTRONG: No, Your Honor. What we're asking is to determine whether or not an individual exercising his constitutional right to make that decision, whether or not that would be licit. We're not asking this Court to enjoin anyone to do anything against those particular beliefs which they might hold.

THE COURT: May I see if I understand you? Are you asking the Court to declare that a request by your client of the doctors to terminate this apparatus is a nonactionable thing?

MR. ARMSTRONG: We're not asking this Court to order the doctors to do anything which they may feel contrary to their beliefs.

THE COURT: You're simply asking the Court to declare that if your client asked the doctors to terminate life, there will be no civil or criminal consequences to attach to that?

MR. ARMSTRONG: That's correct.

THE COURT: Well, it goes beyond that, because they have asked, and the doctor has taken the position, that he will not medically authorize that action. Aren't you really asking us to overrule the doctor's decision?

MR. ARMSTRONG: No. What we're asking, and I believe a fair categorization of the doctor's testimony, is that while he feels that he may be incapable of doing it, there are others who would not feel incapable of doing it. What essentially we are asking for is that if the physicians don't feel that they are capable of doing this, in this instance Dr. Morse and Dr. Javed, that they not interfere with a physician who would be wont to grant the request of the Quinlan family.

THE COURT: Mr. Armstrong, is it not fundamentally correct that in order for you to survive in this action, would it prevail that in the final analysis you want us to declare that the Quinlans have a constitutional right to make this decision? Must we not hold in that fashion in order for you to prevail in this case?

MR. ARMSTRONG: There is another vehicle.

THE COURT: What is it?

MR. ARMSTRONG: If you determine that in the common law best interests of Karen Ann, looking to her set-forth ideals, values, and outlook toward life, that it would be in her best interests to terminate the life-support system at this point, the Court doesn't even have to address itself to the constitutional arguments.

THE COURT: Absent that, however, we must direct our attention to the constitutional right of the Quinlans to make this decision, the decision being to terminate the life of Karen. Isn't that true?

MR. ARMSTRONG: That's correct.

THE COURT: Mr. Armstrong, I gather from your last few answers to questions that in an answer to my previous question you're asking for more than simply the Court's declaration that no adverse consequences will attach to the Quinlans by their making this request. You are also asking the Court to say that no adverse consequences will attach to the physicians if they accede to the Quinlans' request?

MR. ARMSTRONG: Absolutely.

THE COURT: Then in effect you're asking the Court to make a determination that in this case it is legal and without any actionable consequences for the physicians to make a determination and to carry out the determination that the life-sustaining apparatus should be turned off in this case? In other words, you're saying that under these facts and circumstances, if the physician elects to terminate at the request of the parent, there will be no civil, adverse civil or criminal consequences attaching to the physician?

MR. ARMSTRONG: That's correct.

THE COURT: Just a moment. You asked for three things. I take it that you put a lot of thought into them because they seem to go in logical sequence, the first being a prayer for judgment that Karen Ann be declared mentally incompetent, and that the plaintiff be given letters of guardianship with the express power of authorizing a discontinuance of what you there referred to as "all extraordinary means of sustaining the body processes."

MR. ARMSTRONG: That's correct.

THE COURT: And then in the event that's granted, you want the prosecutor, Mr. Collester, to refrain from interference with or criminal prosecution arising out of any relief which the Court might grant. And then in the event that both of those are granted, then you want the doctors to be enjoined from interference with any relief. Now is that the sum and substance of what you seek?

MR. ARMSTRONG: That's correct.

THE COURT: All right. Nothing else?

MR. ARMSTRONG: Nothing else.

CHIEF JUSTICE HUGHES: Mr. Armstrong, along the way of simplicity that you mentioned, I agree that that's the way to attack this problem, and passing the question of competency of Miss Quinlan and the rights of guardianship and mandatory features of instructions to that guardian and so forth, doesn't it come down to this, the long and short of it being: that you ask the Court to declare the law to be, there having been no precedent in any part of the common law that I can figure, that the Court is to declare now that if the doctors stop this procedure and cause death, that it will not result in any civil or criminal sanctions as to such doctors or indeed as to such family members?

MR. ARMSTRONG: That's correct.

THE COURT: So that in effect you're asking the Court, as a court, to make new law.

MR. ARMSTRONG: On these facts, that's correct.

CHIEF JUSTICE HUGHES: On these facts. And that absent any constitutional compulsion to make that new law.

MR. ARMSTRONG: Yes. You can do that through the common law best-interests doctrine.

CHIEF JUSTICE HUGHES: To make new law, without legislation? Wouldn't the Court be legislating, in that case?

MR. ARMSTRONG: No, Your Honor. It would be doing, or reflecting the majesty of the evolution of common law as it has since its inception in England. It's simply addressing itself and drawing an analog from existing cases to circumstances which, because of these particular instances, technological innovations have brought before the Court. I genuinely think that the Court is fully competent to address itself to these types of problems.

THE COURT: Well, Mr. Armstrong, suppose instead of Karen Ann Quinlan being in a deplorable condition in which she is, she were conscious, had cognitive powers, but was on the verge of death from some terminal illness and said, herself, to the doctors and to the hospital that she did not want artificial means of this kind to be employed. What is the law as to that?

MR. ARMSTRONG: Given that circumstance, we would advise that an individual, if death is imminent and the medical measures proposed are futile, in that they offer no hope of cure or any known treatment, then we most assuredly would assert that she a fortiori has a constitutional right to come before the Court.

THE COURT: What is your response, Mr. Armstrong, to those who argue that there is always the possibility of that miracle drug or the miracle remedy which may come to pass between the date that one decides that the person should die and the date that the person perhaps would normally have died with the supportive measures? What is your response to the fact—that we should not concern ourselves with that possibility?

MR. ARMSTRONG: As a broad general principle, that's fine. However, that was investigated thoroughly by the family in concert with Drs. Morse and Javed to find out the existence of any research, of any developments at all that could alleviate the particular irreparable brain damage suffered by Karen. It was found that there is none, nor was any advanced—

THE COURT: Miracles don't come about that way. They just wake up one morning and someone says we have a Salk vaccine. They didn't give "warnings" beforehand. Why is it so impossible that this could come to pass?

MR. ARMSTRONG: Basically, Mr. Justice, those miracles come about as a result of Ford Foundation grants for about one and a half million dollars. There are no grants doing research along these lines to alleviate irreparable brain damage. There simply is no one doing research along those lines.

THE COURT: What if someone were to accidentally just come upon something even though they weren't doing research in this particular area, just accidentally came across something which does the trick?

MR. ARMSTRONG: Well, then we'd all be better off for it.

THE COURT: Including Miss Quinlan?

MR. ARMSTRONG: Most importantly Miss Quinlan.

THE COURT: Now what is your response?

MR. ARMSTRONG: Well, I can only gauge it on the possibility. It's a possibility but not a probability.

THE COURT: And if there is a possibility and if there is this doubt engendered by that possibility, should we not if at all possible resolve all doubts in favor of life, in favor of the continuation of life as to the very last moment?

MR. ARMSTRONG: That is something that should go into the equation when the individual or the individual's family is to make this constitutionally protected decision. Certainly if there is something in the offing along those lines, the individual must take that into consideration; or if the physician knows about it, he should advise the family or the individual of the existence of some research along that line and allow him to assess the probability of it being able to alleviate the situation within which that particular individual finds himself.

THE COURT: Mr. Armstrong, I suspect that philosophically behind your position is something that has not been proven, although you might have attempted to prove it at the trial, and that is the assumption that many physicians without any argument about it every day make decisions to stop giving life-sustaining help to people who are hopelessly ill. Was there an attempt made to prove that? Was there evidence to that effect at the trial?

MR. ARMSTRONG: I think the thrust of the evidence advanced by Dr. Korein is that the requested relief is within the context of medical tradition.

THE COURT: And is being done?

MR. ARMSTRONG: Surely.

THE COURT: Well, that would be—you see, to me that might be influential if it were proven. I've heard that this is so. I've heard that physicians frequently as a matter of daily routine without talking about it make personal decisions in the interest of all concerned not to kill somebody, not to give them a tablet which would kill them, but to stop giving life-sustaining artificial sustenance where it is totally helpless and where the patient is going to suffer more from being kept alive than being terminated—

MR. ARMSTRONG: That's also my understanding.

THE COURT: —and I suppose what you are really arguing here is that the Court should assume that if Karen were able to make the request herself and made it and the physician acceded to that request, he would not be subject to any penalties.

MR. ARMSTRONG: That's one of the thrusts. The other is that if you deem that you haven't sufficient evidence to persuade you that Karen has made that decision, then that you should do the same just interposing the family as the decision maker and all that would follow.

THE COURT: It wouldn't be subject to any penalties if the prosecutor didn't find out about it. The one to ask is the prosecutor, whether in fact he knows, whether it's a matter of common knowledge to him and a source of investigation on his part that he's overlooking. I'm sure he's going to say no. And, Mr. Armstrong, isn't it a fact that if such proofs were developed, proofs that it is common practice for doctors to suspend life-supporting measures and to do other things that you've referred to in order to hasten death, that proofs like this might result in indictments of some form?

MR. ARMSTRONG: Absolutely, Mr. Justice.

THE COURT: Of course they would. Therefore, isn't it naive on our part to expect that anyone will ever prove that this is a common practice despite the fact that down deep we all know it is?

MR. ARMSTRONG: It's very difficult to get a witness to testify to that effect under the glare of litigation, Mr. Justice.

THE COURT: Well, of course they won't because he's testifying to a crime.

MR. ARMSTRONG: Absolutely.

THE COURT: Mr. Armstrong, would it simplify our thinking on this approach if we were to consider a parallel case where, let us say, some patient, Karen, were brought in terribly burned, suffering terrible pain, obviously terminally ill, and the doctor, in his judgment, decided not to apply the life-support respirator and mechanism as a matter of judgment? Would he be any more or less amenable to criminal or civil sanctions in that case, as opposed to a case, let us say, where he happened to be away for the weekend and his assistant applied the life-sustaining mechanisms and the doctor disagreed when he came back on Monday with this procedure—the fact that he has to do the affirmative act of stopping something that has been started—is that any different, logically, than declining to start something?

MR. ARMSTRONG: I think if I could pull us back to this factual situation and say—because here we have had the administration of medical treatment, the respirator. If he makes the decision beforehand in his judgment, and I'm going to say in concert with the patient or his family, that it wouldn't work, it would be the same thing. However, if once you've applied the machine and you see it's futile, a fortiori, that particular decision should be protected because you haven't ruled out the possibility. You've applied it, and you've demonstrated to yourself within the realm of your science—here, medicine—that this machine does nothing. It offers no hope of cure. It's just thwarting and dragging out the natural processes of the body.

CHIEF JUSTICE HUGHES: So that you'd say there is no difference. Is that the idea?

MR. ARMSTRONG: In our circumstance. In the burn case, I don't think you advised me as to whether or not the individual had anything to do with the decision.

CHIEF JUSTICE HUGHES: Well, supposing it's a perception of Dr. Morse upon first seeing Karen that there was no utility whatsoever, aside from prolonging her life for a month or two, in applying the life-sustaining treatment. Would he be any less amenable to criminal or civil sanctions then, or would he be in the realm of the Hippocratic oath responsibility to his professional duties, rather than amenability to the law?

MR. ARMSTRONG: I think he's got to at least come in contact with the individual or his family. They should make that decision. If it's a purely emergent decision, I think that the physicians are, pursuant to the Hippocratic oath, bound to apply those life-sustaining measures.

CHIEF JUSTICE HUGHES: No matter their futility?

MR. ARMSTRONG: Well, if it's totally futile and there's—well, I think—

CHIEF JUSTICE HUGHES: I'm talking about a totally futile case where it is obvious from the doctor's experience and medical knowledge that this patient is either going to die tomorrow or three months from tomorrow, after suffering very bitter pain. If he makes that medical decision, can you conceive that he would be responsible to the law?

MR. ARMSTRONG: If he didn't do it in consort with either the family or the individual, I think he should be.

THE COURT: All right. Now that being so, do you envision perhaps a possibility of a decision being the result or the end product of a combination of the medical profession or specific doctors arriving at a conclusion utilizing judicial guidelines concerning the definition of death? Does this concept at all appeal to you or appear to you as something worthy of this Court's consideration?

MR. ARMSTRONG: What we advance, Mr. Justice Pashman, is that it is the role and function of the physician to advise an individual of his diagnosis, what's wrong with him.

THE COURT: He does that.

MR. ARMSTRONG: From there I'm saying that further I can advise that the physician should advise as to the nature of treatments that are available, what the options are.

THE COURT: Yes, sir?

MR. ARMSTRONG: Then that decision should be made by either the individual or his family.

Oral Argument of James M. Crowley, on Behalf of Appellant Joseph Quinlan

At the outset of Armstrong's argument, he had asked permission from the court to share his time with Mr. James Crowley, an expert in First Amendment law. Crowley was called specifically to argue that Joe Quinlan had a constitutional right, by way of his free exercise of religion, to follow the mentoring of his religious leaders and discontinue the use of any extraordinary means that were being used to sustain Karen Ann.

MR. CROWLEY: Mr. Chief Justice, Honorable Justices, permit me to thank you for extending me the privilege of speaking before this Court on behalf of the Quinlan family. We submit that the Quinlans' decision has a valid claim to constitutional protection not only because it is an exercise of the right of privacy, but also because it is an effectuation of their religious beliefs. Now when such a claim is made, the Court must apply the threefold tasks laid down in *Wisconsin v. Yoder.* First, is the proposed action motivated by sincerely held religious belief? Second, is the proposed action intimately related to daily living? And third, are the beliefs in question shared by an organized group? When the religious nature of a proposed course of action is revealed, the Court must then determine whether any secular state interest is sufficiently compelling to prohibit the proposed action. Joseph Quinlan's claim meets all three *Yoder* tests, and the lower court, we submit, erred in not finding that such a claim was rooted in religious beliefs.

First, the evidence shows him to be a sincerely religious man who as part of his religion believes in the sanctity of life and the perfection of this life in the next and the futility of clinging to this life when hope is gone, in man's ability to know God's will within himself and to carry it out, and in the role of the family in promoting the spiritual good of its members. Second, it is clear that for a religious person nothing is more intimately related to daily life than a consideration and a preparation for the end of it. Third, the testimony of Mr. Quinlan's pastor and the hospital chaplain, the papal allocution admitted into evidence and the official teaching of the Catholic Church contained in the statement of Bishop Casey, which all the Roman Catholic bishops of this state have seconded and which they as friends of this Court have laid before you, make it clear that the course of actions chosen by Mr. Quinlan is actively supported by his church and is a concrete effectuation of its teachings.

THE COURT: May I stop you? It is my understanding that the position of the Catholic Church on this subject is neutral. In other words, it neither advocates nor refuses to advocate the termination of life in a situation of this kind and leaves it to the judgment of those directly concerned.

MR. CROWLEY: This, Your Honor, we submit was the error into which the lower court fell when having considered the evidence it then engaged in what we submit is a constitutionally impermissible weighing of religious belief—that is, an examination of the underlying religious principles and the importance of those principles to the totality of Catholic beliefs.

THE COURT: Are you saying that the teaching is that Mr. Quinlan and his family have the right to make this decision, as opposed to the doctor? Is that what the Church is passing—

MR. CROWLEY: That is how the teaching of the Catholic Church is effectuated—

THE COURT: And they say it's Mr. Quinlan's prerogative to make this determination?

MR. CROWLEY: It's the prerogative of the individual and the family to make life-influencing decisions for themselves and their members.

THE COURT: Mr. Crowley, don't you agree constitutionally though, that in order to evoke the protection of the First Amendment, that it is very well settled that there must be a burden—an underlying burden—that there must be a burden on the free exercise of that person's religion? Isn't that what the cases hold?

MR. CROWLEY: I submit, Your Honor, that there is a burden; but the stronger test is that the exercise—the claimed exercise—has to be a manifest abuse of some societal interest.

THE COURT: Well, Mr. Crowley, the reason I started this interrogation about the position of the Church being neutral, is that in the Jehovah's Witnesses cases you have a situation where the position of the religious adherent is not neutral, but there is an affirmative policy in his religion not to accept treatment. Nevertheless, if the interests of society are sufficiently contrary to the exercise of that religious belief, the courts have had no hesitancy in sustaining the interests of society as against the positive religious beliefs of the Jehovah's Witnesses.

MR. CROWLEY: Fair enough.

THE COURT: Now that being so, why shouldn't that principle apply even more forcefully to a case where the alleged religious interest is, as in this case, neutral and not affirmative.

MR. CROWLEY: Because, Your Honor, I conceive the wall of separation between church and state as being one in which whatever goes on the church side of the wall is not to be interfered with from the state side of the wall. No matter for what reason it goes on, if the church is playing ball on its side of the wall, as long as the ball doesn't go over to the other side and harm some societal interest, then the church should be left alone and people should be left alone with their religious beliefs. Once it impinges on the legitimate societal interests, then the state can step in and—

THE COURT: All right. Now doesn't that then beg the—you would then concede, on the basis of the Jehovah's Witnesses cases, that if the Court's construction of the interests of society in this case are such that the declaratory judgment here sought should be denied, it should make no difference what the religious beliefs of the applicant are?

MR. CROWLEY: Fair enough.

THE COURT: All right. Well, then the issue before us really is, What are the interests of society? And the religious preferences of your client are really irrelevant. Is that not so?

MR. CROWLEY: They are not so irrelevant that he is not entitled to claim an explicitly constitutionally protected right.

THE COURT: Well, there's nothing to prevent him from claiming them, but should the Court give any weight to them if the Court's conception of the interest of society is contrary?

CHIEF JUSTICE HUGHES: When the Court overrules a Jehovah's Witness's religious objection, say, to a transfusion and sees a recovery, either certain or certainly probable—

MR. CROWLEY: Those cases have found that.

CHIEF JUSTICE HUGHES: Doesn't this same thing apply? Would you think the Court should overrule the Jehovah's Witness's religious objection if it were conceded, as in this case, that it was almost hopeless or demonstrably hopeless? I mean, isn't that where the societal interest comes alive, so to speak?

MR. CROWLEY: The societal interest, I believe, is found in a combination of three factors: the nature and the prognosis of the ailment; the nature of the condition, or rather the nature of the treatment; and in the societal responsibilities of the person who is refusing treatment. The nature of the religious beliefs, where it's important for the religion, should have nothing to do with it.

THE COURT: Well, then, is what you are saying really that Catholic freedom of individual choice in this matter is a make-weight which the Court should put into the scales on the side of your client, but not itself be determinative?

MR. CROWLEY: I think it is constitutionally sufficient in itself, because the state has demonstrated no compelling interest, in our view, in forbidding the proposed activity. The cataloged fear— they have made appeals in this thrust and the lower court has heeded those appeals, but there has been no demonstration that in this case a specific societal interest is being harmed.

Oral Argument of Donald G. Collester, the Morris County Prosecutor

CHIEF JUSTICE HUGHES: Mr. Prosecutor, would you assume something for me? Supposing that Dr. Morse, on the night Karen Quinlan was received in that hospital, knew then all that he knows now about her condition and prognosis, and he decided, with the consent let's say of her father and mother, not to apply the life-sustaining apparatus. Would you think of prosecuting him in that case?

MR. COLLESTER: I don't think so, no.

CHIEF JUSTICE HUGHES: You wouldn't have a case, would you?

MR. COLLESTER: I wouldn't have a case at all, obviously.

CHIEF JUSTICE HUGHES: What's the essential difference between a decision not to connect the apparatus, and a decision to disconnect the apparatus? Is there any real difference, in logic?

MR. COLLESTER: Yes, I think there is. I think there is, in two parts. First of all we get into the act-and-omission dichotomy, which here I don't think is really applicable. It's hard to think of something more of an act than literally pulling out a plug, to use an odious phrase associated with this case.

CHIEF JUSTICE HUGHES: Well, let me make it easier for you. Supposing that a fuse blew out, and the doctor said, "Don't bother restoring that fuse."

MR. COLLESTER: I think he's still got the same problem, in terms of exposure.

THE COURT: Or, he didn't replace the oxygen tent.

MR. COLLESTER: I think, under our law right now, there would be exposure to criminal liability—prosecution—as it exists right now, from my reading of it.

THE COURT: You just rebel at the concept, apparently, of affirmatively, as you put it, "pulling this plug," as opposed to all the other measures which will ultimately bring about the same result, and that is death.

MR. COLLESTER: No, I don't—I can see that the criminal law has as one of its basic functions a deterrent. I also think that the law of homicide, in this respect, is relatively clear.

Two months and four days would pass before Chief Justice Hughes and his colleagues would return a decision. Joe Quinlan's attitude became far more peaceful and philosophical during that time. Left alone by the press—for the most part—he began to surmise that whatever happened, God had a greater plan for his family and particularly Karen Ann. Whatever it was, he'd accept it. He reflected on his service in World War II, particularly an experience during the Battle of the Bulge when he was hit by German artillery fire. A fellow soldier carried him away from the corpses surrounding them, saving Quinlan's life. Joe recalls begging the Lord to spare him. He felt he had not accomplished enough for it to be his time. At that time he had no family.

But as Joe Quinlan waited for the New Jersey Supreme Court's decision, his attitude toward death changed greatly:

You can face death when you've done something with your life. I've raised a family now. The next time I face death it'll just be time. Looking back [on that experience in the war], I feel that God was testing me, and sparing me for a role in some larger plan. I began to feel very strongly that Karen Ann [was] part of the plan. And that when we made the decision to let her die in peace, maybe it just wasn't good enough for us to have made it alone. Maybe God wanted everyone to make it, the whole community of doctors and lawyers and everyone. I really think He is using us, running this whole thing. And now when the Supreme Court makes their decision, maybe Karen Ann at last will be able to pass into the loving hands of the Lord. Because He won't punish anyone—especially someone He's using.

The Decision of the New Jersey Supreme Court

Justice Hughes and the other members of the court emerged from seclusion on March 30. The opinion was written, and the following morning at 10 A.M. Paul Armstrong entered the Supreme Court building in Trenton and was given a copy of the fifty-nine-page decision. Quite nervous, Armstrong asked the clerk disseminating the opinion if he might skim it somewhere in private, somewhere with a phone so that he might call the Quinlans. The clerk led him to a large, opulent study, the Supreme Court's inner chambers. Armstrong skimmed from the end of the opinion toward the front. Reading the decision, he wept: the Supreme Court of New Jersey in a unanimous decision had decreed that Joseph Quinlan should be his daughter's guardian and that Karen Ann's right of privacy could be asserted by him.

Chief Justice Hughes wrote the opinion and meticulously set forth the claims and positions of the different parties. He carefully described Karen Ann's condition, the medical treatment rendered, and then discussed the nature of death and the constitutional issues to be resolved:

Since the record has not been expanded, we assume that she is now even more fragile and nearer to death than she was then. Since her present treating physicians may give reconsideration to her present posture in the light of this opinion, and since we are transferring to the plaintiff as guardian the choice of the attending physician and therefore other physicians may be in charge of the case who may take a different view from that of the present attending physicians, we herewith declare the following affirmative relief on behalf of the plaintiff. Upon the concurrence of the guardian and family of Karen, should the responsible attending physicians conclude that there is no reasonable possibility of

Karen's ever emerging from her present comatose condition to a cognitive, sapient state and that the life-support apparatus now being administered to Karen should be discontinued, they shall consult with the hospital "Ethics Committee" or like body of the institution in which Karen is then hospitalized. If that consultative body agrees that there is no reasonable possibility of Karen's ever emerging from her present comatose condition to a cognitive, sapient state, the present life-support system may be withdrawn and said action shall be without any civil or criminal liability therefore on the part of any participant, whether guardian, physician, hospital, or others. We herewith specifically so hold.

The decision provided a series of victories for the Quinlans. In its first step, the court dismissed the argument that Joseph Quinlan did not have standing to assert his case. Normally one can only fight for his own legal rights, and while it is true that he was technically asserting the constitutional rights of his daughter, the court stated that he was "certainly no stranger to the present controversy. His interests are real and adverse and he raises questions of surpassing importance. Manifestly, he has standing to assert his daughter's constitutional rights, she being incompetent to do so." This was a small but necessary opening victory for the Quinlans. If the court had found that Joe Quinlan lacked standing to bring the case, none of the substantive issues would have been decided.

Next, the court rejected the contentions that Karen Ann's free exercise of religion or protection against cruel and unusual punishment were applicable to the controversy at hand. With regard to the free exercise of religion, the Court acknowledged its importance, but found that public interest triumphed over religious exercise that conflicted with important state goals. "Simply stated, the right to religious beliefs is absolute but conduct in pursuance thereof is not wholly immune from governmental restraint." The governmental restraint in this case was the interest in preserving human life. The Quinlans had somewhat expected this reaction, given the *Heston* decision. The Court also refused to plow new ground with the Eighth Amendment's proscription of cruel and unusual punishment. The Court held that the protection applied only to penal sanctions, and they found no precedent in the law "which would justify its extension to the correction of social injustice or hardship."

The majority of Chief Justice Hughes's opinion discussed Karen Ann's right to privacy. Although this right is not explicitly outlined in the Constitution, the 1965 U.S. Supreme Court's decision in *Griswold v. Connecticut* definitively held that a right of personal privacy exists "in the penumbra of specific guarantees of the Bill of Rights," and that certain areas of privacy are guaranteed under the Constitution. Justice Hughes wrote:

> We have no doubt, in these unhappy circumstances, that if Karen were herself miraculously lucid for an interval . . . and perceptive of her irreversible condition, she could effectively decide upon discontinuance of the life-support apparatus, even if it meant the prospect of natural death. . . . We have no hesitancy in deciding . . . that no external compelling interest of the State could compel Karen to endure the unendurable, only to vegetate a few measurable months with no realistic possibility of returning to any semblance of cognitive or sapient life. The only practical way to prevent destruction of that right is to permit the guardian and family of Karen to render their best judgment, subject to the qualifications hereinafter stated, as to whether she would exercise it in these circumstances.

Those were the words that the Quinlans had so desperately waited to hear.

The Effect of the New Jersey Supreme Court Decision

The ruling was a monumental victory for those who saw prolonged and needless suffering by the terminally ill as inhuman. The court's decision was straightforward, and the Quinlans received all of the relief they had requested. Joe Quinlan was appointed Karen Ann's guardian, and with the concurrence of her treating physicians and the ethics committee of the institution in which she was hospitalized, the life support could be withdrawn without criminal liability.

The court carefully and concisely struck down the notion that this flew in the face of modern medical standards. After hearing all of the complicated testimony from the medical professionals, the court simply found that the record spoke to a distinction between curing the ill and comforting the dying. "[Physicians] refuse to treat the curable as if they were dying or ought to die, and . . . they have sometimes refused to treat the hopeless and dying as if they were curable. . . . We think these attitudes represent a balanced implementation of a profoundly realistic perspective on the meaning of life and death and that they respect the whole Judeo-Christian tradition of regard for human life."

Although they admitted that this distinction may be harder to draw in the context of advanced technology and artificial life-sustaining devices, the court once again stated in simple terms a commonsense conclusion to the heightened medical dilemma that had caused many to scratch their heads in the courtroom. "The evidence in this case convinces us that the focal point of decision should be the prognosis as to the reasonable possibility of return to cognitive and sapient life, as distinguished from the forced continuance of that biological vegetative existence to which Karen seems to be doomed." In those few words, the court had carved a neat little passageway through the daunting wall of medical jargon that had clouded the issue for those who wanted merely to comfort Karen Ann in her final days. The simple distinction between those who may be cured, and those who are waiting to die, was the key turning point in the court's summary of the medical concerns in the case. In Karen Ann's case, the court had no difficulty in believing that she was simply waiting to die. Joe Quinlan was now granted the option of ending his daughter's persistent vegetative state.

Whatever Joe Quinlan decided, the opinion continued, "should be accepted by society, the overwhelming majority of whose members would, we think, in similar circumstances, exercise such a choice in the same way for themselves or for those closest to them."

"Our prayers have been answered," Armstrong said into the phone; the Quinlans wept, relieved. Little did they know their struggle was not quite over.

Joe Quinlan was sure that the decision of the New Jersey Supreme Court was, in fact, the will of God, but nevertheless he resolved to be patient with Dr. Morse. "I know how he must be feeling now. He has a different problem here. He has to decide now either to follow orders or to resign. I almost feel sorry for him. We'll give him a few days to make up his mind."

The Quinlans did in fact give him those "few days." Not until April 8, 1976, eight days after the court's decision was handed down, did they contact Dr. Morse and request a meeting. Morse seemed surprised that the Quinlans would want to see him. And while he welcomed the meeting, he acted as if nothing had changed. When the Quinlans asked him when and how he planned to implement the court's decision, Morse answered that he had not read the decision, and that it wouldn't make any difference if he had in fact read it. He informed the Quinlans that he intended to continue to support Karen Ann's life on the respirator, and that he intended to continue to follow his concept of what is standard medical practice. "You know," Morse concluded solemnly, "this is something I will have to live with the rest of my life."

Morse did agree to another meeting to discuss the issue—when he returned two weeks later from a holiday in Puerto Rico. "Trust us," Morse said as he ushered the Quinlans from his office. But any feelings of trust in Morse the Quinlans might have entertained quickly turned to suspicion. In the following weeks, not only did Morse not remove the respirator, but he added new life-sustaining apparatus to the amalgamation of tubes and boxes surrounding Karen Ann's bed. Among these new machines was a body temperature control, implemented, Morse explained, because Karen had an infection and this machine would help to bring down her fever.

After a number of increasingly tense meetings, the Quinlans and Morse came to an agreement that fully satisfied no one. Karen Ann's team of doctors, including Morse, would slowly wean her from the respirator in hopes that she might breathe on her own. Thus the Quinlans' rights would be honored as Karen Ann would no longer be on a respirator, and by the same token, Morse would not violate his code of medical ethics, as his removal of the respirator would not be the direct cause of her death.

By May 22 this had been accomplished. The medical report for that day read: "Doing very well without MA-1 [respirator]. Lungs are clear. [Patient] resting comfortably. Color good. Restful evening. Respiration even and full most of the time."

Remarkably, Karen Ann kept on breathing. Days passed. Then weeks. Joe Quinlan wondered, "What could God be using her for now?" Now that Karen Ann had survived the weaning and was still living, what was the next step?

Since she was off the respirator, there was no need to keep her in a hospital. Karen Ann had to be moved to a long-term health care facility and a new doctor found. Morris View Nursing Home and its director, Richard Watson, would be the final stop for Karen Ann, and were she to near death, no dramatic steps would be taken to revive her. Watson assured the taxpayers of Morris County that no extra personnel would be needed to take care of Karen Ann; she would receive the benefits only of a "general medical and nursing care routine." This consisted of feeding her a commercially packaged formula that was mixed in distilled water and ingested via nasal tube, shifting her body and treating her skin with gastric antacid to fend off further bedsores, cleansing her tracheal area once during each eight-hour shift, changing her catheter, and administering an expectorant and an anticonvulsant medication.

Ironically, the greatest cost to taxpayers would prove to be the armed deputies stationed outside Karen Ann's door twenty-four hours a day, to foil attempts by the media and the public to enter her room.

The move from St. Clare's to the nursing home was complicated by Karen Ann's celebrity status. The Quinlans feared that if news of the transfer leaked to the press, the ensuing crush of photographers could be dangerous to Karen Ann's welfare. Days were spent in the company of local law enforcement authorities in an attempt to properly choreograph the procedure.

The move was planned for 9 P.M., Wednesday, June 9, 1976. The Quinlans arrived at the hospital shortly before the arranged time, trying to appear nonchalant. Unfortunately, the press had been tipped off and they were swarming everywhere. While Karen Ann was safely placed into the ambulance and the drive to the new facility went smoothly enough, those tending to her during the drive were apprehensive about how the handoff would be accomplished at the nursing home.

As the ambulance bearing their daughter arrived at the Morris facility, it began to rain, and then seconds before Karen Ann emerged in her stretcher to be carried through the doors of the new facility, a lightning bolt struck the threshold of the entrance, scattering the press just long enough for Karen Ann to pass through the portals untouched.

The Quinlans visited Karen faithfully and were with her when she died of pneumonia on June 11, 1985, more than nine years after the respirator was disconnected. Julia Quinlan was at her daughter's bedside: "I said the Our Father . . . and I hid my face next to hers and I cried and cried."

At her death, the press once again flooded the airwaves with Karen Ann Quinlan. Cartoonist Paul Conrad of the *Los Angeles Times* drew a cartoon of a beatific Karen Ann wearing angel wings and floating toward heaven. The only incongruity in the cartoon was a liberated wire and a plug that hung out like a long vestigial tail from beneath her robes. The caption beneath read, "Karen Ann Quinlan Is Finally Granted the Right to Die."

KAREN ANN QUINLAN IS FINALLY GRANTED THE RIGHT TO DIE.

Reprinted with permission from Paul Conrad, *Los Angeles Times*, 1985.

A Continuing Legacy

The Karen Ann Quinlan case brought both immediate and lasting consequences for those faced with the impending death of themselves or a loved one. First and foremost, it established binding precedent that remains to this day. If any family find themselves in a position similar to the Quinlans' and desire to bring a patient's comatose existence to a dignified close, they can point to the opinion by Justice Hughes for constitutional support.

A second immediate result of the Quinlan case was public awareness of the "right to die." As a developing issue that had significant consequences for families, doctors, medical institutions, theologians, and philosophers, the question of when and how one may refuse life support took center stage after the decision. In 1976, the California Natural Death Act became law, the nation's first statute granting legal recognition to living wills and protecting physicians from being sued for failing to treat incurable illnesses. Soon after, ten more states passed natural death laws.

In 1980, Pope John Paul II issued the *Declaration in Euthanasia,* which opposed mercy killings but permitted the greater use of painkillers to ease pain and the right to refuse extraordinary means for sustaining life. The "right to die" assumed the national spotlight for a time and also became a political platform for governmental and religious leaders.

One of the most lasting practical consequences of the Quinlan decision was that hospitals and medical facilities across the country were prompted to create ethics committees to give guidance to doctors and families in circumstances similar to those faced by the Quinlans and their doctors.

Another result of the case was the onslaught of advanced directives or living wills. These were documents written while the subject was healthy, but which gave orders about administering life support should the person become terminally ill. Almost unknown before the Quinlan decision, advance directives have become the conventional method of expressing an individual's desire to die naturally should he end up in a comatose state while on life support. As of 2004, advance directive laws had been passed in forty-eight states.

In 1990, the American Medical Association adopted the formal position that with a patient's informed consent through the use of an advance directive, a physician can withhold or withdraw treatment from a patient who is close to death and may also discontinue life support of a patient in a permanent coma.

Another consequence of the Quinlan case is Oregon's assisted-suicide law, which voters have approved twice since 1994. Under strict guidelines, Oregon's law allows physicians to prescribe lethal "cocktails" of narcotics to terminally ill patients. To qualify for physician-assisted suicide under Oregon's law, an adult must be diagnosed as having a life expectancy of less than six months, and a second doctor must find the patient mentally competent and not suffering from depression. The patient must make two oral requests, and a third in writing, for a physician's assistance, and then wait fifteen days before receiving the prescription.

In the first five years following the law's enactment, 129 people in Oregon committed suicide with narcotics prescribed by a physician.

The U.S. Justice Department has mounted significant legal challenges to the Oregon law, repeatedly maintaining that it has the right to ban lethal doses of controlled narcotics. The federal government argues that such narcotics are closely regulated, their use restricted to and intended for medical purposes only. In all likelihood, the fate of the Oregon law will ultimately be decided by the U.S. Supreme Court.

In the end, the life and death of Karen Ann Quinlan was not just about living wills, DNR orders, and extraordinary measures. To Joe and Julia Quinlan it was about returning their daughter to the state where her body could hear "the gentle call that beckoned her to a lasting peace."

CHAPTER TWO

The Amistad *Odyssey*

American Courts Decide If a Free Man Can Be Forced into Slavery

Can [America] become a party to the proceedings for the enslavement of human beings cast upon our shores, and found in the condition of free men . . . ?

—*Roger Sherman Baldwin*

U.S. secretary of state Colin Powell is black; so too is National Security Adviser Condoleezza Rice. Oprah Winfrey is America's highest-paid entertainer; Michael Jordan is perhaps the most beloved sports star of the last twenty years. In the early days of the twenty-first century, some of America's most successful, prominent, and respected citizens—politicians, statesmen, scholars, entertainers, artists, and athletes—are black.

One hundred and thirty-nine years ago, their ancestors might have been human chattel, bought and sold at auction in the American South, until the Civil War forever ended slavery's shameful presence in North America. But the change from property to citizen represented an enormous paradigm shift, one that began not with a war between the states but a series of legal battles fought over definitions: What was a free man? How did a free man become a slave? Could a man become property? Once property, did he retain the right to become free again?

The story of America's slaves gaining their freedom—and of America freeing itself from the horror of slavery—began with the revolt of the Africans aboard the slave ship *Amistad,* and the strength of those slaves, the courage of the men who argued on their behalf, and the integrity of the courts.

A Mean History

Slavery is not a uniquely American institution; accepted as a way of life in much of Western Europe and its colonial holdings throughout the eighteenth century, it survives today in parts of Asia, Africa, and the Middle East. By the end of the eighteenth century, however, the common Western view of slavery as "an ancient and necessary institution" was on the wane.

In 1794, the U.S. government responded to the growing social outcry against slavery by prohibiting American citizens from participating in the slave trade. In 1802, Denmark became the first European nation to completely abolish the slave trade; England soon followed suit. The United States, spurred on by the actions of the European nations, enacted legislation in 1808 forbidding the importation of slaves.

By 1835, France, the Netherlands, Sweden, and even Portugal and Spain—former leaders in the sale of human cargo—agreed to end the international market for slaves. To this end, an international commission, spearheaded by England, attempted to enforce these agreements by capturing slave ships on the high seas, punishing the offending slavers, freeing the captives, and selling the vessels at auction.

Although the European nations and the newly founded United States of America had banned the capture, abduction, and importation of slaves, the institution of slavery itself survived. Those slaves already within the territories of Western nations remained in bondage, their children born into servitude, to be sold and traded as their masters wished. Furthermore, despite the international ban, illegal slave trading continued in the United States and throughout the world. During the first half of the nineteenth century, slavers imported a quarter million slaves into the United States, despite the risk of being convicted of "piracy" and suffering a death sentence.

Spanish and Portuguese merchants were the traders, even after the Spanish government issued an order in 1820 banning the practice. In 1837, Spain issued an order demanding that the captain-general of Cuba (a Spanish colony) stamp out the slave trade on the island. The order, however, was ambiguous. No slaves could be brought into Cuba for transport to another nation, yet the order established two classes of slaves: the *bozal* class included slaves imported from Africa for personal use by a slave owner, if the slave had been in bondage prior to the 1820 prohibition. The *ladino* class included either second-generation slaves or those who had been imported to Cuba prior to the prohibition of 1820. *Bozals* were not to be traded, sold, or shipped by sea, while *ladinos* could be moved around within Spanish territory, if the owner had the "proper" documentation. The people responsible for providing the documentation and enforcing these regulations were prone to "overlook" the rules for a fee; it was not difficult for a slave trader to purchase documents classifying a person as a *ladino,* thereby evading the prohibition on shipping and sale.

The slave trade was—even given the potential penalties and risks—perhaps the most lucrative business of the era. In his 1854 book, *Twenty Years of an African Slaver,* Brantz Mayer described a voyage by a slave ship in 1827 between West Africa and Cuba that resulted in a net profit of more than $41,000, the equivalent of nearly $750,000 today, enough to purchase as many as ten ships in 1827.

The details of the slaver's trade were shocking and brutal. Captive Africans were assembled by a slave trader in a barracoon, or slave pen. When a ship dropped anchor near a barracoon, the trader and the ship's captain would negotiate a price for a set number of slaves. The ship and its crew would then wait until the barracoon contained the agreed-upon number of captives. The Africans were fed a large meal to make them drowsy, then loaded onto the ship, stripped, and placed in the hold.

The conditions belowdecks were atrocious; the holds often measured a scant three feet from ceiling to floor, barely enough space to sit upright. The slaves—chained together in groups of five or ten by the iron collars around their necks—were given two meals a day, in the morning and afternoon. Ten men ate out of a bucket, using their hands to scoop out rice, beans, or yams. A close watch was kept on their dietary habits; any man who failed to eat—damaging the goods—was flogged. Slaves who fell ill were inspected to see if they could be saved; if not, they were thrown overboard.

The Odyssey Begins

In the early spring of 1839, a steady influx of captives kept the barracoon at Lomboko full. One day the slavers tossed a man named Singbe into the slave pen, located in Sierra Leone on the coast of western Africa. Singbe was about twenty-five years old, five feet eight inches tall, a farmer who, with his father, wife, son, and two daughters, had grown rice in the village of Mani. He had left his home several days before on the way to his fields, when he was kidnapped by four other Africans and sold to slavers.

Singbe found himself with a number of other native captives. Gilabaru was another Mende, seized because his uncle's payment to a creditor had failed to arrive. Kimbo was sold to the slavers by his own king. Burna and Kwong were sold to slavers as punishment after they were caught with other men's wives. Fuliwa was sold by another tribe after surviving defeat and capture in battle. Other captives included a small boy, Ka-le, and three little girls, Teme, Kagne, and Margru. All had lost their freedom to other Africans looking to make a profit by selling them to the white slavers. Singbe remained in the barracoon for two months before a slave ship arrived.

When the *Tecora* sailed into the harbor, the captives were stripped, chained in groups of five, and packed so tightly into the hold that one person's head, when lying in rows, was forced upon another person's thigh.

Packed into the hold, they set sail for Cuba. The voyage took nearly three months.

The slave traders smuggled the captive Africans from the *Tecora* into Cuba in small boats, where they were placed in another barracoon. Several days later, Don Jose Ruiz, a Spaniard, claimed he was looking to purchase slaves to add to his family estates near Puerto Príncipe in Cuba—although he may have intended to smuggle them covertly into the southern United States. Ruiz's claim that he wanted to transfer the slaves across Cuba went unchallenged; not particularly surprising, as the governor-general would collect a $15 transfer fee for each of the slaves.

Ruiz picked forty-nine of the captives and paid $450 for each, receiving a document called a *traspaso,* signed and given to him by the governor-general himself. The *traspaso* stated that Ruiz owned and had permission to transport to Puerto Príncipe forty-nine Negro slaves, whom it misclassified as *ladino*—because to be *ladinos* under Spanish law, the slaves would have had to be residents of Cuba prior to 1820.

The Amistad

The captives lined up, collars were fastened about their necks, they were chained in groups and then marched to the Havana docks. As they were loaded onto a ship, each was assigned a Christian name—after all, how could they be residents of Cuba if they didn't have Spanish names?—which was written onto the *traspaso* itself. Singbe became Joseph Cinquez. Then they were put into the hold.

Ruiz met Don Pedro Montez on the dock. Montez, another Spaniard allegedly making the journey to Puerto Príncipe, had booked passage on the ship for himself and the four captive children he had purchased, Ka-le, Teme, Kagne, and Margru.

The *Amistad* was owned and under the command of Captain Ramon Ferrer, who had a crew of two slaves, Antonio and Celestino, and two Spanish sailors. The sailors were responsible for piloting and operating the ship, while Celestino cooked for the crew, passengers, and slaves and maintained the water supply. Antonio was the captain's cabin and errand boy.

Customs officials boarded the *Amistad* for a cursory inspection; Ruiz and Montez each presented their *traspasos,* detailing the number of slaves belonging to each passenger. The customs officials glossed over the *traspasos'* claims that each of the *"ladino"* slaves, including the young children now in Montez's possession, had been in Cuba for at least eighteen years.

The *Amistad* sailed from Havana on June 27. Captain Ferrer noted on the first day that while the weather was good, the winds were wrong. As a result, the *Amistad* would take longer than anticipated to reach its destination. Realizing that the ship carried only four or five days' food for the slaves, Ferrer cut the rations. The captives complained, and when two slaves drank more water than allowed, they were whipped, their wounds treated with salt, gunpowder, and rum. Considered a traditional remedy to prevent infection while at sea, the treatment was excruciatingly painful and left large, hard scars.

By the fourth day at sea, the *Amistad* was fighting its way into the wind. The captives asked Celestino, the slave cook, what would happen to them when they arrived. Celestino told them that the white men would eat them. The stunned captives turned to Singbe, who said, "If we do nothing, we be killed. We may as well die in trying to be free as to be killed and eaten."

The Takeover

On the fifth night, after the crew turned in for the evening, Singbe used a nail he had hidden under his arm to free himself and the others from their chains. The captives burst out of the hold, some armed with machete-like cane knives that were part of the cargo. Captain Ferrer and Celestino were killed during the fight; the two Spanish crewmen fled in a small boat. Singbe considered killing Ruiz and Montez, but a discussion with the other Africans convinced him that without some help they would be unable to sail the *Amistad.*

Montez had at one time been a ship captain and was a capable navigator. Singbe, who made himself understood haltingly through the slave Antonio, told Montez they intended to sail back to Africa, and that he must help them or be killed. Montez agreed to cooperate.

Singbe ordered Montez and Ruiz to sail east to Africa; Montez did so by day, but at night he turned the ship west, hoping to remain near the North American coast, where they'd be discovered by another ship. Later,

Singbe told the others, "They made fools of us." By tacking in the available winds to keep the ship moving, the Spaniards pushed the ship in a more northern than eastern route, even during the day. The Spaniards were helped because the ship, lacking an experienced crew, began deteriorating. The sails tore and were not repaired; the bottom of the ship accumulated barnacles, and it therefore lost speed. June passed into July. July passed into August. Despite occasional stops at small islands to replenish their water supply and gather what little food they could, supplies dwindled. Some of the former captives fell ill and died, while others ate medicines found among the cargo and were poisoned. Meanwhile the surviving Africans began to grow restless and depressed as the schooner zigzagged east and west, slowly moving north as it neared the coast of the United States.

The *Amistad* finally spotted another ship, not far from the entrance to New York's harbor. The captain of the *Blossom* noted the *Amistad*'s poor condition and came alongside, where he could see that the ship was manned by a number of black men. The American captain communicated with Singbe, using improvised signs and Antonio to help translate, learning that the crew needed food and water, which he ordered passed over. The *Blossom* stayed near the *Amistad* overnight, the captain weighing what to do. The next morning, he tried to take the *Amistad* in tow to New York. Singbe and the other Africans, wary of the captain's intentions, attempted to board the *Blossom;* the captain ordered the towline cut, and the *Blossom* sailed away to report the strange vessel they had encountered.

The *Amistad* created a sensation on the East Coast; sightings of the mysterious ship were soon reported in newspapers all along the seaboard. Meanwhile, the desperate Africans, their supplies exhausted, had made no progress toward Africa. Finally, on August 24, the *Amistad* anchored off Culloden Point on the eastern end of Long Island. Singbe decided to send a number of the men ashore to buy or acquire enough food and water for a final grand attempt to reach Africa: they would simply sail east as long as they possibly could. The next morning, a boatload of the men went ashore. They carried goods from the hold of the *Amistad* to offer in trade for provisions, and they even had a supply of gold they had discovered among Captain Ferrer's belongings. However, they were able only to refill their water supply and acquire some potatoes. Singbe himself went ashore the following day, hoping to find someone or somewhere he could get food for the ship. He and the men with him were having only moderate success when they encountered Captains Henry Green and Pelatiah Fordham.

Captives Again

One of the Africans, who had picked up broken English, asked, "What country is this?" Captain Green replied, "This is America." The African asked whether it was a slave country. "No," Captain Green told him, "it is a free country." The Africans were so excited by his response they cheered. They also gave Green what few weapons they were carrying and led him to where they could see the *Amistad* anchored. They traded with Green and his American compatriots for food, telling him they were willing to give Green all the ship's cargo in return for provisions and help in sailing back to Africa. Green seemed agreeable, but whether he would have held up his end of the bargain is unknown; their discussions were interrupted when a U.S. Coast Guard surveying brig, the *Washington,* arrived and pulled alongside.

The commander of the *Washington,* Lieutenant Commander Thomas R. Gedney, sent a small contingent aboard the *Amistad* to investigate. As the group of seven men boarded and ordered all of the Africans on board the ship belowdecks, Singbe rushed back to the ship from shore. However, the armed coastguardsmen had already discovered and freed the Spaniards who were locked below. Ruiz and Montez quickly told the coastguardsmen a tale of mutiny and murder. Ruiz pointed at Singbe and claimed, "These Negroes are my slaves. . . . They have risen and taken the vessel; that is the leader; and I claim your protection." Singbe threw himself over the side. Coast Guard sailors reportedly chased him for thirty minutes while he repeatedly dove and resurfaced in an attempt to escape, until, exhausted, he was pulled into their boat.

Lieutenant Commander Gedney believed fortune had smiled upon him: if the *Amistad* was in the hands of pirates, or at least mutineers, and he seized the ship, he could establish a claim of salvage to both the ship and its cargo. Gedney ordered the *Amistad* towed to New London, Connecticut, where it arrived on the evening of August 27. Gedney sent a message to the United States marshal at New Haven, who then contacted District Judge A. T. Judson; both men arrived in New London the next day, intent on holding an inquiry. Gedney, the marshal, and particularly the judge knew that many questions would have to be addressed. What was the status of the *Amistad*? What was the status of its passengers? Its cargo? Were there grounds for trial on the charge of piracy? Were the Africans slaves, as the Spaniards claimed? In an attempt to answer at least some of these questions, Judge Judson opened his court of inquiry on board the *Washington* on August 29, 1839.

Montez and Ruiz each filed a complaint that "Joseph Cinquez" had led the other slaves in murder and piracy. A manacled Singbe was read an indictment he could not understand. After the judge finished the reading of the indictment, he heard the presentation of evidence. Gedney submitted several bundles of documents discovered aboard the *Amistad,* including the *traspasos* that had been granted to Ruiz and Montez.

Ruiz testified that he had purchased the "slaves" in Havana and was shipping them within Cuba to Puerto Príncipe. However, the bulk of his testimony was centered around the night the Africans had taken the ship and the manner in which he had been held and made to help sail the ship. When Ruiz was finished, the judge called and heard similar testimony from Montez. Finally, the judge, the marshal, Gedney, Ruiz, and Montez made a single circuit of the *Amistad* itself, which was moored next to the *Washington.* When the examination of the decks of the *Amistad* was complete, the group met in the captain's cabin of the *Washington,* where the judge handed down his decision:

> Joseph Cinquez, the leader, and 38 others, as named in the indictment, stand committed for trial before the next Circuit Court at Hartford to be holden [*sic*] on the 17th day of September next. The three girls and Antonio the cabin boy are ordered to give bonds in the sum of $100 each to appear before the said court and give evidence in the aforesaid case.

Neither the Africans nor Antonio had $100 between them, so all were jailed to await the trial. The inquiry concluded, the judge ordered the marshal to transport all the Africans to the New Haven jail.

(Re)Claiming Property

Ruiz and Montez quickly published a notice in the New London newspapers, expressing their gratitude:

> The subscribers, Don Jose Ruiz and Don Pedro Montez, in gratitude for their most unhoped for and providential rescue from the bands of a ruthless gang of African buccaneers and an awful death, would take the means of expressing, in some slight degree, their thankfulness and obligation to Lieutenant Commander T. R. Gedney, and the officers and crew of the U.S. surveying brig *Washington,* for their decision in seizing the *Amistad,* and their unremitting kindness and hospitality in providing for their comfort on board their vessel as well as the means they have taken for the protection of the property. We must

also express our indebtedness to that nation whose flag they so worthily bear, with an assurance that the act will be duly appreciated by our most gracious sovereign, Her Majesty, the Queen of Spain.

The notice was far more than a gracious thank-you for their rescue. The Spaniards were signaling that the Africans were their property, and all others should refrain from claiming salvage rights on the *Amistad* or any of its cargo.

Were the Spaniards likely to prevail? It appeared that they might. In 1839, the U.S. government continued to recognize a property right in slaves, despite the illegality of the slave trade itself. Furthermore, the United States was not without legal precedent in similar matters.

In the autumn of 1797, the crew of the HMS *Hermione* mutinied, murdered the captain and officers, and ran the ship into American water, where they sold it before scattering in the United States. British officials were determined to punish the mutineers, and an intensive search for them ensued. The British consul in Charleston, South Carolina, requested that American authorities arrest a man named Johnathan Robbins and turn him over to British authorities. The consul claimed that Robbins was actually the mutiny's ringleader, Thomas Nash. Robbins-Nash claimed that he was not British but an American citizen who had been seized and impressed into British service. Robbins-Nash believed that he had only been trying to regain the freedom of which he had been illegally deprived, and thus he could not be charged for the mutiny or murders under the British admiralty or criminal laws. However, after listening to Robbins-Nash's argument and the evidence presented by the British consul, the judge ruled that Robbins-Nash was British and ordered him returned to British jurisdiction. Robbins-Nash was taken to the British naval court at Jamaica, where he was convicted and hanged.

It was generally accepted that had Robbins-Nash been found to be an American impressed by the British, he would have been justified in performing any act, including mutiny and murder, to free himself. However, Ruiz and Montez's indictments of the Africans and the presentation of their *traspasos* showed, however falsely, that the "slaves" were all subject to Spanish jurisdiction in Cuba.

Robbins-Nash was not the only significant American precedent. In 1819, the privateer ship *Arraganta,* crewed primarily by Americans, cruised along the coast of West Africa, where it attacked and captured an American ship, two Portuguese ships, and the Spanish ship *Antelope,* carrying 280 captive Africans. With the *Antelope* in tow, the *Arraganta* sailed to Brazil. Before reaching port, the *Arraganta* was shipwrecked, and the survivors, including several captured Americans and Africans, escaped on the *Antelope*. The *Antelope* was later discovered and captured off the coast of Florida by a U.S. government cutter with its illegal "cargo" of Africans. The captain of the cutter filed for salvage rights, while agents of the United States filed claims on behalf of the Africans who had been taken from the American ship. The government agents claimed that the Africans had effectively been transported by Americans in contravention of U.S. slave trade laws, and thus all of the Africans should be freed. The Spanish and Portuguese governments, anxious to reclaim the valuable African captives, also filed claims to the "property" of the *Antelope* and the Portuguese ships.

The American court dismissed the salvage claim of the officer who had recovered the *Antelope* and allowed the U.S. claim only for those Africans who had been taken by the *Arraganta* from the American ship. The rest of the Africans, the court held, were to be returned as property to their Spanish and Portuguese claimants. The case was appealed to the U.S. Supreme Court, which upheld the lower court's decision.

Americans Weigh In

Given these precedents and the testimony and documents Ruiz and Montez provided at the *Amistad* inquiry, it hardly seems surprising that the two Spaniards expected their "property" would be returned to them. Nevertheless, even as the Spaniards anticipated a favorable outcome, Americans puzzled over the case, which had received national notoriety. Even newspapers known for strong anti-abolitionist leanings, such as the *New York Morning Herald,* were reluctant to pronounce the *Amistad* Africans guilty of a crime and questioned the claims of the Spaniards in an editorial published September 2, 1839:

> We despise the humbug doctrines of the abolitionists and the miserable fanatics who propagate them; but if men will traffic in human flesh, steal men from their homes on the coast of Africa, and sell them like cattle at Cuba, they must not murmur if some of the men stealers get murdered by the unfortunate wretches whom they have wronged and stole.

Meanwhile, the Africans were delivered into the custody of Colonel Pendleton, the keeper of the New Haven jail. Mrs. Pendleton took the four young children and put them up in a separate room, away from the main portion of the jail, and Pendleton put the sick prisoners on the third floor of the jail, while the other Africans were placed in cells on the second floor. Willard Gibbs, a professor of languages from Yale University, came to see the captives, hoping that he could determine their homeland and thereby find an interpreter. Curiosity seekers came to gawk at the prisoners, and "entrepreneurs" tried to find a way to capitalize on the sudden fame of the unfortunate Africans. Colonel Pendleton charged one shilling to view the prisoners, promising that the money would go toward the "betterment" of the Africans and pay for their upkeep.

The Reverend Joshua Leavitt, one of New York City's leading anti-slavery activists, traveled to New Haven to visit the imprisoned Africans. In an attempt to communicate with the men, he brought with him a free African fluent in several native languages; unfortunately, he was from the Congo and did not speak Mende, and neither he nor the prisoners understood each other.

Leavitt's descriptions of the prisoners, published in the *Hartford Courant,* reinforced a growing public sympathy for them. Leavitt said that even the "notorious" Singbe seemed a gentle man, not at all the dreaded pirate and murderous mutineer people had originally feared, and despite Singbe's and the other Africans' confusion and growing depression, "They all appear[ed] to be persons of quiet minds and a mild and cheer-ful temper. . . . There are no contentions among them; even the poor children, three girls and a boy, who are in a room by themselves, seem to be uniformly kind and friendly."

Leavitt returned to New York and with another leading abolitionist, Lewis Tappan, formed the Committee on Behalf of the African Prisoners. Tappan, a wealthy and influential merchant, was a member of the New York chapter of the American Anti-Slavery Society. The men met in the office of *The Emancipator,* the periodical published by the Anti-Slavery Society and edited by Leavitt. They used the publication to solicit dona-tions for the support and legal aid of the prisoners. Many Americans were increasingly sympathetic toward the Africans, described in the press as helplessly cast upon the shores of a strange country after countless unknown trials and tribulations. Donations began pouring in, and the committee hired three attorneys, Roger S. Baldwin, Seth P. Staples, and Theodore Sedgwick, to prepare for the approaching trial.

Roger Sherman Baldwin was the grandson of Roger Sherman, a signer of the Declaration of Independence and a member of the Constitutional Convention of 1787, and the son of Simeon Baldwin, a prominent lawyer, former mayor of New Haven, and outspoken opponent of slavery, who helped found the Connecticut Society for the Promotion of Freedom and for the Relief of Persons unlawfully holden [*sic*] in Bondage. Roger Bald-win was a successful attorney known for his dedication to the abolitionist cause, a reputation he'd earned in 1831, facing down an anti-abolitionist mob trying to block the construction of a training school for Negroes in New Haven.

Despite the skill and dedication of the lawyers, there remained a significant obstacle: How could they properly defend their clients when a language barrier prevented all but the most rudimentary communication? Professor Gibbs, the Yale linguistics expert, again visited the prisoners, held up a finger, and said, "One." After a brief pause, one of the Africans replied, "Eta." Encouraged by the breakthrough, Gibbs learned how to count to ten in Mende and began scouring the ports and waterfronts of New Haven and New York for anyone who could understand the language.

Lewis Tappan traveled to New Haven, bringing with him three Africans who spoke several languages among them. One of the three Africans, John Ferry, carried on rudimentary conversations with the prisoners by combining his native language of Bissi with his limited knowledge of the Mende language and the language spoken at the Lomboko barracoon. Tappan wrote happily of finally reaching a breakthrough in communication after so long: "You may imagine the joy manifested by these poor Africans when they heard one of their own color address them in a friendly manner, and in a language they could understand!" Tappan and Ferry also spoke to Singbe. Tappan wrote:

> [Singbe] drew his hand across his throat, as . . . he had done frequently before, and asked whether the people here intended to kill him. . . . He was assured that probably no harm would happen to him—that we were his friends—and that he would be sent across the ocean towards the rising sun, home to his friends. . . . His countenance immediately lost the anxious and distressed expression it had before, and beamed with joy.

Tappan also brought two of the men who had agreed to act as the prisoners' lawyers, Roger Baldwin, who was to be chief counsel for the defense, and Seth Staples. Communicating with the Africans through Ferry, the attorneys began to grasp the full measure of the captives' ordeal. Upon learning the story, the *Hartford Courant* editorialized:

> By the laws of the United States, the African slave trade is declared piracy. . . . It would be very extraordinary then if these men, who were stolen from their own country, and brought away for the purpose of being reduced to a state of slavery, should be punished for using such means as they possessed to extricate themselves.

The attorneys, the abolitionists, and gradually some of the American people were coming to believe that the Africans were not slaves, but free men; not pirates, but victims trying to escape their captors.

The Spanish "Card"

Ruiz and Montez, however, were determined to retrieve their "property." They turned to the Spanish consul in Boston, who in turn wrote to the Spanish minister, Angel Calderon de la Barca. After meeting Ruiz and Montez in New York, de la Barca decided to pressure the U.S. government on their behalf, intimating in a letter to Secretary of State John Forsyth that the courts should not have become involved in what was surely an administrative matter. The Spanish diplomat, after thanking the Americans for the rescue of the Spaniards, suggested that they should have been allowed to claim their "property" immediately after their rescue, rather than leaving it to the courts.

The secretary of state forwarded the letter to President Martin Van Buren, who did not wish to get involved. Van Buren stalled, then asked for more information. It was now September 23, and legal proceedings had begun.

Undeterred by the silence of the U.S. government, the Spanish redoubled their efforts. The Spanish consul in Boston, who received a copy of the letter from de la Barca to Secretary of State Forsyth, traveled to Connecticut to "expedite" matters. There, he met with District Attorney William Holabird and presented much the same case: the Africans were Spanish property and as such should immediately be returned without recourse to the American judicial system. Holabird agreed; it was a matter for the executive branch. The "slaves" must be returned to Spain as agreed in the Spanish-American treaty, because the Africans were considered by Spain to be "rescued merchandise." According to the terms of the treaty between the two nations, all merchandise was to be restored in its entirety.

On September 9, Holabird wrote to the secretary of state, requesting authorization to deliver the Africans immediately to the Spanish. Two days later, Holabird had his answer. He was not to hand them over but was instead instructed to wait and ordered to represent the interests of the government in the case: "You will take care that no proceeding of your circuit court . . . places the vessel, cargo, or slaves beyond the control of the Federal Executive."

The legal proceedings began on Wednesday, September 18, 1839, in the Hartford courthouse. Lawyers, reporters, and curious locals filled the building, and vendors hawked engravings of Singbe and the *Amistad*.

People gathered along the banks of the Connecticut River to watch the arrival of the Africans, and the courtroom was reportedly "filled to suffocation."

Tappan and the abolitionists, through Baldwin and the other lawyers, had asked the circuit court to grant a writ of habeas corpus on behalf of the three small girls. Such a writ would order their immediate release from custody. The defense believed that by limiting their initial efforts to the girls, they could keep the focus on children who had clearly played no role in the mutiny and killings on board the *Amistad* and would generate even more public sympathy for the plight of the captive Africans. Furthermore, if their writ was granted, it would serve as an excellent precedent for freeing the remaining Africans. Finally, a large part of the Spaniards' claim was that the Africans were legally Spanish citizens and *ladino* slaves. Given the girls' young ages and their inability to speak a word of Spanish, the attorneys believed the court would have a difficult time finding that the girls had been legally sold as slaves under Spanish law.

The matter presented a number of complicated issues. The court was faced with the habeas petition from the Africans' attorneys; criminal charges arising from the killings of Captains Ferrer and Celestino; property disputes regarding how to deal with the nonhuman and human "cargo"; admiralty law as a result of both Lieutenant Commander Gedney and Captain Green claiming salvage rights; and jurisdictional issues, District Attorney Holabird citing the 1795 treaty with Spain to argue that the Africans should be turned over to the executive branch and be dealt with according to international law.

Five days after the hearing began, Judge Smith Thompson ruled that the court had no jurisdiction to hear any criminal charges. The judge reasoned that any alleged crimes were against citizens of Spain on a Spanish ship on the open sea, and jurisdiction to hear such a case could reside only in Spain or Spanish possessions. Judge Thompson also refused to grant the habeas writ, explaining, "However abhorrent it may be to our feelings, however desirable that every human being should be set at liberty, we cannot be governed by our feelings, but only by the law." Because slavery "is not only sanctioned by foreign powers . . . but is recognized by the Supreme Court," Thompson could not find that the law must refuse to find the Africans to be slaves at all. To uphold the law then, he regretfully had to hold the Africans until it was decided whether any of the claimants did, in fact, hold a property right in them as slaves. Such a decision, he noted, would be made by the district court when it met in November.

The prisoners were returned to their cells.

Telling Their Story

One finger: "Eta." Two fingers: "Fili." Three fingers: "Kiauwa." Four fingers: "Naeni." Professor Gibbs traveled the wharves and piers in New York City, approaching any blacks he saw, counting in Mende. Gibbs heard that a British cruiser was in the port celebrating a successful trip; it had captured two slave ships while en route to America. The professor made his way to Staten Island, where the ships were quarantined, and went aboard the British ship, where he met a young African. The man, who had been captured and sold into slavery as a child, had been freed when the Portuguese slaver carrying him to America was captured by the British. After returning to Sierra Leone, living at a British mission, and learning English (as well as changing his name to James), he had joined the British cruiser as a member of the crew to act as a seaman and interpreter. James Covey smiled at Gibbs and told him that the words he was saying were numbers in an African language called Mende. Gibbs at last had his man.

Covey was granted permission by his captain to leave and serve as interpreter for the prisoners. At last, the Africans could tell their story without fear of being misunderstood. They clarified the details of their capture and their trips on the *Tecora* and the *Amistad* and spoke of the barracoons, Lomboko and Misericordia. Finally, there seemed adequate testimonial proof that the men were Africans, not Cuban slaves, despite the Spanish claims and documents.

The members of the Anti-Slavery Society were unrelenting in their efforts to free the Africans. Tappan contacted Dr. Richard Robert Madden, the British superintendent of liberated Africans in Havana, Cuba, who had also served on a number of the international commissions created to punish slavers. Madden's work had provided him with unequaled expertise in all aspects of the Cuban slave trade, from importation to the issuance of fraudulent *traspasos* by Cuban officials. Madden agreed to travel to Connecticut to testify on behalf of the African prisoners.

Just when everything seemed to be coming together for the defense, the interpreter, James Covey, became seriously ill and could not travel to Hartford for the November trial. Judge Judson agreed to postpone the trial until January; this, however, presented another problem for the defense. Madden, the expert witness on the Cuban slave trade, could not remain in Hartford through January. The judge allowed the attorneys to conduct a deposition of the witness; that testimony would be used in the trial, instead of requiring his presence for the trial itself. As expected, Madden described a system of fraud, corruption, and cruelty that dominated the slave trade in Cuba.

Meanwhile, the new Spanish minister, Caballero de Argaiz, wrote Secretary of State Forsyth that "public vengeance has not be satisfied, for be it recollected that the legation of Spain does not demand the delivery of slaves but of assassins. Secondly, great injury has been done to the owners . . . and the dignity of the Spanish nation has been offended."

The secretary of state thought it critical that the attorney general intervene to protect America's interests and obligations to a foreign government. This intervention put the American government in the awkward position of being aligned with the Spanish slave traders and against the interests of the Africans of the *Amistad*.

Forsyth wrote to District Attorney Holabird that the *Amistad* case should be handled by the executive branch, not by the courts. Forsyth further instructed Holabird that if the court found in favor of the Spanish, the prisoners were to be handed over to the representatives of Spain immediately. If the court found in favor of the Africans, Holabird was to immediately appeal.

The Trial

The trial began on the morning of January 7, 1840; given the number of lawyers and parties present, it was surprising that so many spectators, including a group of Yale law students who had been given the day off to study the case, managed to find seats in the courtroom. The Africans had three attorneys; the Spaniards, one. The U.S. government's attorney was present, as were Lieutenant Commander Gedney's two lawyers, and Captain Green's one.

A series of witnesses were called on behalf of the prisoners, including James Covey and Professor Gibbs, who testified that they believed the men were free Africans recently captured. Dr. Madden's deposition from November was read into the record. The second day, several of the Africans themselves, including Singbe, testified as Covey translated. Newspapers reported that courtroom spectators listened with "breathless attention" as Singbe and several others told their story of the grueling five months they had endured, most beginning with their capture in Africa and ending, ironically, with their capture in America.

Mixed in with the dramatic testimony of the Africans and Antonio, the Cuban cabin boy, were arguments and testimony concerning treaties and admiralty law. After five days of evidence, testimony, and argument, the court adjourned on January 11, Judge Judson telling the parties that he would have a decision on Monday.

On the morning of Monday, January 13, 1840, the judge read his decision, turning first to the salvage rights. Granting Gedney's claim, he explained that "the services rendered by Lieutenant Gedney were not only meritorious, but highly praiseworthy." Judson found that Gedney's testimony reflected his belief that the *Amistad* was drifting, and his services were such as would "entitle the seizer to his proper allowance." Judson allowed Gedney to collect salvage on one-third of the value of the ship and cargo, but did not include the prisoners as part of that cargo. The judge rejected Captain Green's salvage claim outright.

The judge next turned to the question of the captives. The Africans "were born free and ever have been and still of right are free and not slaves." As such, he found that none of them could be the property of Ruiz or Montez, and as free men they would not be forced to return to Cuba to stand trial under Spanish authorities for murder or piracy, for they revolted only out of a "desire of winning their liberty." He concluded, "Singbe and Gilabaru shall not sigh for Africa in vain. Bloody as may be their hands, they shall yet embrace their kindred." He ordered that they be placed under the control of the executive branch and returned to Africa. Upon hearing the news, the Africans, who had remained in their cell for much of the trial except when called upon to testify, cheered, shouted, and fell to their knees in joy.

However, as ordered by Secretary of State Forsyth, Holabird appealed Judge Judson's decision to the circuit court. Denied bail, the prisoners continued their captivity in the cells of New Haven, awaiting now the decision of the circuit court.

Within months the circuit court of appeals upheld Judge Judson's decision granting the Africans their freedom. Yet, once again bowing to the pressure of the Spanish government, the United States filed an appeal, this time to the U.S. Supreme Court. And once again, the Africans waited in their cells in New Haven.

Roger Baldwin continued as chief counsel for the Africans. However, Baldwin and the committee of abolitionists felt they needed a person of greater stature to argue the case in the Supreme Court. In October 1840, Lewis Tappan visited John Quincy Adams at his home in nearby Massachusetts.

Adams was the son of John Adams, the second president of the United States and had himself been the sixth president. A Harvard graduate and a member of the bar for fifty years, Adams had been a successful attorney; professor at Harvard; senator from Massachusetts; minister to Berlin under President Thomas Jefferson; and minister to Russia and England and secretary of state under President James Monroe.

Though not known as an abolitionist, Adams frequently introduced petitions in Congress to abolish slavery or prevent persons born in the

United States from being sold into slavery. He continued to fight the practice, despite the infamous "gag" resolutions adopted by Congress at the behest of the pro-slavery members, beginning in 1836. Adams tried to force the legislative body to address slavery by immediately "tabling" every such petition introduced, without committee examination or printing.

Adams resisted Tappan at first—he was seventy-four, and even though still a congressman, he had not argued before the Supreme Court for thirty years—but by the end of the month, he agreed to represent the Africans. In November, Adams and Baldwin conferred and agreed that Baldwin would write the legal brief and that they would share oral arguments.

As one postponement of the case followed another, it would be February 20, 1841, before they would be pitted against U.S. attorney general Henry Gilpin, a recent appointee of President Van Buren's and to whom fell the duty of arguing for the executive branch in its fight to uphold what it believed was its obligations to Spain.

Oyez! Oyez!

Chief Justice Roger Taney took the bench before a varied audience. Curious spectators and tourists mingled with dedicated followers of the case, who were in turn split on both sides of the slavery debate. Conversely, some of the most interested parties were not present at all. Ruiz and Montez had returned to Cuba, relying upon the Spanish minister, who had a delegation in attendance. Lewis Tappan was also absent, forced away for business reasons. Most conspicuously, the Africans themselves were absent; all requests for permission for some of them to sit as spectators for the trial had been disapproved.

Arguments before the Supreme Court in the nineteenth and early twentieth century had an entirely different texture from those today. For example, the lawyers' statements in *Amistad* were more akin to speeches, which the lawyers delivered without interruption. However, in more modern cases (see *Falwell v. Flynt,* Chapter 6), the attorneys must fend off constant inquiries from the justices. This change was incremental, and as they became more involved in the actual "argument," it served both the court and the parties in that the justices could direct the lawyers' attention precisely to their concerns and thus better focus the inquiry. Although the Supreme Court of 1841 would not pepper the lawyers with questions, it would listen with acute interest.

Attorney General Gilpin would begin, followed by Baldwin and then Adams. Gilpin had three primary concerns: First, the integrity and importance of maintaining international treaties. Second, the concern that the executive branch, through President Van Buren and Secretary of State Forsyth, was attempting to preempt the role of the courts. And finally, the primary issue of whether human beings can be considered mere property.

Gilpin thus first focused on the importance of meeting treaty obligations:

> In this situation, the executive government looks to its treaty stip-ulations, the most solemn and binding compacts that nations know among each other, and the obligations of which can never be treated lightly, so long as good faith forms the first duty of every commu-nity. Those stipulations entered into in 1795 provide, in the first place, that each party to the treaty, the United States and Spain, shall "endeavor, by all means in their power, to protect and defend all ves-sels and other effects belonging to the citizens or subjects of the other, which shall be within the extent of their jurisdiction."
>
> Now these are stipulations too clear to be misunderstood; too imperative to be wantonly neglected. Could we not ask of Spain the fulfillment of every one of them towards our own citizens? If so, were we not bound, at least, to see that, through some public func-tionary, or by some means in which nations fulfill mutual obligations, they were performed by us to the subjects of Spain whenever the cause should arise?
>
> Did it arise in this case? Here were unquestionably, as the repre-sentative of Spain believed and stated, a vessel and effects of subjects of that country within our jurisdiction; here was a vessel and mer-chandise rescued, as he alleged, from the hands of robbers, brought into one of our ports, and already in the custody of public officers. Did not a treaty stipulation require the United States to "endeavor, by all means in their power, to protect and defend" this property? Did not a treaty stipulation require us to "extend to them all favor, pro-tection, and held"? Did not a treaty stipulation bind us to "restore, entire, the property to the true proprietors, as soon as due and suffi-cient proof should be made concerning the same"? If not, then is there no force and meaning in language; and the words of solemn treaties are an idle breath, of which nations may be as regardless as of the passing wind.

Attorney General Gilpin then turned his attention to the question of whether the executive branch had the right and the authority to become involved.

An attempt is made by argument to prove that the government of the United States had no right to interpose. And why not? It is said, because there is no law giving this power, and it cannot be implied; because in a question of private property it must be left to the parties alone to prosecute their rights, and the parties in this case were already doing so for themselves; and because it was an interference and encroachment of the executive on the province of the Court, not sanctioned by any precedent. These are the grounds that have been taken.

Yet every instance of interposition of foreign functionaries, consuls, and others affords a precedent. They have no right of property. They are no parties in interest. They interpose in behalf of the citizen. It will hardly be denied that where the foreign functionary may come into our courts to prosecute for the party in interest, our own functionaries may do the same.

It seems clear, then, that these objections to the duty of the executive to interpose, where the property to be restored is in the custody of the Court, cannot be sustained either by principle or authority.

Viewed, then, on every ground of treaty obligation, of constitutional duty, of precedent, or of international intercourse, the interposition of the executive in the mode adopted, so far from being "unnecessary and improper," was one of duty and propriety, on receiving from the Spanish minister his official representation, and from the district attorney the information that the matter was already in charge of the Court.

Gilpin then turned to the delicate argument of the status of the Africans themselves.

If slaves then, were property by the laws of Spain, it might be justly concluded that, even if they were not so recognized by the United States, still they are property within the meaning of the treaty, because the intention of the treaty was to protect the property of each nation. But, in fact, slaves were, and are, as clearly recognized by them to be property, as they ever were by Spain. Our citizens hold them as property; buy and sell them as property; legislate upon them as property. State after state has been received into this Union, with the solemn and deliberate assent of the national legislature, whose constitutions, previously submitted to and sanctioned by that legislature, recognize slaves as merchandise; to be held as such, carried as such from place to place, and bought and sold as such.

It has been argued that this government never has recognized property in slaves. To this it is answered, that if no other proof could be adduced, these acts of the national government are evidence that it has done so. The Constitution of the United States leaves to the states the regulation of their internal property, of which slaves were, at the time it was formed, a well-known portion. It also guaranteed and protected the rights of the states to increase this property, up to the year 1808, by importation from abroad. How, then, can it be said, that this government never has recognized this property?

But it is contended that, although they may have been recognized as property by the two nations, they were not such property as was subject to restoration by the treaty. Now, to this it may be answered, in the first place, that every reason which can be suggested for the introduction of the treaty stipulations to protect and restore property, applies as fully to slaves as to any other. It is, in states where slavery exists, a valuable species of property; it is an object of traffic; it is transported from place to place.

It is submitted, then, that so far as this Court is concerned, there is sufficient evidence concerning this property to warrant its restoration pursuant to the provisions of the treaty with Spain; and that, therefore, the judgment of the Court below should be reversed, and a decree made by this Court for the entire restoration of the property.

Gilpin's well-reasoned and well-supported argument presented a compelling case that, regardless of the moral issues involved, the international community can only function properly when nations abide by the terms of their agreements. And a dispute involving persons or property of a particular country should, in fact, be resolved by that nation. Gilpin was well advised to stay clear of the moral propriety of the slave trade, "however much we may abhor the African slave trade," and focus on the propriety of international cooperation. And indeed precedent and prevailing practices strongly favored his position. It was then left for Baldwin and Adams to deal with harsh precedent and the compelling argument that the treaties between nations are nearly sacrosanct.

Argument by Roger Baldwin on Behalf of the Amistad *Slaves*

This case is not only one of deep interest in itself, as affecting the destiny of the unfortunate Africans whom I represent, but it involves considerations deeply affecting our national character in the eyes of the whole civilized world, as well as questions of power on the part of the government of the United States which are regarded with anxiety and alarm by a large portion of our citizens. It presents, for the first time, the question whether the government, which was established for the promotion of justice, which was founded on the great principles of the Revolution, as proclaimed in the Declaration of Independence, can, consistently with the genius of our institutions, become a party to proceedings for the enslavement of human beings cast upon our shores and found in the condition of free men within the territorial limits of a free and sovereign state.

In the remarks I shall have occasion to make, it will be my design to appeal to no sectional preferences and to assume no positions in which I shall not hope to be sustained by intelligent minds from the South as well as from the North. Although I am in favor of the broadest liberty of inquiry and discussion—happily secured by our Constitution to every citizen, subject only to his individual responsibility to the laws for its abuse—I have ever been of the opinion that the exercise of that liberty by citizens of one state, in regard to the institutions of another, should always be guided by discretion and tempered with kindness.

If the government of the United States could appear in any case as the representative of foreigners claiming property in the Court of Admiralty, it has no right to appear in their behalf to aid them in the recovery of fugitive slaves, even when domiciled in the country from which they escaped, much less the recent victims of the African slave trade who have sought an asylum in one of the free states of the Union.

The recently imported Africans of the *Amistad,* if they were ever slaves, which is denied, were in the actual condition of freedom when they came within the jurisdictional limits of the state of New York. They came there without any wrongful act on the part of any officer or citizen of the United States. They were in a state where, not only no law existed to make them slaves, but where, by an express statute, all persons are declared to be free. They were under the protection of the laws of a state which, in the language of the Supreme Court, "has the same undeniable and unlimited jurisdiction over all persons and things within its territorial limits, as any foreign nation when that jurisdiction is not surrendered or restrained by the Constitution of the United States."

The American people have never imposed it as a duty on the government of the United States to become actors in an attempt to reduce to slavery men found in a state of freedom by giving extraterritorial force to a foreign slave law. Such a duty would not only be repugnant to the feelings of a large portion of the citizens of the United States, but it would be wholly inconsistent with the fundamental principles of our government and the purposes for which it was established, as well as with its policy in prohibiting the slave trade and giving freedom to its victims.

If these Africans had been taken from the possession of their Spanish claimants and wrongfully brought into the United States by our citizens, a question would have been presented similar to that which existed in the case of the *Antelope,* but when men have come here voluntarily, without any wrong on the part of the government or citizens of the United States in withdrawing them from the jurisdiction of Spanish laws, why should this government be required to become active in their restoration? They appear here free men. They stand before our courts presumed to be free. They stand before our courts on equal ground with their claimants, and when the courts, after an impartial hearing with all parties in interest before them, have pronounced them free, it is neither the duty nor the right of the executive of the United States to interfere with the decision.

We deny that Ruiz and Montez, Spanish subjects, had a right to call on any officer or court of the United States to use the force of the government or the process of law for the purpose of again enslaving those who have thus escaped from foreign slavery and sought asylum here. We deny that the seizure of these persons by Lieutenant Gedney for such a purpose was a legal or justifiable act.

If a foreign slave vessel, engaged in a traffic which by our laws is denounced as inhuman and piratical, should be captured by the slaves while on her voyage from Africa to Cuba, and they should succeed in reaching our shores, have the Constitution or laws of the United States imposed on our judges, our naval officers, or our executive the duty of seizing the unhappy fugitives and delivering them up to their oppressors? Did the people of the United States, whose whole government is based on the great principles of the Revolution, proclaimed in the Declaration of Independence, confer upon the federal, executive, or judicial tribunals the power of making our nation accessories to such atrocious violations of human rights? Is there any principle of international law which requires it? Are our courts bound—and if not, are they at liberty—to give effect here to the slave trade laws of a foreign nation, to laws affecting strangers never domiciled there, when, to give them such effect, would be to violate the natural rights of men? These questions are answered in the negative by all the most approved writers on the laws of nations.

By the law of France, the slaves of their colonies, immediately on their arrival in France, become free. By the law of the state of New York, a foreign slave escaping into that state becomes free, and the courts of the United States, in acting upon the personal rights of men found within the jurisdiction of a free state, are bound to administer the laws as they would be administered by the state courts in all cases in which the laws of the state do not conflict with the laws or obligations of the United States. The United States as a nation have prohibited the slave trade as inhuman and piratical, and they have no law authorizing the enslaving of its victims. And that laws of a nation have no force beyond its own territories, except so far as it respects its own citizens who owe it allegiance, is too familiarly settled to need the citation of authorities.

But it is claimed that if these Africans, though "recently imported into Cuba," were by the laws of Spain the property of Ruiz and Montez, the government of the United States is bound by the treaty to restore them and that, therefore, the intervention of the executive in these proceedings is proper for that purpose. It has already, it is believed, been shown that even if the case were within the treaty, the intervention of the executive as a party before the judicial tribunals was unnecessary and improper, since the treaty provides for its own execution by the courts, on the application of the parties in interest.

The Spanish treaty, on which the attorney general has principally relied, provides "that all ships and merchandise, of what nature so ever, which shall be rescued out of the hands of pirates or robbers, on the high seas, shall be brought into some port of either state, and shall be delivered to the custody of the officers of that port, in order to be taken care of, and restored entire to the true proprietors, as soon as due and sufficient proof shall be made concerning the property thereof." To render this clause of the treaty applicable to the case under consideration, it must be assumed that under the term *merchandise* the contracting parties intended to include slaves, and that slaves, themselves the recent victims of piracy, who, by a successful revolt, have achieved their deliverance from slavery on the high seas and have availed themselves of the means of escape of which they have thus acquired the possessions—are to be deemed "pirates and robbers," "from whose hands" such "merchandise has been rescued."

It is believed that such a construction of the words of the treaty is not in accordance with the rules of interpretation which ought to govern our courts and that when there is no special reference to human beings as property, who are not acknowledged as such by the law of comity of nations generally but only by the municipal laws of the particular nations which tolerate slavery, it cannot be presumed that the contracting parties intended to include them under the general term *merchandise.* As has already been remarked, it may well be doubted whether such a stipulation would be within the treaty-making power of the United States. It is to be remembered that the government of the United States is based on the principles promulgated in the Declaration of Independence by the Congress of 1776 "that all men are created equal; that they are endowed by their Creator with certain inalienable rights; that among these are life, liberty, and the pursuit of happiness; and that to secure these rights governments are instituted."

By "merchandise rescued from pirates," the contracting parties must have had in view property, which it would then be the duty of the public ships of the United States to rescue from its unlawful possessors because, if it is taken from those who are rightfully in possession, the capture would be wrongful, and it would be our duty to restore it. But is it a duty which our naval officers owe to a nation tolerating the slave trade to subdue for their kidnappers the revolted victims of their cruelty? Could the people of the United States, consistently with their principles as a nation, have ever consented to a treaty stipulation in which would impose such a duty on our naval officers? A duty which would drive every citizen of a free state from the service of his country? Has our government, which has been so cautious not to oblige itself to surrender the most atrocious criminals who have sought asylum in the United States, bound itself, under the term *merchandise,* to seize and surrender fugitive slaves?

The phraseology of the entire article in the treaty clearly shows that it was intended to apply only to inanimate things or irrational animals, such as are universally regarded as property. It is "merchandise rescued from the hands of pirates and robbers on the high seas" that is to be restored. There is no provision for the surrender of the pirates themselves, whom it is lawful for and the duty of all nations to capture and punish. If these Africans were "pirates" or sea robbers whom our naval officers might lawfully seize, it would be our duty to detain them for punishment, and then what would become of the "merchandise"?

But they were not pirates. Cinquez, the master spirit who guided them, had a single object in view. That object was, not piracy or robbery, but the deliverance of himself and his companions in suffering from unlawful bondage. They owed no allegiance to Spain. They were on board the *Amistad* by constraint. Their object was to free themselves from the fetters that bound them in order that they might return to their kindred and their home. In so doing, they were guilty of no crime for which they could be held responsible as pirates. Suppose they had been impressed American seamen who had regained their liberty in a similar manner. Would they in that case have been deemed guilty of piracy and murder?

The United States, as a nation, is to be regarded as a free state, and all men being presumptively free, when "merchandise" is spoken of in the treaty of a free state, it cannot be presumed that human beings are intended to be included as such.

In the interpretation of treaties we ought always to give such a construction to the words as is most consistent with the customary use of language; most suitable to the subject, and to the legitimate principles of the government; such a construction as will not lead to injustice to others or in any way violate the laws of nature. These are, in substance, the rules of interpretation. The construction claimed in behalf of the Spanish libelants, in the present case, is at war with them all.

It would be singular indeed if the tribunals of a government which has declared the slave trade "piracy" and has bound itself by a solemn treaty with Great Britain, in 1814, to make continued efforts "to promote its entire abolition, as a traffic irreconcilable with the principles of humanity and justice," should construe the general expressions of a treaty which since that period has been revised by the contracting parties, as obliging this nation to commit the injustice of treating as property the recent victims of this horrid traffic, more especially when it is borne in mind that the government of Spain, anterior to the revision of the treaty in 1819, had formally notified our governments that Africans were no longer the legitimate objects of trade.

The law of nature and the law of nations bind us as effectually to render justice to the African as the treaty can to the Spaniard. Before a foreign tribunal, the parties litigating the question of freedom or slavery stand on equal ground, and in a case like this, where it is admitted that the Africans were recently imported, and consequently never domiciled in Cuba, and owe no allegiance to its laws, their rights are to be determined by the law which is of universal obligation, the law of nature.

Baldwin finished his argument late Tuesday, and the Court adjourned for the day. Baldwin's summation was precise, and many felt that if the legal precedents were the primary concern, Baldwin's argument should carry the day. Co-counsel John Quincy Adams characterized Baldwin's argument as "sound and eloquent," but Adams was not completely satisfied. Historians have since suggested that although Baldwin's points of law were excellent, it did not take into account the current mood and attitudes of the United States. Point for point it was sound, but it did not acknowledge the importance of the issue to be decided before the court itself, much less the impact that the decision would have on both the Africans and upon American society. The *Amistad* case was of greater proportion and further reach than the immediate facts and points of law could suggest, and Adams felt these concerns had to be addressed when he rose on Wednesday, February 24, to address the court with his argument.

In his memoirs, Adams remembered the moment: "I had been deeply distressed and agitated 'til the moment when I rose; and then my spirit did not sink with me." Adams chose not to speak specifically as a lawyer; Baldwin had already shown the strength of the legal argument on behalf of their clients; rather, Adams spoke as a leader, and he let his strength of will come through in his argument as a social, moral, and political voice, hoping to guide the court.

Argument by President John Quincy Adams on Behalf of the Amistad Slaves

In rising to address this Court as one of its attorneys and counselors, regularly admitted at a great distance of time, I feel that an apology might well be expected where I shall perhaps be more likely to exhibit at once the infirmities of age and the inexperience of youth, than to render those services to the individuals whose lives and liberties are at the disposal of this Court which I would most earnestly desire to render. But as I am unwilling to employ one moment of the time of the Court in anything that regards my own personal situation, I shall reserve what few observations I may think necessary to offer as an apology till the close of my argument on the merits of the question.

I therefore proceed immediately to say that, in a consideration of this case, I derive, in the distress I feel both for myself and my clients, consolation from two sources—first, that the rights of my clients to their lives and liberties have already been defended by my learned friend and colleague in so able and complete a manner as leaves me scarcely anything to say, and I feel that such full justice has been done to their interests, that any fault or imperfection of mine will merely be attributed to its true cause; and secondly, I derive consolation from the thought that this Court is a court of justice. And in saying so very trivial a thing I should not on any other occasion, perhaps, be warranted in asking the Court to consider what justice is. Justice, as defined in the *Institutes of Justinian,* nearly two thousand years ago, and as felt and understood by all who understand human relations and human rights, is "the constant and perpetual will to secure to every one his own right."

And in a court of justice, where there are two parties present, justice demands that the rights of each party should be allowed to himself, as well as that each party has a right, to be secured and protected by the Court. This observation is important, because I appear here on behalf of thirty-six individuals, the life and liberty of every one of whom depend on the decision of this Court. The Court, therefore, I trust, in deciding this case, will form no lumping judgment on these thirty-six individuals, but will act on the consideration that the life and the liberty of every one of them must be determined by its decision for himself alone. From the day when the vessel was taken possession of by one of our naval officers, they have all been held as close prisoners, now for the period of eighteen long months, under custody and by authority of the courts of the United States. I trust, therefore, that before the ultimate decision of this Court is established, its honorable members will pay due attention to the circumstances and condition of every individual concerned.

When I say I derive consolation from the consideration that I stand before a court of justice, I am obliged to take this ground because, as I shall show, another department of the government of the United States has taken, with reference to this case, the ground of utter injustice, and these individuals for whom I appear, stand before this Court, awaiting their fate from its decision, under the array of the whole executive power of this nation against them, in addition to that of a foreign nation. And here arises a consideration, the most painful of all others; in considering the duty I have to discharge, in which, in supporting the action to dismiss the appeal, I shall be obliged not only to investigate and submit to the censure of this Court, the form and manner of the proceedings of the executive in this case, but the validity, and the motive of the reasons assigned for its interference in this unusual manner in a suit between parties for their individual rights.

At an early period of my life it was my fortune to witness the representation upon the stage of one of the tragic masterpieces of the great dramatist of England, or I may rather say of the great dramatist of the world, and in that scene which exhibits in action the sudden, the instantaneous fall from unbounded power into irretrievable disgrace of Cardinal Wolsey, by the abrupt declaration of displeasure and dismission from the service of his king, made by that monarch in the presence of Lord Surry and of the lord chamberlain; at the moment of Wolsey's humiliation and distress, Surry given vent to his long-suppressed resentments for the insolence and injuries which he had endured from the fallen favorite while in power, and breaks out into insulting and bitter reproaches, till checked by the chamberlain, who says, "Oh! my lords; press not a falling man too far: 'tis Virtue." The repetition of that single line, in the relative position of the parties, struck me as a moral principle, and made upon my mind an impression which I have carried with me through all the changes of my life, and which I trust I shall carry with me to my grave.

It is, therefore, peculiarly painful to me, under present circumstances, to be under the necessity of arraigning before this Court and before the civilized world, the course of the existing administration in this case. But I must do it. That government is still in power, and thus, subject to the control of the Court, the lives and liberties of all my clients are in its hands. And if I should pass over the course it has pursued, those who have not had an opportunity to examine the case and perhaps the Court itself, might decide that nothing improper had been done, and that the parties I represent had not been wronged by the course pursued by the executive.

The charge I make against the present executive administration is that in all their proceedings relating to these unfortunate men, instead of that justice, which they were bound not less than this honorable Court itself to observe, they have substituted sympathy!—sympathy with one of the parties in this conflict of justice, and antipathy to the other. Sympathy with the white; antipathy to the black.

All the proceedings of the government, executive and judicial, in this case had been founded on the assumption that the two Spanish slave dealers were the only parties aggrieved—that all the right was on their side and all the wrong on the side of their surviving self-emancipated victims. I ask Your Honors, was this justice? It was not so considered by Mr. Forsyth [the secretary of state] himself. It was sympathy, he so calls it, for the letter referring to the proceedings of this government from the very first intervention of Lieutenant Gedney, he says, "Messrs. Ruiz and Montez were first found near the coast of the United States, deprived of their property and of their freedom, suffering from lawless violence on their persons, and in imminent and constant danger of being deprived of their lives also."

The national sympathy with the slave traders of the barracoons is officially declared to have been the prime motive of action of the government. The sympathy of the executive government, and as it were of the nation, in favor of the slave traders, and against these poor, unfortunate, helpless, tongueless, defenseless Africans, was the cause and foundation and motive of all these proceedings and has brought this case up for trial before Your Honors.

For I inquire by what right, all this sympathy, from Lieutenant Gedney to the secretary of state, and from the secretary of state, as it were, to the nation, was extended to the two Spaniards from Cuba exclusively, and utterly denied to the victims of their lawless violence. By what right was it denied to the men who had restored themselves to freedom and secured their oppressors to abide the consequences of the acts of violence perpetrated by them, and why was it extended to the perpetrators of those acts of violence themselves? When the *Amistad* first came within the territorial jurisdiction of the United States, acts of violence had passed between the two parties, the Spaniards and Africans on board of her, but on which side these acts were lawless, on which side were the oppressors, was a question of right and wrong, for the settlement of which, if the government and people of the United States interfered at all, they were bound in duty to extend their sympathy to them all; and if they intervened at all between them, the duty incumbent upon this intervention was not of favor, but of impartiality—not of sympathy, but of justice, dispensing to every individual his own right.

I know of no law, but one which I am not at liberty to argue before this Court, no law, statute, or constitution, no code, no treaty, applicable to the proceedings of the executive or the judiciary, except that law [pointing to the copy of the Declaration of Independence, hanging against one of the pillars of the courtroom], that law, two copies of which are ever before the eyes of Your Honors. I know of no other law that reaches the case of my clients, but the law of nature and of nature's God on which our fathers placed our own national existence. The circumstances are so peculiar that no code or treaty has provided for such a case. That law, in its application to my clients, I trust will be the law on which the case will be decided by this Court.

The Africans were in possession and had the presumptive right of ownership; they were in peace with the United States; the courts have decided, and truly, that they were not pirates; they were on a voyage to their native homes. They had acquired the right, and so far as their knowledge extended, they had the power of prosecuting the voyage; the ship was theirs and, being in immediate communication with the shore, was in the territory of the state of New York and entitled to all the provisions of the law of nations, and the protection and comfort which the laws of that state secure to every human being within its limits.

In this situation, Lieutenant Gedney, without any charge or authority from his government, without warrant of law, by force of firearms, seizes and disarms them, then being in the peace of that commonwealth and of the United States, drives them on board the vessel, seizes the vessel and transfers it against the will of its possessors to another state. I ask in the name of justice, by what law was this done? Even admitting that it had been a case of actual piracy, which your courts have properly found it was not, there are questions arising here of the deepest interest to the liberties of the people of this Union, and especially of the state of New York. Have the officers of the U.S. Navy a right to seize men by force, on the territory of New York, to fire at them, to overpower them, to disarm them, to put them on board of a vessel and carry them by force and against their will to another state, without warrant or form of law? I am not arraigning Lieutenant Gedney, but I ask this Court, in the name of justice, to settle it in their minds, by what law it was done, and how far the principle it embraces is to be carried.

The whole of my argument to show that the appeal should be dismissed is founded on an averment that the proceedings on the part of the United States are all wrongful from the beginning. The first act, of seizing the vessel, and these men, by an officer of the navy, was a wrong. The forcible arrest of these men, or a part of them, on the soil of New York, was a wrong. After the vessel was brought into the jurisdiction of the District Court of Connecticut, the men were first seized and imprisoned under a criminal process for murder and piracy on the high seas. Then they were libeled by Lieutenant Gedney as property, and salvage claimed on them, and under that process were taken into the custody of the marshal as property. Then they were claimed by Ruiz and Montez and again taken into custody by the court.

The Spanish minister then demanded that the vessel should be set at liberty, and the Negroes sent to Cuba to be tried. And he is so confident in the disposition of the United States in favor of this demand that he even presumes the president of the United States had already immediately dispatched an order to the court in Connecticut, to stay its proceedings and deliver up the Negroes, to the government of Spain.

What combination of ideas led to that conclusion, in the mind of Mr. Calderon [the Spanish minister], I am not competent to say. He evidently supposes the president of the United States to possess what we understand by arbitrary power—the power to decide cases and to dispose of persons and of property at his own discretion, and without the intervention of any court. What led him to this imagination I am unable to say.

In what capacity does he demand that the president of the United States should place himself? Is it a demand to deliver up these people as property? No. Is it that they should deliver them to the minister himself, as the representative of the Spanish government, to be disposed of according to the laws of Spain? No. It demands of the chief magistrate of this nation that he should first turn himself into a jailer, to keep these people safely, and then into a tipstaff to take them away for trial among the slave traders of the barracoons. Was ever such a demand made upon any government? He must seize these people and keep them safely and carry them, at the expense of the United States, to another country to be tried for their crimes! Where in the law of nations is there a warrant for such a demand?

May it please Your Honors—if the president of the United States had arbitrary and unqualified power, he could not satisfy these demands. He must keep them as a jailer; he must then send them beyond seas to be tried for their lives. I will not recur to the Declaration of Independence—Your Honors have it implanted in your hearts—but one of the grievous charges brought against George III was that he had made laws for sending men beyond seas for trial. That was one of the most odious of those acts of tyranny which occasioned the American Revolution. The whole of the reasoning is not applicable to this case, but I submit to Your Honors that, if the president has the power to do it in the case of Africans and send them beyond seas for trial, he could do it by the same authority in the case of American citizens. By a simple order to the marshal of the district, he could just as well seize citizens of the United States, on the demand of a foreign minister, and send them beyond seas for trial before a foreign court. The Spanish minister further demands, "That if, in consequence of the intervention of the authorities of Connecticut, there should be any delay in the desired delivery of the vessel and the slaves, the owners both of the former be indemnified for the injury that may accrue to them."

M. Calderon de la Barca then refers to several treaty stipulations in support of his demand, and particularly the eighth, ninth, and tenth articles of the Treaty of 1795, continued in force by the treaty of 1819. Article eight is a provision for vessels with their owners, driven into port by distress. Who was the Spanish owner here with his ship? There was none. I say the Africans were here with their ship. If you say the original owner is referred to, in whose name the ship's register was given, he was dead, he was not on board and would not claim the benefit of this article. The vessel either belonged to the Africans, in whose possession it was found, and who certainly had what is everywhere the first evidence of property. The truth is, this article was not intended to apply to such a case as this, but to the common case, in regard to which it has doubtless been carried into execution hundreds of times, in meeting the common disasters of maritime life.

Next we have article nine: "All ships and merchandise, of what nature so ever, which shall be rescued out of the hands of any pirates or robbers, on the high seas, shall be brought into some port of either state, and shall be delivered to the custody of the officers of that port, in order to be taken care of, and restored entire to the true proprietor, as soon as due and sufficient proof shall be made concerning the property thereof."

Was this ship rescued out of the hands of pirates and robbers? Is this Court competent to declare it? The courts below have decided that they have no authority to try, criminally, what happened on board the vessel. They have then no right to regard those who forcibly took possession of the vessel as pirates and robbers. If the sympathies of Lieutenant Gedney, which the secretary of state says had become national, had been felt for all the parties, in due proportion to their sufferings and their deserts, who were the pirates and robbers? Were they the Africans? When they were brought from Lomboko against the laws of Spain, against the laws of the United States, and against the law of nations, so far as the United States, and Spain, and Great Britain, are concerned, who were the robbers and pirates? And when the same voyage, in fact, was continued in the *Amistad,* and the Africans were in a perishing condition in the hands of Ruiz, dropping dead from day to day under his treatment, were they the pirates and robbers? This honorable Court will observe from the record that there were fifty-four Africans who left Havana. Ruiz says in his libel that nine had died before they reached our shores. The marshal's return shows that they were dying day after day from the effects of their sufferings. One died before the court sat at New London. Three more died before the return was made to the court at Hartford—only seventeen days— and three more between that and November. Sixteen fell victims before November, and from that time not one has died. Think only of the relief and benefit of being restored to the absolute wants of human nature. Although placed in a condition which, if applied to forty citizens of the United States, we should call cruel, shut up eighteen months in a prison, and enjoying only the tenderness which our laws provide for the worst of criminals, so great is the improvement of their condition from what it was in the hands of Ruiz, that they have perfectly recovered their health, and not one has died; when, before that time, they were perishing from hour to hour.

At the great day of accounts, who is to be responsible for those sixteen souls that died? Ruiz claims those sixteen as his property, as merchandise. How many of them, at his last hour, will pass before him and say, "Let me sit heavy on thy soul tomorrow"?

Who, then, are the tyrants and oppressors against whom our laws are invoked? Who are the innocent sufferers, for whom we are called upon to protect this ship against enemies and robbers? Certainly not Ruiz and Montez.

But, independently of this consideration, the article cannot apply to slaves. It says ships and merchandise. Is that language applicable to human beings? Will this Court so affirm? It says they shall be restored entire. Is it a treaty between cannibal nations, that a stipulation is needed for the restoration of merchandise entire, to prevent parties from cutting off the legs and arms of human beings before they are delivered up? The very word *entire* in the stipulation is of itself a sufficient exclusion of human beings from the scope of the article. But if it was intended to embrace human beings, the article would have included a provision for their subsistence until they are restored, and an indemnification for their maintenance to the officers who are charged with the execution of the stipulation. And there is perhaps needed a provision with regard to the institutions of the free states, to prevent a difficulty in keeping human beings in the custom house, without having them liable to the operation of the local law, the habeas corpus, and the rights of freedom.

But with regard to article nine, I will speak of my own knowledge, for it happened that on the renewal of the treaty in 1819, the whole of the negotiations with the then minister of Spain passed through my hands [Adams was secretary of state at that time], and I am certain that neither of us ever entertained an idea that this word *merchandise* was to apply to human beings.

May it please Your Honors, there is not one article of the treaty that has the slightest application to this case, and the Spanish minister has no more ground for appealing to the treaty, as a warrant for his demand, than he has for relying on the law of nations.

I have now, may it please the Court, examined the letter of the Spanish minister demanding the interposition of the national executive to restore these unfortunate Africans to the island of Cuba. And now I may inquire of Your Honors, what, in your opinion, was the duty of the secretary of state, on receiving such a letter? And in the first place, what did he do?

His first act was to misrepresent the demand, and to write to the district attorney in Connecticut, directing him to pursue a claim for the possession of these people on behalf of the United States, on the ground that the Spanish minister had demanded their delivery to him, as the property of Spanish subjects, and ordering him to take care that no court should place them beyond the control of the executive. That is what he did. And the consequence is the case now before the Court.

We should inquire what answer the Spanish minister ought to have received from the American secretary. I aver that it was the duty of the secretary of state to show the Spanish minister that all his demands were utterly unacceptable, and that the government of the United States could do nothing of what he required. It could not deliver the ship to the owner, and there was no duty resting on the United States to dispose of the vessel in any such manner. And as to the demand that no salvage should be taken, the Spanish minister should have been told that it was a question depending exclusively on the determination of the courts, before whom the case was pending for trial according to law. And the secretary ought to have shown the Spanish minister that the demand for a proclamation by the president of the United States, against the jurisdiction of the courts, was not only unacceptable but offensive—it was demanding what the executive could not do, by the Constitution. It would be the assumption of a control over the judiciary by the president, which would overthrow the whole fabric of the Constitution; it would violate the principles of our government generally and in every particular; it would be against the rights of the Negroes, of the citizens, and of the states.

The secretary ought to have done this at once, without waiting to consult the president, who was then absent from the city. The claim that the Negroes should be delivered was equally unacceptable with the rest; the president has no power to arrest either citizens or foreigners. But even that power is almost insignificant compared with that of sending men beyond seas to deliver them up to a foreign government. The secretary should have called upon the Spanish ambassador to name an instance where such a demand had been made by any government of another government that was independent. He should have told him that such a demand was treating the president of the United States, not as the head of a nation, but as a constable, a catchpole—a character that it is not possible to express in gentlemanly language.

But what did the secretary do in fact? He barely replies to Mr. Calderon [the Spanish minister] that he had sent his letter to the president for his consideration, and that "no time will be needlessly lost, after his decision upon the demand it prefers shall have reached me, in communicating to you his views upon the subject."

And now, from that day to this, the secretary of state has never answered one of these demands, nor arrested one of these misapprehensions, nor asserted the rights and the honor of the nation against one of these most extraordinary, unacceptable, and insolent demands. He has degraded the country, in the face of the whole civilized world, not only by allowing these demands to remain unanswered, but by proceeding, I am obliged to say, throughout the whole transaction, as if the executive were earnestly desirous to comply with every one of the demands.

There is a complete answer to all these demands of the Spanish legation: "The Constitution and laws have secured the judicial power against all interference of the executive authority." That is very true. The laws of the state of New York, of which the Constitution and laws of the United States and their treaties with foreign powers form a part, afford to Messrs. Ruiz and Montez all the necessary means for the security of their rights, and therefore "render unnecessary any agency on the part of" the executive. There is a perfect answer, worthy of an American statesman.

The attorney general says the courts of no country execute the penal laws of another. I may ask, does any nation execute the slave laws of another country? Is not the slave system as peculiar as the revenue system or the criminal code? These men were found free, and they cannot now be decreed to be slaves but by making them slaves. By what authority will this Court undertake to do this? What right has Ruiz to claim these men as his property when they were free, and so far from being in his possession when taken, he was in theirs. If there is no right of visitation and search by the cruisers of one nation over those of another, by what right has this ship been taken from the men who had it in their possession?

Now, here I take issue that the vessel was engaged in the slave trade. The voyage in the *Amistad* was a mere continuation of the original voyage in the *Tecora*. The voyage in its original intention was not accomplished until the slaves had reached their final destination on the plantation. This is the principle universally applicable to coasting vessels. I say further that the object of Ruiz and Montez was illegal, it was a part of the voyage from Lomboko, and when they fell into the hands of Lieutenant Gedney, they were steering in pursuance of that original voyage. Their object was to get to Puerto Príncipe, and of course the voyage was to them an unlawful one. The object of the Africans was to get to a port in Africa, and their voyage was lawful. And the whole character of the affair was changed by the transactions that took place on board the ship. The late attorney, however, comes to the conclusion that the courts of the United States cannot proceed criminally against these people, that the provisions of the acts of Congress against the slave trade are not applicable to Ruiz and Montez, and so he recurs to the ninth article of the Treaty of 1795. I have nothing to add to what I have before said respecting the treaty. It can have no possible application in this case.

The attorney general now comes to a conclusion as to what is to be done. That these men, being at that time in judicial custody of the courts of the United States, should be taken out of that custody, under an order of the president, and sent beyond seas by his sole authority! The cabinet adopted that opinion; why, then, did they not act upon it? Why did not the president send his order to the marshal to seize these men and ship them to Cuba or deliver them to the order of the Spanish minister? I am ashamed! I am ashamed that such an opinion should ever have been delivered by any public officer of this country, executive or judicial. I am ashamed to stand up before the nations of the earth, with such an opinion recorded as official, and what is worse, as having been adopted by the government—an opinion sanctioning a particular course of proceeding, unprecedented among civilized countries, which was thus officially sanctioned, and yet the government did not dare to do it. Why did they not do it? If this opinion had been carried into effect, it would have settled the matter at once, so far as it related to these unfortunate men. They would have been wrested from that protection, which above all things was their due after they had been taken into custody by order of the Court, and would have been put into the power of "public vengeance" at Havana. Yet there was not enough. There seems to have been an impression that to serve an order like that would require the aid of a body of troops. The people of Connecticut never would, never ought to have suffered it to be executed on their soil, but by main force. So the Spanish minister says his government has no ship to receive these people, and the president must therefore go further, and as he is responsible for the safekeeping and delivery of the men, he must not only deliver them up, but ship them off in a national vessel, so that there may be no habeas corpus from the state courts coming to the rescue as soon as they are out of the control of the judiciary. The suggestion, which first came from the district attorney, that the Court would undoubtedly place the Africans at the mercy of the executive, is carried out by an announcement from the secretary of state, of an agreement with the Spanish minister to send them to Cuba in a public ship.

A celebrated state prisoner, when going to the scaffold, was led by the Statue of Liberty, and exclaimed, "O Liberty! How many crimes are committed in thy name!" So we may say of our gallant navy, "What crimes is it ordered to commit! To what uses is it ordered to be degraded!"

Will this Court please to consider for one moment the essential principle of that opinion? Will this Court inquire what, if that opinion had been successfully carried into execution, would have been the tenure by which every human being in this Union, man, woman, or child, would have held the blessing of personal freedom? Would it not have been by the tenure of executive discretion, caprice, or tyranny? Had the precedent once been set and submitted to, of a nameless mass of judicial prisoners and witnesses, snatched by executive grasp from the protective guardianship of the supreme judges of the land at the dictate of a foreign minister, would it not have disabled forever the effective power of the habeas corpus? Well

was it for the country—for the president of the United States himself that he paused before stepping over this Rubicon!—that he said,
"We will proceed no further in this business." And yet, he did not
discard the purpose, and yet he saw that this executive trampling at
once upon the judicial authority and upon personal liberty would
not suffice, either to satisfy the Spanish minister or to satiate the
public vengeance of the barracoon slave traders.

Is it possible that a president of the United States should be ignorant that the right of personal liberty is individual. That the right to
it of every one is his own *jus sum;* and that no greater violation of his
official oath to protect and defend the Constitution of the United
States could be committed, than by an order to seize and deliver up
at a foreign minister's demand thirty-six persons, in a mass, under
the general denomination of all the Negroes, late of the *Amistad.*
That he was ignorant, profoundly ignorant of this self-evident truth,
inextinguishable till gilt-framed Declarations of Independence shall
perish in the general conflagration of the great globe itself, I am constrained to believe—for to that ignorance, the only alternative to
account for this order to the marshal of the District of Connecticut
is willful and corrupt perjury to his official presidential oath.

Lawless and tyrannical—may it please the Court, truth, justice, and
the rights of humankind forbid me to qualify these epithets—lawless
and tyrannical as this order thus was upon its face, the cold-blooded
cruelty with which it was issued was altogether congenial to its spirit—
it was to be executed only in the event of the decision of the Court
being favorable to the pretended application of the Spanish minister.

Was ever such a scene of Lilliputian trickery enacted by the rulers
of a great, magnanimous, and Christian nation? Contrast it with
that act of self-emancipation by which the savage, heathen barbarians
Cinquez and Grabeau liberated themselves and their fellow suffering
countrymen from Spanish slave traders, and which the secretary of
state, by communion of sympathy with Ruiz and Montez, denomi-
nates lawless violence. Cinquez and Grabeau are uncouth and barbarous names. Call them Harmodius and Aristogiton, and go back
for moral principle three thousand years to the fierce and glorious
democracy of Athens. They too resorted to lawless violence
and slew the tyrant to redeem the freedom of their country. For
this heroic action they paid the forfeit of their lives;
but within three years the Athenians expelled their tyrants themselves, and in gratitude to their self-devoted deliverers decreed that
thenceforth no slave should ever bear either of their names. Cinquez

and Grabeau are not slaves. Let them bear in future history the names of Harmodius and Aristogiton.

This review of all the proceedings of the executive I have made with the utmost pain, because it was necessary to bring it fully before Your Honors, to show that the course of that department had been dictated, throughout, not by justice but by sympathy—and a sympathy most partial and unjust. And this sympathy prevailed to such a degree, among all the persons concerned in this business, as to have perverted their minds with regard to all the most sacred principles of law and right, on which the liberties of the people of the United States are founded; and a course was pursued, from the beginning to the end, which was not only an outrage upon the persons whose lives and liberties were at stake, but hostile to the power and independence of the judiciary itself.

[Adams then drew the court's attention to a recent well-publicized article that editorialized the *Amistad* case was one of "importance" to the "southern states."] What was the purpose or intent of that article, I am not prepared to say, but it was evidently calculated to excite prejudice, to arouse all the acerbities of feeling between different sections of this country, and to connect them with this case, in such a manner as to induce this Court to decide it in favor of the alleged interests of the southern states, and against the suppression of the African slave trade.

It is not my intention to review the piece at this time. It has been done, and ably done, by more than one person. And after infinite difficulty, one of these answers has been inserted in the same journal in which the piece appeared. I now wish simply to refer Your Honors to the original principle of slavery as laid down by this champion of the institution. It is given by this writer as a great principle of national law and stands as the foundation of his argument. I wish, if Your Honors deem a paper of this kind, published under such circumstances, worthy of consideration in the decision of a case, that Your Honors would advert to that principle and say whether it is a principle recognized by this Court, as the ground on which it will decide cases. The truth is, that property in man has existed in all ages of the world, and results from the natural state of man, which is war. When God created the first family and gave them the fields of the earth as an inheritance, one of the number, in obedience to the impulses and passions that had been implanted in the human heart, rose and slew his brother. This universal nature of man is alone modified by civilization and law.

Is there the principle on which a particular decision is demanded from this Court on behalf of the southern states? Is that a principle recognized by this Court? Is it the principle of that Declaration [of Independence]? It is alleged in the journal article that war gives the right to take the life of our enemy, and that this confers a right to make him a slave, on account of having spared his life. Is that the principle on which these United States stand before the world? That Declaration says that every man is "endowed by his Creator with certain inalienable rights," and that among these are life, liberty, and the pursuit of happiness. If these rights are inalienable, they are incompatible with the rights of the victor to take the life of his enemy in war, or to spare his life and make him a slave. If this principle is sound, it reduces to brute force all the rights of man. It places all the sacred relations of life at the power of the strongest. No man has a right to life or liberty if he has an enemy able to take them from him. There is the principle. There is the whole argument of this paper.

Now I do not deny that the only principle upon which a color of right can be attributed to the condition of slavery is by assuming that the natural state of man is war. The bright intellect of the South clearly saw that without this principle for a cornerstone, he had no foundation for his argument. He assumes it therefore without a blush, as Hobbes assumed it to prove that *government* and *despotism* are synonymous words. I will not here discuss the right or the rights of slavery, but I say that the doctrine of Hobbes that war is the natural state of man, has for ages been exploded, as equally disclaimed and rejected by the philosopher and the Christian. That it is utterly incompatible with any theory of human rights, and especially with the rights which the Declaration of Independence proclaims as self-evident truths. The moment you come to the Declaration of Independence, that every man has a right to life and liberty, an inalienable right, this case is decided. I ask nothing more in behalf of these unfortunate men than this Declaration.

[Here Adams discussed the Antelope decision. And while the court's ruling in *Antelope* was ultimately contrary to his position, Adams pointed out errors in the opinion, then distinguished it from the position of the Africans and found support in Chief Justice Marshall's conclusion.]

The principle common to these cases is that the legality of the capture of a vessel engaged in the slave trade depends on the law of the country to which the vessel belongs. If that law gives its sanction to the trade, restitution will be decreed; if that law prohibits it, the vessel and cargo will be condemned as good prize.

It was by the application of this principle, to the fact, that, at the time when the *Antelope* was taken by the *Arraganta,* the slave trade, in which the *Antelope* was engaged, had not yet been made unlawful by Spain, that the Supreme Court affirmed so much of the decree of the circuit court as directed restitution to the Spanish claimant of the Africans found on board the *Antelope* when captured by the *Arraganta.*

But by the same identical principle, applied to the case of the *Amistad,* if, when captured by Lieutenant Gedney, she and her cargo had been in possession of the Spaniards, and the Africans in the condition of slaves, the vessel would have been condemned, and the slaves liberated, by the laws of the United States; because she was engaged in the slave trade in violation of the laws of Spain. She was in possession of the Africans, self-emancipated, and not in the condition of slaves. That, surely, could not legalize the trade in which she had been engaged. By the principle asserted in the opinion of the Supreme Court, declared by Chief Justice Marshall, it would have saved the vessel, at once, from condemnation and from restitution and would have relieved the Court from the necessity of restoring to the Africans their freedom. Thus the opinion of the Supreme Court, as declared by the chief justice, in the case of the *Antelope,* was a fact, an authority in point, against the surrender of the *Amistad,* and in favor of the liberation of the Africans taken in her, even if they had been, when taken, in the condition of slaves. How monstrous, then, is the claim upon the courts of the United States to re-enslave them, as thralls to the Spaniards Ruiz and Montez! Or to transport them beyond the seas, at the demand of the minister of Spain!

I said when I began this plea that my final reliance for success in this case was on this Court as a court of justice; and in the confidence this fact inspired that, in the administration of justice, in a case of no less importance than the liberty and the life of a large number of persons, this Court would not decide but on a due consideration of all the rights, both natural and social, of every one of these individuals. I have endeavored to show that they are entitled to their liberty from this Court. I have avoided, purposely avoided, and this Court will do justice to the motive for which I have avoided, a recurrence to those first principles of liberty which might well have been invoked in the argument of this cause. I have shown that Ruiz and Montez, the only parties in interest here, for whose sole benefit this suit is carried on by the government, were acting at the time in a way that is forbidden by the laws of Great Britain, of Spain, and of the United States, and that the mere signature of the governor-general of Cuba ought not to prevail over the ample evidence in the case that these Negroes were free and had a right to assert their liberty. The review of the case of the *Antelope,* and my argument in behalf of the captives of the *Amistad,* is closed.

May it please Your Honors: On the seventh of February, 1804, now more than thirty-seven years past, my name was entered, and yet stands recorded, on both the rolls, as one of the attorneys and counselors of this court. Five years later, in February and March 1809, I appeared for the last time before this Court, in defense of the cause of justice and of important rights, in which many of my fellow citizens had property to a large amount at stake. Very shortly afterwards, I was called to the discharge of other duties—first in distant lands, and in later years, within our own country, but in different departments of her government.

Little did I imagine that I should ever again be required to claim the right of appearing in the capacity of an officer of this Court; yet such has been the dictate of my destiny—and I appear again to plead the cause of justice, and now of liberty and life, in behalf of many of my fellow men, before that same Court, which in a former age I had addressed in support of rights of property. I stand again, I trust for the last time, before the same Court, but not before the same judges—nor aided by the same associates—nor resisted by the same opponents. As I cast my eyes along those seats of honor and of public trust, now occupied by you, they seek in vain for one of those honored and honorable persons whose indulgence listened then to my voice. Marshall, Cushing, Chase, Washington, Johnson, Livingston, Todd—where are they? Where is that eloquent statesman and learned lawyer who was my associate counsel in the management of that cause, Robert Goodloe Harper? Where is that brilliant luminary, so long the pride of Maryland and of the American bar, then my opposing counsel, Luther Martin? Where are they all? Gone! Gone! All gone! Gone from the services which, in their day and generation, they faithfully rendered to their country. From the excellent characters which they sustained in life, so far as I have had the means of knowing, I humbly hope, and fondly trust, that they have gone to receive the rewards of blessedness on high. In taking, then, my final leave of this bar, and of this Honorable Court, I can only ejaculate a fervent petition to heaven, that every member of it may go to his final account with as little of earthly frailty to answer for as those illustrious dead, and that you may, every one, after the close of a long and virtuous career in this world, be received at the portals of the next with the approving sentence—"Well done, good and faithful servant; enter thou into the joy of thy Lord."

John Quincy Adams's argument on behalf of the "unfortunate Africans" was the crowning achievement of a distinguished record of service to his country. Former president Adams's argument before the Supreme Court accomplished the goals he had set forth: First, and foremost, it captured and exploited the moral high ground. Second, it pointed out the repugnant position of the executive branch in first kowtowing to a foreign power and second in virtually running roughshod over the courts. Third, he turned the Supreme Court's recent holding in *Antelope,* which many viewed as binding precedent contrary to the interests of the Africans, around to actually support his position. And finally he invoked the clarion call of justice and beseeched the justices to be "virtuous."

Judgment Day

More than a week later, at noon on March 9, 1841, the decision was announced. Adams immediately wrote to Baldwin, who had returned to New Haven, "The decision of the Supreme Court in the case of the *Amistad* has this moment been delivered by Judge Story. The captives are free."

Justice Story, writing for the court, reviewed the facts of the case, and summed up the positions succinctly:

> The cause has been very elaborately argued, as well upon the merits as upon a motion on behalf of the appellees to dismiss the appeal. On the part of the United States, it has been contended, 1. That due and sufficient proof concerning property has been made to authorize the restitution of the vessel, cargo, and Negroes to the Spanish subjects on whose behalf they are claimed pursuant to the treaty with Spain, of the 27th of October, 1795. 2. That the United States had a right to intervene in the manner in which they have done, to obtain a decree for the restitution of the property, upon the application of the Spanish minister. These propositions have been strenuously denied on the other side.

Justice Story briefly reviewed the points made in Gilpin's argument, stressing that the argument claimed that the Africans must only be returned under the treaty if they were to "fall within the description of merchandise." The court, Story wrote, believed:

It is clear, in our opinion, that neither of . . . the essential facts and requisites has been established in proof. . . . It is plain beyond controversy, if we examine the evidence, that these Negroes never were the lawful slaves of Ruiz or Montez, or of any other Spanish subjects. They are natives of Africa, and were kidnapped there, and were unlawfully transported to Cuba, in violation of the laws and treaties of Spain, and the most solemn edicts and declarations of that government. By those laws, and treaties, and edicts, the African slave trade is utterly abolished; the dealing in that trade is deemed a heinous crime; and the Negroes thereby introduced into the dominions of Spain are declared to be free. Ruiz and Montez are proved to have made the pretended purchase of these Negroes with the full knowledge of all the circumstances. . . . If, then, these Negroes are not slaves, but are kidnapped Africans, who, by the laws of Spain itself, are entitled to their freedom, and were kidnapped and illegally carried to Cuba, and illegally detained and restrained on board of the *Amistad;* there is no pretense to say that they are pirates or robbers.

The court asserted that it was responsible for the protection of the rights of individuals, and that "supposing that these African Negroes not to be slaves, but kidnapped, and free Negroes . . . the United States are bound to respect their rights as much as those of Spanish subjects." The court finally acknowledged that the captives, who had waited so long, were "declared to be free, and . . . dismissed from the custody of the Court."

The Supreme Court affirmed the decisions of the lower courts, with the exception of the earlier order that the Africans be at the disposal of the president to be returned to Africa. Instead, the court held that they were truly free. They could go or remain as they chose, free men.

Surprisingly, despite the power of Adams's argument, when the official records of the *Amistad* case were published, the court noted that the arguments of Attorney General Henry Gilpin and Roger Baldwin had been given the greatest weight in their deliberations. The judges claimed that "many of the points presented by Mr. Adams, in the discussion of the case, were not considered by the Court essential to its decision, and were not taken notice of in the opinion of the Court."

Tappan arranged for the newly freed Africans to move to a predominantly abolitionist community in Farmington, Connecticut, while arrangements were made and money raised to take them back to Africa. For approximately eight months, the men remained in Farmington, where the Africans were expected to attend lectures on English and

Christianity and were responsible for tending gardens to help feed themselves.

The abolitionists took Singbe and some of his compatriots on a publicity tour, exploiting their celebrated victory for the abolitionist cause. However, as time passed, the Africans became depressed and homesick. Concerns were heightened further when in the summer of 1841, one of the men, Foone, drowned amid rumors of suicide; he had frequently spoken of his mother and Africa.

Finally, by fall of 1841, the money necessary to charter a ship to Africa had been raised. The plan was for the men and six missionaries to sail on the *Gentleman,* disembark at Sierra Leone, and travel overland into Mende country to establish a mission. On November 17, the Africans sailed from Farmington to New York City, where their ship awaited. For several nights, the abolitionists held large revivals in churches across Manhattan. At each, Singbe rose and gave a speech in Mende, translated into English by one of his shipmates, thanking those who had befriended them and promising to pray for them.

On Thursday, November 25, the Africans boarded the *Gentleman.* While the ship was towed out of the harbor, Lewis Tappan, the missionaries, and a handful of other abolitionists met in the cabin of the tugboat to say farewell to their friends. They prayed together, sang a hymn, then Singbe and Tappan each spoke. They recited the Lord's Prayer, then the missionaries and the former slaves climbed aboard the *Gentleman.*

The ship sailed east for fifty days, arriving at Sierra Leone in mid-January 1842. After two and a half years, the Africans were finally home and truly free.

Most of them walked away from the mission, never to be seen again. Others remained in contact with at least some portion of the Western world. Kinna became an ordained minister, but chose to remain in his homeland with his several wives. Margru, one of the little girls, grew up and returned to the United States, studied at Oberlin College, and then returned to work at a series of African missions. Singbe—one of those who walked away from the mission—returned to the small mission outpost, known as Mo Tappan. In 1879, he passed away, a free man.

After Amistad

Today, few would argue the "rightness" of the Supreme Court decision. It was, in its day, an admirably strong stand against the harsh cruelty of slavery, a stand for the rights of the oppressed, one that differentiated between people born free and simple merchandise or property. Nevertheless, as so often happens, "rightness" and "efficacy" diverged in the *Amistad* case. In solving one portion of this complex legal puzzle, in focusing on and answering the question whether the Africans were free men or merchandise, the court's decision did not address the other issues the case brought before it; in fact, the court, noting that it could dispose of the case "upon the merits" of the property claims, specifically circumvented the issues of the relationships between the executive, legislative, and the judicial branches, as well as the question of the integrity of international treaties themselves.

The *Amistad* case provoked sharp divisions in Congress, the beginning of twenty years of heated debates that would end in civil war. Congress saw a number of bills introduced in response to Spain's continued pressure for reimbursement and threats to abrogate its treaties with the United States in "reciprocation." Each resulted in sharply divided responses from representatives of Northern and Southern states. Eight presidents attempted—with varying degrees of enthusiasm—to mollify the Spanish. Some administrations, notwithstanding the Supreme Court's decision, attempted to pay reparations for the Spaniards' "slaves"; their efforts failed, as Northern congressmen refused to back legislation, treaties, or other provisions involving any mention of the continued *Amistad* claims.

Fortunately, in the end, the principles underpinning the *Amistad* case survived. Although it took more than forty years—until 1884—for Spain to officially drop its claim, the United States consistently refused to recognize a claim that had no basis "in justice or moral right," as noted by Secretary of State William Seward on behalf of President Lincoln. Seward's reasoning echoed that expressed by John Quincy Adams in his argument before the court twenty years before.

Twenty-three years after the *Amistad*'s unwilling passengers returned to their homes, free men, the United States released its slaves from bondage. The Thirteenth Amendment to the Constitution, ratified in 1865, officially abolished slavery and involuntary servitude throughout the United States and its territories. Three years later, the Fourteenth Amendment granted national and state citizenship to all people born or naturalized in the United States, thus vesting the rights and privileges of citizenship in the African-American population.

The *Amistad* decision put slavery—its cruelty, its injustice—at the center stage of American politics for years to come. The decision, affirming that men and women born free were inalienably, unalterably free, no matter the color of their skin, was a catalyst for monumental change. The coming struggle would pit brother against brother, tear the country apart, shed the blood of more Americans than any war in the nation's history, in an effort to wash away the awful stain and stench of two hundred years of slavery from the nation's soil.

CHAPTER THREE

Enemy Within

Radio Star John Henry Faulk
Challenges the McCarthy-Era Blacklist

It is clear, ladies and gentlemen, that communism is the great enemy, not only of our country and of all the free world, but of all decency. The shortest distance between the cradle and the grave is communism. . . . The question is whether we will permit our government to protect us . . . , or whether we are going to permit private vigilantes like this gentleman seated here with the thin mouth and the blue suit with a hidden microphone in his lapel. That is the question: Are you going to permit private vigilantism for profit?

—Louis Nizer, from his closing argument on behalf of Faulk

It was 1955, and John Henry Faulk—like America itself—was flush with success, enjoying the unimaginable prosperity that came with the end of a global war ten years before and something called a "police action" in faraway Korea.

Faulk was running his own radio show on WCBS, in the very heart of bustling New York City. From his office window he could see the crowded streets, an occasional '55 Ford Thunderbird, its newly designed tail fins and shiny chrome drawing the eye, gaudy and brash.

Americans were hot for entertainment, and radio and television were only too eager to please. Carl Perkins shot to the top of the charts begging the girls not to step on his footwear in "Blue Suede Shoes," and Elvis Presley debuted his lament "Heartbreak Hotel" as he began his ascent to the rock-and-roll throne.

In the midst of this teenage assault on the airwaves, Faulk's comedic personality and instantly recognizable Texas accent were honey to the ears of weary parents, relaxing throughout the New York metropolitan region, drinks in hand after a rough day. Faulk, like his listeners, enjoyed spending time with his wife and three children watching *I Love Lucy* or *Father Knows Best* on their new televisions.

World War II had ended, and Americans were still riding high on their victory over the Axis powers. But a new enemy had risen from the ashes of conflict, as former allies in the fight against facism squared off. The Soviet Union lowered an iron curtain across Eastern Europe, and Red China entered the fray, sending waves of troops against American GIs in the frozen mountains of Korea. After the unconditional surrender of Germany and Japan, the negotiated peace settlement at Panmunjom was a shock to Americans, and a reminder that new superpowers were vying for supremacy on the world stage.

Fear of communism motivated Americans; children started the school day with the Pledge of Allegiance, and their parents—ready to take up arms against anyone or anything that threatened their way of life— proclaimed their loyalty to the United States with pride.

John Henry Faulk had no reason to suspect that this rising tide of paranoia and patriotism would soon claim his fame, fortune, and perhaps, his freedom.

A Hot War Ends, a Cold War Begins

America's fear of communism began with the Bolshevik revolution during World War I, but active animosity was set aside during the slaughter of World War II. The Nazi juggernaut headed east for Moscow, the Japanese hit the American fleet in Pearl Harbor, and Joseph Stalin was transformed from tyrant to courageous "Uncle Joe," fighting the facist foe.

As the allies closed in on Berlin, plans for war-ravaged Europe were already being drawn up. President Franklin Delano Roosevelt, frail and weary, traveled to Yalta in February 1945, for a meeting with British prime minster Winston Churchill and Premier Stalin. When details of the secret meeting were released, it appeared that Stalin had gotten the best of FDR, putting in place the groundwork for more than forty years of Soviet domination of Eastern Europe. Two months later, the American president was dead of a cerebral hemorrhage.

President Harry Truman led the country in the last months of the war, meeting with Churchill and Stalin at Potsdam; at this conference he revealed to the allies the existence of the atomic bombs and his intention to use them against the Japanese.

In the years after the end of the war, the Soviets began a series of moves designed to force the Americans out of the Western section of Berlin. Truman, determined not to be bullied by Stalin, but unwilling to risk all-out conflict, publicly declared, "We will stay in Berlin." The Soviets put in place a blockade, preventing the delivery of food or coal to the residents of the Western-controlled zones. The Americans used massive airpower to supply food to the besieged Berliners—earning the affection of the former enemies a mere three years after their defeat—and the crisis eased.

On August 29, 1949, Truman—and the American public—received notice that the United States' unrivaled dominance of the postwar world had come to an end: the Soviets had detonated their first nuclear weapon. Whatever thoughts the president might have had about using military force to loosen Stalin's grip on the nations of Eastern Europe were now moot.

The Cold War had begun, and both sides hunkered down for the decades-long battle about to be waged on the margins by the superpowers and their proxies. Many Americans believed the threat posed by the communists was not limited to Eastern Europe, but was part of a more ambitious agenda: the overthrow of the United States of America.

America's legislative branch was not immune to the growing fear of communism. In response to the perceived threat to the United States by the international communist movement, Congress scrambled to create investigative committees and loyalty review boards to question suspected communists. In the House of Representatives, this concern was addressed through the House Un-American Activities Committee (HUAC). Formed in 1938 to investigate individuals and organizations suspected of having communist ties, HUAC's prewar attacks on the Roosevelt administration led to its marginalization during the war years. With the Soviets and the Americans now at dagger's point around the globe, HUAC was about to get a new lease on life.

HUAC: Bigger, Badder

The congressmen serving on HUAC had a broad mandate: to ensure that the persons they investigated were not dangerous to the public or America as a whole. As far as anyone could tell, *dangerous* was subjectively defined by the committee members, allowing nearly anyone to be brought before the committee for questioning.

J. Edgar Hoover, the director of the Federal Bureau of Investigation, placed suspected communists under government surveillance; he compiled a catalog of nearly half a million Americans he thought posed a possible security hazard to the United States; the vast majority were merely politically liberal—harmless to U.S. security. Hoover provided name after name for investigation by HUAC, the result being the deportation of hundreds of innocent Russians, sent back to the very regime HUAC—and Hoover—claimed to abhor.

Believing that celebrities had the ability to influence the American people as a result of their fame, HUAC set its sights on Hollywood in 1947, issuing subpoenas to more than forty witnesses who were expected to testify on the extent to which communism had infiltrated the film industry. Although some Hollywood stars—including Gregory Peck, Humphrey Bogart, and Danny Kaye—appeared before the committee and said they believed such questioning violated the First Amendment right to freedom of speech and assembly, others willingly testified and "named names." HUAC would not be deterred.

Although many members of the filmmaking community—directors, actors, and screenwriters—*had* been members of the Communist Party, many having joined during the Great Depression of the 1930s, such political party membership and attendance at their meetings was not illegal.

Ten of the witnesses called before the committee refused to answer any questions and—when the Supreme Court refused to reverse their convictions—were imprisoned for contempt of Congress, for terms ranging from six months to one year. Director Edward Dmytryk, and writers Dalton Trumbo, Alvah Bessie, Herbert Biberman, Lester Cole, Ring Lardner, Jr., John Howard Lawson, Albert Maltz, Samuel Ornitz, and Adrian Scott were among those imprisoned. When the "Hollywood Ten" were released from jail, they found the Hollywood studios unwilling to hire them. Afraid of further attention from Congress—after assuring legislators the studios did not knowingly employ communists—the studio heads blacklisted the unrepentant Ten.

HUAC subpoenaed hundreds of suspected communists for questioning. Roy Cohn, one of the committee's most aggressive attorneys, attacked the character of each witness, probing personal habits, demanding to know the names of the witness's friends, asking for lists of organizations to which the witness belonged, and sometimes going so far as to ask about a witness's sexual preference—on the assumption that, because homosexuality carried such a stigma, homosexuals were more likely to be security risks, as they could be targeted for blackmail because of their secret.

Cohn, a former assistant U.S. attorney, was one of four prosecutors in the trial of Julius and Ethel Rosenberg, who were convicted of spying for the Soviets and passing on the details of the American atomic weapons program to their handlers. Cohn played a key role in convincing the trial judge to impose the death sentence on the couple. Although the execution of the Rosenbergs remains a focal point of the American left even today, declassified documents released after the fall of the Soviet Union— as well as the autobiography of the Rosenbergs' Soviet spymaster—reveal they were in fact guilty.

The Rosenberg verdicts earned Cohn a place in the Truman administration, where he prosecuted espionage cases for the Justice Department until his 1953 appointment to HUAC.

HUAC cast a wide net in its search for communists; it was not uncommon for a witness to be labeled "pro-communist" merely for being a member of the American Civil Liberties Union (ACLU), and belief in racial equality immediately drew suspicion from some committee members. The chairman of one loyalty review board summed up the attitude of the day saying, "Of course the fact that a person believed in racial equality doesn't prove that he's a communist, but it certainly makes you look twice, doesn't it?"

Not to be outdone by the House of Representatives, the Senate created its own investigative panel, the Senate Committee on Government Operations; the most aggressive subset of the committee, the Permanent Subcommittee on Investigations, was chaired by Senator Joe McCarthy, a Republican from Wisconsin. Acting on the recommendation of his friend, FBI director Hoover, McCarthy appointed former HUAC attorney Roy Cohn to the Committee on Government Operations.

Born in 1908, McCarthy had early on learned the power of innuendo and false accusation. In 1939, only thirty and out of law school a mere four years, he decided to run for circuit court judge. McCarthy falsely accused his opponent of being senile and guilty of financial corruption; he won the election, took a seat on the Wisconsin bench, and then took an active role in his cases.

Soon after donning his judge's robes, McCarthy acquitted Quaker Dairy of unfair price practices on the grounds that the law would expire in six months, then destroyed a critical portion of the court record—earning a rebuke from the Wisconsin Supreme Court, but his decision could not be overturned on appeal. When World War II broke out, McCarthy temporarily traded his robe for marine fatigues. A first lieutenant, McCarthy headed to the Pacific as an intelligence officer, where he flew on combat missions as an observer.

McCarthy resigned his commission after the war, resumed his duties as a judge, and decided to run for a seat in the U.S. Senate. In 1946, he challenged longtime senator Robert La Follette for the Republican nomination, and in a tight race eked out a victory. In his typical fashion, McCarthy fought a dirty campaign, harshly criticizing La Follette for not joining the armed forces during the war, overlooking that La Follette was almost fifty years old in 1941. La Follette, his career in tatters, retired from politics and soon after committed suicide. McCarthy handily defeated the Democratic candidate in the general election, becoming—at thirty-eight—the youngest member of the U.S. Senate.

McCarthy soon developed a flair for using the press to garner headlines, ridiculing other senators and proclaiming his disdain for New Deal politics. Rumors began surfacing that McCarthy, tagged as a loudmouth, had taken bribes from the Pepsi-Cola Company, that his tales of heroic exploits as a gunner on bombing missions were lies, and that he was being investigated for tax evasion. Realizing his credibility was suffering, McCarthy latched on to a surefire way to divert attention from his own troubles and ride the rising tide of anticommunist hysteria.

In a February 1950 speech to a West Virginia women's group, McCarthy claimed Secretary of State Dean Acheson knew that more than two hundred State Department employees were communists. In response, the Democratic-controlled Senate formed a committee to investigate his charges; McCarthy could not produce the name of a single current State Department employee, and the committee issued a report stating it was unable to confirm any of his accusations. Unbowed, he continued his attacks. In 1952, with the Republicans now in control of the Senate, McCarthy gained his seat on the committee that would introduce the American public to "McCarthyism."

It worked like this: Hoover would provide the information the senator needed to smear a suspect's reputation. McCarthy would voice the accusations through the newspapers and in Congress, and Cohn would then prosecute the suspect on charges of cooperating with subversive communist forces.

Americans targeted by either HUAC or the Subcommittee on Investigations became pariahs overnight, their careers destroyed when their names landed on the infamous blacklist. Employers, rather than risk guilt by association, simply found a reason to fire the accused and hire someone else. When McCarthy's tactics were called into question, he would turn on the accuser, claiming his critics were subversives.

Have a Care, Be AWARE

Following McCarthy's lead, private organizations were created to eliminate from American society communists, communist sympathizers, and other groups considered subversive. One such self-appointed group, AWARE, Inc., was founded by Vincent Hartnett—an obscure script editor—and a group of New York actors. AWARE operated as a privately run version of the Subcommittee on Investigations by gathering "information" on various radio or television personalities and publishing its findings in a bulletin insinuating that such persons were communist or pro-communist, leaving the accused to prove their innocence. AWARE was primarily interested in the actions of media personalities because, it reasoned, celebrities had considerable public access in which to spread their pro-communist propaganda.

AWARE's bulletins—just like McCarthy's accusations—resulted in the taint of communism attaching to any person named, whether or not it was true. The fear of communism ran so deep that movie studios fired targeted celebrities, even if the star had a large earning potential; it was simply too much of a gamble to be associated with communism or persons whose names were associated with communism.

AWARE's interest in radio and television stars necessitated its involvement with the American Federation of Television and Radio Artists (AFTRA). In the early 1950s, AFTRA—the union representing radio and television personalities—espoused AWARE's anticommunist cause, its primary concern becoming tracking and fighting communism, rather than representing union members. Supported by AWARE's positive press, the same governing board of AFTRA was elected year after year without opposition, until 1954, when a slate of candidates challenged the incumbents. Not only were the insurgents defeated, they were labeled communists by AWARE, taking a page from the McCarthy playbook. AWARE circulated its bulletin about the defeated candidates to all employers in the radio and television industries; suddenly the candidates who had lost the election also lost their jobs. AWARE had established that anyone who opposed it would do so at his own peril, and that any studio that employed one of the listed would not be free of suspicion either. The AFTRA blacklist had begun.

A crucial component of AWARE's policy of intimidation was complete deniability; no person could definitively point to the group as being behind a firing. AWARE was insulated while the employers did the dirty work. Rather than make an issue of political affiliation, an employer would wait until the employee committed some trivial error, then fire him for it. The author of AWARE's bulletins, the group's cofounder Vincent Hartnett, became a master of innuendo and insinuation, never giving quite enough information to form the basis for a libel suit.

Hartnett, with the aid of information given him by the FBI, had earlier published a book, *Red Channels,* wherein he cited circumstantial evidence against a list of persons whom he considered subversive and a communist threat. Although the book's opening declared that persons listed in *Red Channels* were not necessarily communists, and despite Hartnett's being a private citizen without license from the government to investigate communist activities, the book caused havoc for the people whose names appeared within. Many television and radio station executives kept a copy of *Red Channels* in their desk drawer to screen potential employees.

Through AWARE, Hartnett established himself as a private-sector judge of who was and who was not a communist. Those executives responsible for hiring and firing in the television and radio industry occasionally sought Hartnett's approval before hiring a star to avoid AWARE's bad press. After a time, Hartnett began charging for this service. A "consulting" fee was required to run a background check on each name submitted by a potential employer. The service was so lucrative, Hartnett's $75-a-week salary ballooned to an annual income of more than $26,000—more than $160,000 in today's dollars.

When employers grumbled about the arrangement, Hartnett had Laurence Johnson explain the consequences of failing to request "clearance" for each employee, and the penalty for questioning Hartnett's assessment of a potential employee's patriotism. Johnson, a white-haired grocer in his seventies from Syracuse, New York, owned a chain of six supermarkets and had indirect control over thousands of products, in his role as an official in the National Association of Supermarkets. During the 1950s, major sponsors of radio and television stations were frequently food or grocery product lines. If an employer refused to request a background check, or worse, if the employer was refused clearance for a particular actor and used him anyhow, Johnson would put pressure on the show's sponsors to withdraw their support.

He would explain to the sponsor that they ought not support a communist-sympathizing station that had refused the advice of the knowledgeable Hartnett. Johnson would also point out that he could ruin the product's name permanently by telling customers that the proceeds supported communism. In several instances, Johnson called the sponsor and explained that he was going to put questionnaire boxes next to the sponsor's product asking customers to indicate whether they would rather buy an item whose proceeds went to support communism or instead a competitor's product, conveniently located three feet from the questionnaire display.

Although the FBI was the primary source of Hartnett's information, he also relied on informants. One informant's testimony had been largely responsible for the convictions of several people accused of being communist sympathizers. Johnson would pass on the informant's names to Hartnett, and he continued to rely on the names, even after the informant was indicted for perjury after admitting he had simply fabricated testimony.

Although employers denied there was a blacklist, a television or radio star listed in AWARE's bulletin could seldom, if ever, gain another position. Directors William Wyler, Billy Wilder, and John Huston, screenwriter Philip Dunne, and actors Humphrey Bogart, Danny Kaye, and Gregory Peck survived, despite their denunciations of McCarthyism, but other would-be stars vanished into the night, their careers prematurely curtailed by the effects of the blacklist. The rules of McCarthyism declared that one accused of communism was guilty until proven innocent.

The Faulk Challenge

John Henry Faulk was infuriated by the blacklist. What had happened to innocent until proven guilty? What about freedom of speech? And what about allowing the American public to make up their own minds about politics, rather than forcing all persons into the same cookie-cutter credo? Faulk believed that it was America's ability to allow each person to have a different opinion that made the nation great. Without this pluralistic theme, America would be a land where a man wasn't free to disagree with the government and become a place that did not tolerate diversity. Wasn't communism's ban on independent thought the very reason that the U.S. government was combating it in the first place?

These concerns prompted Faulk to join with a few other AFTRA members in January 1956 to run against the current board members, Faulk running for the second vice president's spot. Faulk's group called themselves the Middle-of-the-Road Party, and their platform was that communism was a frightful thing, but so too were the McCarthy-like tactics used by AWARE to fight it. The Middle-of-the-Road Party strongly opposed the blacklisting instigated by AWARE and sought to focus less on communism and more on fairly representing the AFTRA members' financial interests.

Although it was difficult for AFTRA members to openly support the Middle-of-the-Road slate for fear of repercussions from AWARE, disgust with the blacklist carried Faulk and his partners to victory. The Middle-of-the-Road Party swept into office, winning twenty-seven of the thirty-five seats on the board, including the position of president, vice president, and second vice president. Unfortunately, it would not be enough. The eight seats not carried by the Middle-of-the-Road Party were still held by AWARE's proxies, and they offered stiff resistance to every suggestion from Faulk's party, causing a rift in the AFTRA membership.

In mid-February, AWARE lived up to its fearsome reputation among the union's members, issuing yet another bulletin. This time their target was the Middle-of-the-Road Party, particularly John Henry Faulk, the man who had received the most votes of the candidates daring to question AWARE's omnipotence. In typical McCarthyite fashion, AWARE lashed out with its weapon of choice, innuendo.

The AWARE bulletin portrayed AWARE as the lone bastion in the fight against communism, attacking the Middle-of-the-Road Party and asking why it had chosen to oppose AWARE when AWARE worked tirelessly to fight communism. It questioned the loyalty of everyone who joined the Middle-of-the-Road Party and suggested that using the term *blacklisting* for AWARE's tactics was merely an attempt to frighten union members while subversive communist forces infiltrated the union. AWARE then directly discussed Faulk:

John Henry Faulk was further quoted as saying that "all [middlers] were chosen for their opposition to Communism as well as their opposition to AWARE." In most cases, this may well be true. But how about Faulk himself? What is his public record? . . .

(1) According to the *Daily Worker* [the Communist Party's official paper] of April 22, 1946, "Jack Faulk" was to appear at Club 65, 13 Astor Place, N.Y.C.—a favorite site of pro-communist affairs.

(2) According to the *Daily Worker* of April 17, 1947, "Johnny Faulk" was to appear as an entertainer at the opening of "Headline Cabaret," sponsored by Stage for Action (officially designated a Communist front). . . .

(3) According to the *Daily Worker* of April 5, 1948, "John Faulk" contributed cabaret material to "Show-Time for Wallace," revues staged by the Progressive Citizens of America (officially designated a Communist front) in support of Henry A. Wallace's candidacy for the president of the U.S. Although Wallace was the officially endorsed candidate of the CP, by no means are all his supporters Communist or pro-Communists. What is in question here is support of any candidate given through a Communist-front setup.

(4) A program dated April 25, 1946, named "John Faulk" as a scheduled entertainer (with identified Communist Earl Robinson and two non-Communists) under the auspices of the Independent Citizens Committee of the Arts, Sciences and Professions (officially designated a Communist front, and predecessor of the Progressive Citizens of America).

(5) Vol. 3, Nos. 1 & 2, of the Bulletin of People's Songs (officially designated a Communist front) named Faulk as one who had sent greetings to People's Songs on its second anniversary.

(6) "Johnny Faulk" was listed in a circular as an entertainer or speaker (with Paul Robeson and two others) to appear at "Spotlight on Wallace" to be held in Room 200 of the Jefferson School of Social Science on February 16, 1948. The Jefferson School has been found by the Federal Government to be what it is, the official training school of the Communist conspiracy in New York.

(7) "John H. Faulk" was a U.S. sponsor of the American Conti-

nental Congress for Peace, staged in Mexico City, September 5–10, 1949, as shown by the official "call." The Congress was later described by the HUAC as "another phase in the Communist world 'peace' campaign, aimed at consolidating anti-American forces throughout the Western Hemisphere."

Faulk read the bulletin, five single-spaced pages in all, with a mix of shock, fear, and anger. AWARE never once directly accused Faulk of being a communist, yet their innuendo implied precisely that. Faulk had never supported communism, but the juxtaposition of his name with the words *communist front* made it sound as though he had. Several of the events Hartnett reported on never took place, and none of the organizations sponsoring events that Faulk did attend were "officially designated" communist fronts—Hartnett had merely made it up. Hartnett even used his FBI connections to get the Middle-of-the-Road Party denounced by HUAC and Faulk subpoenaed to testify before the committee.

Hartnett increased the pressure, circulating the rumor Faulk was being investigated by the government as a possible communist subversive. Hartnett was relentless. He sent copies of the bulletin to every radio station, producer, manager, and sponsor supporting Faulk. Laurence Johnson, meanwhile, visited offices up and down Madison Avenue, demanding Faulk's sponsors withdraw their support immediately or be faced with a boycott of their products. In one fell swoop AWARE had linked communism with Faulk's name, put Faulk's job in real jeopardy, and destroyed the power of the new AFTRA board, as union members scrambled to disassociate themselves from the slate.

On April 11, 1956, the annual AFTRA board meeting was held at the New York City Center. There was a record turnout, the audience littered with pro-AWARE union members sitting in small groups, seeming to glare directly at Faulk. One at a time, those who wished to speak were given the opportunity. Former Middle-of-the-Road Party members took the microphone and denounced their association with the party. Some union members even claimed that the slate was holding secret meetings to discuss the infiltration of communism into AFTRA. Faulk was furious, but when he took the microphone, his denials seemed to fall on deaf ears. Ed Sullivan, vehemently pro-AWARE and a television heavyweight, sat among a large group of AFTRA members and pointed at Faulk, scoffing in open disdain.

Faulk returned to his office at WCBS and almost immediately received a call from a *Variety* columnist asking if he had any comments on the AFTRA meeting. He was stunned. How did the reporter get word so quickly? The reporter replied that he had been told what would happen at the meeting the previous day, by a source he would prefer not to name. Faulk stood, staring blankly at the silent receiver in his hand. The challenge to his patriotism was entirely unfounded, and yet the public might very well believe it because he refused to come forward and swear up and down that he was not a communist. Mere denial was not enough; AWARE demanded that he crawl, beg for forgiveness for a sin he had not committed. His wife and three children depended on him, and he began to wonder if he could continue to support them if WCBS succumbed under the pressure of the blacklist and fired him. For a moment Faulk thought back, wondered where he could have gone wrong. What had he done to merit this vicious attack?

As the dial tone buzzed angrily in the receiver, the answer came to him: nothing. He had done nothing but run against AWARE on the union ballot. He had done nothing but have the audacity to disagree with AWARE's puppets. Furious that AWARE gave itself a license to ruin the careers of others, Faulk slammed the receiver down and strode resolutely from his office. If AWARE thought John Henry Faulk would take this without a fight, they were grievously mistaken.

Early Days

Faulk was born August 21, 1913, the son of Henry and Mattie Faulk and the fourth of five children. Faulk's father, a lawyer, taught him early on to stand up for what he believed in. He was troubled by the racial inequities of life in 1920s Texas, as he struggled to understand why his black pals were not allowed to attend his high school and weren't welcome in many of the homes in Austin.

Faulk and his siblings had the run of a large, drafty house on the poor side of town. Although Mr. Faulk could afford a house in Austin, he preferred to raise his children in the country, where the family could have a few chickens, a cow, a family dog, and bit of land for them to play on. Mr. Faulk owned some property nearby, which he rented to tenants too poor to live anywhere else. Mrs. Faulk was constantly bringing apples, bread, toys, and an occasional chicken to help out people who depended on the Faulks' generosity to survive.

Mr. Faulk could have served as the model for Atticus Finch. He litigated torts, defended murderers, and had an abiding interest in the civil rights of the large black community in Austin. During the Great Depression, Mr. Faulk often defended people for free.

Both Mr. and Mrs. Faulk were vehement opponents of the Ku Klux Klan, much to the surprise of many of their townsfolk. The Faulks were viewed as eccentrics because they frequently had black visitors, including John Henry's best friend, Snooky Bates. The two boys were inseparable. Although other white families might be shunned for acting like the Faulks, the family's steadfast attendance at the local Methodist church kept them in the good graces of their neighbors.

John Henry spent his days with Snooky down at the creek or rambling in the woods. Eventually, he began disappearing for a couple of days at a time. Mrs. Faulk adopted a regular practice of walking down to Snooky Bates's house to retrieve her absent son. It wasn't long after John Henry entered the first grade that the grim realities of racism began to make themselves apparent to him. John Henry's elementary school did not admit blacks, and John Henry's playtime with Snooky grew shorter and shorter during the school year.

When John Henry turned sixteen, an unfortunate accident left him blind in one eye. He was swimming in the creek with some friends and dried his face on an old towel lying on the bank. Several days later, his eyes began to hurt. The doctor diagnosed conjunctivitis, but John Henry's mother took him to a specialist in Dallas. John Henry had contracted a gonorrheal infection from the towel, blinding him and nearly requiring removal of the eye.

Having lost his vision in one eye, John Henry had trouble with depth perception and was no longer as proficient at sports and outdoor activities as he had been. Depressed, he turned to books and began devouring literature of all sorts. He read Thoreau, whom his father admired so, and the writings of Madison and Jefferson. His father told him that Madison was the true genius of the First Amendment, and that the First Amendment "was the one that contained all our great freedoms."

In 1932, John Henry enrolled as a freshman at the University of Texas. He had anticipated becoming a lawyer like his father, but, after two years of classes, turned instead to literature and folklore. Here he met J. Frank Dobie, the "cowboy professor." John Henry was drawn to Dobie because of his unorthodox teaching practices and his open disdain for authority. The two began a friendship that would last until Dobie's death.

While John Henry was studying folklore and working on a master's thesis on the sermons of black ministers, Mr. Faulk was diagnosed with liver cancer. John Henry returned home in the fall of 1939 to spend the last few weeks of his father's life with him. In September, Mr. Faulk passed away; his body remained on display at the Methodist church for longer than usual, to allow both whites and blacks time to mourn—separately.

The following year, John Henry finished his master's thesis, "Ten Negro Sermons," and submitted it to the English Department. The thesis took an inordinate amount of time to read, because John Henry used phonetic spelling to accurately convey the flavor of the preachers' speech patterns. His thesis preserved the rapidly diminishing art of giving a "Negro sermon," at least that's what Congress thought. Shortly after the thesis was completed, it was published and archived in the Library of Congress as a work worth protecting.

John Henry's labors in the English Department earned him a part-time job at the University of Texas, where he taught English and amused his class with Texas tales using his ever-growing list of impersonations. One of his students, a talented blond woman studying piano and voice in the Fine Arts School, was especially impressed with John Henry's stories. Within six weeks of meeting, Hally Wood and John Henry were married.

Off campus, war raged around the world. Rejected by the army due to his bad eye, John Henry was determined to put his energy to work fighting fascism. In 1942 he left his position at the University of Texas to join the war effort in the merchant marine. The next couple of years found John Henry crewing supply ships, dodging torpedoes; joining the American Red Cross division in Egypt; becoming a member of the American Civil Liberties Union; and finally enlisting in the army, after admissions requirements were lowered. John Henry was soon assigned to Camp Swift, near Austin, and served as liaison between the local civilian community and the soldiers.

Encouraged by his fellow soldiers at Camp Swift, John Henry began working on a radio script in his free time. Through a friend working at WCBS, the CBS station in New York City, John Henry got an interview. The station's executives thought this talented newcomer was just the sort of entertainer that would hit it big in New York, and after John Henry was discharged from the army in 1946, they offered him a contract to appear on his own program. John Henry had a weekly show called *Johnny's Front Porch,* in which he compared life in Texas to life in the Big Apple, using the characters that he had worked so long in developing. Although the show was not a smash hit, New Yorkers slowly began warming up to John Henry Faulk.

The stress of moving to New York City, in addition to his absence during the war, had taken a toll on the marriage. Although the Faulks had just welcomed a newborn daughter, Cynthia, they were not happy. When John Henry found love letters written to his wife, he knew it was over; they divorced in 1947. The following year, John Henry met a slim, dark New Yorker named Lynne. The two dated seriously for about six weeks before marrying.

These years marked an important time, not only for John Henry but for the country as well. Richard Nixon, a Republican candidate for Congress, labeled his opponent a "pinko" and a "Red" and won a seat in Congress. The Hollywood Ten were convicted and jailed. The chairman of HUAC proclaimed that communism was like the antichrist and was "older than Christianity . . . it hounded and persecuted its savior during his earthly ministry, inspired his crucifixion, derided him in his dying agony, and then gambled for his garments at the foot of the cross." The U.S. attorney general began administering "loyalty tests" to all potential federal workers and kept a list of those who did not pass as suspected subversives. John Steinbeck's *Grapes of Wrath* was banned from school libraries and burned as communist propaganda.

John Henry and Lynne began a happy marriage; soon, they had two children. After working at another radio station for a time, John Henry returned to WCBS to run his own morning show. The program, featuring music, weather, and a healthy dose of storytelling, was a four-hour-long hit. For the next six years, *The John Henry Faulk Show* kept New Yorkers close to the radio and laughing.

John Henry's comedic personality was in high demand, and he began appearing on television. He flew to Washington, D.C., to emcee a party attended by many senators and other high-profile politicians. Although John Henry's performance drew riotous laugher, one senator appeared unimpressed with the Texas comedian, remaining stonily silent: Joseph McCarthy. Wary of the blacklisting practices in the radio and television industries, John Henry believed his patriotic record kept him free of suspicion. In a letter to his mentor and friend J. Frank Dobie, John Henry expressed his mixed feelings about his success: "It looks like I'll be sailing along up here for quite a spell, unless McCarthy decides to crack my knuckles for un-McCarthy-like thoughts."

There was good reason to be cautious. These were times when one could be blacklisted for belonging to the Anti-Nazi League or the committee to end segregation in major league baseball. AWARE, Inc., had used part of the proceeds from Hartnett's book, *Red Channels,* to publish a book telling suspected subversives how to clear their name. Working both sides of the issue, AWARE began raking in royalties from this book, as the blacklisted scrambled to find ways to escape the taint and work again. While the suspected subversives struggled to find employment, those not yet on the list found they were being followed home from union meetings by AWARE members scrutinizing a suspect's every movement. Some found their trash had been sifted through; a few even discovered that "anticommunists" had broken into their homes and planted bugs to record their conversations. Against this backdrop, John

Henry Faulk decided he'd had enough and joined with several others in challenging AWARE. And when AWARE turned its frightful focus on John Henry in an attempt to destroy his hard-earned career, Faulk was determined to find a lawyer to set things right.

Finding an Advocate

An acquaintance was an associate in the offices of Louis Nizer, perhaps the most famous trial lawyer in Manhattan, if not the country. The associate discussed the matter with Nizer, who agreed to meet with Faulk the following morning to discuss the suit.

The law offices of Phillips, Nizer, Benjamin, and Krim occupied an entire floor of the Paramount Building. As Faulk entered Nizer's spacious office, he focused first on the gleam of a broad, well-polished desk, and then upon the athletic figure rising from behind it. Nizer was of medium height, powerfully built, and light on his feet as he crossed the room to shake Faulk's hand. Faulk was immediately put at ease by the genial attorney and settled into a heavy leather chair.

When Faulk finished telling his story, Nizer paused, then explained to Faulk just how difficult a case of this nature was. Nizer emphasized that it would take years to complete; that AWARE would likely make conditions much harder on Faulk than at present; and that the trial would be arduous and expensive. Faulk said he understood, but remained steadfast in his belief that AWARE had to be forced to take responsibility for its actions. For Faulk, the outcome of the trial mattered not only to him, but also to the dozens of other actors and actresses, radio personalities, and media entertainers whose careers had been destroyed by AWARE's campaign of implication and accusation.

Nizer waited a moment, as though choosing the perfect words, then smiled warmly at Faulk before saying, "I have deliberately tried to discourage you. I don't want you to be misled that this would be an easy case. It won't be. This action will be a long one. But you will win in the end. I will represent you." Nizer's even tone evoked a confidence— without arrogance—that lifted Faulk's spirits.

Fortunately Faulk had chosen his counsel well, for this was not the first, nor the last, time that Nizer would stand without flinching beneath the bright lights of public scrutiny.

The Boy Orator

Louis Nizer was born in London on February 6, 1902, and traveled with his mother to New York in 1905. Like many other immigrants, he entered the United States through Ellis Island; unlike the others, he was dressed in a blue velvet Lord Fauntleroy suit, a hat (complete with pom-pom), and was toting a tennis racket through the gate. Nizer and his mother were greeted with a barrage of hugs, kisses, and tears from his father, who had come across only the year before to set up a cleaning and dyeing shop in Brooklyn.

The Nizer family credo was hard work and persistence. Nizer's father worked eighteen to twenty hours a day in the shop, giving up on sleep entirely when orders began to back up. Nizer's mother spent her days trimming lace or pressing clothes in the shop's back room. Nizer would spend his evenings after school studying and trimming yard after yard of lace while he and his mother sang songs and told jokes to make the work go faster.

Poverty was common in Nizer's neighborhood, and many of his class-mates suffered through their years of school without enough to eat or the most basic of medical care. Tuberculosis was a common killer of young children, and several families near the Nizers lost young children to it. By the time he was twelve, Nizer began to attract attention when, stand-ing on a street corner near his home, he railed against the appalling con-ditions in his neighborhood.

The "boy orator," as Nizer was called by his listeners, always drew a crowd and was soon recruited to speak for the Socialist Party on poverty. Nizer now reached audiences from the back of a flatbed pickup, elevated so that all listeners could see his earnest face. By the time Nizer was fif-teen he had turned his speaking abilities to asking audiences to buy war bonds in support of the United States in World War I. Nizer was so suc-cessful that he received a certificate of merit from the government.

This period of "soapboxing" gave Nizer insights into how to persuade his listeners. Persuasion, Nizer realized, required describing the victims of poverty—or any other cause—so that the audience members actually empathized with them and imagined exactly what the victims looked like as they struggled under their burdens. It required an honesty and forth-rightness that would appeal to the integrity of his audience.

Nizer's neighborhood had a band of toughs who ruled the streets. Their leader was a fifteen-year-old bully named Leo. Leo's favorite activ-ity was to beat up all the kids in the neighborhood who did not show him sufficient deference. Walking with a swagger that was as exaggerated as his Brooklyn accent, he would sometimes pummel one of his own gang members just to display his dominance. Nizer tried to steer clear of Leo.

One day while heading home from school, an unsuspecting Nizer rounded a corner to come face-to-face with Leo's gang. Nizer endured a savage beating from the tough, but refused to give up. Nizer slammed into the larger boy's body, knocking him back. Leo pulled out a pair of brass knuckles, but Nizer twisted Leo's wrist and kicked them away. As the shouts of onlookers gave way to shocked silence, Nizer took one last jab at Leo before walking away. Nizer had a busted lip, one eye swollen shut, and a broken rib, but he was victorious.

Although he received a stern lecture about fighting from his father and was stuck in bed for a week to heal, the time alone gave Nizer an opportunity to think about what the fight had meant. Leo was a seemingly insurmountable opponent, one every kid in the neighborhood quaked before. Yet Nizer, a boy much smaller than Leo, had conquered him. Years later, after receiving news that Leo had been convicted of a capital crime and executed at Sing Sing, Nizer described the fight as a turning point in his life, a point at which he realized that "he who will not be beaten can't be beaten. Sheer *will* can triumph over great odds."

Nizer entered Columbia College, and while there, he competed for the Curtis Oratorical Award, the highest prize given by the college for a speaking competition. After several elimination rounds, four finalists were chosen. Nizer delivered a speech on disarmament and made the finals. The last round was held before students, faculty, the townsfolk, and the contestants' parents. Nizer delivered his piece with the firm confidence of a seasoned professional and won.

Nizer entered the Curtis Oratorical competition again, only to be warned by his professor that he would be handicapped by his prior win, and that the judges would likely handle him less delicately than his inexperienced competitors. Undaunted, Nizer delivered a stunning speech against capital punishment and became the first person ever to win the competition more than once.

In addition to his athletic and oratorical pursuits, Nizer retained a rigorous academic calendar. His work ethic left little time for socializing, but he felt that the time spent with his crew team or his speech class provided him with all the social interaction he needed. Inheriting his father's steady drive, Nizer was a student who could not keep still, always moving on to some new task. His junior year, he qualified to teach English at the college and took on a night position instructing non-English-speaking students.

A year and a half later, Nizer enrolled at Columbia law school and after graduating and passing the bar found himself unable to get a job. A recession had greatly limited opportunities for new lawyers.

Nonetheless, there was a first case, and it came through Nizer's father, who brought home three potential clients. The three men explained that they owned property on the west side of Ellery Street in Brooklyn, where pushcart vendors sold their goods. The city had passed an ordinance allowing pushcarts only on the east side of Ellery Street. This ordinance had the effect of making property on that side very valuable, since customers visited the shops there while looking at the pushcarts. Property on the west side experienced a drop in value after the ordinance was passed. The men wanted the ordinance overturned, but after interviewing three other lawyers they could get no one to take their case.

Undaunted by being their fourth choice, Nizer agreed to take the case for $500. He learned all he could about the rules that govern the passage of a city law. He drafted not only his own arguments but the arguments he thought the city would make and developed counterarguments for them. He interviewed dozens of property owners, pushcart peddlers, and city employees; he investigated other areas of the city where pushcarts were found; and he peered down at Ellery Street from the rooftops to study pedestrian traffic patterns.

At trial, Nizer painted a picture of the city's arbitrary application of this ordinance to Ellery Street, while allowing every other street to have pushcarts on both sides. Nizer convinced the judge that the ordinance was arbitrary and was simply an attempt to inflate property values on the east side of Ellery Street to favor the politically connected property owners.

The city appealed the judge's decision to the court of last resort, the New York Court of Appeals. Nizer would have to argue before none other than the United States' preeminent jurist, Chief Judge Benjamin N. Cardozo.

Cardozo's decisions remain among the most eloquent and best reasoned, even today. Nizer compared arguing before Cardozo to the feeling a musician would have after having studied Beethoven's genius for his entire life and then being forced to play a musical piece before the master himself. Nizer knew that Cardozo had all the knowledge of the law that would apply in the case, and so Nizer tried to explain what Cardozo had little knowledge of, the facts. Nizer's organization of his argument was well received by the esteemed jurist, and the city was once again soundly trounced.

Nizer's success brought him to the attention of Louis Phillips, a lawyer who ran his own law firm. Phillips, who had known Nizer's parents in London, offered Nizer a position and offered him $20 per week, in addition to a percentage of whatever clientele Nizer could bring in. Nizer accepted and began searching for his own clients. After two years, Nizer was made a full partner.

Over the next twenty-five years, the law firm of Phillips and Nizer grew into one of the most prestigious in Manhattan. Nizer represented

Elizabeth Taylor in a libel suit against a paper that printed misinformation about her children and won her a judgment. He helped rewrite an entire screenplay to excise portions based on the life of Nobel Prize winner Sinclair Lewis, thus allowing his client to avoid an injunction prohibiting the scheduled production of the play. Nizer was called upon by President Johnson to file a libel suit against the *Saturday Evening Post* for claiming the president used racial slurs, although Nizer later persuaded the president to ignore the statement and not file suit.

Nizer's career was well established, and his services were in high demand. From his office high above Manhattan, the world looked good to Louis Nizer. He believed in the power of hard work, persistence, and goodwill; he quoted Voltaire explaining the need for man to do good things for one another: "We must not be guilty of the good things we did not do." Nizer believed this and tried to look past the probable compensation that he would receive from a client, focusing instead on the good that would come out of a suit.

Faulk "Ponies Up"

Faulk left Nizer's office relieved that one of the best lawyers in the country was representing him. Faulk believed that the lawsuit would take some time, and while he might be precluded from further television appearances by the blacklist, he and Lynne and their three children could make it on what he earned on his WCBS radio show until the whole affair blew over.

Faulk called a few loyal Middle-of-the-Road Party members and assured them that AWARE's days of interference with AFTRA were numbered. One friend congratulated Faulk, then asked how much of a retainer Nizer had charged. Faulk tried to brush the question aside, but his friend confronted him with grim reality. Nizer was a "million-dollar attorney," and that meant he would charge a large retainer, probably between $50,000 and $100,000.

Faulk called Nizer and asked about the retainer. The attorney explained that a case of this length and complexity would have considerable out-of-pocket expenses that would have to be paid. Nizer told Faulk that he had tried to keep the retainer as low as was practical, because he knew Faulk had a family to care for. The retainer would be $10,000.

Faulk expressed his thanks before hanging up, but did not tell Nizer that he had nowhere near that much in his bank account. Faulk was just beginning litigation, and he was already up against a wall trying to find a way to raise the necessary money.

While sitting in his office at WCBS thinking about how he would explain his lack of a retainer to Nizer, Faulk was called to the upstairs office of a friend who also worked at WCBS, the most famous journalist in America, Edward R. Murrow. Murrow asked him why he looked so despondent, and Faulk explained the situation. Murrow was taken aback; he had assumed that WCBS was footing the bill for Faulk's lawsuit, since it was work-related.

Faulk told Murrow that WCBS wanted him to drop the suit and avoid implicating WCBS in any bad press that might come from fighting AWARE. Murrow told Faulk to call up Nizer and tell him that he would have his retainer in the morning. When Faulk told Murrow that he couldn't possibly borrow such a large sum when there was no guarantee that he would ever be able to repay him, Murrow said, "Let's get this straight, Johnny. I am not making a personal loan to you of this money. I am investing this money in America. Louis Nizer must try this case. These people must be brought into court. This blacklisting racket must be exposed. This is a very important suit. I don't know whether even you realize how important it is."

With the first hurdle cleared, *Faulk v. AWARE, Laurence Johnson, and Vincent Hartnett* was filed in the New York State Supreme Court on June 26, 1956.

Faulk initially received a great deal of fan mail from his listeners, telling him that he was doing the right thing, asking why the television and radio industries had not taken care of this themselves, and expressing outrage that the issue had to be taken to court at all. Faulk was heartened by the letters and was sure that once companies like WCBS saw the steps he was taking, they would jump on the bandwagon. Faulk believed that the increased circulation of his name might actually make him more popular than ever.

Nothing could have been further from the truth.

When the television and radio networks got wind of Faulk's suit, they avoided him as though he had just contracted "highly contagious mumps." He was more controversial than ever, and controversy equaled death in McCarthy's America. Faulk's television offers dried up, and his sponsors slowly began to pull their advertising from his radio show. Faulk was informed by his manager that until the lawsuit was over, he might as well face the fact that no work outside of his contract with WCBS would be forthcoming.

Meanwhile, the defendants were preparing for battle with their newly hired attorney, Godfrey Schmidt. Through their attorney, AWARE answered Faulk's complaint by claiming that Faulk had no cause of action for a conspiracy-to-libel claim. AWARE stated that there was no libel because it had never actually called Faulk a communist. Further, AWARE claimed that it had merely given a list of events that Faulk had attended, and that any misstatement was the result of honest mistake and not malicious intent.

Nizer challenged the answer as unresponsive, and the judge agreed. The judge held that AWARE had raised an issue of communism through innuendo and clearly called into question Faulk's patriotism through a libel per se. This early ruling was a huge win for Faulk's case, because the only defense to a libel per se is "truth." For AWARE to escape liability for its acts, it would be forced to show that Faulk actually was a communist or pro-communist as indicated by his actions or words and not by implication.

In December of 1956, WCBS surprised Faulk by renewing his contract for another five years. Although it contained a provision allowing the network to fire Faulk for any reason, he believed that WCBS was implicitly giving him a vote of confidence. Faulk was surprised to see that the AFTRA union members did not seem quite so confident. Though he remained on the board of directors, he was vastly outnumbered by AWARE loyalists, who repealed nearly every measure passed by Faulk's board the year before, reinstituting loyalty checks and a rule that forbade "pro-communists" from being members.

Overwhelmed by the pending lawsuit, his sudden drop in income, and the feeling that he was an outcast among the circle who had previously supported him, Faulk decided to take a break. He took Lynne and his children on a short trip to Jamaica. Getting away from New York was just what the Faulks needed, and they returned feeling much more optimistic. They would make it on Faulk's WCBS salary if they were careful, and they could reestablish old friendships when the lawsuit blew over. While Lynne was busy unpacking the family's luggage, the telephone rang and Faulk answered. He had been fired.

A crucial part of blacklisting was to get rid of controversial employees for seemingly valid reasons. A company could not afford to invite a lawsuit by stating "suspicion" as the reason for discharge. In Faulk's case, WCBS compiled some statistical data suggesting that Faulk's ratings were slipping. To avoid a scene, WCBS waited for Faulk to go on vacation before delivering the bad news.

Faulk discussed the data with one of his managers at WCBS, also a trusted friend, and was told what he had already assumed. The data was bogus. Faulk had been a tremendous money earner for WCBS; his ratings remained higher than those of almost every other show on the station; and he had managed to hold a steady audience despite a downturn in the station's overall ratings.

How could Faulk support his family? His business manager made out a budget, but the Faulks would have to cut expenses "right to the bone" to even see them through the next three months. Faulk began searching for work immediately. He made a detailed list of everyone he could think of who might be in a position to get him a job. He went on interview after interview, even flying to Minneapolis for a weekend when one of his contacts appeared to be offering him a job. He was taken out to dinner, introduced to the cast members of a television show in production, and promised that good things were coming.

Faulk was repeatedly assured by numerous companies that he would be contacted soon with an offer. In every instance, the promises were hollow. At best, Faulk would receive a phone call giving some excuse for why he couldn't be hired at present.

Lynne began working in the advertising department of a firm that sold bathroom fixtures. Though she was complimented on the quality of her work, she was fired when her employer learned of Faulk's lawsuit against AWARE. She eventually found a job as a waitress; it didn't pay much, but it did pay something. The family was struggling.

The lawsuit progressed at what seemed like a snail's pace. The defendants found one excuse after the next for why their depositions could not be taken. Their lawyer was frequently unavailable. Worst of all, Hartnett had used his FBI contacts to report Faulk as a suspected pro-communist. The FBI passed this information along to HUAC; Faulk soon received a subpoena. This provided more ammunition for AWARE, who circulated the news that Faulk was being investigated by HUAC as a suspected communist.

Finally, the day for defendants' depositions arrived. Hartnett was to be examined first, then Johnson, and perhaps a couple of AWARE members. Hartnett entered the room puffing on a large cigar. He was of medium height and thin, with a cocky walk. He and Faulk locked eyes for a moment. It was the first time either of the men had seen the other. Vincent Hartnett had tried to destroy Faulk without even knowing who he was, and Faulk had tried to defend himself against the foe with no face. Now, both men had a chance to size each other up.

Nizer broke the tension by shaking hands with Schmidt, Hartnett's lawyer, and explaining how the questioning would go. Hartnett draped himself in a chair, slouching and sucking on his cigar. He gave curt, easy answers to Nizer's questions. Slowly, the story began to unravel. As Nizer asked more and more questions, Hartnett's responses grew more irritable. Finally, Nizer asked a question phrased in a way that accused Hartnett of libel.

"Mr. Nizer," Hartnett snapped, "I would remind you that I'm not on the witness stand, and you're not a district attorney."

Nizer eyed Hartnett intently for a few moments, and then said, "Do I understand, sir, you presume to instruct me in the conduct of this examination? Are you, sir? How dare you impudently speak of district attorneys and witnesses! You, sir, who have sat as judge, jury, prosecuting attorney, and executioner on the lives and careers of hundreds of loyal, innocent victims! You, sir, who have drawn the noose of starvation around the neck of that innocent man sitting there, seeking to starve his children and destroy his reputation. You dare, sir, instruct me in the conduct of this case?"

The cold tone of Nizer's eloquent reply left Schmidt and Hartnett speechless. Hartnett opened and closed his mouth, trying to form a response, but Schmidt placed his hand on Hartnett's shoulder to silence him. Hartnett tried to put his cigar back into his mouth, but stuck it in his left ear by mistake. Schmidt told Nizer that his comments were unnecessarily harsh, and Nizer quipped that he didn't need any instruction from him either. The rest of the deposition went without a hitch; Hartnett obediently answered every question that Nizer asked.

After the deposition, Nizer and Schmidt talked. Schmidt said that "a small sum, perhaps $10,000," could be raised if Faulk chose to drop the suit. Nizer talked to Faulk about the possibility of settling. Nizer offered to waive all of Faulk's legal fees and allow him to keep the settlement.

Faulk looked thoughtful for a moment, then rejected this option. Faulk wanted to challenge the institution of blacklisting itself; that was the purpose of filing a conspiracy charge against the defendants. Faulk was not interested in merely recouping his personal loss.

It had now been two full years since the lawsuit was filed. The Faulks were scraping by on what Lynne earned as a waitress and what Faulk could scrounge up selling encyclopedias and mutual fund shares door-to-door. Faulk had been offered a job at a radio station in San Francisco, but when he pressed to find out when the job would begin, they canceled, claiming that their schedule was overbooked. However, contained within the cancellation letter was another letter addressed to the Mutual Broadcasting Company. Faulk thought at first that the secretary had meant to send him a copy of the letter and had mailed off the original by mistake. But when he read the letter, Faulk realized that he had never been meant to see it at all. Written by the station manager, it asked how Faulk was doing with his lawsuit. It plainly stated that the station might not be interested in hiring Faulk if he was still "controversial." At Nizer's suggestion, Faulk photocopied the letter and sent the original back to the secretary informing her that she had mistakenly mailed him a letter meant for someone else. Through this coincidence, Faulk had the first hard evidence that the notoriety spawned by AWARE's lies had cost him a job.

HUAC delayed Faulk's appearance for unknown reasons. Their involvement made it difficult for Faulk to concentrate on his lawsuit and his family, because an investigation by HUAC was no small matter—you could be thrown in prison on the basis of a "wrong answer" if HUAC decided to prosecute. Faulk decided that the subpoena was baseless and was intended merely to intimidate him.

Faulk's younger sister, Texana, stepped up to help her now infamous brother. Texana still lived in Austin, where she led the life of a typical housewife. Like the rest of the Faulks, she had strong political views and a willingness to get her hands dirty defending them. Texana began a letter-writing campaign.

She had townsfolk, family friends, contacts Faulk had in New York, Faulk's radio-show fans, and everyone else she could think of write letters to HUAC begging them to dismiss the subpoena against Faulk. It took several months, but finally the letters paid off. The subpoena was withdrawn. Faulk was relieved to have HUAC off his mind for the time being.

Meanwhile, Nizer was making excellent progress with the case, collecting depositions from parties whose testimony would be crucial at the trial. It seemed that Nizer's skill had completely intimidated Schmidt, who no longer offered much resistance to Nizer's demands. Faulk's case was rapidly being buttressed. And then without warning, Schmidt was off the case, and a new team of attorneys were brought aboard. They were Thomas Bolan and his partner, ex-HUAC attorney and once right-hand man to Senator McCarthy, Roy Cohn.

Cohn, called the "scourge of subversives" by many, had informed Nizer that the case would have to remain "as is" for a few months. When asked why, Cohn informed Nizer that he was going overseas for a while and wouldn't be back until late in the year.

Faulk was outraged and demanded, "How can Cohn make a decision like that on his own?" Nizer understood Faulk's frustration, but Cohn convinced the court to allow him the delay. To Faulk, every week of scrimping by was a terrible hardship, and it seemed as if the defendants were intentionally trying to squeeze him to the point of dropping the suit.

Cohn returned from Europe late that year but continued to stall. Nizer finally was able to secure a court order forcing Cohn to allow Nizer to proceed with the depositions in a timely fashion. When Nizer was through collecting his depositions, Cohn began his delaying tactics again.

Nizer returned to court, asking the judge to force Cohn to expediously complete his own depositions, and finally in August 1961, just over five years after the suit was filed, Cohn and Bolan were ready to depose Faulk.

Cohn's office was located high above Wall Street, and as the elevator shot Nizer and Faulk skyward, Nizer gave his client some words of encouragement. He told Faulk to remember at all times that he had "right and justice on [his] side" and to "answer all questions honestly and straightforwardly" without being evasive. As Faulk and Nizer got off the elevator and entered Cohn's office, Faulk saw something that made his stomach turn. It was a floor-to-ceiling photograph of Cohn leaning over the shoulder of Senator McCarthy and whispering something in his ear while McCarthy scanned the room before him with suspicion. To Faulk, this picture "symbolized the McCarthy era" of suspicion and accusation that had been the scourge of his life for the past five years. Steeling himself, Faulk sat down and answered the questions hurled at him.

The trial was scheduled to begin on April 3, 1962. And the six days before were busy, as Faulk used his time trying to recruit witnesses who would testify against AWARE. Nizer was wise to leave the majority of this duty to Faulk. The fear of being blacklisted was a difficult hurdle to overcome, but Faulk's personality, sincerity, and personal relationships with the people he called made it harder for potential witnesses to decline. Faulk secured the testimony of Kim Hunter. Hunter had won an Academy Award for her performance in *A Streetcar Named Desire,* but her career was destroyed when AWARE mistakenly accused her of being a communist and blacklisted her from any further work. Even Eleanor Roosevelt, a friend of Faulk's for many years, agreed to testify, but Nizer vetoed the idea, deciding that the risk to Mrs. Roosevelt's failing health was too great.

The Trial Begins

His legs numb with anxiety, Faulk rose to his feet as the bailiff announced the entrance of the tall, gentle-looking man who would preside over the trial, Judge Abraham Geller. Geller was a white-haired man in his fifties, given to peering over the rim of his glasses when attorneys tried his patience. His black robes were immaculately pressed and billowed slightly behind him as he climbed the stairs to his bench. Judge Geller was known for the strict discipline he required in the courtroom. He demanded absolute silence, perfect decorum on the part of counsel, and utter stillness from witnesses while being administered the oath. Despite these stern requirements, Judge Geller was extremely courteous toward counsel, witnesses, and the jury, evincing a sort of kindliness toward all within his courtroom.

After a lengthy jury selection—many jurors had to be excused due to their professed dislike and bias against Roy Cohn—the trial was ready to begin. Cohn's partner, Bolan, would handle the majority of the trial because Cohn was busy elsewhere.

Nizer and Faulk took their place on one side of a long table at the front of the courtroom. When Bolan and Hartnett entered, they sat down at the same table directly opposite Faulk. Laurence Johnson, claiming illness, was not present, nor would he be for the remainder of the trial.

Faulk did not realize that he and Nizer would be sitting at the same table as the defendants. For the next fourteen weeks, Faulk would have to sit no more than four feet away from the man who had destroyed his career, driven him out of town, and forced him to beg for charity from his friends. Faulk tried not to look across the table, instead focusing on the piles of papers that Nizer was industriously organizing into neat stacks.

Nizer's opening statement drew a full house. The air inside the court-room grew stiflingly hot as the hours passed. Nizer began by explaining Faulk's background, his Texas upbringing, his service in the merchant marine, army, and Red Cross. Nizer talked about Faulk's family, describing the intense patriotism that the Faulk family embodied. Nizer told how Faulk had built his career, and how it was wrenched away from him. He delved into Faulk's personality as well, describing him as possessing a "quiet American grit," unique in the hustle and bustle of New York.

Nizer laid out the entire case to the jury and the audience, the rising and falling tones of his voice drawing listeners into the rhythm of his words. When he finished his opening statement and the court took a recess for lunch, audience members flooded to the front of the room, offering praise and handshakes. Nizer gently brushed them away as he and his assistants took Faulk out of the humid courthouse for a much needed lunch break.

Upon returning to the courtroom, Bolan rose and prepared to deliver his opening. Faulk looked around the courtroom and commented to one of Nizer's assistants that it was only about a third as full as it had been that morning. The assistant grinned proudly and pointed at Nizer, explaining that the audience had come to see Nizer's opening, and Bolan was seen as merely a sidelight of the proceedings. Faulk looked at Nizer for a moment, the attorney's head bowed low over a stack of documents, and felt relief. The opening statements would prove to set the standard for the rest of the trial, because for the next fourteen weeks Nizer would outshine the opposition in every aspect of the trial.

Between Nizer's direct examination and Bolan's cross-examination, Faulk spent nearly four weeks on the witness stand. Faulk told Nizer that being on the witness stand was unbelievably stressful, every wiggle of his in his chair scrutinized by the jury. After the first few hours of gentle questioning by Nizer, however, Faulk began to feel more at ease.

Bolan, however, was less than pleasant, accusing Faulk of being little more than a disc jockey, asking him if he intentionally exaggerated his Texan accent. Faulk remained calm and did his best to answer the questions.

As Bolan's cross-examination blurred from one week into the next, Faulk began losing sleep; when he managed to drift off, he could do nothing but dream of giving faulty answers or ruining his case with a poorly worded response.

When Faulk was finally done testifying, Nizer brought on witnesses to corroborate the story that Faulk's testimony had laid out.

Over the next few weeks, witness after witness was called. Some testified as to the prices that Hartnett charged for "clearing" performers; others explained the ridiculous practice of blacklisting children as young as seven for being pro-communist. Nizer called witnesses who explained the connection between Johnson's control of sponsors and Hartnett's blacklisting of entertainers. Experts showed how much Faulk would likely have made if he had continued in the entertainment industry. Actress Kim Hunter gave the jury a tearful account of how AWARE had destroyed her career and forced her to beg for forgiveness in public, before "clearing" her and allowing her to work again.

When Nizer was through, he had assembled a compelling and appalling picture of how Hartnett and Johnson had ruined the lives of every entertainer who dared oppose their tactics. Now, the defense brought on their own witnesses to attempt to show that Hartnett and Johnson were really the innocents that they claimed to be.

Bolan began with witnesses who attempted to minimize Faulk's popularity. In one of many blunders during the trial, Bolan relied on an article describing Faulk as disc jockey, rather than a radio star. Bolan had apparently either forgotten what the rest of the article said or had not read the whole thing, because farther down on the page was a description of the blacklisting practices used by AWARE. As the article had been introduced as a piece of evidence, Nizer was permitted to read the anti-AWARE statement to the jury, while Bolan sat and listened in dejected silence.

In another bad turn for the defense, Nizer cross-examined a witness who testified that AWARE's bulletins were balanced and reliable. Nizer drew from the witness an admission not only that the sources AWARE relied on were questionable, but also that Hartnett had intentionally omitted any mention of Faulk's fierce patriotism because it detracted from the insinuation that Faulk was pro-communist. With each witness the defense put forth, Nizer drew more blood.

Finally, Vincent Hartnett swaggered up to the witness stand, took his seat, and folded his arms across his chest. Onlookers said his face bore a look of skeptical insolence, his thin mouth drawn tight into a hard line. As Bolan questioned him, Hartnett tipped back in his chair in mock-boredom and reeled off his answers in a quick, succinct style. Once in a while, Hartnett would take small pink cards from his pocket and jot something down with his pencil. Bolan assumed that Hartnett was taking notes on his own testimony.

Once Bolan finished his questioning of Hartnett, Nizer began his cross-examination. Through a clever series of questions, Nizer got Hartnett to admit that he did not trust HUAC's judgment about which organizations were pro-communist, then forced Hartnett to admit that it was precisely these classifications that AWARE relied on when writing the bulletins targeting Faulk. Hartnett testified that AWARE's technique of classifying people as pro-communist on the basis of which organizations they patronized would have resulted not only in President Eisenhower being blacklisted, but also Hartnett himself.

Nizer's careful questioning elicited from Hartnett that the names of persons who opposed AWARE were "leaked" to the FBI through Hartnett's contacts, so that additional pressure could be brought to bear in the form of a HUAC subpoena.

Nizer established that Hartnett wrote articles under an alias in which he praised the works and actions of "one Vincent Hartnett."

Finally distracted by Hartnett's continual practice of writing on the little pink cards, Nizer asked him what he was doing. Hartnett answered that he was keeping a record of who entered the courtroom to watch the trial. The implication that Hartnett was planning to use these cards to label observers of the Faulk trial as Faulk supporters and thus pro-communist was clear to all—including the jury.

The finale came when Bolan, attempting to rehabilitate Hartnett's credibility on redirect, asked Hartnett whose names he had written down on the pink cards. Hartnett listed off a few names and pointed out a man who he claimed had sat down next to Lynne Faulk. Nizer then rose and asked Hartnett to point out who Lynne Faulk was. Hartnett did so, and Nizer—with dramatic flair—asked the woman her name. She stood and answered, "Helen Soffer. S-O-F-F-E-R." The courtroom erupted; reporters ran to the phones to get the story into print; the audience began chatting; and the jurors looked at each other in disbelief. Hartnett explained he had never actually met Lynne Faulk, but that a certain reporter had told him who she was.

Nizer called the reporter as a witness; he testified that he had not spoken a word to Hartnett since the trial began, and he had certainly never pointed out who Mrs. Faulk was.

His voice filled with sarcasm, Nizer asked Hartnett, "Sir, is that an example of the accuracy with which you have identified your victims for the past ten years?"

During trial, Laurence Johnson's health became an issue. Despite repeated requests, Johnson had refused to appear to testify, claiming that he had an injured esophagus, which made it difficult for him to sit upright. Nizer, who had evidence that Johnson had been on a lengthy nationwide tour and driven up and down the eastern seaboard several times in the past year alone, was not impressed. Surely a man who was well enough to attend to his business and take vacations was also well enough to withstand a few hours of testimony. Nizer even offered to allow Johnson to take breaks as often as he needed if he would only appear to testify; Johnson refused.

This issue was important because, if a defendant failed to appear without some acceptable reason, the jury was permitted to draw the strongest assumption against that defendant that the evidence would support. In this case, an assumption like that would subject Johnson to almost certain liability. Both Bolan and Nizer brought in experts to testify as to Johnson's health. Naturally, Bolan's expert testified that Johnson could suffer severe injury if he was forced to testify, while Nizer's expert testified that Johnson and the many other people like him with the same condition led normal lives and merely watched their diet to control their esophageal problems. It would be up to the jury to decide which expert they would believe.

When the testimony was concluded, the lawyers made their closing arguments. As counsel for the plaintiff, Nizer had the luxury of the last argument.

Faulk was not prepared for just how harsh Bolan's closing argument would be. Bolan rose and readjusted the pile of exhibits and evidence that he would need while talking to the jury. The beginning of Bolan's speech proceeded as Faulk had expected, but Bolan then launched into an onslaught of insults that made Faulk feel weak.

Mr. Faulk has deliberately lied to you on numerous occasions in this case on matters of great importance. There are so many lies that it is hard to list them all. I will give you about nine or ten for a start and mention many more throughout my summation.

. . . I submit that on this series of lies, they are so deliberate, so flagrant, that you could question anything Mr. Faulk told you at this trial, but I am going to give you quite a few others that are almost as bad, if not worse in some cases. . . .

And as is evident throughout much of his testimony Mr. Faulk when he knew—when he believed that there wasn't any occasion to contradict him. . . . He wanted to show you that he was quite a performer before the alleged libel, before the publication of Exhibit 41 [the AWARE bulletin]. The fact is that it wasn't until after the publication of Exhibit 41 that Mr. Faulk really got sponsors. . . .

I submit that Mr. Faulk got more publicity out of this lawsuit, as a result of this lawsuit, than he had ever had before in his life. He had never been mentioned to any extent at all in the New York newspapers.

. . . Mr. Faulk's lies spread over a tremendous area. Every area in which he testified, he lied or exaggerated. . . .

This is another hoax which the plaintiff is seeking to perpetrate at this trial. The plaintiff, from the start of his career, has been primarily a radio disc jockey and nothing else. . . . His ability or lack of ability was very well known in the industry. . . . The fact is that Mr. Faulk was not a star performer. He was ranked third or fourth amongst the radio disc jockeys in New York.

As Bolan went on and on, Faulk's heart sank. He "realized that it would be impossible ever to communicate to anyone, even [his] dearest friends, how utterly crushing this experience was."

Nizer was not immune to the pain that Faulk was suffering. In the six years that Nizer had been working on the Faulk trial, he had learned a lot about John Henry. Nizer knew that Faulk had pride, not the preening, pompous sort, but the quiet confidence of a man who bounced back no matter what came his way.

Nizer gripped his seat, his knuckles white with frustration, waiting for Bolan to finish. The attorney's tirade against Faulk hardened Nizer's resolve to make his closing argument as forceful as possible. Nizer was ready to "turn the sword back upon them and avenge the new as well as old injuries."

Nizer and his assistants did not sleep that night, and when the team arrived at the courthouse the next morning, they were greeted by a courtroom filled to bursting. The buzz was nearly deafening as the team made their way to the front of the room and arranged their papers for the final day. Faulk relaxed, telling himself that no further evil could come out of this trial. Nizer would speak, the jury would decide, and it would finally be all over.

Judge Geller appeared, and the courtroom fell silent. The audience seemed to hold their breath in anticipation of greatness, and rising slowly from his chair, Nizer did not disappoint.

Closing Argument of Louis Nizer

May it please Your Honor, Mr. Foreman, ladies and gentlemen of the jury:

First, and very earnestly and sincerely, not just as lip service, let me thank you on behalf of John Henry Faulk, my client, myself, and my associates as counsel, for the extraordinary dedication to duty and patience that you have shown in serving on this case.

This is not the ordinary service that you have rendered. It is far beyond the call of duty; we understand it fully. You have been deprived of your regular attendance to your business and great sacrifice. We have been conscious of it, sensitive to it. You have been deprived of practices, going to your homes at regular hours, and this is far beyond the call of duty. We are very grateful, irrespective of any subject of the merits of this controversy, for what you are serving and doing.

I think there is one compensation that you may derive from this which is also of an extraordinary nature, and that is that this is a historic case, and that you are participating in a case which has historic implications. It is a case by John Henry Faulk against these defendants, but certain cases involve extraordinary principles.

There are in the history of litigation just a few of these, sometimes only one a generation, and I want to say also in all candor that if, during these long ten weeks, I have at any time taxed your patience because of the zeal of an advocate, asked more questions when perhaps it was clear to you, or had some contentions with counsel, I apologize for that.

You must understand that we too have been under strain. For six years we have waited for this day, six years. We have worked during those six years day and night. You see the exhibits, the documents, the unraveling of that which was very difficult to prove in a courtroom under oath; and so we too have been under strain, including the fact that last night there was no sleep at all.

It has been a great responsibility, which we take very earnestly and you ought to have, I hope, the satisfaction that your word, whatever it be when this case is over, will have significance in the history of litigation nationally and, I think, internationally.

The last day was a very bitter day for us yesterday because we would have thought that, after everything that happened in this courtroom there could have been a different position taken by the defendants. I would expect them to defend themselves, but they didn't have to spill their malice and hate in this courtroom until I felt I was neck deep in mud yesterday. When a man has no generosity in his heart, he has real heart disease; and I think the defendants yesterday demonstrated the malice with which this case from the first moment has been steeped in.

So [the defendants] stood bare in this courtroom as libelers who had destroyed this man and his family. Don't you think it would have been the decent thing under those circumstances for the defendant to take the usual, proper position for a defendant, "I was wrong, I am sorry"; a little repentance, "but I didn't mean it, please don't so tax me too heavily." That is a proper stance for these defendants.

But, no, even under those circumstances, they came into this court and called my client a liar for coming into court and testing his rights. Any man would have had to hold on to himself under those circumstances. I admire Mr. Faulk for just keeping silent under that attack, because I had to grip my seat.

The first thing I would like to do, ladies and gentlemen, is to put this case in the large perspective in which it belongs. I want to put the proper frame around it. In the first place, there is no issue of communism in this case. John Henry Faulk, from the first moment that he could understand and breathe, has been anticommunist, and no one has proved otherwise. One of the bad days we had, and I will never forgive the defendants for this, was when they cross-examined him for hours: "Did you know Ina May Bull in Austin, Texas?" "Did you know there was a communist meeting? Were you there?"

And he said no, no, no. Wouldn't you think they would bring in Ina May Bull, or was it just bull? Wouldn't you think after you accuse a man of having attended communist cell meetings in Austin, Texas, with those questions, despite the fact that His Honor advised you and instructed you are not to draw any inference from these questions, what was the purpose of these questions? It is like having a woman on the stand and saying, "Weren't you unfaithful in Austin, Texas?" and then forgetting about it. You don't ask that kind of question unless you have some evidence. You don't say to a man, "Did you ever rob a bank in Baltimore?" and then forget about it. If you make that kind of an accusation, you ought to come clean and have some evidence; and they have enough investigators. They couldn't prove a shred.

So communism is not an issue. We detest communism. Every one of our witnesses too. Suskind said, "I wouldn't touch a communist with a ten-foot pole."

It is clear, ladies and gentlemen, that communism is the great enemy, not only of our country and of all the free world, but of all decency. The shortest distance between the cradle and the grave is communism, and I don't know how any man can believe in communism when communism doesn't believe in any man.

There is no issue here of communism. The question is whether we will permit our government to protect us under proper judicial procedures, or whether we are going to permit private vigilantes like this gentleman seated here with the thin mouth and the blue suit with a hidden microphone in his lapel. That is the question: Are you going to permit private vigilantism for profit?

If he was a real patriot and he dug up any evidence, he would have sent it to the FBI like all of us should. The issue is not communism at all. It is private vigilantism, and the only time that Mr. Bolan came near to touching the issue in this case is when he told you yesterday all about the Fifth Amendment fellows.

He said, "If a man take the Fifth Amendment, haven't we a right, when I want to employ the man, to take it into consideration?"

Why, you don't need the Fifth Amendment. I as an individual employer can refuse to hire anybody because I don't like the color of his tie. I can refuse to hire anybody because I don't like his speech, I don't like the way he dresses. That is my privilege as an American, but that isn't blacklisting. That doesn't mean that I send around a list to all the employers that this man will go to, and they all agree that they can't hire this man. That is what this evil is about.

And the question is not whether somebody should have a right to reject a man who took the Fifth. The question is whether Mr. Hartnett can send around a list to all the agencies and sponsors and put them into their grips and say, "If you use this man, we are going to see to it that you get pressure from the American Legion Post 41 and the Veterans Action Committee," and thus, by a concerted conspiracy, hit a man behind his back when he doesn't know what has hit him, deprive him of his livelihood.

And why? He never faced any accuser. The only time we have had a chance is by waiting six years to come into this courtroom and struggle through every witness, objection after objection, and then we are maligned for coming into an American court. We are told we are liars. We had no right to be here, I suppose.

The real issue in this case, ladies and gentlemen, is that there are people who try to take the law into their hands. They try to because they have fanatic beliefs, but in this case there was no fanaticism; it was malice. Even as fanatics, they didn't think Faulk was a communist. They struck at Faulk for another reason, which I am going to give you. That is what makes it malicious. But when they struck at other people, they did it fanatically, and if people can take the law into their own hands that way, then the Ku Klux Klan is a good organization.

They too think the government isn't doing enough. You heard Mr. Hartnett testify that is the philosophy of these people. Mr. Hartnett said it's unrealistic to depend on the government. I couldn't believe my ears. He actually said it from the witness stand.

And there you had an insight into the evil that we are striking at, private vigilantes taking the law into their own hands. And what is the result? There is an ironic fact in this, ladies and gentlemen. It means that they are following communist techniques under the guise of fighting communism; because when you and your neighbor are not safe from somebody who doesn't like you, and he tips off Mr. Johnson or Mr. Hartnett and he can, through these organizations, ruin you in your enterprise and your business or writing a letter behind your back to an employer, and you suddenly find yourself economically strangled, which is what happened to Mr. Faulk—he didn't earn one cent at his profession in 1958, 1959, 1960. Mr. Bolan forgot all about that. When you find you are strangled because your neighbor or someone who is fanatical can take these measures against you without recourse, without your facing an accuser, without you showing you are innocent, then you have communism under the guise of fighting communism.

And these people crushed dozens of people. We have perhaps hundreds. We have listed them here, and Mr. Bolan criticizes us for talking about other people than Faulk. We alleged a conspiracy to control the radio and television industry, and it was our duty to show you that this happened to all sorts of artists.

And [Mr. Hartnett] who, if you hadn't met him in the courtroom and seen him cross-examined, you would think this was some great powerful figure—all these dictators, they shrink when you see them.

That is the kind of action and conspiracy which operates here, and there are bones on these roads of wonderful artists, men and women in their profession, crushed by this.

And we have had the courage—I say "we"—I mean Mr. John Henry Faulk—you rarely find them. The reason I am spilling out my heart and feelings in this case is because when do you find that kind of American? Everybody rushes to shelter. Why put up the fight? Why should I starve with my children for the industry? I know Americanism is being violated, but why is it my duty to be a martyr? But this man, from the first moment, said, "I am going to see this thing through if I have to drive a taxi." It takes courage on the part of Mr. Faulk, and the suffering which you have a right to award him damages for, cannot be described in a courtroom. You just cannot describe what happens to three children the ages of seven, five, and four when their daddy is deemed to be disloyal and can't get a job, and the neighbors stop inviting them, and his friends are just a little colder; maybe there is something to this.

So the issue in this case, putting it in the proper framework, is, can Mr. Johnson control, as we have alleged and proven, the entire radio and television industry?

This is dangerous, ladies and gentlemen. It is far more dangerous than the communists are. This is far more dangerous, to permit the culture, the entertainment medium, to be controlled by a few people for profit. That is the real issue; that is the framework.

[Faulk] is a liberal Democrat, always was, never had any interest in the Communist Party. And I must stop again to interrupt myself. All this talk about the Fifth Amendment fellows, Mr. Faulk never took the Fifth Amendment. Mr. Faulk never had any occasion to. He never testified before any House Un-American Activities Committee. Nobody ever called him. He wasn't even in *Red Channels* when Mr. Hartnett was the author of it in 1950. They didn't put him in. And in 1950, *Red Channels,* that was a year after all of these specifications; so if he had them, why didn't he put them in? Because he knew he was clean. He put these false charges in to strike at Faulk and destroy him because Faulk was threatening them with the Middle-of-the-Roaders. And that's why Mr. Hartnett and all the directors of AWARE and Mr. Johnson met. They met and decided to destroy this man before he destroyed their income, their illegitimate income. That is the reason for the malice in this case.

This isn't even a case of mistaken fanaticism. You know, someone once said that a fanatic is a man who, having lost sight of his objective, redoubles his efforts. Now, they didn't lose sight of their objective. This was very calculated. They wanted to destroy Faulk because, in destroying Faulk, that blacklisting could continue and they could collect the sums. Hartnett testified before the House Un-American Activities Committee about Kim Hunter. They asked him some embarrassing questions, and they said, "Well, you were asking for two hundred dollars," and he said—forgive me for this language, I am quoting him—"Wouldn't I be an ass not to collect money when her agent was making fifty g's?" This is his language, "fifty g's."

What kind of language is that? Is this the language of a responsible, important man who is trying to be patriotic, or does it have a smell, has it got the tone of the kind of thing it is? "Her agent is getting fifty g's. Why can't I get into their racket and hold her up for just two hundred bucks?"

You know, this thing would be funny except for the fact that every artist gave up his dignity. Every artist gave up his self-respect. You either knuckled under to the Hartnetts and to the Johnsons or you were out of work, and very few people wanted to do what Faulk did and not have food to eat in order to bring this case to trial. And I am not exaggerating. The record shows, the last day we read in, he is in the so-called advertising business in Austin, Texas. That is a fine name for it. His wife, Lynne, who is in this courtroom, and himself, worked day and night, Saturdays and Sundays, and they made forty-seven hundred dollars last year, and they are in debt over their heads with three children.

How many artists want to do that in order to stand up to these people? And you have a chance; that is why I say this case is historic. You have a chance in this case to give a clarion call to the world on this, to make an award of punitive damages in several million dollars, of compensatory damages over a million dollars. It doesn't matter whether it can be collected or not. Let the word get out that this kind of thing must stop.

Give by your verdict a clear answer to the kind of un-Americanism which this case represents. Aren't we free people? Do we have to knuckle under? Would you, before you get a job, before you draw a wonderful artistic cover, do you want Mr. Jones or Mr. Smith to pass upon you so that you can't earn your livelihood if he thinks you are not a good American?

Now I am going to do this, ladies and gentlemen, before the

lunch hour. I am going to trace this conspiracy by date. I am going to show you how this conspiracy to get at Faulk was planned step by step, and let me explain something about this if I may. It is very rare, when you charge a conspiracy among people, that you have direct evidence, because the old classic story is the conspirators getting together in a cellar by candlelight. Well, you are not there to take a picture of them.

[Hartnett and Johnson] sensed in that early date when the Middle-of-the-Road slate was nominated, it was like a reform administration coming into a corrupt city. All the evil elements get very busy: "We've got to do something. There is a new administration that may put us out of business."

And the blacklisting business of Mr. Hartnett and Mr. Johnson was being threatened by a slate that said, "We are running on an anti-blacklisting and anti-communist slate." That is why they called themselves the Middle-of-the-Road, against the blacklisters and against communism.

Now see what happens. As soon as AWARE was condemned by the union—remember, they passed a resolution condemning AWARE for interfering, and responsible newspapers began to write articles on the subject. There is in evidence Exhibit 49, this column . . . "Not long ago the American Federation of Television and Radio Artists, the terror-stricken union of radio and TV performers, took a courageous and long overdue stand by condemning the viciously un-American practice of blacklisting actors."

And at the end, "Other sponsors have cravenly given in and hired only actors approved by this little wolf pack of vigilantes."

Doesn't this remind you of the old technique of journalism when you write a terrible article about an executive and say this man is running around with blondes? Then you go up to the executive and say, "You know, I have to write this article."

But the other fellow asks, "Well, now, can't you kill that article? It isn't true."

The journalist replied, "Well, we have a right as journalists. We heard it."

The executive asked again, "Well, what could I do?"

The journalist said, "Well, if you want me to protect your firm against having its windows broken or something like that, if you will pay me five thousand dollars a year for protection, I'd kill it."

People have been indicted for that. That is blackmail. Have we been too strong in our complaint when we said this is a racketeering practice? Now back to my conspiracy.

Something very like a state of terror spread through the union. Actors who might have sought AFTRA office were afraid to do so. Many members have told me that they were afraid to speak at AFTRA meetings for fear that their names would be noted and their opportunities for work would diminish. Several have told me they were afraid even to attend the meetings.

And incidentally, [AWARE] had to approve children. [Hartnett] admitted that, a five-year-old child. Remember Suskind testifying he looked high and low for a good child actress? She was rejected because her father was supposed to have a significant communist-front record. And Hartnett seriously, with those thin, cruel lips, on the stand says, "Well, you know, they start these children very young in these organizations."

Mr. Hartnett suggests they reprint two *Daily Worker* columns which have nothing to do, of course, with Faulk. He never read the *Daily Worker,* never saw it in his life.

To reprint two *Daily Workers* with a few comments and send it to all the advertising agencies. What was the purpose of that? To choke Mr. Faulk. Mr. Hartnett concocts a whole series of lies, and he starts preparing drafts. Now, we know they are all lies now, don't we? There is not a truth in any of them. The Court has stricken out the defense of truth or partial truth. And he draws a draft, and when we examined the documents and I asked him to present the draft, this is what was presented. This is not the original exhibit, but I will use it; it's a photostat. Notice it. It's a half a page cut off with a scissors. It says number two at the top. It isn't even the first page.

I asked him how big was this draft, the first draft. He said it was fifty percent bigger than Exhibit 41. You know how big Exhibit 41 is. You have seen this thing. It's a whole bunch of these pages, you know [indicating]. It was fifty percent larger than this.

Now, I said to him, "Where is the rest of it? You cut off a half a page. This is all you have?"

Do you think he says it's lost? No. Do you think he says it's misplaced? No. He says he destroyed it. He destroyed the first draft. When? After this lawsuit was begun. This is incredible. After the lawsuit was begun he destroyed it. So [Hartnett] admits that after this suit is begun he goes to his file and destroys the other ten, fifteen, twenty pages, and this is all that happens to be left. He cut out half a page to show he had something. Now, why did he destroy it? You don't go to that length after a suit is begun to destroy an important document. I asked him, "Didn't you know this is important?"

We are dealing with malice. See, if we had this first draft, ladies and gentlemen, we would show you the malice, because before the lawyers got at it you would see the poison spill out of this man; and he knew it. Lord knows what was in that document.

So they destroy it, but I ask you: Is this honest conduct? And secondly, what are they trying to hide in destroying the first draft of Exhibit 41, and doesn't this prove malice conclusively?

This is the conspiracy spelled out date by date, and the reason I spell it out for you, ladies and gentlemen, is that there was malice in all this. This is not a case in which Mr. Hartnett mistakenly thought that Mr. Faulk was a pro-communist. He knew he wasn't. He was going after him to stop the reform movement from coming into the union that would do away with Mr. Hartnett's racket, and that is malicious. That is personal hatred.

What did [CBS] decide to do? Let's get a big affidavit up. Let's have Faulk swear once more that he is a very good American. Incidentally, this is pretty humiliating. How would you like to every Monday and Wednesday sign an affidavit that you are a good, loyal American, you are not a communist spy? But to save his job, CBS says, "Go ahead, make an affidavit."

Now, Mr. Bolan has been telling you that this affidavit was not a complete denial. I don't know how anybody could be more forthright. I will have to read just one or two paragraphs to you. I am trying to be brief.

This is Mr. Faulk in this affidavit, which CBS used. Remember what this affidavit was for. They gave it to their own salesmen so that when they went out to sell Mr. Faulk, they had an affidavit in their pocket in case the fellow said, "I can't use Faulk. I hear he is a communist." "Well, look at his affidavit."

That is a fine way to sell. How would you like to sell anything, merchandise or a person, and have an affidavit under your arm in case the fellow says he is a traitor. This is what they put him through.

What is there in this affidavit, for Lord's sake, that can give any comfort to Mr. Bolan's argument that he didn't deny everything? When he said that "I do not consider the allegations made by AWARE of any relevance," what he meant was, how can you say a man is a communist, even if all these charges were true, because he attended an *Amsterdam News* function at Club 65. Does that make him a communist? Or he entertained at a cabaret on one evening for a Wallace function? Does that make him a communist? Suppose it was all true; it wouldn't mean anything. That is what he was saying, and he was right. Would it mean anything? Is this the way you prove a man is not a good American?

One man testified to something; two words stuck in my head. One of the experts said, "From the moment that this attack on his loyalty came out, he was a walking corpse." Do you remember that phrase? "He was a walking corpse." It would take a year, but he was through. He was like a man who had cancer. He was doomed to die in a year or fourteen months, and Mr. Bolan stands here and says, "But wasn't he living during that year?" He was living, but he was surely cut off from this profession as if he had been dropped that very day.

Now I go to Exhibit 41, and believe me, my friends, I am not going to go through these items to show they are not true. We are past that. They are false. I am going to go through them for one purpose, and I want to announce my purpose.

I believe the learned Court has studied the law on this complex subject of libel and has been instructing you throughout the trial—a very fine procedure, I think, to help juries and help lawyers—we get much erudition from it. I believe—I don't want to encroach on the Court's province—that you will be instructed that recklessness in publishing something proves malice. When a man prints something that destroys your character and reputation, he must check, he must be careful. If we didn't set that standard, what would happen to our reputations, any of us?

I am going through these items not to show that they were false. I am going through these items to show that they were *deliberately* false, that they were *recklessly* published; that they were published *without* checking. That is my purpose.

You know, I perhaps will leave this subject with one word, to give you the enormity of this thing. Suppose I said about one of you, so-and-so attended a function with a notorious communist writer from *Pravda* on such and such a date, period; published it.

Well, some people would say, "That's a funny thing. This man is one of the worst communist fellows." Then it comes out that where you attended with this fellow was at a press conference at the White House; there were one hundred and fifty other fellows there, and so was the communist there, so was the communist from *Pravda* there, and so were you as a good American.

But I leave out the fact that it's a press conference at the White House with President Kennedy. I just say you attended with a notorious communist. That's what they did here, and it isn't an accident. It is maliciously designed to destroy his character, and it isn't just his character they destroyed—I am coming to that. There are three children who suffer because of that destruction of their father's reputation in every way, not only physically.

Mr. Hartnett testified that if he hasn't a document, generally— you see, he forgot about this—he doesn't think he should publish anything. That is how careful a consultant he is for his twenty or hundred dollars that he charges. In this case, he then later admitted in five out of the seven instances he didn't have a document, but he still published it.

Why did he make an exception in this case? Because he was after Faulk, and he never knew that we would be after him and dig up all of these documents.

They were not easy. This is like a web constructed of pieces of cloth that we have to weave together over six years. It wasn't easy to piece this together, and Mr. Hartnett thought he'd get away with it as he did in other cases.

Since it is no more important because we know now that this isn't true, I just remind you that Mr. Hartnett, on the examination, said, and I quote, "I was fed"—this is the investigator—"I was fed a barrel of misinformation." And when he read the correction on that part of the testimony, he never changed that sentence. He never said he didn't say, "I was fed a barrel of misinformation."

These are the people who sell patriotism for profit. They don't really go after the communists. This has been an old story. The demagogues raise a lot of fuss and get publicity. They don't capture communists. The only communists that have been captured have been by governmental authorities and indicted and tried.

But the McCarthys and the other committees haven't yet caught one, and Mr. Hartnett and the AWARE group never caught a single communist; and if they were there, they were lax because they should have gotten them under the constitutional provision. They never even started a proceeding, and that is conceded.

Let me stress this: when we walked into the examination before trial on this suit, that was the first time that Mr. Hartnett had ever laid eyes on Mr. Faulk or Faulk on Mr. Hartnett. Isn't that extraordinary? This man's life is destroyed by this man, and they have never met. He wasn't after Mr. Faulk as an individual. He was a party of the Middle-of-the-Road group, and he was out to destroy him. He didn't even know who he was.

May I pause to tell you an aphorism? I think it was G. K. Chesterton who wrote, "If we have something unimportant to do, like building a bridge or a great scientific experiment, then we get specialists." That is if you have something *unimportant* to do.

But if you have something *important* to do, like deciding right and wrong and doing justice, you get twelve people who apply their common sense, their wisdom that comes down from centuries of experience to each of us. And he wound up with, I think, a very emotional sentence: "After all, isn't that what the founder of Christianity did? He gathered twelve around him."

We depend upon your common sense in this thing, which is the highest form of wisdom. And because we have respect, we don't insult your intelligence the way I think the defendants have with their arguments.

Faulk, in trouble, turns to Fred Mitchell. He says, "I need some work. Can you get it for me?" Mitchell consults his own talent departments. He says, "You know, I am going to be blunt with you about this," Mitchell testified. He said, "You are just controversial and you are dead. You won't get anything."

Faulk says, "Why don't you put me on without my name? I will just broadcast and you won't say 'John Henry Faulk,' " and Mitchell laughs. He says, "With your voice and accent, you are going to disguise yourself?" You remember that bit of testimony? He says, "Don't be foolish." Take that under consideration. [Faulk] became a pariah. He was like a leper.

I again beg your indulgence—please grant me a little more time without holding it against me, because I am running longer than I should. I will try to finish within half an hour or less, but after six years, give me this opportunity to do my full—every task I can for my client in this case. I hope you will grant me that indulgence, because I am about to discuss damages, which is the climax in practical terms of what you can do.

I have told you that the most important word in this case is *unemployability,* and we presented eight experts, eight of the outstanding figures in radio and television on that subject. They didn't present one. Why didn't they call an expert?

Mark Goodson, who is the king, as he was referred to by Mr. Bolan in his summation, of the popular type of show, the panel show, you remember him, testified as follows on unemployability, before I get to amounts:

"I would say in general that nonclearability means unemployability. Innocence or guilt was never brought up, because the facts of the matter were never discussed. When a name was not cleared, it was difficult to get further information. A sponsor is in business to sell goods. He has no interest in being involved in causes. He does not want controversy. The favorite slogan along Madison Avenue is 'Why buy yourself a headache?' It is the advertising agency's job to see to it that the products are sold, and the advertising agency can lose a great deal. It can lose the account. The choice between Performer A, who is noncontroversial, and Performer B, about whom there is any kind of cloud whatsoever, the natural instinct, business basis, is to use the noncontroversial personality. Again, a favorite saying is 'There are a lot of other actors, a lot of other performers. Why bother with this one? Why buy a headache?' "

Mr. Dickler: "Controversial means some people have written letters or made telephone calls to an agency or a network. Generally, the letters or the telephone calls which threaten a boycott of the program or product. That is controversial. It doesn't have anything to do with the truth or the falsity of what the accusations are, or what the motivation of the accuser is, whether they are honest or dishonest. Controversial means possibly troublesome. When the phrase *in trouble* is used in the business, they meant that they might be troublesome, and therefore you might just as well not borrow trouble. And if you are an advertising agency or a network employer, 'Go get somebody else who isn't troublesome.' "

And on unemployability, listen to Suskind:

"The broadcasting industry is incredibly and unusually sensitive and frightened. It is an industry dedicated to promoting goodwill. The slightest whisper about an artist is damning and is murderous to the career of that artist."

That is why Mr. Faulk can't earn a penny in all these years, not one cent.

He is unemployable until, perhaps, your verdict will give him a new, fresh start, at least to begin. It will take him five years to get where he was.

And I come to perhaps the most extraordinary demonstration of why you should allow him heavy damages, as I will soon indicate, and that is the show called *Leave It to the Girls,* on the NBC national network, and later on the ABC national network, and he was the moderator. Aside from being a guest for many months, he was the moderator for six months—moderator.

Why do I stress this? Because this show got a review from the editor in chief of *Variety,* Abel Green, which is considered, as you know, the bible of television. Listen to this in a really outstanding expert magazine: "The boffo impact of *Leave It to the Girls* generally, and their inaugural guest, the Dixie drawling man about panels, John Henry Faulk in particular, result in a zingy half hour made particularly so by Faulk's uninhibited, thoroughly natural, and genuinely good-humored foiling with Eloise McElhone, Vanessa Brown, and Lisa Ferraday. All were articulate and witty in their answers, but Faulk provided the most spontaneous fund as the gallant yet unyielding vis-à-vis. He was relaxed, natural, knew how to shade his satire, and emerged so warm a personality that if he's been gainfully employed in the medium, as he has been in actuality"—let me read that again—"if he's been gainfully employed in the medium, as he has been in actuality, he should cast his iconoscopes on wider wavelengths. In actuality, that's just what he did Saturday night, catching a nighttime audience to great personal advantage."

The reason I mention this is, this is like the Academy Award for television personality, and every expert who testified, Collingwood, Mark Goodson, Hilton, said they had read this and they were entranced with the potential of this man. He had a brilliant career in television, which was cut off instantly. Forget the radio for a minute, where he stayed on a year. He never earned a cent thereafter, but television was cut off, and that's where I ask you to give your compensatory damage.

Libel is an injury to reputation and character. The law takes a very serious view of it. If an automobile runs you over, that's a wrong, but it only breaks a bone. Even that isn't as serious as destroying your reputation. In an automobile accident, all you can recover is the loss for your broken arm, loss of earnings, and anguish and pain. That is all.

But the law, in its wisdom, says when somebody destroys your reputation and character, we leave it to a jury if there is malice to give another kind of damage in addition to the first kind, and that is called punitive damages, smart money. Not *smart* in the sense of clever; *smart,* it hurts. You slap somebody's wrist and it smarts. And the idea of the law is, in order to discourage other citizens from doing this same thing to reputation, you can give punitive damages. The jury is given that right.

And so there are two kinds of damages in a libel, unlike all others. The law in its wisdom for centuries has seen the wisdom of this. You first decide how much is lost in income. That is his television income, his radio income, and the pain and anguish that he had suffered. That is the regular kind of injury, as if the automobile ran him over.

And then in addition to that, in a separate category, in your discretion, according to your wisdom, depending on the degree of malice and the wrong of this case, to make a lesson of it for all the future that it can't happen again, you can give punitive damages in such amount as you wish; and I am going to indicate what we respectfully ask of you in both categories.

On the subject of how much Mr. Faulk would have earned in television, Mr. Charles Collingwood said the real income for any artist is television, and Faulk's reputation as a television personality was outstanding, because he knew it; he had appeared with him on many shows on television. He said that the plaintiff would have a progressive career in television if it hadn't been cut off because, one, he has an amusing anecdotal style and a pleasing personality. And I must read to you what Mr. Goodson says about Mr. Faulk's earnings:

"If a person has not been exposed for any substantial period of time, his value is definitely diminished. He becomes an unknown all over again, and it is harder today to start an unknown than it was back in the 1950s when prices were lower. He would certainly not be able to pick up where he left off. . . ."

I asked him about what that kind of artist earns, so that you would have an expert opinion, something to go on.

"A hundred thousand dollars up to a million dollars a year if you were talking about earnings. I would say that Faulk would have fallen probably between the $150,000 and $500,000 mark if he had continued as he was."

So here is, I think, the greatest expert in the world on this subject, who says you can't give it down to a penny because it depends on so many circumstances, the competition, all sorts of things, but the range is $150,000 to $500,000 a year. That was cut off like a knife when they libeled him, that he would have earned beginning that time, according to Mark Goodson, and you saw the kind of man, the reliability, the responsibility. He was under oath.

Listen to Garry Moore:

"John Henry Faulk had a rare sort of talent. There are only a handful of people in the business who function the way John Henry Faulk is capable of functioning. These are generally referred to as personalities, because it is hard to pinpoint the kind of talent as opposed to dancer or singer or acrobat. It is a kind of talent which has a great sustaining quality, because you may have a different singer each week or a different dancer, but the host, the master of ceremonies, personality is a continuing job. He is there every week. His employment is far steadier than that of the people in other categories. It is a talent that is very hard to duplicate."

We have asked for a million dollars' damages in this case, although we go way over it. We think that was a conservative estimate on the basis of all these experts, and we ask at your hands nothing else, no compromise, a million dollars of actual compensatory damages against all the defendants.

Now, punitive damages. We think in view of the malice that has been shown in this case, and the suffering that has gone on, that you should award severe punitive damages.

We think that punitive damages should be awarded against each of the defendants, in addition to the million dollars of compensatory damages, a million dollars separately for each of the defendants as a lesson to others to stop blacklisting and free the industry and not destroy people's lives. We ask for a million dollars at your hands for punitive damages separately for each of the defendants.

You cannot re-create this pain and anguish at a jury box. I have to leave it to your hearts. And you know, there is no law that has ever been written that is as good as the law in your heart, and that is the law I am asking you to apply in this case.

[Faulk] says, "You see, we had packed everything in the house, and the kids, the children, my wife, we were all ready to go to Texas, and therefore we didn't have a choice. We couldn't stay in New York. We had given up the apartment. So we took off to Texas. We got down there."

Before that he had testified that he had been served with a dispossess notice; he couldn't pay his rent, so you can see why he couldn't stay on. And he testified that he had been living on the charity and goodwill of some good people who gave him these moneys, and right to this day, or he couldn't live with his children at that; and his wife is working.

Before they got down to Texas, for the first time in ten years his wife, who is a housewife and has given him these three children, goes out as a saleslady in a fixture place to help earn a living while he tries to get a job, and he goes home and takes care of the children. Now they are out in Texas. They have finally been reduced to that little place in the world where he was born. A little final haven he thinks he may have.

The next year he earned twenty-five hundred dollars, he says, and of course, having earned twenty-five hundred dollars, you can imagine how much he was in debt for the expenses and everything. The year after that, not one cent. The year after that, not one cent. In 1960, not a cent. In 1961, not a penny. In 1962, not a penny from radio or television.

And what has he been able to eke out from his so-called advertising business except his debts? Well, I told you the last year, 1961, forty-seven hundred dollars net, and of course you can imagine how inadequate that is, and what his loans are, which he said were heavy to the bank and everyone else.

He has these three children. The Court asked their ages because he knew it was a proper factor in this case. He answered, "There is Johanna, she is my oldest child. She was seven then, and Evelyn was six, and Frank Dobie, my son, was four." They attended schools here. They had to be uprooted and taken there.

I will not go on with the rest of the terrible story of this man's ordeal, but now I place his life in your hands. I place his wife's life and his three children's lives in your hands, very literally, because this man's reputation is either going to be restored by a verdict that will ring to the world, or he will be besmirched all over again.

I leave to your hands the doing of full justice, and if you do that, ladies and gentlemen, you can sleep well because God will be awake. Thank you.

There was a moment of silence as Nizer's words seemed to hang in the air, then the courtroom was filled with the excited whispering of the audience. Judge Geller called for order, then announced a brief recess. Nizer and Bolan followed the judge into his chambers. There was a problem.

Trouble Arises

Laurence Johnson had been found in a hotel room in the Bronx, dead, apparently of old age. Because no verdict had been reached, could his estate still be held liable if the jury awarded damages? Nizer and his legal team lost another night of sleep preparing a brief arguing that the claim against Johnson's estate did not expire with his death. Judge Geller was persuaded by Nizer's argument and ordered the executor of Johnson's estate to stand in as a replacement defendant.

Bolan immediately told several reporters about Johnson's death. Judge Geller called them into his chambers and asked if they would delay printing the story for one day, to prevent the jurors from reading about the death in the papers and being influenced by it. The reporters refused to hold back the story, and Judge Geller was forced to sequester the jury. The judge did not want to deceive the jury; he explained that Johnson was dead, but that any harm he had caused did not die with him. Rather, Johnson's estate was just as liable for Faulk's injuries as it was when Johnson was alive. Judge Geller cautioned the jury not to allow this change in the circumstances to dissuade them from doing justice.

When the jury was reconvened the following day, Judge Geller explained to the jury that the defendants had been charged with conspiracy to commit libel. The defendants' only defense was to prove that the charges against Faulk were true. Judge Geller took that issue from the jury. He explained that the defense had provided insufficient evidence to meet this burden, and thus the jury should only consider whether damages should be mitigated by the defendants' actions. This was a significant ruling in that the "truth defense" was now lost to the defendants. Now it only remained for the jurors to decide how culpable each of the defendants was.

Judge Geller described the two types of damages available in the suit as compensatory and punitive. Compensatory damages are intended to compensate a plaintiff for losses suffered as a result of the libel. If the damage was found to be substantial, then substantial compensatory damages should be awarded. Punitive damages are meant to deter a defendant from committing misconduct and to dissuade other potential wrong-doers from committing the same act. If the jury found that the defendants acted with malice, then the jurors were free to award substantial punitive damages.

Judge Geller explained that damages against each defendant should be awarded only if the jury found each defendant to have taken part in the conspiracy to libel. He further explained to the jury that a partial defense of reliance might allow the award of a lesser amount of punitive damages. This partial defense could only be used if the jury found that the defendants had reasonably relied on their sources of information after a careful and thorough check of the information's integrity and validity. If, however, the jury found that the defendants had acted with malice, then there could be no partial defense of reliance, and the jury was free to award punitive damages within reason. No punitive damages could be awarded against Laurence Johnson's estate because Johnson was dead and could not be deterred from future misconduct.

In one fell swoop, Judge Geller had destroyed Bolan's entire case. Through his instructions, he changed the issue from whether damages should be awarded to how much damages should be awarded. Faulk found it ironic that Bolan had been working on the case for nearly six years only to have all his efforts thrown out in the last hour. At 5:35 P.M. the jury was released to deliberate, and Faulk and Nizer went to a quiet restaurant to get some dinner.

While Faulk was picking at his food and trying hard not to talk about the case, an announcement was made: something was happening at the courthouse. Faulk and Nizer raced back.

The Jury Speaks

The jury had a question: Could they award more than the million dollars that Nizer had asked for? Nizer fell back in his chair, stunned, as the judge explained the law to the jurors. No jury had ever asked if they could award more than Nizer had asked for. He explained to Faulk that the largest jury award in a libel verdict had been half a million dollars. They told each other that the jury could have asked that question for any number of reasons. The two men paced the halls of the courthouse for the next two hours, waiting for any word on the deliberations.

Finally, Nizer and Faulk saw a commotion at the courtroom door. Errand boys were sent running to inform all parties that the jury had reached a verdict. Despite the late hour—it was after 11:30 P.M.—the courtroom was packed.

Nizer and Faulk watched the jurors file back into the box and scrutinized their faces for any sign of what was to come. The panel, weary after months of trial, appeared emotionless. The court clerk looked around carefully to make sure everyone was present and finally asked if the jury had reached a verdict. The foreman replied that they had. "And how do you find?" asked the clerk.

"We, the jury, have arrived at our decision in favor of Mr. Faulk. We have awarded the plaintiff, Mr. Faulk, compensatory damages in the sum of one million dollars against AWARE, Inc., Mr. Vincent Hartnett, and the estate of the late Mr. Laurence Johnson. We have also awarded the plaintiff, Mr. Faulk, punitive damages in the sum of $1,250,000 against AWARE, Inc., and $1,250,000 against Mr. Hartnett."

The audience seemed to remember to breathe all at once. Then a wave of whispering rippled across the room. Bolan demanded a poll of the jury. Only one juror out of twelve had opposed the damages award, but this was of little consequence, as only ten jurors are required to agree in civil trials. The crowd seemed to vibrate with excitement, and when Judge Geller finally adjourned the proceedings, the room exploded in pandemonium. The crowd divided into those who dashed for the door to spread the word and those well-wishers who surged forward to congratulate Nizer and Faulk—including the jurors, who, freed from their roles as disinterested observers, could now warmly greet the man for whom they had felt such sympathy during the trial. Several members of the jury were crying as they shook his hand, and Faulk's eyes welled up as he greeted them.

Faulk and Nizer embraced and clapped each other on the back, struggling not to break down in front of the press. The men were so exhausted—the sleepless nights having taken their toll—that they ruled out the idea of any celebratory party afterward, deciding instead to go with the rest of the legal team for an hour's quiet chat before heading home.

On their way out of the courtroom, Nizer found himself facing Vincent Hartnett. Hartnett looked desperate, his eyes wide; he seemed thinner and taller than when the trial had begun. Before Nizer could speak, Hartnett leaned forward and began talking in a half-whispered rasp, "We will appeal. Now, Mr. Nizer, it is all in God's hands!"

Nizer raised his eyebrows skeptically and replied, "What makes you think it hasn't been there all the time?" The attorney then turned and left to join his client.

Faulk had triumphed. Although he had a $3.5 million verdict—the largest damage award to date—what mattered to him most was that America now knew that blacklisting would not be tolerated. Nizer arranged a settlement with Johnson's estate. Apparently, the businessman was secretly deep in debt, his entire estate not worth even a fraction of the million-dollar judgment. Nizer accepted $175,000.

Hartnett followed through on his threatened appeal. Although damages against AWARE and Hartnett were reduced to $500,000, every other aspect of the trial was affirmed. Hartnett continued his efforts for a new trial, but after dragging the case through two appeals courts and unsuccessfully seeking certiorari from the U.S. Supreme Court, he ran out of judges to whom he could make his case. Unfortunately, Hartnett and AWARE were insolvent; none of the $500,000 could be collected.

Nizer's firm had spent nearly half a million dollars during the trial, but Nizer was not going to take all of Faulk's settlement money. Nizer paid the $25,000 required by the court for filing fees and courtroom usage, then split the balance of the cash with Faulk. Nizer insisted—over Faulk's objections—that his client take the $75,000 to pay off all of his debts and start over, freed from the bill collectors. The two men had just endured the ordeal of a lifetime; they were happy to return to their families for a well-deserved rest.

More Than a Lawsuit

Faulk v. AWARE, Inc. was not merely a case about libel. Libel had existed as a cause of action for centuries, but this was different because Faulk's suit challenged more than traditional libel law. This case took on the McCarthyism system of sly accusation and suspicion. It challenged the idea that one could be presumed guilty until proven innocent. It proclaimed that Americans had the right to speak freely, the right to associate with whatever organizations they chose. Nizer summed up McCarthyism's toll as "the destruction of the inviolate right to be presumed innocent until proven guilty; to be confronted by one's accuser and have the right to examine and answer; above all, to prevent the invasion of man's right to think and speak without fear."

Another, less well-remembered victim of McCarthyism was the Fifth Amendment right against self-incrimination. The Fifth Amendment guarantees that "no person . . . shall be compelled in any criminal case to be a witness against himself." Witnesses subpoenaed to appear before HUAC were questioned about their association with the communist movement. Many were not even remotely communist sympathizers, but any attempt to remain silent would result in contempt charges and a prison sentence. Witnesses who admitted their membership in the Communist Party risked being labeled as spies or security threats.

Witnesses faced three options: tell the truth and risk being imprisoned for mere association with "forbidden" institutions; refuse to answer questions and be imprisoned for contempt; or lie. Not surprisingly, many chose the last option. HUAC often demanded that those giving testimony provide the names or identities of other "subversives" as a good-faith showing that the witness truly was patriotic. Put under this kind of pressure, with the threat of prison time hanging over their heads, some witnesses named names, implicating coworkers.

Faulk's victory helped reestablish the principle that guilt could no longer be presumed when a witness chose to remain silent. Faulk wanted to keep his political beliefs to himself, to be able to choose a path of moderation without being branded a subversive. The jury in the Faulk case found this expectation reasonable.

Faulk's trial forced his accusers into the bright light of day. No longer would the purveyors of baseless accusations be permitted to launch their attacks from the safety of anonymity. If a witness was evasive and contradictory, as Hartnett had been, a jury would have the option of evaluating his testimony accordingly.

Finally, the Faulk case had a tremendous impact on America's vision of the First Amendment. During the height of the McCarthy era, although Americans had a right to speak freely, criticizing HUAC or belonging to an organization like the American Civil Liberties Union might result in one's being blacklisted, ostracized, and possibly subjected to criminal investigation.

With McCarthy's death and Faulk's victory, all of this began to change. Faulk's trial showed the public that it could question the vestiges of McCarthyism without fear. Through Nizer's closing argument, Americans had a chance to hear an uninterrupted explanation of why blacklisting was an evil that had to be eliminated. Nizer's righteous indignation was an electrifying indictment of the corruption that threatened the freedoms GIs had been called upon to defend during World War II. And John Henry Faulk became an example of the kind of man who was a true patriot, having a robust faith in America's ability to withstand a challenge, and to entertain differing beliefs, and an understanding that freedom of speech included the right not only to have unpopular opinions, but to speak them without fear of retribution.

Out of the Darkness, into the Light

After the verdict against AWARE, the fear the organization had inspired evaporated and membership plummeted. Hartnett too was diminished. His credibility destroyed both by his defeat in court and by the newspaper articles recounting his contradictory testimony, he faded from view. Without a front man following the trial, AWARE was dissolved not long after.

Shortly before Faulk filed his suit, the U.S. Senate took action against Joe McCarthy, censuring him 65 to 22 for his actions in front of the committee investigating his abuses of his legislative authority. The senator lost his post as chairman of the Subcommittee on Investigations not long after and found himself stripped of power. Depressed, McCarthy's drinking increased; he died of cirrhosis in 1957.

Roy Cohn moved on to a New York law firm, where he ran a high-powered practice. Cohn amassed huge debts and was investigated by the IRS, which said he owed more than $3 million in unpaid taxes. Cohn was disbarred for unethical conduct and died of AIDS in 1986.

HUAC survived the end of the McCarthy era, continuing its pursuit of communist influences in America, albeit with less aggressive tactics than McCarthy's. HUAC changed its name, but was never able to completely free itself of the taint associated with the memory of the senator from Wisconsin. Congress dissolved the committee in 1975.

With the fall of the Berlin Wall in 1989 and the subsequent dissolution of the Soviet Union in the 1990s, the fear of communism began to disappear from the American psyche.

As for Nizer and Faulk, the trial marked six unforgettable years. They had gained each other's friendship and together fought the evils of the blacklist. Both men believed that after the trial, Faulk's talents would be in high demand. No offers came. Network television and radio may not have been frightened by the blacklist anymore, but they had long since forgotten John Henry Faulk; he was yesterday's news. Absence from the entertainment industry usually becomes permanent, and this applied to Faulk. The constant stress of the trial—exacerbated by the Faulks' financial woes—took a toll on the Faulks' marriage. Although Lynne and Faulk had recently welcomed their fourth child, they decided to divorce.

Not one to wallow in self-pity, and still as charming as ever, Faulk soon met a high-spirited Englishwoman; the couple married in 1965, had a son, and spent the rest of their lives together. Faulk died of cancer in 1990. He was seventy-six.

John Henry Faulk remained firmly convinced that the blacklist was one of America's greatest tragedies. Ignored by the entertainment industry, he began a new career, traveling the country, lecturing on the blacklist and McCarthyism. Faulk often quoted his lifelong friend J. Frank Dobie, recalling his belief that "forced orthodoxy through death, suppression, exile, derision, banning of books, starvation, and all the other methods of self-righteous and conforming respectability has never been the answer."

In 1975, CBS bought the television rights to *Fear on Trial,* Faulk's book about his experiences while on the blacklist. The televised drama—featuring George C. Scott as Nizer and William Devane as Faulk—was well received by the public and critics alike, taking home an Emmy Award for writing. CBS, basking in the critical acclaim, never offered Faulk the opportunity to return to the airwaves from which the network had fired him twenty years before.

CHAPTER FOUR

A Woman's Rightful Place

Susan B. Anthony Casts a Vote and Battles for the Ballot

[That little man in black says] woman can't have as much rights as man because Christ wasn't a woman. Where did your Christ come from? . . . From God and a woman. Man has nothing to do with him.

—*Sojourner Truth*

The only alleged ground of illegality of the defendant's vote is that she is a woman. If the same act had been done by her brother under the same circumstances, the act would have been not only innocent, but honorable and laudable; but having been done by a woman it is said to be a crime. The crime therefore consists not in the act done, but in the simple fact that the person doing it was a woman and not a man. I believe that this is the first instance in which a woman has been arraigned in a criminal court, merely on account of her sex.

—*Henry R. Selden, attorney for Susan B. Anthony*

Is there a man who will not agree with me, that to talk of freedom without the ballot, is mockery—is slavery—to the women of this Republic?

—*Susan B. Anthony*

The eighteenth-century British legal commentator William Blackstone succinctly assessed the historical relationship between men and women: "Husband and wife are one, and that one is the husband." A little more than a hundred years later, American women found themselves with fewer rights than the recently freed slaves, for a constitutional amendment not only removed the latter's chains, but granted them access to the ballot box. The suffragettes of the post–Civil War era would wait more than fifty years to take part lawfully in the democratic process. But Susan B. Anthony refused to wait, and she took up her cause armed with only a ballot and a relentless moral standard. She voted in the election of 1872 and changed history by breaking the law and challenging it through a trial that would garner national attention.

By twenty-first-century standards, what the feminist radicals of the 1800s sought was modest. But to gain any voice, generations of brave and forward-thinking people faced public ridicule and condemnation. They championed their unpopular cause of equality in the face of hundreds of years of legal and societal subjugation. Today, every American citizen over the age of eighteen can vote. Yet for the female half of the population, this right was not stated in the U.S. Constitution and was not established until well into the twentieth century. Women's suffrage was the product of decades of struggle and unrest, and its central figure was Susan B. Anthony.

Women's rights have occupied an awkward position in American history. As a social cause, women's suffrage was the undercard to both the abolitionist and black suffrage movement during the bulk of the nineteenth century. Suffragists and reformers for both causes were fighting oppression and inequality, and the commonality of goals often created a political synergy through the fusion of the two causes.

Both schools of antebellum reformists had common characteristics of radical thought and idealism founded on philosophies such as William Lloyd Garrison's secular visions of equality among all people. The Civil War ushered in an era of change in the American social landscape, yet strangely, after the war, the feminists found themselves deserted by many of the abolitionist champions, many of whom now focused their efforts solely on black rights and suffrage. Indeed, many civil rights leaders felt that the push for African-American suffrage would be hindered by the additional burden of the "women's cause." Black suffrage was an arduous struggle in its own right, and the added baggage of another controversial issue seemed destined to sink both efforts. Though some reformists remained loyal to both suffrage causes, and most probably supported women's rights in their hearts, feminism needed new heroes. From the ashes of the post–Civil War reconstruction era, new leaders for the feminist cause needed to emerge.

The Abolitionist and Feminist Movements of the Early 1800s

The feminist movement was one of three major American social movements during the nineteenth century; both the antislavery and the labor movements were also closely tied to America's growing pains. But women's rights were not achieved by a series of independent and escalating protests that eventually caused a political compromise. The changes were actually the response to the economic, political, and social limitations placed upon women. The elements of reform were spurred by society's impatience with and hostility toward women's oppression.

Nowhere in the nineteenth century could this deliberate subjugation/gender disparity be seen more clearly than in married women. According to Blackstone, the "legal existence of women is suspended during the marriage, or at least is incorporated and consolidated into that of the husband; under whose wing, protection and cover, she performs everything." Unmarried women faced a life of aging alone, as "old maids."

In the first half of the nineteenth century, women's rights had actually declined since the American Revolution. The American colonial period allowed women who owned property to make arrangements to vote. Though it was an atypical arrangement, some women were permitted to protect their interests or even run a business. Ironically, the Constitution ended this, and once peace had been established in the aftermath of the Revolution, the scant women's rights that did exist faded away.

Not surprisingly the early voices of the feminist movement were almost exclusively male and abolitionist. Frederick Douglass, the escaped slave and renowned orator, was the editor of *The North Star,* an antislavery paper. William Lloyd Garrison, publisher of *The Liberator,* spent most of his life devoted to the antislavery cause and was among the most radical thinkers of the time, insisting that all slaves must be freed and allowed to integrate into society. And George Thompson, a British abolitionist, helped pass antislavery legislation through Parliament and later lectured extensively with Garrison, echoing his "radical" abolitionist views. Their philosophies, while primarily focused on black civil rights and the abolition of slavery, were adopted by feminist reformers.

The feminist movement, which began some three decades before the Civil War, paralleled the antislavery movement of the time. The men and women who would later champion women's rights viewed the support blacks had received as exactly the type of momentum their cause needed to generate to be successful. But the feminist movement was different in some key areas. While women sought to change the social structure to emancipate themselves from dependency, they had to be dutiful in their roles as wives and mothers. This paradox—of seeking change while being dependent upon the status quo—made it difficult for women who wished to maintain a family or who were dependent upon their husbands for income to become politically active. Feminists who had families had to find other ways to voice their feelings and frustrations. Literature had quietly reflected the discontentment with the female condition for years, but the outlet of books was too subtle an approach for the militant, truly radical feminists.

Elizabeth Cady Stanton, one of the first women to pick up the gaunt-let, was the prototypical radical feminist. Stanton's curious and difficult split of loyalties between family duties and the feminist cause are illus-trated in this excerpt from a letter to Susan B. Anthony:

I can generalize and philosophize easily enough of myself; but the details of the particular laws I need, I have not time to look up. You see, while I am about the house, surrounded by my children, wash-ing dishes, baking, sewing, etc., I can think up many points, but I cannot search books, for my hands as well as my brains would be necessary for that work. . . . I seldom have one hour undisturbed in which to sit down and write.

Born Elizabeth Cady, she was the daughter of a prominent New York judge and, amid a wealthy upbringing, became an unlikely early leader of women's rights. She was educated at the finest seminary school in the area and married abolitionist Henry Brewster Stanton. Over time she aligned herself with other prominent abolitionists including Lucretia Mott, William Lloyd Garrison, and Wendell Phillips. Eventually she met and formed a lifelong bond with Susan B. Anthony.

Despite the demands on her time and energy that went with raising a family, Stanton and her contemporary, Lucretia Mott, still generated waves in the political and social scene. On July 19, 1848, the two women took the first step toward organizing the women's rights movement by assembling a convention in Seneca Falls, New York. Anthony, who would eventually come to be the leader of the movement, was not yet an integral part of it.

The historical significance of this event to the women's rights move-ment cannot be overstated. Historians point to the Seneca Falls Conven-tion and Susan B. Anthony's trial as the galvanizing events preceding the eventual recognition of women's suffrage. At Seneca Falls, for the first time, the movement stepped out on its own, without taking a backseat to the abolitionists. Yet Stanton and Mott originally decided that, to be taken seriously by the public, a man needed to preside over the gather-ing. Though some women had been involved in the abolitionist move-ment for decades, their role was primarily that of silent support. It was considered improper for a Christian woman to be vocal or outspoken about her beliefs, particularly on something so controversial. But as the convention grew closer, the women came to believe that a woman should be at the forefront; Abigail Bush was ratified as president of the conven-tion and was chosen to preside over the meeting.

The first Seneca Falls Convention, held at the Wesleyan Methodist Chapel, began on a tenuous note, Abigail Bush trembling with fear as she stood on the podium, waiting to address the gathering of several hundred people. But her confidence grew as she spoke and she earned praise and admiration for her presence as president. Bush's efforts and the gamble Stanton and Mott made in selecting a woman to speak garnered added attention as well as criticism for the radical defiance the convention represented.

The substantive purpose of the meeting, to craft and ratify a formal declaration of rights, resulted in the "Declaration of Sentiments and Resolutions," signed by more than a hundred women and men. The document outlined the grievances and issues women faced and included a list of goals for the emerging women's movement, primarily focusing on suffrage. In this document it was further declared that future women's rights conventions and meetings were necessary to ensure continuing progress toward equality.

Prior to Seneca Falls, the women's rights movement had had disjointed support and an uncoordinated band of followers because it was generally regarded by mainstream society as secondary to the emancipation of the slaves. Early feminists disseminated their philosophies and beliefs by writing to one anther. But at Seneca Falls, the participants vowed to be organized in their efforts and stern in their demands. Henceforth, protests would be publicly visible, and women would raise their own voices in the leadership of the cause. Stanton insisted that the duty of women was not uncertain or passive: "The duty of the women of this country [is] to secure to themselves the sacred right to the elective franchise." Seneca Falls represented the venting of centuries of frustration, and it galvanized the adherents of the women's rights movement to a focused cause with definite goals.

But the Seneca Falls Convention did not have the immediate revolutionary impact that Stanton, Mott, and the others had hoped. And while the next decade brought steady progress, the gains made were unremarkable, given the bold advances the feminists envisioned. Meanwhile, the unrest caused by abolitionists and the strain between the North and the South would soon erupt in the most savage fighting in American history, the Civil War. The feminist momentum was put on hold as Americans turned all attention to supporting their respective war efforts.

An Average Girl from an Average Family

Susan Brownell Anthony, born in western Massachusetts on February 15, 1820, was the second child of Daniel and Lucy Anthony. Her family was of ordinary means, industrious—in keeping with her father's Quaker heritage. Her mother had quietly accepted her role as a traditional wife.

As a child, Susan Anthony did nothing to hint at the rebellious, fiery character that would typify her later life. Neither a tomboy nor a daddy's girl, she was just an average child. Susan enjoyed the benefits of an education that may not have been possible fifty or one hundred years earlier, when child labor was more prevalent. But being of working-class origins, Susan and her five siblings were expected to contribute to the family. Susan seemed to accept her place within the household without complaint. A Quaker maxim exemplified her positive, industrious outlook as a young girl:

All work and no play, makes Jack a dull boy,
All play and no work, makes Jack a mere toy.

So when the young Susan had completed her considerable chores and duties, she would wander in the fields behind her house picking flowers or simply enjoying the afternoon. She loved nature and displayed a keen interest in the animals of Berkshire Hills, Massachusetts.

During her mother's fourth pregnancy, Susan and her two younger sisters were sent to stay with her paternal grandparents. Her grandfather was a strong believer in the importance of a child's education, and during the short stay he not only taught Susan to read, but subjected her to extensive lessons for hours each day. Susan's eyes, however, suffered from the intense schedule, and she became badly cross-eyed after the six-week visit. When she returned home, her parents kept her away from reading for months, hoping it would restore the alignment of her eyes. The respite was partially successful; her condition improved, but her left eye remained slightly misaligned for the remainder of her life. This imperfection not only impaired her reading ability, but damaged her self-confidence, as she felt forever insecure about her appearance.

Susan's father built and operated a small textile mill, which produced cotton cloth using power looms. Young teenage girls operated the machines because theirs was the cheapest available labor, at $1.50 per week, plus room and board. Because Daniel Anthony's mill contained only twenty looms, he could not afford a boardinghouse for the young girls, as was the usual practice in the industry. Instead, about half of the girls stayed in the Anthony house, and the other half at Daniel's sister's house. Over time the girls became like family to the Anthonys, who welcomed them into their lives and treated them well. This arrangement had a strong impact on Susan and her sisters, who were exposed to the differences between wage-earning working women and traditional married women like their mother. The wage-earning girls had the benefit of independence, but it came with a heavy trade-off: a six-day workweek. In contrast, married women were totally dependent upon their husbands' income and generosity, but usually only had to perform household duties.

When she was eleven, Susan became familiar with her father's business and suggested that he replace a boy who was acting as a supervisor with a particularly bright young girl. Susan had observed that the girl had better knowledge of the machines and of the business than the boy she wanted replaced. But her father refused, explaining that a woman had no business overseeing a mill.

Quakers, however, had a different view when it came to education, which they viewed as the right of every child, regardless of gender. When Susan returned home from the district school upset that she would not be taught division because she was female, Daniel withdrew all his children and organized a home-schooling system. Teaching alone at first, he eventually hired a woman named Mary Perkins to teach full-time. Perkins was a well-educated product of the Ipswich Academy, a prominent school in Massachusetts, which taught contemporary instruction techniques. During the day, she taught the Anthony children, and at night she offered classes for the mill workers.

Perkins brought a new perspective to Susan. She was now exposed to a female figure who was educated and occupying a role traditionally reserved for college-educated men. Young Susan was so influenced by Perkins that she herself took up small teaching assignments in town. She would teach children during the summer when the male teachers took better-paying farm jobs. Her interest in education eventually convinced her father to pay the sizable $125 tuition to send her to an all-female boarding school. But unlike male universities that rewarded diverse activities, the Quaker seminary school she attended was restrictive. Susan was unhappy there; she was torn between the academics she enjoyed and the homesickness that dominated her thoughts. She had no way to focus her energy, and she withdrew from any friends she had made early in her stay there. She became a loner, increasingly depressed.

Then one day in 1838, ten years prior to Seneca Falls, a speaker she had heard about for her entire life came to address the academy. Lucretia Mott, a leading female abolitionist, spoke to the girls about the value and importance of education and the power it provides, and Anthony felt the impact of Mott's antislavery beliefs.

Shortly after Mott delivered her address, however, Susan was forced to withdraw from the academy and return home. The family business, which had been struggling for years, had collapsed. The Anthonys were forced to sell almost all their possessions—their house, their books, their tools, and even most of their clothes—to pay the debts they had incurred. Susan returned to teaching to help pay for the losses. And at that point, Susan B. Anthony's formal education ended, and adulthood began. As biographer Kathleen Barry noted, "All of this prepared her for but did not guarantee that she would become a most uncommon representative of the common woman."

Susan had always shown a strong commitment to her family. She admired her parents and worked hard to care for her sisters. The Anthony sisters had been closely bonded for many years. But when the son of her father's former business partner began courting Guelma, her older sister, the dynamic was threatened. Susan did not view Guelma's suitor as an equal, fit for her sister's hand. Susan quietly protested her sister's marriage and eventually became disenchanted with the institution of marriage itself.

Her decision not to marry later set her apart from many of her feminist counterparts. The Quaker tradition, however, was somewhat different from that of many other Christian religions, in that it had long recognized the value of the single woman. As a result, Anthony may have been under less pressure from her family to marry than her peers. Likewise, as an educated woman, Anthony possessed greater freedom than most others. Teachers of the time tended to be more independent, a result of respect for their profession and the steady salary it provided.

She never saw a need to surrender her identity through marriage, and indeed she despised its inequities, formed by tradition and ingrained in the legal landscape of nineteenth-century American marital laws. As already noted, the entirety of the married couple was the identity of the husband. Assets and autonomy were vested in him, and the woman's role was undoubtedly a subservient one. By her early twenties, Anthony had already begun formulating a philosophy that no person should be forced to submit to any such servitude.

As a young teacher, Anthony's character was slowly forged through the independence provided by her profession. Because she was single, she could create her own identity and agenda, not merely contribute to a husband's. Her political philosophy began to reflect this independence. Anthony saw autonomy and independence as inalienable rights that all people deserved; slaves and women both deserved the opportunity to achieve whatever their personal potentials made possible. She eventually decided that she would never marry and subject herself to a life of subservience and an identity defined by her husband.

By the 1850s Anthony was in her thirties and was committed to the causes of abolition and feminism, traveling extensively to attend meetings and the lectures of Garrison and George Thompson. She had also taken part in the Underground Railroad and had personally assisted several of the estimated 150 escaped slaves who passed through Rochester, New York, on the way to Canada.

In 1852, Anthony met the woman with whom she would be eternally linked. Anthony and Elizabeth Cady Stanton had learned of each other years before and had long shared a mutual respect. When they finally met, the attraction was immediate and enduring. The women had an immediate bond based upon shared beliefs, despite their contrasting lifestyles. Stanton was open, enthusiastic, and insightful, while Anthony was independent and serious. Over the years, Stanton's education and well-developed philosophies made her an ideal complement to Anthony's strong-willed presence. Their openness and acceptance of each other would forge a friendship that would last fifty years, until Stanton's death.

The Postbellum Years and the Fourteenth Amendment

Immediately after the Emancipation Proclamation, Stanton and Anthony organized the Women's National Loyal League (WNLL). The WNLL was the first national organization devoted to women's suffrage and sought enfranchisement by way of a constitutional amendment.

In 1865 the states ratified the Thirteenth Amendment, granting former slaves freedom and citizenship but withholding the vote. In December of 1865, Congress introduced the Fourteenth Amendment, and in the middle of the following year passed it along for state ratification. The amendment indirectly gave blacks the right to vote by forcing former Confederate states to enfranchise them or lose a proportional share of their congressional delegations. However, the amendment was only a partial victory, because the new law would not necessarily provide full federal protection if states chose to ignore the amendment. While it represented an incremental advancement of black civil rights by granting complete citizenship, it was seen as a political compromise for abolitionists because it did not grant full, unequivocal rights to blacks.

Abolitionists and suffragists had long looked to the Republican Party as the champion of their causes. The Republican-inspired Fourteenth Amendment essentially killed two birds with one stone—it asserted federal dominance over Confederate states and freed the slaves in the process. Abolitionists felt the amendment actually fell well short of their ideological and long-term goals, yet they were stuck with it as the lesser of two evils. Because the Republicans adopted it as part of their official 1866 election platform, abolitionists and suffragists were forced to support it, realizing that a Republican victory was the more pressing priority.

However, this compromise had a devastating affect on Stanton and Anthony's push for women's suffrage. The feminist cause had already been deferred by the Civil War, when all efforts were focused on the fight to preserve the Union. Now, the abolitionists had effectively left the feminists behind, separating the causes.

Wendell Phillips, the abolitionist leader, informed feminist activists that his organization would temporarily delay its support for the women's movement. Believing that the black struggle was itself more than his group could handle, he remarked, "I hope in time to be as bold as Stuart Mill and add to that last clause 'sex'! But this hour belongs to the Negro. As Abraham Lincoln said, 'one war at a time.'"

Stanton confided in Anthony her fears: "I have argued constantly with Phillips . . . but I fear one and all will favor enfranchising the negro without us. [The] woman's cause is in deep water."

The split between the two movements revealed how unprepared the feminist cause was to strike out on its own. While it had piggybacked on the flourishing abolitionist network during the antebellum years, the women's rights movement had failed to develop a separate presence. The nascent Women's National Loyal League lacked the organizational framework, leadership experience, and sound following the abolitionists had acquired.

Stanton and Anthony were all too aware of these challenges. Likewise they were concerned with the wording of the Fourteenth Amendment. The Republican Congress had chosen the word *male* rather than *people* or *persons,* giving an explicit division to the sexes for the first time in constitutional history. The net effect was a per se rule authorized by the Constitution to maintain the disfranchisement of women and continue them as second-class citizens.

So, while the Fourteenth Amendment would represent an advancement for the civil liberties of one group fighting for suffrage, it distinctly set back another group. Upon learning of the wording of the proposed Fourteenth Amendment, Stanton and Anthony drew up a petition and gathered more than a hundred thousand signatures. "We ask that you extend the right of suffrage to Woman . . . and thus fulfill your constitutional obligation 'to guarantee to every state in the Union a Republican from of government.'" Past efforts by local feminist organizations had been directed at lobbying state legislatures. But the WNLL, for the first time in history, appealed directly to Congress, praying for sympathy from some of the Republican congressmen or senators.

Their efforts were futile, and by early 1866 it was clear that the Fourteenth Amendment would include the word *male* and exclude any progress for women—more than a symbolic slap in the face to the WNLL and the feminist cause. Later in 1866, Anthony and Stanton attempted to persuade Wendell Phillips to change his mind and merge the American Anti-Slavery Society with their group. Phillips refused, reiterating his belief that only one suffrage cause should be pursued at a time. Undeterred, Anthony and Stanton held their first postwar convention in May of 1866, where the delegates unanimously declared that their goal was universal suffrage and voted to rename their organization the American Equal Rights Association.

By 1868, the Fourteenth Amendment was ratified into law and a proposed amendment providing explicit constitutional protection of voting rights for all men was beginning to take shape. Meanwhile, the women's movement, shunted to the backwaters of the American political landscape, was splintering. Differences between the radicals, led by Anthony and Stanton, and the conservatives, led by Henry Blackwell and his wife, Lucy Stone, were taxing the ERA's previous solidarity. The problems first surfaced in 1867, when the Kansas state legislature put two issues on the November election—blacks' and women's suffrage. Anthony, Stanton, Blackwell, Stone, and many others led a nine-month-long campaign to support both referendums.

Kansas had long been opposed to slavery and thus had relatively strong support for black rights. In terms of women's rights, Kansas was generally regarded as second only to New York in its progressive advancement of women. But instead of the success for which the feminists and blacks had hoped, disaster struck. The Republican Party leaders, upon whom the feminists had relied, rejected the Equal Rights Association's universal suffrage stance, choosing to support only black suffrage. Some Republicans even began an openly antifeminist stance, opposing the female suffrage movement altogether.

Outraged and desperate, many feminists turned to the Democrats and aligned themselves with the anti-Negro policy they supported. Ultimately, with the once-allied suffragist groups now warring, a disastrous result was realized: both referendums failed and the feminist movement fractured into two opposing factions—one wing aligning with the Republican deferral of sexual equality and the Anthony/Stanton–led wing willing to dissolve a forty-year partnership between blacks and women.

From the abortive effort in Kansas two new organizations were formed by 1869. Blackwell and Stone's American Woman Suffrage Association (AWSA) remained aligned with the dominant Republican Party and black suffragists such as Frederick Douglass. Anthony and Stanton headed the National Woman Suffrage Association (NWSA), which insisted upon equality and inclusion.

The more radical NWSA opted not to support the pending vote on the Fifteenth Amendment, which would enfranchise black men, because it lacked any voting rights for women. Nonetheless, the Republican Party and the black suffragists won their war by 1870 with the ratification of the Fifteenth Amendment. This left women's rights as the final battle for the surviving yet divided armies of suffragists.

Despite the division between the two groups, their collective effort increased national sympathy for women's suffrage. Although competing politically in terms of the means to the end, they shared a common goal, which prevented all-out warfare. By this time, Anthony was being paid to lecture and was using the funds to support the cause, notably by starting the first woman's suffrage paper, a weekly called *The Revolution*. Anthony struggled to keep it afloat, enduring a series of financial setbacks and harsh attacks from Lucy Stone and Frederick Douglass.

Anthony refused to retaliate, realizing that their shared goals were greater than her personal pride. She said, "I want you to know that it is impossible for me to lay a straw in the way of any one who personally wrongs me—if only that one will work nobly for the cause. They may try to hinder my success but I never theirs." She even attended the AWSA conventions, though her presence was frequently criticized and always controversial.

Despite the attacks, Anthony sought the common ground, and in 1886 she surprised the AWSA audience by standing and approaching the podium when Lucy Stone finished her speech. Her bold move filled the room with applause. When the crowd finally quieted down, Anthony called for national action and put the women's cause ahead of her fate and her organization:

Women must not cease to demand a Sixteenth Amendment of the Constitution, giving suffrage to all conditions of men and women. I ask of the convention, at this early stage, not only to demand the favorable action of state legislatures, but of Congress. I care not if this association shall crush out the organization of which I am a member, and the Revolution to which I have given years' labor, for if this association will come up to its great work and accomplish it so help me high heaven, I will be content.

The Suffragists Get Their Day in Court

Throughout these turbulent years, the U.S. Supreme Court had remained surprisingly quiet on the issues of women's rights. Article III of the Constitution dictates the limits of the federal judiciary. Though the public perceives the Supreme Court as omnipotent because it wields the power to uphold or overturn laws by declaring them unconstitutional, there are definite limits to this power. Namely, the Constitution provides that only true cases and controversies will be heard. Thus the Court will not simply provide advisory opinions on its interpretations of either laws or constitutional questions. As such, it was not until 1871 that the first case of gender discrimination appeared before the Supreme Court.

Myra Bradwell attempted to use the privileges and immunities clause of the Fourteenth Amendment to gain membership to the Illinois Bar Association. She directly challenged an Illinois law that forbade females from receiving a law license or practicing law. Her attorney maintained that the practice of law was a "privilege" of citizenship and was, therefore, protected by the Fourteenth Amendment and further, that the denial of her attempt to practice law was a blatant and unlawful form of discrimination.

The Supreme Court's majority opinion found against Bradwell and voiced the conservative sentiments of the time:

> The civil law, as well as nature herself, has always recognized a wide difference in the respective spheres and destinies of man and woman. Man is, or should be, woman's protector and defender. The nature and proper timidity and delicacy which belongs to the female sex evidently unfits it from many of the occupations of civil life. . . . The family institution is repugnant to the idea of a woman adopting a distinct and independent career from that of her husband. . . . The paramount destiny and mission of women are to fulfill the noble and benign offices of wife and mother. This is the law of the creator. . . . It is within the province of the Legislature to ordain what offices, positions and callings shall be filled and discharged by men.

A Daring Move

Following the crushing defeat suffered in Bradwell's case, suffragettes knew they needed to regain momentum, and on a cool New York November morning, Susan B. Anthony, leading her three sisters, marched confidently. They walked into a barbershop, which had been converted to a registry office for the day, and insisted that all four of them had the right to register to vote in the upcoming election. The election inspectors denied their request.

Undeterred, Anthony read them the text of the Fourteenth Amendment and excerpts from the New York State Constitution. The three men, all young enough to be Anthony's sons, refused to let the women register. Then she changed her tactics: "If you still refuse us our rights as citizens, I will bring charges against you in criminal court and I will sue each of you personally for large, exemplary damages."

Having gained the registrars' attention, Anthony explained that she had consulted Judge Henry Selden, a highly respected Rochester jurist, and had money to back her if it came to a legal fight. The inspectors, confused and stunned by Anthony's persistence and unaware that she was actually thousands of dollars in debt and monetarily incapable of waging any civil battle, hesitantly allowed the women to register. Anthony then personally assured the young men that she would assist them in any legal struggles they might face. By afternoon, when the story had leaked to the media, there were rumors that the defiant women and the inspectors would all be arrested.

Early in the morning of November 5, 1872, Anthony led a group of women, including three of her sisters, down to the polls, where the four sisters voted. Anthony had her national issue. And while she was by no means the first woman to have tried to vote, her prominence made her the most significant figure to have done so. Anthony took great pride in her action. She wrote Stanton:

Well I have been & gone & done it!! Positively voted the Republican ticket straight this a.m. at 7 o'clock—& swore my vote in at that. Was registered on Friday & 15 other women followed suit in this ward, then on Sunday some 20 or thirty other women tried to register, but all save two were refused. All my three sisters voted— Rhoda De Garmo too. Amy Post was rejected & she will immediately bring action for that, similar to the Washington action, & Hon Henry R. Selden will be our Counsel. He has read up the law & all of our arguments & is satisfied that we are right & ditto the Old Judge Selden (his elder brother). So we are in for a fine agitation in Rochester on the question; I hope the morning's telegrams will tell of many women all over the country trying to vote. It is splendid that without any concert of action so many should have moved here so impromptu. Haven't we wedged ourselves into the work pretty fairly & fully? & now that the Repubs have taken our votes—for it is the Republican members of the Board—the Democratic paper is out against us strong & that scared the Dem's on the registry board. How I wish you were here to write up the funny things said & done. Rhoda De Garmo told them that she wouldn't swear or affirm, "but would tell the truth," & they accepted that. When the Democrat said my vote should not go in the box, one Republican said to the other, "What do you say Marsh!" "I say put it in!" "So do I," said Jones, and "we'll fight it out on this line if it takes all winter." If only now all the suffrage women would work to this end of enforcing the existing constitution—supremacy of national law over state law—what strides we might make this winter. But I'm awful tired; for five days I have been on the constant run, but to splendid purpose, so all right. I hope you voted too.

Affectionately,
Susan B. Anthony

Twenty-three days later, a warrant was issued for Anthony's arrest, and the federal marshal gave her the option of turning herself in. Anthony refused, insisting that she would not go down to the court voluntarily because she was innocent of any crime. When the marshal appeared at her home to escort her, she declared that if she was to be arrested, she wanted to be handcuffed like any male criminal. The marshal sheepishly declared handcuffs were not necessary and reluctantly escorted her to the courthouse, where she found that each of the three inspectors had been arrested as well. All were charged, and though bail was posted, Anthony refused bail and remained in jail.

Henry R. Selden, the source of much of Anthony's legal advice, was to represent her. Resembling a diminutive Abraham Lincoln, Selden was highly respected throughout New York, where he had served as the first Republican lieutenant governor in 1857, following a stint as state reporter for the New York State Court of Appeals, New York's highest court. He later served as an associate judge on the same Court of Appeals and was then elected to the legislature in 1865. Selden, an abolitionist, had a reputation as an activist in both his legal career and his tenure in the legislature. His views made him a thorn in the side of Democrats and an ally to the suffragists—especially his friend Susan B. Anthony, whom he highly respected.

Selden believed in a woman's right to vote, based on the same legal interpretation upon which Anthony had relied, and he had advised her of that belief. Stanton quoted Selden: "There is law enough not only to protect you in the exercise of your right to vote, but to enfranchise every woman in the land." His support would be crucial to Anthony's case. He worked on her defense with John Van Voorhis, neither attorney charging for their services, though Anthony insisted on paying what she could.

Selden's first maneuver was to file a writ of habeas corpus claiming his client's incarceration was illegal because she had committed no crime. The court not only denied the writ, but doubled the bail to $1,000. Anthony would not pay, refusing to cooperate with a legal system that did not recognize her as a true citizen, but Selden posted the bail over her objection, claiming quietly that he could not stand to see a woman jailed. Posting bail was, however, a crucial error—by freeing Anthony, they had lost their ability to appeal the denial of their habeas petition to the Supreme Court. Anthony, upon learning of this error, rushed back to the courtroom to cancel the bond, but it was too late.

While awaiting trial in New York State court, Anthony once again defied the authorities and voted in a local election. A trial date of May 13, 1873, was set regarding the first "offense." Anthony and Selden were now faced with a strategic decision: Should they seek a jury trial or opt for a judge sitting alone? Selden believed a judge would be more likely to acquit her and end the controversy quickly, but Anthony disagreed. She saw a jury trial as a better opportunity to plead her case to common men—women, of course, did not sit on juries—and avoid being at the mercy of the legal system she so vehemently distrusted.

Anthony began a publicity campaign, traveling around Monroe County declaring her innocence and protesting the oppression of women, delivering her stump speech some twenty-nine times in thirty days.

> Friends and fellow citizens: I stand before you tonight, under indictment for the alleged crime of having voted at the last presidential election, without having a lawful right to vote. It shall be my work this evening to prove to you that in thus voting, I not only committed no crime, but, instead, simply exercised my citizen's right, guaranteed to me and all United States citizens by the national Constitution, beyond the power of any state to deny.
>
> Our democratic-republican government is based on the idea of the natural right of every individual member thereof to a voice and a vote in making and executing the laws. We assert the province of government to be to secure the people in the enjoyment of their unalienable rights. We throw to the winds the old dogma that governments can give rights. Before governments were organized, no one denies that each individual possessed the right to protect his own life, liberty, and property. And when one hundred or one mil-

lion people enter into a free government, they do not barter away their natural rights; they simply pledge themselves to protect each other in the enjoyment of them, through prescribed judicial and legislative tribunals. They agree to abandon the methods of brute force in the adjustment of their differences, and adopt those of civilization.

Nor can you find a word in any of the grand documents left us by the fathers that assumes for government the power to create or to confer rights. The Declaration of Independence, the United States Constitution, the constitutions of the several states, and the organic laws of the territories, all alike propose to protect the people in the exercise of their God-given rights. Not one of them pretends to bestow rights.

"All men are created equal, and endowed by their Creator with certain unalienable rights. Among these are life, liberty, and the pursuit of happiness. That to secure these, governments are instituted among men, deriving their just powers from the consent of the governed."

Here is no shadow of government authority over rights, nor exclusion of any class from their full and equal enjoyment. Here is pronounced the right of all men, and "consequently," as the Quaker preacher said, "of all women," to a voice in the government. And here, in this very first paragraph of the declaration, is the assertion of the natural right of all to the ballot; for, how can "the consent of the governed" be given if the right to vote be denied.

Surely, the right of the whole people to vote is here clearly implied. For however destructive to their happiness this government might become, a disfranchised class could neither alter nor abolish it, nor institute a new one, except by the old brute-force method of insurrection and rebellion. One-half of the people of this nation today are utterly powerless to blot from the statute books an unjust law, or to write there a new and a just one.

The women, dissatisfied as they are with this form of government, that enforces taxation without representation; that compels them to obey laws to which they have never given their consent; that imprisons and hangs them without a trial by a jury of their peers; that robs them, in marriage, of the custody of their persons, wages, and children; are this half of the people left wholly at the mercy of the other half, in direct violation of the spirit and letter of the declarations of the framers of this government, every one of which was based on the immutable principle of equal rights to all?

By those declarations, kings, priests, popes, aristocrats, were all alike dethroned, and placed on a common level, politically, with the lowliest born subject or serf. By them, too, men, as such, were deprived of their divine right to rule, and placed on a political level with women. By the practice of those declarations all class and caste distinction will be abolished; and slave, serf, plebeian, wife, woman, all alike, bound from their subject position to the proud platform of equality.

The preamble of the federal constitution says:

"We, the people of the United States, in order to form a more perfect union, establish justice, insure domestic tranquility, provide for the common defence, promote the general welfare, and secure the blessings of liberty to ourselves and our posterity, do ordain and establish this constitution for the United States of America."

It was we, the people, not we, the white male citizens, nor yet we, the male citizens; but we, the whole people, who formed this Union. And we formed it, not to give the blessings of liberty, but to secure them; not to the half of ourselves and the half of our posterity, but to the whole people—women as well as men. And it is downright mockery to talk to women of their enjoyment of the blessings of liberty while they are denied the use of the only means of securing them provided by this democratic-republican government—the ballot.

In all the penalties and burdens of the government (except the military), women are reckoned as citizens, equally with men. Also, in all the privileges and immunities, save those of the jury box and ballot box, the two fundamental privileges on which rest all the others.

The United States government not only taxes, fines, imprisons, and hangs women, but it allows them to register ships and take out passport and naturalization papers. Not only does the law permit single women and widows to the right of naturalization, but Section 2 says, "A married woman may be naturalized without the concurrence of her husband."

I wonder the fathers were not afraid of creating discord in the families of foreigners.

And again: "When an alien, having complied with the law, and declared his intention to become a citizen, dies before he is actually naturalized, his widow and children shall be considered citizens, entitled to all rights and privileges as such, on taking the required oath." If a foreign-born woman by becoming a naturalized citizen is entitled to all the rights and privileges of citizenship, is not a native-born woman, by her national citizenship, possessed of equal rights and privileges?

The only question left to be settled, now, is: Are women persons? And I hardly believe any of our opponents will have the hardihood to say they are not. Being persons, then, women are citizens, and no state has a right to make any new law, or to enforce any old law, that shall abridge their privileges or immunities. Hence, every discrimination against women in the constitutions and laws of the several states is today null and void, precisely as is every one against Negroes.

Is the right to vote one of the privileges or immunities of citizens? I think the disfranchised ex-rebels, and the ex–state prisoners will agree with me, that it is not only one of them, but the one without which all the others are nothing. Seek first the kingdom of the ballot, and all things else shall be given thee, is the political injunction.

Webster, Worcester, and Bouvier all define citizen to be a person, in the United States, entitled to vote and hold office. Prior to the adoption of the Thirteenth Amendment, by which slavery was forever abolished, and black men transformed from property to persons, the judicial opinions of the country had always been in harmony with these definitions. To be a person was to be a citizen, and to be a citizen was to be a voter.

If the Fourteenth Amendment does not secure to all citizens the right to vote, for what purpose was that grand old charter of the fathers lumbered with its unwieldy proportions? The Republican Party, who drafted the document, pretended it was to do something for black men; and if that something was not to secure them in their right to vote and hold office, what could it have been? For, by the Thirteenth Amendment, black men had become people, and hence were entitled to all the privileges and immunities of the government, precisely as were the women of the country.

Those newly freed men were in possession of every possible right, privilege, and immunity of the government, except that of suffrage, and hence, needed no constitutional amendment for any other purpose. What right, I ask you, has the Irishman the day after he receives his naturalization papers that he did not possess the day before, save the right to vote and hold office? And the Chinamen, now crowding our Pacific coast, are in precisely the same position.

What privilege or immunity has California or Oregon the constitutional right to deny them, save that of the ballot? Clearly, then, if the Fourteenth Amendment was not to secure to black men their right to vote, it did nothing for them, since they possessed everything else before. But, if it was meant to be a prohibition of the states to deny or abridge their right to vote—which I fully believe—then it did the same for all persons, white women included, born or naturalized in the United States; for the amendment does not say all male persons of African descent, but all persons are citizens.

But, however much the doctors of the law may disagree as to whether people and citizens, in the original Constitution, were one and the same, or whether the privileges and immunities in the Fourteenth Amendment include the right of suffrage, the question of the citizen's right to vote is settled forever by the Fifteenth Amendment. "The citizen's right to vote shall not be denied by the United States, nor any state thereof; on account of race, color, or previous condition of servitude." How can the state deny or abridge the right of the citizen, if the citizen does not possess it? There is no escape from the conclusion that to vote is the citizen's right, and the specifications of race, color, or previous condition of servitude can, in no way, impair the force of the emphatic assertion, that the citizen's right to vote shall not be denied or abridged.

There is an old saying that "a rose by any other name would smell as sweet," and I submit if the deprivation by law of the ownership of one's own person, wages, property, children, the denial of the right as an individual to sue and be sued, and to testify in the courts, is not a condition of servitude most bitter and absolute, though under the sacred name of marriage?

Does any lawyer doubt my statement of the legal status of married women? I will remind him of the fact that the old common law of England prevails in every state in this Union, except where the legislature has enacted special laws annulling it. And I am ashamed that not one state has yet blotted from its statute books the old common law of marriage, by which Blackstone, summed up in the fewest words possible, is made to say, "Husband and wife are one, and that one is the husband."

Thus may all married women, wives, and widows, by the laws of the several states, be technically included in the Fifteenth Amendment's specification of "condition of servitude," present or previous. And not only married women, but I will also prove to you that by all the great fundamental principles of our free government, the entire womanhood of the nation is in a "condition of servitude" as surely as were our revolutionary fathers, when they rebelled against old King George.

Women are taxed without representation, governed without their consent, tried, convicted, and punished without a jury of their peers.

And is all this tyranny any less humiliating and degrading to women under our democratic-republican government today than it was to men under their aristocratic, monarchical government one hundred years ago? There is not an utterance of old John Adams, John Hancock, or Patrick Henry, but finds a living response in the soul of every intelligent, patriotic woman of the nation. Bring to me a common-sense woman property holder, and I will show you one whose soul is fired with all the indignation of 1776 every time the tax-gatherer presents himself at her door. You will not find one such but feels her condition of servitude as galling as did James Otis when he said:

"The very act of taxing exercised over those who are not represented appears to me to be depriving them of one of their most essential rights, and if continued, seems to be in effect an entire disfranchisement of every civil right. For, what one civil right is worth a rush after a man's property is subject to be taken from him at pleasure without his consent? If a man is not his own assessor in person, or by deputy, his liberty is gone, or he is wholly at the mercy of others."

And yet one more authority; that of Thomas Paine, than whom not one of the revolutionary patriots more ably vindicated the principles upon which our government is founded:

"The right of voting for representatives is the primary right by which other rights are protected. To take away this right is to reduce man to a state of slavery; for slavery consists in being subject to the will of another; and he that has not a vote in the election of representatives is in this case. The proposal, therefore, to disfranchise any class of men is as criminal as the proposal to take away property."

Is anything further needed to prove woman's condition of servitude sufficiently orthodox to entitle her to the guaranties of the Fifteenth Amendment?

Is there a man who will not agree with me, that to talk of freedom without the ballot, is mockery—is slavery—to the women of this Republic? . . . I admit that prior to the rebellion, by common consent, the right to enslave, as well as to disfranchise both native and foreign-born citizens, was conceded to the states. But the one grand principle, settled by the war and the reconstruction legislation, is the supremacy of national power to protect the citizens of the United States in their right to freedom and the elective franchise, against any and every interference on the part of the several states. And again and again have the American people asserted the triumph of this principle, by their overwhelming majorities for Lincoln and Grant.

This marvelously crafted and constitutionally sound speech was not the spontaneous rant of a firebrand, unnerved on the eve of her trial. Susan B. Anthony had thought about her cause for thirty years; she had read legal treatises and was well versed in constitutional law. She took on the courts' extension of full rights to blacks via the Fourteenth and Fifteenth Amendments and applied and interpreted the precise language of those amendments to include women. She defined women as citizens and servants now emancipated, thereby analogizing her status as a woman to that of an emancipated slave. They were once both servants to the white male, but only the former slaves now enjoyed the full rights of citizenship.

Anthony, now in her fifties, collapsed from exhaustion during one of her speeches. Her condition was so serious that she was hospitalized, and some newspapers reported that she had died. Anthony knew any rumors of weakness would damage her cause and frighten her own aged mother, so she mustered the wherewithal to return to the rigors of her planned tour almost immediately.

The presiding judge was not amused by Anthony's obvious attempts to taint the jury pool, ordering the trial moved to Ontario County and resetting the trial date to June 17, 1873. Anthony simply shifted her speaking tour and once again hit the road. This time she embarked on an appeal to Ontario County's public, visiting a different town each day with a fellow suffragette, Matilda Joslyn Gage. Anthony repeated her speech twenty-one more times, concluded her campaign on June 16, the day before the trial was slated to begin in Canandaigua, the county seat. An excerpt from one of Gage's speeches delivered in Canandaigua, marks the gravity of the issue:

The eyes of all nations are upon us; their hopes of liberty are directed towards us; the United States is now on trial by the light of its own underlying principle. Its assertion of human right to self-government lies a hundred years back of it. The chartered confirmation and renewal of this assertion has come up to our very day, and though all the world looked on and wondered to see us crush the rebellion of '61, it is at this hour, at this soon coming trial of Miss Anthony at Canandaigua, before the Supreme Court of the Northern District of New York, it is at this trial that republican institutions will have their grand test, and as the decision is rendered for or against the political rights of citizenship, so will the people of the United States find themselves free or slaves, and so will the United States have tried itself, and paved its way for a speedy fall, or for a long and glorious continuance.

Miss Anthony is today the representative of liberty. In all ages of the world, and during all times, there have been epochs in which some one person took upon their own shoulders the hopes and the sorrows of the world, and in their own person, through many struggles, bore them onward. Suddenly or gradually, as the case might be, men found the rugged path made smooth and the way opened for the world's rapid advance. Such an epoch exists now, and such a person is Susan B. Anthony.

To you, men of Ontario County, has come an important hour. The fates have brought about that you, of all the men in this great land, have the responsibility of this trial. To you, freedom has come looking for fuller acknowledgment, for a wider area in which to work and grow. Your decision will not be for Susan B. Anthony alone; it will be for yourselves and for your children's children to the latest generations.

You are not asked to decide a question under favor, but according to the foundation principles of this republic. You will be called upon to decide a question according to our great charters of liberty—the Declaration of Independence and the Constitution of the United States.

You are to decide, not only on a question of natural right, but of absolute law, of the supreme law of the land. You are not to decide according to prejudice, but according to the Constitution. If your decision is favorable to the defendant, you will sustain the Constitution; if adverse, if you are blinded by prejudice, you will not decide against women alone, but against the United States as well.

No more momentous hour has arisen in the interest of freedom, for the underlying principles of the republic, its warp and woof alike, is the exact and permanent political equality of every citizen of the nation, whether that citizen is native born or naturalized, white or black, man or woman. And may God help you.

The Trial of Susan B. Anthony

Federal judge Ward Hunt, who was to preside over Anthony's trial, had recently been appointed to the bench with the assistance and backing of U.S. senator Roscoe Conklin, a longtime opponent of women's rights. Anthony's supporters feared Hunt would simply do as the senator directed.

Susan B. Anthony's trial on the charge of illegally voting in a federal election was a succinct affair, taking just two days—a surprisingly brief time for an issue of such constitutional importance. The courtroom quickly filled to capacity, the audience including former president Millard Fillmore, who had grown up near Canandaigua and was currently living in Buffalo, seventy-five miles to the west. The press provided extensive coverage, including caricatures, some vicious, of the defendant.

"The Woman Who Dared"

The prosecutor, Richard Crowley, called the young men whom Anthony had bullied into allowing her to register. Their testimony came in without objection and established that Anthony did, in fact, vote. When the defense began its response, Selden acted as a witness on Anthony's behalf, testifying that he had advised her to vote. He then attempted to call Anthony to the stand. The prosecution objected, stating that she was incompetent to act as a witness because she was a woman. Judge Hunt agreed and did not allow her to testify, despite Selden's strong objection.

Subsequent testimony by a witness for the prosecution seemed to prove that Anthony had registered to vote before consulting Selden; her attorney objected when the prosecution tried to admit the defendant's statement, reasoning that if she could not testify, her words should also be excluded. Unswayed, Judge Hunt allowed the testimony.

Because Anthony was precluded from testifying, the testimony was quickly concluded and the trial moved into closing arguments. And here Henry Selden proved to be a worthy champion.

Closing Argument of Henry Selden on Behalf of Susan B. Anthony

The defendant is indicted under the nineteenth section of the Act of Congress of May thirty-first, 1870, for "voting without having a lawful right to vote."

The only alleged ground of illegality of the defendant's vote is that she is a woman. If the same act had been done by her brother under the same circumstances, the act would have been not only innocent, but honorable and laudable; but having been done by a woman it is said to be a crime. The crime therefore consists not in the act done, but in the simple fact that the person doing it was a woman and not a man. I believe this is the first instance in which a woman has been arraigned in a criminal court, merely on account of her sex.

Women have the same interest that men have in the establishment and maintenance of good government; they are to the same extent as men bound to obey the laws; they suffer to the same extent by bad laws and profit to the same extent by good laws; and upon principles of equal justice, as it would seem, should be allowed equally with men, to express their preference in the choice of lawmakers and rulers. But however that may be, no greater absurdity, to use no harsher term, could be presented, than that of rewarding men and punishing women, for the same act, without giving to women any voice in the question which should be rewarded, and which punished.

I am aware, however, that we are here to be governed by the Constitution and laws as they are, and that if the defendant has been guilty of violating the law, she must submit to the penalty, however unjust or absurd the law may be. But courts are not required to so interpret laws or constitutions as to produce either absurdity or injustice, so long as they are open to a more reasonable interpretation. This must be my excuse for what I design to say in regard to the propriety of female suffrage, because with that propriety established there is very little difficulty in finding sufficient warrant in the Constitution for its exercise.

This case, in its legal aspects, presents three questions:

1. Was the defendant legally entitled to vote at the election in question?
2. If she was not entitled to vote, but believed that she was, and voted in good faith in that belief, did such voting constitute a crime under the statute before referred to?
3. Did the defendant vote in good faith in that belief?

If the first question be decided in accordance with my views, the other questions become immaterial; if the second be decided adversely to my views, the first and third become immaterial. The two first are questions of law to be decided by the court, the other is a question for the jury.

My first position is that the defendant had the same right to vote as any other citizen who voted at that election. Miss Anthony, and those united with her in demanding the right of suffrage, claim, and with a strong appearance of justice, that upon the principles upon which our government is founded, and which lie at the basis of all just government, every citizen has a right to take part, upon equal terms with every other citizen, in the formation and administration of government.

This claim on the part of the female sex presents a question the magnitude of which is not well appreciated by the writers and speakers who treat it with ridicule. Those engaged in the movement are able, sincere, and earnest women, and they will not be silenced by such ridicule, nor even by the villainous caricatures of Nast. On the contrary, they justly place all those things to the account of the wrongs which they think their sex has suffered. They believe, with an intensity of feeling which men who have not associated with them have not yet learned, that their sex has not had, and has not now, its just and true position in the organization of government and society. They may be wrong in their position, but they will not be content until their arguments are fairly, truthfully, and candidly answered.

In the most celebrated document which has been put forth on this side of the Atlantic, our ancestors declared that "governments derive their just powers from the consent of the governed." Blackstone says, "The lawfulness of punishing criminals is founded upon this principle: that the law by which they suffer was made by their own consent; it is a part of the original contract into which they entered when first they engaged in society; it was calculated for and has long contributed to their own security."

Quotations, to an unlimited extent, containing similar doctrines from eminent writers, both English and American, on government, from the time of John Locke to the present day, might be made. Without adopting this doctrine which bases the rightfulness of government upon the consent of the governed, I claim that there is implied in it the narrower and unassailable principle that all citizens of a state, who are bound by its laws, are entitled to an equal voice in the making and execution of such laws.

The mastery which this doctrine has acquired over the public mind, has produced as its natural fruit, the extension of the right of suffrage to all the adult male population in nearly all the states of the Union; a result which was well epitomized by President Lincoln, in the expression "government by the people for the people."

This extension of the suffrage is regarded by many as a source of danger to the stability of free government. But, I believe it furnishes the greatest security for free government, as it deprives the mass of the people of all motive for revolution; and that government so based is most safe, not because the whole people are less liable to make mistakes in government than a select few, but because they have no interest which can lead them to such mistakes, or to prevent their correction when made.

On the contrary, the world has never seen an aristocracy, whether composed of few or many, powerful enough to control a government, who did not honestly believe that their interest was identical with the public interest, and who did not act persistently in accordance with such belief; and, unfortunately, an aristocracy of sex has not proved an exception to the rule. The only method yet discovered of overcoming this tendency to the selfish use of power, whether consciously or unconsciously, by those possessing it, is the distribution of the power among all who are its subjects. Short of this the name *free government* is a misnomer.

This principle, after long strife, is generally recognized on this side of the Atlantic, as far as relates to men; but when the attempt is made to extend it to women, political philosophers and practical politicians, those "inside of politics," two classes not often found acting in concert, join in denouncing it. It remains to be determined whether the reasons which have produced the extension of the franchise to all adult men, do not equally demand its extension to all adult women. If it be necessary for men that each should have a share in the administration of government for his security, and to exclude partiality, it would seem to be equally, if not more, necessary for women, on account of their inferior physical power: and if, as is persistently alleged by those who sneer at their claims, they are also inferior in mental power, that fact only gives additional weight to the argument in their behalf, as one of the primary objects of government, as acknowledged on all hands, is the protection of the weak against the power of the strong.

I can discover no ground consistent with the principle on which the franchise has been given to all men, upon which it can be denied to women. The principal argument against such extension is based upon the position that women are represented in the government by men, and that their rights and interests are better protected through that indirect representation than they would be by giving them a direct voice in the government. That men, not individually, but collectively, are the natural and appropriate representatives of women, and that, notwithstanding cases of individual wrong, the rights of women are, on the whole, best protected by being left to their care.

It must be observed, however, that the cases of cruelty and injustice of men are the result of ages of legislation by these assumed protectors of women. The wrongs were less in the men than in the laws which sustained them, and which contained nothing for the protection of the women.

But passing this view, let us look at the matter historically and on a broader field.

If Chinese women were allowed an equal share with men in shaping the laws of that great empire, would they subject their female children to torture with bandaged feet, through the whole period of childhood and growth, in order that they might be cripples for the residue of their lives?

If Hindu women could have shaped the laws of India, would widows for ages have been burned on the funeral pyres of their deceased husbands?

If Jewish women had had a voice in framing Jewish laws, would the husband, at his own pleasure, have been allowed to "write his wife a bill of divorcement and give it in her hand, and send her out of his house"?

Would women in Turkey or Persia have made it a heinous, if not capital, offense for a wife to be seen abroad with her face not covered by an impenetrable veil?

Would women in England, however learned, have been for ages subjected to execution for offenses for which men, who could read, were only subjected to burning in the hand and a few months' imprisonment?

The principle which governs in these cases, or which has done so hitherto, has been at all times and everywhere the same. Those who succeed in obtaining power, no matter by what means, will, with rare exceptions, use it for their exclusive benefit. Often, perhaps generally, this is done in the honest belief that such use is for the best good of all who are affected by it. A wrong, however, to those upon whom it is inflicted, is none the less a wrong by reason of the good motives of the party by whom it is inflicted.

The condition of subjection in which women have been held is the result of this principle; the result of superior strength, not of superior rights. Superior strength, combined with ignorance and selfishness, but not with malice. It is a relic of the barbarism in the shadow of which nations have grown up. Precisely as nations have receded from barbarism, the severity of that subjection has been relaxed. So long as merely physical power governed in the affairs of the world, the wrongs done to women were without the possibility of redress or relief; but since nations have come to be governed by laws, there is room to hope, though the process may still be a slow one, that injustice in all its forms, or at least political injustice, may be extinguished.

No injustice can be greater than to deny to any class of citizens not guilty of crime, all share in the political power of a state, that is, all share in the choice of rulers, and in the making and administration of the laws. Persons to which such share is denied, are essentially slaves, because they hold their rights, if they can be said to have any, subject to the will of those who hold the political power. For this reason it has been found necessary to give the ballot to the emancipated slaves. Until this was done their emancipation was far from complete. Without a share in the political powers of the state, no class of citizens has any security for its rights, and the history of nations to which I briefly alluded, shows that women constitute no exception to the universality of this rule.

Great errors, I think, exist in the minds of both the advocates and the opponents of this measure in their anticipation of the immediate effects to be produced by its adoption. On the one hand it is supposed by some that the character of women would be radically changed—that they would be unsexed, as it were, by clothing them with political rights, and that instead of modest, amiable, and graceful beings, we should have bold, noisy, and disgusting political demagogues, or something worse, if anything worse can be imagined. I think those who entertain such opinions are in error. The innate character of women is the result of God's laws, not of man's, nor can the laws of man affect that character beyond a very slight degree. Whatever rights may be given to them, and whatever duties may be charged upon them by human laws, their general character will remain unchanged. Their modesty, their delicacy, and their intuitive sense of propriety, will never desert them, into whatever new positions their added rights or duties may carry them.

A person deprived of political rights is essentially a slave, because he holds his personal rights subject to the will of those who possess the political power. This principle constitutes the very cornerstone of our government—indeed, of all republican government. Upon that basis our separation from Great Britain was justified. "Taxation without representation is tyranny." This famous aphorism of James Otis, although sufficient for the occasion when it was put forth, expresses but a fragment of the principle, because government can be oppressive through means of many appliances besides that of taxation. The true principle is, that all government over persons deprived of any voice in such government, is tyranny. That is the principle of the Declaration of Independence.

We were slow in allowing its application to the African race, and have been still slower in allowing its application to women; but it has been done by the Fourteenth Amendment, rightly construed, by a definition of "citizenship," which includes women as well as men, and in the declaration that "the privileges and immunities of citizens shall not be abridged."

If there is any privilege of the citizen which is paramount to all others, it is the right of suffrage; and in a constitutional provision, designed to secure the most valuable rights of the citizen, the declaration that the privileges and immunities of the citizen shall not be abridged, must, as I conceive, be held to secure that right before all others.

It is obvious, when the entire language of the section is examined, not only that this declaration was designed to secure to the citizen this political right, but that such was its principal, if not its sole object, those provisions of the section which follow it being devoted to securing the personal rights of "life, liberty, property, and the equal protection of the laws."

The clause on which we rely, to wit: "No state shall make or enforce any law which shall abridge the privileges or immunities of citizens of the United States," might be stricken out of the section, and the residue would secure to the citizen every right which is now secured, excepting the political rights of voting and holding office. If the clause in question does not secure those political rights, it is entirely nugatory, and might as well have been omitted.

It has been said, with how much or how little truth I do not know, that the subject of securing to women the elective franchise was not considered in the preparation, or in the adoption of these amendments. It is wholly immaterial whether that was so or not. It is never possible to arrive at the intention of the people in adopting constitutions, except by referring to the language used.

It is not a new thing for constitutional and legislative acts to have an effect beyond the anticipation of those who framed them. It is undoubtedly true, that in exacting the Magna Charta from King John, the barons of England provided better securities for the rights of the common people than they were aware of at the time, although the rights of the common people were neither forgotten nor neglected by them. It has also been said, perhaps with some truth, that the framers of the original Constitution of the United States built better than they knew; and it is quite possible that in framing the amendments under consideration, those engaged in doing it have accomplished a much greater work than they were at the time aware of. I am quite sure that it will be fortunate for the country, if this great question of female suffrage, than which few greater were ever presented for the consideration of any people, shall be found, almost unexpectedly, to have been put at rest.

Although not directly connected with the arguments as to the right secured to women by the Constitution, I deem it now proper to allude briefly to some of the popular objections against the propriety of allowing females the privilege of voting. I do this because I know from past experience that these popular objections, having no logical bearing upon the subject, are yet, practically, among the most potent arguments against the interpretation of the Fourteenth Amendment, which I consider the only one that its language fairly admits of.

It is said that women do not desire to vote. Certainly many women do not, but that furnishes no reason for denying the right to those who do desire to vote. Many men decline to vote. Is that a reason for denying the right to those who would vote?

Another objection is, that the right to hold office must attend the right to vote, and that women are not qualified to discharge the duties of responsible offices. I beg leave to answer this objection by asking one or more questions. How many of the male bipeds who do our voting are qualified to hold high offices? How many of the large class to whom the right of voting is supposed to have been secured by the Fifteenth Amendment, are qualified to hold office? Whenever the qualifications of persons to discharge the duties of responsible offices is made the test of their right to vote, and we are to have a competitive examination on that subject, open to all claimants, my client will be content to enter the lists, and take her chances among the candidates for such honors.

Another objection is that engaging in political controversies is not consistent with the feminine character. Upon that subject, women themselves are the best judges, and if political duties should be found inconsistent with female delicacy, we may rest assured that women will either effect a change in the character of political contests, or decline to engage in them. This subject may be safely left to their sense of delicacy and propriety.

I humbly submit to Your Honor, therefore, that on the constitutional grounds to which I have referred, Miss Anthony had a lawful right to vote; that her vote was properly received and counted; that the first section of the Fourteenth Amendment secured to her that right, and did not need the aid of any further legislation.

But conceding that I may be in error in supposing that Miss Anthony had a right to vote, she has been guilty of no crime, if she voted in good faith believing that she had such a right. This proposition appears to me so obvious, that were it not for the severity of the consequences which may follow a conviction, I should not deem it necessary to discuss it.

To make out the offense, it is incumbent on the prosecution to show affirmatively, not only that the defendant knowingly voted, but that she voted knowing that she had no right to vote. That is, the term "know-ingly," applies not to the fact of voting, but to the fact of want of right.

We cannot conceive of a case where a party could vote without knowledge of the fact of voting, and to apply the term *knowingly* to the mere act of voting, would make nonsense of the statute. This word was inserted as defining the essence of the offense, and it lim-its the criminality to cases where the voting is not only without right, but where it is done willfully, with a knowledge that is without right. Short of that there is no offense within the statute. This would be so upon well-established principles, even if the word *knowingly* had been omitted, but that word was inserted to prevent the possi-bility of doubt on the subject, and to furnish security against the inability of stupid or prejudiced judges or jurors to distinguish between willful wrong and innocent mistake.

If the statute had been merely, that "if any election for representa-tive in Congress any person shall vote without having a lawful right to vote, such person shall be deemed guilty of a crime," there could have been justly no conviction under it, without proof that the party voted knowing that he had not a right to vote. If he voted innocently supposing he had the right to vote, but had not, it would not be an offense within the statute. An innocent mistake is not a crime, and no amount of judicial decisions can make it such.

I concede, that if Miss Anthony voted, knowing that as a woman she had no right to vote, she may properly be convicted, and that if she had dressed herself in men's apparel, and assumed a man's name, or resorted to any other artifice to deceive the board of inspectors, the jury might properly regard her claim of right, to be merely col-orable, and might, in their judgment, pronounce her guilty of the offense charged, in case the constitution has not secured to her the right she claimed. All I claim is, that if she voted in perfect good faith, believing that it was her right, she has committed no crime. An innocent mistake, whether of law or fact, though a wrongful act may be done in pursuance of it, cannot constitute a crime. The con-demnation of Miss Anthony, her good faith being conceded, would do not less violence to any fair administration of justice.

One other matter will close what I have to say. Miss Anthony believed, and was advised that she had a right to vote. She may also have been advised, as was clearly the fact, that the question as to her right could not be brought before the courts for trial, without her voting or offering to vote, and if either was criminal, the one was as much so as the other. Therefore she stands now arraigned as a criminal, for taking the only steps by which it was possible to bring the great constitutional question as to her right, before the tribunals of the country for adjudication. If for thus acting, in the most perfect good faith, with motives as pure and impulses as noble as any which can find place in Your Honor's breast in the administration of justice, she is by the laws of her country to be condemned as a criminal, she must abide the consequences. Her condemnation, however, under such circumstances, would only add another most weighty reason to those which I have already advanced, to show that women need the aid of the ballot for their protection.

Upon the remaining question, of the good faith of the defendant, it is not necessary for me to speak. That she acted in the most perfect good faith stands conceded.

Thanking Your Honor for the great patience with which you have listened to my too extended remarks, I submit the legal questions which the case involves for Your Honor's consideration.

Selden had covered all the bases from Blackstone to Locke to Lincoln and answered all the criticism—even the most absurd ("their inferior physical power . . . and their inferior mental power . . . gives additional weight to the argument in their behalf . . . for the protection of the weak against the power of the strong"); women's interests are better protected through indirect representation by men ("men . . . are the natural and appropriate representatives of women"); the vote would radically change women for the worse ("that instead of modest, amiable, and graceful beings, we should have bold, noisy, and disgusting political demagogues")—then turned back to the Declaration of Independence and the Constitution ("life, liberty, property, and the equal protection of the laws").

Selden was comprehensive and thorough. And once he had completed the portion of his argument that Anthony had an absolute right to vote and thereby broke no law, he turned to the claim that even if she was wrong in her belief, she was nonetheless not guilty if she in good faith believed she was right. This last argument was most likely designed to give the jurors—the all-male jurors—the option of acquitting Anthony without necessarily validating her claim of women's suffrage.

Unfortunately, Selden's attempt to raise and then deflect commonly held prejudices, and his efforts aimed at putting the defense's case on sound constitutional footing for the jurors' consideration, fell on deaf ears. Immediately on the heels of the prosecution's two-hour closing argument, Judge Hunt unfolded the paper containing a decision he had obviously prepared in advance and read:

I have given this case such consideration as I have been able to, and, that there might be no misapprehension about my views, I have made a brief statement in writing.

The right of voting, or the privilege of voting, is a right or privilege arising under the constitution of the state, and not of the United States. The qualifications are different in the different states. Citizenship, age, sex, residence, are variously required in the different states, or may be so. If the right belongs to any particular person, it is because such person is entitled to it by the laws of the state where he offers to exercise it, and not because of citizenship of the United States. If the State of New York should provide that no person should vote until he had reached the age of thirty-one years, or after he had reached the age of fifty, or that no person having gray hair, or who had not the use of all his limbs, should be entitled to vote, I do not see how it could be held to be a violation of any right derived or held under the Constitution of the United States.

We might say that such regulations were unjust, tyrannical, unfit for the regulation of an intelligent state; but if rights of a citizen are thereby violated, they are of that fundamental class derived from his position as a citizen of the state, and not those limited rights belonging to him as a citizen of the United States.

The rights appertaining to this subject are those first under article one, paragraph two, of the United States Constitution, which provides that electors of representatives in Congress shall have the qualifications requisite for electors of the most numerous branch of the state legislature, and second, under the Fifteenth Amendment, which provides that the right of a citizen of the United States to vote shall not be denied or abridged by the United States, or by any state, on account of race, color, or previous condition of servitude.

If the legislature of the State of New York should require a higher qualification in a voter for a representative in Congress than is required for a voter for a member of the Assembly, this would, I conceive, be a violation of a right belonging to one as a citizen of the United States. That right is in relation to a federal subject or interest, and is guaranteed by the federal Constitution. The inability of a state to abridge the right of voting on account of race, color, or previous condition of servitude, arises from a federal guaranty. Its violation would be the denial of a federal right—that is a right belonging to the claimant as a citizen of the United States.

This right, however, exists by virtue of the Fifteenth Amendment. If the Fifteenth Amendment had contained the word *sex,* the argument of the defendant would have been potent. She would have said, an attempt by a state to deny the right to vote because one is of a particular sex, is expressly prohibited by that amendment. The amendment, however, does not contain that word. It is limited to race, color, or previous condition of servitude.

The Fourteenth Amendment gives no right to a woman to vote, and the voting by Miss Anthony was in violation of the law.

If she believed she had a right to vote, and voted in reliance upon that belief, does that relieve her from the penalty? It is argued that the knowledge referred to in the act relates to the knowledge of the illegality of the act, and not to the act of voting; for it is said that she must know that she voted. Two principles apply here: first, ignorance of the law excuses no one; second, every person is presumed to understand and to intend the necessary effects of his own acts.

Miss Anthony knew that she was a woman, and that the constitution of this state prohibits her from voting. She intended to violate that provision—intended to test it, perhaps, but certainly intended to violate it. The necessary effect of her act was to violate it, and this she is presumed to have intended. There was no ignorance of any fact, but all the facts being known, she undertook to settle a principle in her own person. She takes the risk, and she cannot escape the consequences.

No system of criminal jurisprudence can be sustained upon any other principle. Assuming that Miss Anthony believed she had a right to vote, that fact constitutes no defense if in truth she had not the right. She voluntarily gave a vote which was illegal, and thus is subject to penalty of the law.

Upon this evidence I suppose there is no question for the jury and that the jury should be directed to find a verdict of guilty.

And with that, Judge Hunt directed the clerk to enter up a verdict of guilty. Selden objected, attempting to poll the jurors, but Judge Hunt foreclosed any discussion, stating, "Take the verdict, Mr. Clerk." The clerk then said, "Gentlemen of the jury, hearken to your verdict, as the Court has recorded it. You say you find the defendant guilty of the offense whereof she stands indicted, and so say you all."

To this the jury made no response, and the jurors were immediately dismissed. One journalist covering the trial reported that one juror immediately upon being dismissed spoke up and told Judge Hunt that the verdict was not his, nor that of the rest, and that if he could have spoken, he would have answered, "Not guilty." The position of many in support of women's suffrage was also clear in words of another journalist: "She has voted and the American Constitution has survived the shock. Fining her one hundred dollars does not rule out the fact that . . . women voted, and went home, and the world jogged on as before."

Judge Hunt's position, however, was also clear: the purpose of juries in the American legal system is to weigh the admissible evidence and serve as determiners of the facts. Judge Hunt, by his ruling, found no facts in dispute and, therefore, determined it appropriate to dispense with the jury. And to that extent he was correct. With no factual issues in dispute and with only questions of law remaining, it was within his discretion to pull the case from the jurors and resolve any questions of law himself.

It can be argued, however, that a fact *was* in dispute. If Anthony truly believed she had a legal right to vote, then she had no intent to break the law—specifically no intent to vote illegally—and so a fact was in dispute.

Nonetheless, the only true issue was the constitutional issue, and Judge Hunt was not going to leave that to the jurors, who could have ignored the law and found for the defendant based on the reasoning set forth in Selden's brilliant argument. Indeed, Selden's argument was designed to elicit that response; Selden and his client were seeking jury nullification of the judge's instructions on the law.

The defense strategy may well have worked. Newspapers polled some of the jury members, who responded that they would have found Anthony not guilty, thus confirming the earlier report of the vocal juror.

All that remained was for Judge Hunt to sentence the defendant. But Susan B. Anthony, hardly in awe of the jurist or the court, gave little deference to his authority, and in her exchange with Judge Hunt she seized the opportunity to express her views, an opportunity she had been denied at trial.

JUDGE HUNT: (Ordering the defendant to stand up) Has the prisoner anything to say why sentence shall not be pronounced?

ANTHONY: Yes, Your Honor, I have many things to say; for in your ordered verdict of guilty, you have trampled underfoot every vital principle of our government. My natural rights, my civil rights, my political rights, my judicial rights, are all alike ignored. Robbed of the fundamental privilege of citizenship, I am degraded from the status of a citizen to that of a subject; and not only myself individually, but all of my sex are, by Your Honor's verdict, doomed to political subjection under this, so-called, form of government.

JUDGE HUNT: The Court cannot listen to a rehearsal of arguments the prisoner's counsel has already consumed three hours in presenting.

ANTHONY: May it please Your Honor, I am not arguing the question, but simply stating the reasons why sentence cannot, in justice, be pronounced against me. Your denial of my citizen's right to vote is the denial of my right of concert as one of the governed, the denial of my right of representation as one of the taxed, the denial of my right to a trial by a jury of my peers as an offender against law, therefore, the denial of my sacred rights to life, liberty, property, and—

JUDGE HUNT: The Court cannot allow the prisoner to go on.

ANTHONY: But Your Honor will not deny me this one and only poor privilege of protest against this high-handed outrage upon my citizen's rights. May it please the Court to remember that since the day of my arrest last November, this is the first time that either myself or any person of my disfranchised class has been allowed a word of defense before judge or jury—

JUDGE HUNT: The prisoner must sit down—the Court cannot allow it.

ANTHONY: All of my prosecutors, from the eighth ward corner grocery politician, who entered the complaint, to the United States marshal, commissioner, district attorney, district judge, Your Honor on the bench, not one is my peer, but each and all are my political sovereigns; and had Your Honor submitted my case to the jury, as was clearly your duty, even then I should have had just cause of protest, for not one of those men was my peer; but, native or foreign born, white or black, rich or poor, educated or ignorant, awake or asleep, sober or drunk, each and every man of them was my political superior; hence, in no sense, my peer. Even, under such circumstances, a commoner of England, tried before a jury of lords, would have far less cause to complain than should I, a woman, tried before a jury of men. Even my counsel, the Honorable Henry R. Selden, who has argued my cause so ably, so earnestly, so unanswerably, before Your Honor, is my political sovereign. Precisely as no disfranchised person is entitled to sit upon a jury, and no woman is entitled to the franchise, so, none but a regularly admitted lawyer is allowed to practice in the courts, and no woman can gain admission to the bar—hence, jury, judge, counsel, must all be of the superior class.

JUDGE HUNT: The Court must insist—the prisoner has been tried according to the established form of law.

ANTHONY: Yes, Your Honor, but by forms of law all made by men, interpreted by men, administered by men, in favor of men, and against women; and hence, Your Honor's ordered verdict of guilty, against a United States citizen for the exercise of "that citizen's right to vote," simply because that citizen was a woman and not a man. But, yesterday, the same man-made forms of law declared it a crime punishable with a thousand-dollar fine and six months' imprisonment, for you, or me, or any of us, to give a cup of cold water, a crust of bread, or a night's shelter to a panting fugitive as he was tracking his way to Canada. And every man or woman in whose veins coursed a drop of human sympathy violated that wicked law, reckless of consequences, and was justified in so doing. As then, the slaves who got their freedom must take it over, or under, or through the unjust forms of law, precisely so, now, must women, to get their right to a voice in this government, take it; and I have taken mine, and mean to take it at every possible opportunity.

JUDGE HUNT: The Court orders the prisoner to sit down. It will not allow another word.

ANTHONY: When I was brought before Your Honor for trial, I hoped for a broad and liberal interpretation of the Constitution and its recent amendments, that should declare all United States citizens under its protecting ægis—that should declare equality of rights the national guarantee to all persons born or naturalized in the United States. But failing to get this justice—failing, even, to get a trial by a jury not of my peers—I ask not leniency at your hands—but rather the full rigors of the law.

JUDGE HUNT: The Court must insist— (Anthony sat down.) The prisoner will stand up. (Anthony stood.) The sentence of the Court is that you pay a fine of one hundred dollars and the costs of the prosecution.

ANTHONY: May it please Your Honor, I shall never pay a dollar of your unjust penalty. All the stock in trade I possess is a ten-thousand-dollar debt, incurred by publishing my paper—*The Revolution*—four years ago, the sole object of which was to educate all women to do precisely as I have done, rebel against your man-made, unjust, unconstitutional forms of law, that tax, fine, imprison, and hang women, while they deny them the right of representation in the government; and I shall work on with might and main to pay every dollar of that honest debt, but not a penny shall go to this unjust claim. And I shall earnestly and persistently continue to urge all women to the practical recognition of the old revolutionary maxim that "resistance to tyranny is obedience to God."

JUDGE HUNT: Madam, the Court will not order you committed until the fine is paid.

Again the judge found himself in a dilemma: he had ordered a fine; Anthony refused to pay it. Ordinarily, a defendant—convicted of a crime and defying the judge—would have been thrown in jail for contempt of court. However, if Hunt ordered her imprisoned, she would again be eligible for appeal on a habeas corpus petition to the U.S. Supreme Court. Keenly aware of this risk, Hunt ordered that Anthony pay a symbolic fine, one the courts were powerless to enforce.

In a sense, the trial of Susan B. Anthony was a reflection of how women were treated throughout contemporary American society. She would not be tried by a representative jury of her peers because women were excluded from jury service. Judge Hunt would not allow Anthony to testify in her own defense, ruling that, as a woman, she was not competent to act as her own witness. Despite the vehement objection of her attorney, this articulate woman was precluded from taking the witness stand and explaining her actions to the jurors. It is unclear whether this was the rule or the custom in federal court. It seems as though women were simply prohibited from testifying in a federal trial, but this is contradicted by the fact that Anthony later testified at the trial of the three registrars. Furthermore, why did Selden try to have her testify if in fact he knew that rules of court precluded it?

Anthony kept her promise and remained in Canandaigua for the trial of the three election inspectors, all of whom were convicted and fined $25, one without even appearing in court. They were imprisoned on February 26, 1874, when they—like Anthony—refused to pay the fines. Anthony appealed to Senator Sargent for a pardon for the men; President Grant granted the request. The senator next tried to get the Senate to pay her fine, a request swiftly denied by the unsympathetic legislators.

Susan B. Anthony had gambled and lost in the courtroom. But her eight-month legal battle would eventually enjoy greater success in the court of public opinion. Anthony and her views were now known by virtually every American with any interest in current affairs. Portrayed in the press as both a fearless martyr and a defiant criminal, Susan B. Anthony would forevermore represent the face of the suffragette movement.

The Aftermath

Anthony's troubles did not end with her trial; her personal life was a mess. Guelma, her oldest sister, died after a prolonged struggle with tuberculosis. The legal proceedings prevented Anthony from remaining on the lecture circuit, and looking after her sister as she lay dying kept her at home. Bills began to accumulate, both for Anthony and *Revolution,* leaving creditors with little choice but to file suit. Desperate to avoid financial collapse, she borrowed money and settled with most of her creditors.

The issue of women's suffrage finally made its way to the U.S. Supreme Court, litigated not by Anthony but by another woman, Virginia Minor, who tried to vote in the presidential election of October 1872. The registrar of voters had turned her away from the polling place because she was a woman. Her husband, Francis Minor, filed suit in the state court of Missouri, alleging that the registrar deprived his wife of her legal right to vote. The Missouri court granted a motion to dismiss by the defendant, affirmed by the Missouri Supreme Court, relying upon the U.S. Supreme Court's opinion in *Bradwell v. Illinois* as binding authority. Undaunted by their loss in the Missouri courts, the Minors petitioned the U.S. Supreme Court to hear their case, and the justices granted their petition.

The State of Missouri's attorneys were so confident that the *Bradwell* case would control the Supreme Court's decision, they did not even file an opposing legal brief.

The Minors' argument relied upon the Fourteenth Amendment and the same reasoning Selden used on Anthony's behalf. The Supreme Court, however, disagreed, holding that the Fourteenth Amendment did not bestow any new rights upon the citizens. Furthermore, voting rights were properly controlled by the state legislatures, which had the power to limit suffrage as they saw fit. The last three paragraphs of the opinion, however, hinted at the court's awareness of the argument favoring women's suffrage. Nonetheless, their holding exemplified what was a common view of constitutional law in the nineteenth century: the Supreme Court could not simply consider an argument of public policy if it was unfounded in law:

> Our province is to decide what the law is, not to declare what it should be. . . . If the law is wrong, it ought to be changed; but the power for that is not with us. The arguments addressed to us bearing upon such a view of the subject may perhaps be sufficient to induce those having the power, to make the alteration but they ought not to

be permitted to influence our judgment in determining the present rights of the parties now litigating before us. No argument as to woman's need of suffrage can be considered. It is not for us to look at the hardship of withholding. Our duty is at an end if we find it is within the power of a state to withhold.

It was now evident that that Supreme Court would not extend the vote to women, leaving the suffrage supporters only one remedy—a constitutional amendment.

Momentum was building. That same year, the Women's Christian Temperance Union was founded and allied itself with suffrage groups. The states were confronting the issue; Michigan had a women's suffrage law on the ballot, similar to the failed Kansas legislation. The measure was defeated by fifteen thousand votes but represented the strongest public showing thus far—forty thousand votes, almost 40 percent of men, were in favor of women's suffrage. Anthony's campaign was slowly winning the war, and she characterized the Michigan defeat as "a grand triumph, not a failure."

Finally, in 1878, six years after Anthony and Minor tried to vote, Congress introduced a constitutional amendment enfranchising women: "The right of citizens of the United States to vote shall not be denied or abridged by the United States or by any State on account of sex." But the road to ratification was neither smooth nor short; the proposed amendment stalled for decades.

The Western states leaned toward ratification, while the South fought against approval. In July of 1890, Wyoming was admitted to the Union and became the first state with a constitution guaranteeing women's voting rights. Utah and Colorado soon followed, and women's suffrage failed by a slim margin in California. That same year, two major suffrage groups, the National Woman Suffrage Association and the American Woman Suffrage Association, put aside their disagreements and joined forces as the National American Woman Suffrage Association (NAWSA).

By 1900, Susan B. Anthony, now the icon of the women's movement, was an old woman. Despite her age and failing health, she traveled each year to Washington, D.C., for NAWSA's annual meeting. She made her last yearly trek to the capital in 1902, at the age of eighty-two.

At Elizabeth Cady Stanton's funeral that year, a photograph of Anthony rested on the casket. Discussing her dear friend's death, Anthony said, "The voice is hushed that I have longed to hear for fifty years."

Anthony's final public appearance was in Washington, D.C., on February 15, 1906. Her fiery demeanor dimmed by the toll of the sixty-year struggle, she symbolically passed the torch to the next generation of suffragists, declaring they must persevere and succeed, because "failure is impossible!" Anthony wanted the women's cause—and not its leader—to be the focus of national attention. Knowing her death was imminent, she instructed mourners months before that "when it is a funeral, remember that there should be no tears. Pass on, and go on with the work." She died March 13 at her home in Rochester, New York, ten thousand people turning out to mourn the loss of their champion.

Six years later, ex-president Theodore Roosevelt's Bull Moose Party became the first national political party to support women's suffrage, but it wasn't until 1920—one hundred years after Anthony was born and forty-two years after its introduction—that the Nineteenth Amendment to the Constitution was ratified by the states. Women finally had the vote.

Susan B. Anthony's life, her unflagging determination, and her trial brought a woman's right to vote to the forefront of American political discourse, radically and permanently altering the rights and status of women in American society. Almost fifty years after her trial, fourteen years after her death, and some 130 years after the Constitution was ratified, the Nineteenth Amendment finally secured for women the right to vote.

CHAPTER FIVE

The Truth Shall Set You Free

The English Crown and Colonial Government
Try Muzzling Newspaper Publisher John Peter Zenger
and the Fledgling American Press

> . . . it is pretty clear that in New York, a man may make very free
> with his God, but he must take special care what he says of his gov-
> ernor.
>
> —*Andrew Hamilton, in his closing argument*
> *on behalf of John Peter Zenger*

Americans watched in awe as a dejected Richard Nixon waved good-bye, climbed aboard the presidential helicopter, and left behind the ruins of his presidency. Less than two years after his landslide victory in the election of 1972, Nixon was gone, a lifetime's work erased, a result of his arrogance, paranoia, and a bungled burglary at an office building in the Watergate complex.

Two journalists had set in motion a chain of events that had brought down the most powerful politician in the world. When *Washington Post* reporters Carl Bernstein and Bob Woodward began work on the story of the break-in and resulting cover-up, they did so without fear of arrest, even when it became clear the crime led back to the White House. They knew that the First Amendment protected them, gave them shelter from the wrath of an angry president.

But where did they get the right to criticize the government? Did the First Amendment spring forth fully formed from the minds of the founding fathers, or was there a story behind its declaration that a free press was an essential guarantor of liberty? Who first challenged a government's right to restrict speech and impose penalties for publishing one's opinion?

The answers are found in the first decades of the eighteenth century, forty years before the American Revolution, when a young immigrant printer named John Peter Zenger challenged a tyrannical English governor by printing articles criticizing his administration. The trial of John Peter Zenger validated—for the first time in the New World—the concepts of free speech and free press that formed the backbone of the American Bill of Rights.

Coming to America

In the early days of the eighteenth century, Europeans seeking escape from the rigid social and class structure of Europe looked west. North America, with its French and English colonies, promised great opportunity for those willing to chance the crossing and the risk of leaving behind the Old World for the New.

In 1710, the Zenger family left Germany with their daughter, Catharina, their younger son, Johannes, and their elder son, thirteen-year-old John Peter, bound for the British colonies. The journey from Europe was arduous; meager accommodations, scant provisions, and minimal medical care took their toll on the family. John Peter's father died during the voyage, making the teen the eldest male in the family and leaving his mother to care for her children, alone in a foreign land.

The Zengers arrived in the small but growing New York City. John Peter, who neither spoke nor understood English, was immediately apprenticed to New York's sole printer, William Bradford. Apprenticeships were the common method of learning a trade during the colonial era. Young men joined an established tradesman in a binding contractual relationship: the apprentice would live with his "master" as a member of the family, receiving training, food, clothing, and shelter, for which the apprentice would give his labor for a set time. Zenger was bound to remain with and obey Bradford for eight years.

Zenger satisfied the terms of his apprenticeship and, now twenty-one, moved to Maryland and established his own printing business. He met a young woman, married, and soon fathered a son. His domestic bliss was short-lived; his wife died, and Zenger, now twenty-five and a single parent, closed up shop and returned to Manhattan.

He entered into a partnership with his former employer and mentor, William Bradford, but within a year they went their separate ways. Zenger opened his own printing shop, and New York now had two printers.

Early New York Politics

The Manhattan of 1730 bore little resemblance to today's metropolis. Fifteen hundred homes dotted the area then known as New York City, and reports from the colony's lone newspaper, William Bradford's *New York Weekly Gazette,* claimed that quail could be found and shot just east of today's Broadway. Rising up to form the young city's skyline were the colonial fort, City Hall, the governor's house, and numerous churches. Only ten thousand people called New York home; seventeen hundred were slaves.

Rough-and-tumble New York politics were not born in the modern era; the political scene in John Peter Zenger's time was particularly tumultuous. Colonial New York was governed in part by a crown-appointed governor and his council of ministers, generally made up of the wealthiest, most influential men, and by an elected assembly. In the early 1700s, a political split developed between the council and the assembly.

Lewis Morris, appointed by the governor as chief manager for colonial matters, led one faction. Wealthy and politically influential in the colonies of New York and New Jersey, Morris also served as a judge and would later sit as chief justice of New York's Supreme Court. One grandson would sign the Declaration of Independence, another would help draft and sign the Constitution.

As chief manager for the governor, Morris waged an ongoing attack on another prominent New York political figure, Stephen DeLancey. DeLancey, a self-made merchant of French Huguenot origin, represented the growing—and wealthy—mercantile class, whose interests included trading with the French colony in Quebec. The French in turn traded with the Indians, which strengthened the French position and weakened the power of the governor.

The merchants' growing wealth and influence fueled a political struggle, with the DeLancey faction battling to wrest control of the colonial government from Morris and his allies. The power struggle sometimes included personal attacks and resulted in the splintering of New York's political culture. The two distinct groups would survive until the 1730s, and their rivalry finally played itself out on the legal stage with John Peter Zenger in the lead role.

In 1731, the crown-appointed governor died, and as was the custom, the senior member of the governor's council, Rip Van Dam, rose to assume the mantle of governor until King George II appointed a replacement. Shortly after Van Dam assumed the position of temporary governor, the king appointed William Cosby to become the new governor of the New York and New Jersey colonies.

An Abuse of Office

Cosby was a privileged Anglo-Irish aristocrat with powerful connections and previous service to the English king as governor of Minorca, a small Mediterranean island. His performance ought not to have inspired confidence in his abilities; Minorcan residents repeatedly complained of Cosby's incompetence, but their grievances fell on deaf ears in England.

However, Cosby soon exceeded the tolerance even of his well-placed friends when he seized the goods of a Spanish merchant, sold them at auction, kept the proceeds, and doctored the records to cover his tracks. England was pursuing cordial relations with Spain, and such an affront to a Spanish national was bound to have diplomatic repercussions. Cosby was removed from his post and recalled to England.

Cosby awaited another posting, undaunted by his firing, unconcerned that his greed had sparked a diplomatic incident. Despite his past failures, Cosby's connections won him the New York/New Jersey governorship. Once appointed, he did not immediately set sail; he stayed in England, tending to personal financial and political matters, and as a result, Rip Van Dam served as the colonial governor for seventeen months.

Cosby finally arrived in New York on August 1, 1732, and immediately began alienating influential members of the city's political, economic, and social circles. First, upon hearing that the assembly had voted him a £750 gift for helping defeat the sugar tax while in London (a feat for which Cosby deserved little, if any, credit), he complained to subordinates and his own council until the assembly raised the amount to £1,000. Next, Cosby engaged in a dispute with the Morris faction, setting the stage for the Zenger trial.

Cosby delivered a decree to Rip Van Dam, still the senior member of the council, ordering that he pay Cosby half of all salary and fees collected by the office of New York governor during the time between which Cosby was appointed in July of 1731 and the time that he actually arrived in the colony in August of 1732. Ample precedent existed for such a request, as traditionally the acting governor only retained one-half of the salary while sitting as governor. However, the time between Cosby's appointment and his arrival was unusually long and, it was noted, due to personal rather than governmental demands. Making matters worse, Cosby demanded the amount by an order—rather than requesting it in a more personal manner.

His dignity offended, Van Dam refused to pay, and Cosby sued the former acting governor, a much respected member of the colony's political and social scene. However, Cosby faced a number of problems in his suit: he could have sued in a common-law court, but he realized that any jury in such a forum would hold decidedly pro–Van Dam sentiments, given his status in the community and the fact that Cosby was an outsider. Alternatively, Cosby might have sued in the chancery, the court designed to resolve civil disputes. But in that court the governor sat as judge; thus Cosby would have been forced to preside over his own litigation, an inherent conflict of interest.

For these reasons, Cosby, without the consent or authority of the popularly elected assembly, executed an order giving the New York Supreme Court jurisdiction over the case and ordered Richard Bradley, the attorney general of New York, to bring the suit in the king's name.

No precedent existed for the colony's Supreme Court acting as a trial court in such a matter. When the case convened, the jurists included Chief Justice Lewis Morris (the same Lewis Morris who held considerable social and political clout); Justice James DeLancey, a relation of Morris's old political foe, Stephen DeLancey; and Justice Frederick Philipse, an ally of the old DeLancey faction and a wealthy merchant who made his money—in part—from the slave trade.

Van Dam's attorney, James Alexander, argued the Supreme Court lacked jurisdiction even to try the case. Alexander maintained that Cosby had manipulated the law, countermanded the authority of the popularly elected assembly, and thus usurped the power of the people of New York. Chief Justice Morris—who had an interest in the outcome, as he had acted as interim governor for New Jersey and might be asked to pay half of his salary to Cosby—ended the litigation when he issued an opinion that the Supreme Court had no jurisdiction, lacking the consent of the assembly.

Cosby, infuriated by Morris's ruling and his insubordination, penned a letter questioning his judgment, his integrity, and demanding a copy of the decision. Morris not only provided Governor Cosby with the requested copy, he also published it for the public to read. Cosby, enraged by Morris's act of public defiance, proclaimed the legal decision erroneous and outside the bounds of his office, then removed Morris from the bench, a position Morris had held for nearly eighteen years. Acting quickly, Cosby elevated James DeLancey to chief justice, promoted Philipse to second justice, and refused to appoint a third officer to fill the remaining seat.

In effect, Governor Cosby had attempted to rig his own trial, and when that failed, he downsized the court on his own authority. By leaving the DeLancey faction in control of the court, Cosby succeeded in revitalizing the political feud between the Morrises and the DeLanceys and their backers. The Morris faction was now the popular, antigovernor party, and the DeLancey interest became the governor's party.

Despite his removal from the court, Lewis Morris would not fade into political obscurity and in October 1733 stood for election as assemblyman. Morris faced a Cosby/DeLancey loyalist for the seat. As was customary, both candidates marched to the polling place with large groups of their supporters in tow. The Morris backers had an obvious numerical superiority, and the governor-appointed sheriff demanded that all in attendance swear a loyalty oath in support of the King, George II. Numerous Quakers, all of whom supported Morris, objected; their religious beliefs prohibited them from swearing oaths. Quakers had historically been allowed to affirm their loyalty, but on this occasion the sheriff insisted. When the Quakers refused, the sheriff denied their right to vote. Thus, Morris lost thirty-eight votes but still prevailed in the election by eighty votes.

That Cosby's sheriff had disenfranchised respected members of the community served to emphasize the arbitrary and capricious nature of the governor's administration. Morris and James Alexander were now intent on more than simple political opposition to Cosby's regime; their party decided to take their grievances directly to the people.

Publisher Zenger

Since there was but one newspaper in the colony, William Bradford's *New York Weekly Gazette,* and since that paper was sponsored, largely written, and censored directly by the Cosby administration, the opposition party needed an independent vehicle to wage its attacks on the governor.

Peter Zenger operated the only other printing press in New York; the popular party sought out Zenger and employed his services to publish a weekly opposition newspaper, to be called *The New York Weekly Journal.*

The stated purpose of *The New York Weekly Journal* was the recall of Governor Cosby and his replacement with a more qualified and suitable candidate. Cosby had given them ample cause. In thirteen months, the governor had sued a council member; circumvented established law and practice by expanding the jurisdiction of the Supreme Court for his own political and economic gain; removed a popular and long-serving justice of the New York Supreme Court; altered the colony's court system by reducing the number of justices on the Supreme Court (both of whom now supported the governor); and attempted to alter the outcome of an election.

James Alexander, Lewis Morris, and the rest of Cosby's opposition meant to arouse public sentiment against the governor, forcing London to remove him from office. Alexander wrote, "[We mean] to expose him and those ridiculous flatteries with which [his subordinates] loads our other newspaper."

On November 5, 1733, John Peter Zenger's *New York Weekly Journal* appeared on the streets of New York for the first time. It consisted of four pages and cost three shillings. Zenger's name appeared on the front of the paper as its printer, and his was the only name in the paper—not a pseudonym. Zenger likely wrote no articles and edited no text.

Alexander, an erudite writer and accomplished master of satire, wrote the majority of the articles and served as the editor in chief. Many other articles, editorials, columns, and advertisements were penned by Morris, his son, Lewis Morris, Jr., and friend and political ally Cadwallader Colden.

Zenger's contribution and dedication to the *Journal,* however, should not be discounted—his name appeared on a petition carried by Lewis Morris to England in an attempt to oust Governor Cosby. And while he had no formal schooling, Zenger knew the printing business. By the time he began publishing the *Journal,* he had more than twenty years in the trade and was no doubt fully aware of the laws of criminal defamation. Moreover, Zenger knew the material that he published was extremely inflammatory. To set the type, Zenger had to read every word printed in his paper. Even if his limited English diminished his ability to comprehend the exact meaning of many articles, it cannot be said that he did not understand that the *Journal* he published contained personal and political attacks on the governor's administration and that making such attacks, either in print or in speech, might lead to prosecution.

The New York Weekly Journal was the first known opposition newspaper in the American colonies. It represented independent ideas and the freedom to criticize without the permission of or censorship by governmental authorities. The *Journal* was independently funded, written, edited, and distributed, unique characteristics for early-eighteenth-century North American colonial society.

The *Journal* not only utilized the right to speak and print freely but promoted that right as well. In the second edition, an article spoke directly of the liberty of the press, espousing the virtue of free thought and the right to disseminate and receive news without interference. Through Zenger's paper, the popular party spoke for the right to print their paper and spoke against Governor Cosby's administration every Monday without restraint.

Articles often made direct reference to Cosby and his lackey Francis Harison. One of Harison's duties was to ensure the state-sponsored *Weekly Gazette* portrayed Governor Cosby in the most favorable light. In addition to editor and censor, Harison had held a number of other appointed positions since arriving in the colonies in 1710, including recorder, judge of the admiralty, and member of the governor's council. Harison's ability to cultivate relationships with important and influential political figures, resulting in his own financial gain, was a thing to behold. Harison had discovered—through one of his many offices—that fifty thousand acres on the colonial border were to be turned over from New Jersey to New York. He then urged friends in England to buy up the land—while at the same time using the now rising values created by the speculation that he had encouraged to secure notes to purchase much of the land for himself. Under Cosby's administration, Harison served up flattering articles about the governor without shame, while using his influence to amass a fortune, much to the general distaste of New Yorkers.

When the popular party founded the *Journal,* Harison found himself a constant target of Alexander's satirical wit. One article made reference to Harison as a "large spaniel some five feet five inches tall that strayed from his kennel, dropping fulsome panegericks [*sic*] at the *Gazette.*"

According to the *Journal,* "the spaniel, once a good Christian, has now taken to abusing mankind in a heathenish manner," and the colony would benefit greatly if someone would return him to his cage. Harison, for his part, was not a man of letters, and his columns written in reply were no match for the intellect of Alexander and Morris.

However, the primary focus of the *Journal* was the governor himself. Issue one began by recounting the governor's attempt to circumvent New York election law and the will of the people by manipulating the outcome. The election was reported as a triumph not only for Lewis Morris, but also for democratic ideals and fair play. Another early issue alluded to Cosby and his management of the colony:

> A supreme magistrate may be conceived to injure his subjects, if in his dealings with them, he treats them either not as subjects, or not as men. The duty of a supreme magistrate respects either the whole people or particular persons; and thus much he owes to the whole people, that he procures the good and safety of the community, according as laws direct and prescribe. Therefore he injures the whole people, if he evades or suffer these laws to be evaded to their hurt.

Another edition attacked Cosby for his refusal to ensure defendants received jury trials.

An article, likely written by Lewis Morris, attacked Governor Cosby, saying, "A Governor turns rogue, does a thousand things for which a small rogue would have deserved a halter; and because it is difficult if not impracticable to obtain relief against him, therefore it is prudent to keep in with him and join in the roguery. . . . A Governor does all he can to chain you, and it being difficult to prevent him, it is prudent in you (in order to preserve your liberty) to help him put them on and rivet them fast."

In September 1734, the *Journal* accused Cosby of voting as a member of the council, demanding bills from the assembly be presented to his office prior to their delivery to the council, and of adjourning the assembly in his own name rather than the name of the king. These acts led the Board of Trade, the governing body for colonial matters, to censure Cosby and warn him against future transgressions.

The *Journal*'s broadsides at Governor Cosby proved so popular with New Yorkers that by issue twelve Zenger added a Thursday edition. The unceasing attacks and the success of the *Journal* infuriated the governor. He harbored little doubt as to the identity of his tormentors. In letters to the London Board of Trade, Cosby wrote, "Cabals were form'd against the Government and a meeting of their factious men is still held several nights in a week at a private lodging [in] which I have discover'd Alexander always present and Morris."

In his letter of December 6, 1734, Cosby wrote that Morris, Van Dam, and Alexander treated his administration with disdain and that "a press supported by him [Alexander] and his party began to swarm with the most virulent libels." But Cosby was not satisfied with silencing James Alexander; he intended to quiet all opposition. If Cosby had arrested and charged Alexander, the others—Morris, Colden, and Van Dam—could have continued their attacks in the *Journal*. Alexander might even continue the campaign from his jail cell. But Zenger presented a safer target. With the printer in jail, Cosby's hope was that the printing press would grind to a halt.

To convict Alexander, Cosby would need direct evidence to tie him to the paper, to prove that he was actually behind the libels; Zenger presented less of a challenge—his name appeared on the paper. Zenger also made a more attractive target because of his social status. Whereas Alexander was a wealthy and well-known member of the colony, Zenger was merely an obscure German immigrant. Alexander would likely garner far more public support than the printer.

All that was needed to convict for seditious libel was to prove that the accused printed and published the libels. Zenger was Cosby's man, and the governor intended to make an example of him, bringing down the popular party and crushing opposition to his regime.

Because the paper was independent and neither relied upon government sanction nor bowed to an appointed censor, Alexander felt compelled to continually make the case for a free press, including articles on freedom of the press and speech. Side by side would be an article attacking the Cosby administration for abuses of power, and another justifying the author's right to print and speak of political officials in a public forum.

Alexander frequently printed the "Letter of Cato," a series of essays written in England by political philosophers Thomas Gordon and John Trenchard. They proposed that citizens must, for a government to function to their benefit, have the right to speak, print, and inquire about the government's actions. Cato's letters stated that only an informed electorate and citizenry could adequately choose officials and direct the government for the common good, and the only way to inform the citizens was to provide an open forum for the free flow of information and discussion.

The Governor Strikes Back

In 1735, theories of a free press would be put to the test. Cosby ordered Chief Justice James DeLancey to obtain an indictment against Zenger for seditious libel. Twice in late 1734, DeLancey appeared before a grand jury and read the charge, as well as selections from the *Journal* that he alleged met the common-law definition of seditious libel. One article read:

> Your appearance in print, at last, gives pleasure to many [referring to Cosby], though most wish you had come fairly into the open field, and not appeared behind retrenchments of the supposed laws against libeling and of what other men have said and done before: These retrenchments, gentlemen, may soon be shewn to you and all men, to be weak, and to have neither law nor reason for their foundation, so cannot long stand you in stead: Therefore, you had much better as yet leave them, and come to what the people of this city and province think on the points in question; they think, as matters now stand, that their liberties and properties are precarious, and that slavery is like to be installed upon them and their posterity, if some things are not amended; and this they collect from many past proceedings.

DeLancey also read from a second *Journal* article:

> One of our neighbors [from New Jersey] being in company, observing the strangers [of New York] full of complaints, endeavored to persuade them to remove to New Jersey; to which it was replied, they would be leaping out of the frying pan and into the fire: for says he, we both are under the same governor, and your Assem-

bly have shown with a witness what is to be expected from them; one who was then moving to Pennsylvania to which place it is reported several considerable men are removing, expressed in terms very moving, much concern for the circumstances of New York, seemed to think them very much owing to the influence that some men had in the administration, said that he was now going from them, and was not to be hurt by any measures they should take, but could not help some concern for the welfare of his countrymen, and should be glad to hear that the Assembly would exert themselves as became them, by showing that they have the interest of their country more at heart, than the gratification of any private view of their members, or being at all affected by the smiles or frowns of a governor, both which ought equally to be despised, when the interests of their country is at stake.

You, says he, complain of the lawyers, not I think the law itself is at an end. We see men's seeds destroyed, judges arbitrarily displaced, new courts erected, without the consent of the legislature, by which it seems to me, trials by jury are taken away when a governor pleases, men of known estates denied their votes, contrary to the received practice, the best expositor of any law: Who is there in that province, that call anything his own, or enjoy any liberty longer than those in the administration will condescend to let them do it, for which reason I have left it as I believe more will.

Despite the derogatory tone of the articles, the grand jury twice refused to indict anyone involved with the *Journal*. Cosby, unbowed by obvious public sentiment against him, next sent an order to the assembly requesting that the hangman burn the *Journal,* as it contained statements derogatory of the king's representatives. The assembly, after some debate on the matter, ordered the resolution tabled. When Cosby sent the order to the assembly a second time, the assembly simply ignored it altogether.

Governor Cosby next sent Francis Harison to convince the local magistrate that he should order the *Journal* burned. The magistrate quickly denied Harison's request, forbidding anyone within his authority from participating in the act. Cosby then brought the matter in front of his own council, where, in the presence of only nine of the twelve members, and with Councillors Van Dam and Alexander notably absent, finally obtained an order to burn the newspaper. Harison and the sheriff had to bring in a slave to burn the *Journal* in front of City Hall. No one turned out for the burning, other than the governor's men and the slave.

On November 2, 1734, the governor's council, this time with only eight members present, issued a warrant for the arrest of Zenger on the charge of printing and publishing seditious libels. After ignoring two grand juries, two occasions on which the assembly refused to take action, and the noticeable lack of popular opinion in favor of such a move, Cosby finally apprehended his man.

The sheriff arrested John Peter Zenger on November 2, 1734. At the bail hearing on November 23, Zenger was represented by James Alexander and William Smith. Chief Justice James DeLancey, the same judge promoted in the Van Dam case when Governor Cosby removed Lewis from the bench, presided. Zenger's counsel cited numerous authorities to support a reasonable bail amount, including the Magna Charta and the Habeas Corpus Act, which directed that bail be set according to the nature of the offense and the wealth of the prisoner.

Despite Zenger's status as a father and a citizen, as well as his own sworn testimony that his personal worth was less than £50, not including his printing equipment and the clothes on his back, bail was set at £400. Unable to produce this hefty amount, Zenger would spend the next nine months incarcerated. The governor clearly wanted to keep Zenger from his printing business and shut down the *Journal*. He succeeded in the former, but failed in the latter; the popular party continued to write, and with the help of Zenger's family, the paper missed only a single issue.

The grand jury was scheduled to sit only until January, at which point, unless charged, Zenger would have to be freed. However, on the last day of the term, with the grand jury unwilling to bring a formal indictment, the prosecutor circumvented the grand jury and brought formal charges by way of an information.

Seditious Libel

And so, in January 1735, John Peter Zenger sat in jail, facing charges of printing seditious libels against the king's government and officials. It is important to note that the kind of libel at issue in this case was a criminal offense, with incarceration a real possibility, unlike the modern libel cause of action, where the relief sought is monetary damages.

Criminal libel has traditionally fallen into four categories: blasphemous libel or defamation of religion; obscenity; private libel, which applies to private individuals; and seditious libel or defamation of the government.

Seditious libel has proven difficult to adequately define; its seemingly ambiguous nature allowed officials to tailor their own definitions to prosecute politically bothersome individuals. Zenger's jury would ultimately be instructed that seditious libel was "scandalizing the government by reflecting on public officials or offices or those entrusted with administration of public affairs, by publishing material tending to breed a dislike of their governors, or by alienating the affections of the people in any way."

While "truth is an absolute defense" to libel in the twenty-first century, at the time of Zenger's trial, the truth of the statements made the crime even worse. As contemporaneous scholars reasoned, people are more likely to believe the truth, and true statements are likely to breed a deeper and more sustained contempt, thus rendering more damage upon the victim. Since Zenger did, in fact, paint the material, his defense faced a difficult, if not impossible, battle given the law of seditious libel.

On April 15, 1735, the information against John Peter Zenger was brought before the court. The charge was that Zenger did "falsely, seditiously, and scandalously print and publish, a certain false, malicious, seditious scandalous libel, entitled *The New York Weekly Journal,* containing the freshest advices, foreign and domestic; in which libel (concerning his excellency the said Governor, and the Ministers and Officers of the King) among other things therein contained are these words . . ." The information went on to list the libelous words printed and published in *The New York Weekly Journal* in five separate editions.

The alleged libels contained in the indictment included claims that the people of New York feared for their liberties and properties at the hands of the governor; that they feared slavery at the hands of his administration; that certain citizens of New York considered moving to or had moved to Pennsylvania to escape the Cosby administration; and that the people of New York saw judges arbitrarily displaced, new courts erected without the consent or permission of the legislature, and men denied their right to vote. The information charged that these words, printed in *The New York Weekly Journal* by Zenger, disturbed the peace of the province, injured the governor and his ministers, and injured the king.

Zenger's counsel, Alexander and Smith, answered the allegations with their bill of exceptions. They challenged Governor Cosby's right to act without the consent of the legislature in maintaining the court in its current condition, and the court's right to exist and hear the case, as it was a direct result of Cosby's usurpation of power and authority. Alexander and Smith intended to turn the trial into a public condemnation of Cosby and his administration, as well to set forth the legal justification of their work in the *Journal.*

Chief Justice DeLancey asked Zenger's counselors if they appreciated the nature and consequences of the exceptions that they had brought. Both men answered that they did. William Smith went so far as to state he had such confidence in his right to object to the commission of a judge—if he believed that commission to be illegitimate—that he would wager his life upon that right. Alexander and Smith said they stood prepared to argue their exceptions to the information, if the court would hear those arguments. DeLancey recessed the proceedings until the next morning.

Alexander and Smith
Discharged and Disbarred

On the next day, April 16, 1735, Chief Justice DeLancey and Justice Philipse reconvened. Without allowing Alexander or Smith to speak, the chief justice ruled that the court would neither hear nor allow the exceptions, then added, "We must go from the bench or you from the [bar]." DeLancey then issued an order excluding Alexander and Smith from the current case and from practicing in front of the New York Supreme Court in the future. The clerk entered the order into the record and read the ruling publicly. And with a gavel blow, DeLancey disbarred James Alexander and William Smith.

It was a devastating blow to Zenger and his defense. These men—lawyers and intellectuals—had orchestrated the entire campaign against Cosby and were now relegated to the sidelines of a trial presided over by judges in the governor's pocket. Zenger, left with few options, asked for appointed counsel; DeLancey obliged by appointing John Chambers. Although by all accounts an able defense attorney, Chambers belonged to the governor's party.

On July 29, 1735, the lawyers began selecting a jury. This generally consisted of the court pulling forty-eight names from the freeholders' book; about a thousand landowners in New York at the time were "fit" for jury duty, all male and all white. Each side would then strike one name from the list, alternating turns, until twelve names remained: these names composed the jury. At least three of the men chosen were known supporters of the Morris-Alexander faction, and the Dutch ancestry of some others meant that the jury might at the very least be sympathetic to Zenger's plight and perhaps even downright hostile to Cosby, the English governor.

Andrew Hamilton Steps Forward

Attorney General Bradley opened the prosecution's case by reading the indictment and telling the jury that the charges would be proven against Zenger. In the defense opening statement, John Chambers maintained that great latitude should be given to individuals in their speech and writings, and that the prosecution would fail in their attempt to prove the necessary elements of libel.

As Chambers was speaking, a man rose from the gallery and stepped forward, interrupting him, and addressed the court. He said his name was Andrew Hamilton and he had come from Philadelphia to represent Zenger. Andrew Hamilton was widely regarded as the finest trial lawyer in the North American colonies and had been urged by Alexander and Morris to come to Zenger's defense. Whether his dramatic entry into the case was planned or a matter of circumstance attributable to the uncertain nature of travel in 1735 America is lost to history.

Hamilton was born in Scotland and educated at St. Andrews University. He began his postgraduate study at the University of Glasgow, where he became embroiled in political intrigues. Hamilton secretly changed his name to Trent and booked passage to Virginia, where he began studying law. By the time he began practicing law, he felt safe enough to cast aside his alias and reclaim his birth name.

In 1712, the Penn family, perhaps the best-known name in the colonies, retained the services of Andrew Hamilton to represent them in a land dispute over title to Delaware. That a family as prestigious as the Penns would employ his services to settle a dispute over a vast tract of land when the adverse party was the king of England, speaks volumes of Hamilton's ability and notoriety as an attorney. A letter sent by James Logan to William Penn reported, "Codd [the attorney for King James II's interest] was baffled at ye Court by the Dexterity of our Lawyer's [Hamilton's] Management." Hamilton litigated numerous cases in Maryland, Delaware, and Pennsylvania in the next decade, firmly establishing himself as the premier trial lawyer in the colonies. In 1713, Hamilton traveled to London on business and was admitted to practice at Gray's Inn, the most popular and best respected of the Inns of Court. Upon his return from London, now as a British barrister and personal adviser to the Penn family, the Baltimores employed Hamilton "for the purpose of codifying and reorganizing the colony's judiciary laws."

Hamilton's practice eventually led him to take up residence in Philadelphia, where he soon became the attorney general of Pennsylvania. Hamilton later resigned his position to travel once more to London, where, over two years, he met and became friendly with Benjamin Franklin. Franklin, in his autobiography, said, "Among my friends in the House I must not forget Mr. Hamilton, before mentioned. . . . He interested himself for me, strongly in that instance, as he did in many others afterwards, continuing his patronage until his death."

Hamilton had heard about Zenger's plight soon after Alexander and Smith were disbarred and agreed, on short notice, to travel to New York and take the case. Hamilton was long a student of politics and took this opportunity to defend not just a man, but also a principle of law and of politics. Moreover, he enjoyed the opportunity to try a case that would profoundly affect the state of the law and the power structure of New York. Perhaps he sensed that this would be his finest moment.

Due largely to the shortness of time and to Alexander's expertise in the matter, Hamilton used Alexander's brief and defense strategy throughout the trial. Thus, many accolades for any brilliance in the arguments themselves should go to Alexander, while one should give credit to Hamilton for the oratory and lawyering skills employed in the courtroom.

Early Scrimmage: Is Truth a Defense?

Hamilton deftly took the reins from defense counsel Chambers and began Zenger's defense in a most surprising fashion, by admitting that John Peter Zenger had in fact printed and published the material in question:

> May it please Your Honor; I am concerned in this cause on the part of Mr. Zenger the defendant. The information against my client was sent me, a few days before I left home, with some instructions to let me know how far I might rely upon the truth of those parts of the papers set forth in the information, and which are said to be libelous. And though I am perfectly of the opinion with the gentleman [Chambers] who has just now spoke, on the same side with me, as to the common course of proceedings, I mean in putting Mr. Attorney [Bradley] upon proving, that my client printed and published those papers mentioned in the information; yet I cannot think it proper for me—without doing violence to my own principles—to deny the publication of a complaint, which I think is the right of every freeborn subject to make, when the matters so published can be supported with truth; and therefore I'll save Mr. Attorney the trouble of examining his witnesses to that point; and I do, for my client, confess, that he both printed and published the two news papers set forth in the information, and I hope in so doing he has committed no crime.

This was an extremely risky gambit since the law did not recognize truth as a defense. Hamilton and shadow defense counsel Alexander and Morris knew that their only chance of success lay in admitting the publication but arguing that because it was truthful it *should not* be criminal. As a result of the defense's concession about publication, Zenger's trial was quite unusual. Neither side called any witnesses.

As Hamilton had envisioned, the entire trial consisted of oral arguments in front of Justice DeLancey and more importantly the jury. With this strategy, Hamilton severely disrupted Attorney General Bradley's plan. Bradley had intended the proof of printing and publication as his primary case against Zenger. Once Hamilton admitted that Zenger did indeed print the *Journal,* Bradley felt that the case was all but won. He dismissed his witnesses and moved for the jury to return a special verdict. That is, Bradley wanted the jury to determine only the matter of printing and publication, which Hamilton now admitted, and leave the question of whether the words printed were libelous to the court as a matter of law. If Bradley could get the jury to make such a finding, the case would be lost for Zenger; he was sure that DeLancey, sitting as chief justice, would return a verdict favorable to the governor.

Hamilton, however, was a formidable foe and not about to concede—even though the law of libel was completely opposed to his position:

I hope it is not our bare printing and publishing a paper, that will make it a libel: you will have something more to do, before you make my client a libeler; for the words themselves must be libelous, that is, false, scandalous, and seditious or else we are not guilty.

Hamilton—defying all precedent—was attempting to shift the lines of battle, from the content of the words to the question of their truth. Bradley responded with overwhelming legal authority intended to show that by writing or speaking ill of the government or of governmental officials, the libeler brought scandal upon that government, a sacred thing among men, and broke both the established laws of man and God. The words, he reminded the jury, speak for themselves. Hamilton, prepared for precisely this type of argument, responded:

May it please Your Honor; I agree with Mr. Attorney Bradley that government is a sacred thing, but I differ very widely from him when he would insinuate that the just complaints of a number of men, who suffer under a bad administration, is libeling that administration. Had I believed that to be law, I should not have given the court the trouble of hearing anything that I could say in this cause. As it is become my duty to be both plain and particular in this cause, I beg leave to bespeak the patience of the court.

I was in hopes, as that terrible court, the English Star Chamber, where those dreadful judgments were given, and that law established, which Mr. Attorney has produced for authorities to support this cause, was long ago laid aside, as the most dangerous court to the liberties of the people of England that ever was known in that kingdom; that Mr. Attorney knowing this, would not have attempted to set up a Star Chamber here, nor to make their judgments a precedent to us: for it is well-known that what would have been judg'd treason in those days for a man to speak, I think, has since not only been practiced as lawful, but the contrary doctrine has been held to be law.

Hamilton linked the precedents supporting the state's position to the reviled Star Chamber, a court utilized by English monarchs for political trials. The Star Chamber tried cases without a jury and often employed torture to elicit confessions from defendants. Although it was abolished in 1641, its precedents were binding law at the time of the Zenger trial.

Hamilton made frequent reference to the Star Chamber as he argued for a fundamental change in the law of libel, namely the defense of truth and the right of the jury to render a general verdict on the entire information, rather than observing a limitation to the matters of publication.

Hamilton and Bradley debated the merits of truth as defense to libel, in the presence of a jury growing ever more sympathetic to Zenger's position.

MR. HAMILTON: For though I freely acknowledge that there are such things as libels, yet I must insist at the same time that what my client is charged with is not a libel; and I observed just now, that Mr. Attorney in defining a libel, made use of the words "scandalous, seditious, and tend to disquiet the people"; but whether with design or not I will not say, he omitted the word *false.*

MR. BRADLEY: I think I did not omit the word *false:* but it has been said already that it may be a libel, notwithstanding it may be true.

MR. HAMILTON: In this I must still differ with Mr. Attorney; for I depend upon it, we are to be tried upon this information now before the court and jury, and to which we have pleaded not guilty, and by it we are charged with printing and publishing a certain false, malicious, seditious, and scandalous libel. This word *false* must have some meaning, or else how came it there? I hope Mr. Attorney will not say, he put it there by chance, and I am of opinion his information would not be good without it. But to shew that it is the principal thing which, in my opinion, makes a libel, I put the case, [if] the information had been for printing and publishing a certain true libel, would that be the same thing?

Or could Mr. Attorney support such an information by any precedent in the English law? No, the falsehood makes the scandal, and both make the libel. And to shew the Court that I am in good earnest, and to save the court's time, and Mr. Attorney's trouble, I will agree that if he can prove the facts charged upon us to be false, I'll own them to be scandalous, seditious, and a libel. So the work seems now to be pretty much shortened, and Mr. Attorney has now only to prove the words false, in order to make us guilty.

MR. BRADLEY: We have nothing to prove; you have confessed the printing and publishing; but if it was necessary, as I insist it is not, how can we prove a negative?

This was a monumental error by the prosecution. By his question he implicitly conceded his position that the issue was simply publication. Hamilton was quick to seize the advantage by engaging Bradley's rhetorical question, thus shifting the argument to proof of truth and away from simply establishing publication.

MR. HAMILTON: I did expect to hear that a negative cannot be proved; but everybody knows there are many exceptions to that general rule: for if a man is charged with killing another, or stealing his neighbor's horse, if he is innocent, in the one case, he may prove the man said to be killed, to be really alive; and the horse said to be stolen, never to have been out of his master's stable, and this I think is proving a negative. But we will save Mr. Attorney the trouble of proving a negative, and take the *onus probandi* upon ourselves, and prove those very papers that are called libels to be true.

Even though Hamilton had offered to take the initiative from the prosecutor, Chief Justice DeLancey, ever the governor's man, recognized that this shift in the argument would prove fatal to the prosecutor and joined the debate.

MR. CHIEF JUSTICE: You cannot be admitted, Mr. Hamilton, to give the truth of a libel in evidence. A libel is not to be justified; for it is nevertheless a libel that it is true.

MR. HAMILTON: I am sorry the court has so soon resolved upon that piece of law; I expected first to have been heard to that point. I have not in all my reading met with an authority that says we cannot be admitted to give the truth in evidence, upon an information for a libel.

MR. CHIEF JUSTICE: The law is clear that you cannot justify a libel.

MR. HAMILTON: I own that, may it please Your Honor, to be so; but, with submission, I understand the word *justify* there, to be a justification by plea, as it is in the case upon an indictment for murder, or an assault and battery; there the prisoner cannot justify, but plead not guilty: yet it will not be denied but he may, and always is admitted, to give the truth of the fact, or any other matter, in evidence, which goes to his acquittal; as in murder, he may prove it was in defense of his life, his house, and in assault and battery, he may give in evidence that the other party struck first, and in both cases he will be acquitted. And in this sense I understand the word *justify*, when applied to the case before the Court.

MR. CHIEF JUSTICE: I pray shew that you can give the truth of a libel in evidence.

MR. HAMILTON: I am ready, both from what I understand to be the authorities in the case, and from the reason of the thing, to shew that we may lawfully do so. But here I beg leave to observe that informations for libels is a child, if not born, yet nursed up, and brought to full maturity, in the Court of Star Chamber.

Note that as this exchange continued, Hamilton's true aim in pursuing this argument was not to actually win the ruling of the court. Hamilton knew that the deck was stacked against him in the person of Chief Justice DeLancey. Hamilton's genuine intention was to provide a rational basis for truth as a defense to libel, so that *when* DeLancey did rule against him, the jury would have heard Hamilton's argument and witnessed the seemingly unfair and arbitrary ruling of Governor Cosby's chief justice.

MR. CHIEF JUSTICE: Mr. Hamilton, you'll find yourself mistaken; for in *Coke's Institutes* you'll find informations for libels, long before the Court of Star Chamber.

MR. HAMILTON: I thank Your Honor; that is an authority I did propose to speak to by and by; but as you have mentioned it, I'll read that authority now. I think there cannot be a greater, at least a plainer, authority for us, than the judgment in the case of *John de Northampton*. Now, sir, by this judgment it appears the libelous words were utterly false, and there the falsehood was the crime, and is the ground of that judgment: And is not that what we contend for? Do not we insist that the falsehood makes the scandal, and both make the libel? And how shall it be known whether the words are libelous, that is, true or false, but by admitting us to prove them *true*, since Mr. Attorney will not undertake to prove them false? Besides, is it not against common sense that a man should be punished in the same degree for a true libel, if any such thing could be, as for a false one? I know it is said that truth makes a libel the more provoking, and therefore the offense is the greater, and consequently the judgment should be the heavier. Well, suppose it were so, and let us agree, for once, that truth is a greater sin than falsehood: yet as the offenses are not equal, and as the punishment is arbitrary, that is, according as the judges in their discretion shall direct to be inflicted; is it not absolutely necessary that they should know whether the libel is true or false, that they may by that means be able to proportion the punishment?

For, would it not be a sad case if the judges, for want of a due information, should chance to give as severe a judgment against a man for writing or publishing a lie, as for writing or publishing a truth? And yet this as monstrous and ridiculous as it may seem to be, is the natural consequence of Mr. Attorney's doctrine, that truth makes a worse libel than falsehood, and must follow from his not proving our papers to be false, or not suffering us to prove them to be true.

Chief Justice DeLancey, recognizing he was overmatched by Hamilton's verbal talents, tossed the gauntlet back to Bradley.

MR. CHIEF JUSTICE: Mr. Attorney, you have heard what Mr. Hamilton has said, and the cases he has cited, for having his witnesses examined, to prove the truth of the several facts contained in the papers set forth in the information. What do you say to it?

MR. BRADLEY: The law in my opinion is very clear; they cannot be admitted to justify a libel; for, by the authorities I have already read to the Court, it is not the less a libel because it is true. I think I need not trouble the Court with reading the cases over again; the thing seems to be very plain.

Unimpressed by Bradley's uninspired and perfunctory response, DeLancey felt compelled to reenter the fray.

MR. CHIEF JUSTICE: Mr. Hamilton, the Court is of opinion, you ought not to be permitted to prove the facts in the papers. These are the words of the book: "It is far from being a justification of a libel that the contents thereof are true, or that the person upon whom it is made had a bad reputation, since the greater appearance there is of truth in any malicious invective, so much the more provoking it is."

MR. HAMILTON: These are Star Chamber cases, and I was in hopes that practice had been dead with the Court.

MR. CHIEF JUSTICE: Mr. Hamilton, the Court have delivered their opinion, and we expect you will use us with good manners; you are not to be permitted to argue against the opinion of the Court.

MR. HAMILTON: With submission, I have seen the practice in very great courts, and never heard it deemed unmannerly to—

MR. CHIEF JUSTICE: After the Court have declared their opinion, it is not good manners to insist upon a point, in which you are overruled.

MR. HAMILTON: I will say no more at this time; the Court I see is against us in this point; and that I hope I may be allowed to say.

MR. CHIEF JUSTICE: Use the Court with good manners, and you shall be allowed all the liberty you can reasonably desire.

Hamilton was therefore precluded from producing evidence establishing the truth of the material in Zenger's newspaper. Of course Hamilton expected as much, given that had DeLancey allowed it, Hamilton would have embarked on a line of argument in which he would have turned the trial into a public attack on the governor.

Hamilton continued, untroubled by DeLancey's ruling, knowing he needn't prove the truth of the material printed in the *Journal* to win acquittal for Zenger. The jurors were Hamilton's audience; he knew that those men were all New Yorkers. They all lived and worked under the administration and had presumably read the *Journal* and were familiar with the deeds they recounted. Each man undoubtedly held opinions regarding the truth or falsity of those statements.

A brazen Hamilton accordingly ignored the court's admonition and addressed the jury directly, appealing to them as witnesses to the facts of the case, to note the truth of the articles, which the defense had been denied the right to prove.

MR. HAMILTON: I thank Your Honor. Then, gentlemen of the jury, it is to you we must appeal, for witnesses to the truth of the facts we have offered and are denied the liberty to prove; and let it not seem strange that I apply myself to you in this manner, I am warranted so to do both by law and reason. The law supposes you to be summoned out of the neighborhood where the fact is alleged to be committed; and the reason of your being taken out of the neighborhood is, because you are supposed to have the best knowledge of the fact that is to be tried. And were you to find a verdict against my client, you must take upon you to say, the papers referred to in the information, and which we acknowledge we printed and published, are false, scandalous, and seditious; but of this I can have no apprehension. You are citizens of New York; you are really what the law supposes you to be, honest and lawful men; and, according to my brief, the facts which we offer to prove were not committed in a corner; they are notoriously known to be true; and therefore in your justice lies our safety. And as we are denied the liberty of giving evidence, to prove the truth of what we have published, I will beg leave to lay it down as a standing rule in such cases, that the suppressing of evidence ought always to be taken for the strongest evidence; and I hope it will have that weight with you. But since we are not admitted to examine our witnesses, I will endeavor to shorten the dispute with Mr. Attorney, and to that end, I desire he would favor us with some standard definition of a libel, by which it may be certainly known, whether a writing be a libel, yea or not.

The prosecutor responded yet again with his recitation to the jury of the accepted definition of libel, including that a libel is no less a libel where the words are expressed in a scoffing or ironic manner.

MR. HAMILTON: Aye, Mr. Attorney; but at standard rule have the books laid down, by which we can certainly know, whether the words or the signs are malicious? Whether they are defamatory? Whether they tend to the breach of the peace, and a sufficient ground to provoke a man, his family, or friends to acts of revenge, especially those of the ironical sort of words? And what rule have you to know when I write ironically? I think it would be hard, when I say, such a man is a very worthy honest gentleman, and of fine understanding, that therefore I meant he was a knave or a fool.

MR. BRADLEY: I think the books are very full; that such scandal as is expressed in a scoffing and ironical manner makes a writing as properly a libel, as that which is expressed in direct terms; as where a writing, in a taunting manner says, reckoning up several acts of charity done by one, says, you will not play the Jew or the hypocrite, and so goes on to insinuate; that what he did was owing to his own glory, which kind of writing is as well understood to mean only to upbraid the parties with the want of these qualities, as if it had directly and expressly done so. I think nothing can be plainer or more full than these words.

MR. HAMILTON: I agree the words are very plain, and I shall not scruple to allow when we are agreed that the words are false and scandalous, and were spoken in an ironical and scoffing manner, that they are really libelous; but here still occurs the uncertainty, which makes the difficulty to know what words are scandalous, and what not; for you say, they may be scandalous, true or false; besides, how shall we know whether the words were spoke in a scoffing and ironical manner, or seriously? Or how can you know whether the man did not think as he wrote? For by your rule, if he did, it is no irony, and consequently no libel.

MR. CHIEF JUSTICE: Mr. Hamilton, do you think it so hard to know when words are ironical, or spoke in a scoffing manner?

MR. HAMILTON: I own it may be known; but I insist, the only rule to know is, as I do or can understand them; I have no other rule to go by, but as I understand them.

MR. CHIEF JUSTICE: That is certain. All words are libelous or not, as they are understood. Those who are to judge of the words, must judge whether they are scandalous or ironical, tend to the breach of the peace, or are seditious: there can be no doubt of it.

It seemed as if Chief Justice DeLancey had been forced by Hamilton's logic to agree that it was proper to judge and evaluate the words, not simply the fact of the publication. While Hamilton knew that the law as of the early eighteenth century mandated that the judge decide whether words satisfied the legal elements of libel, Hamilton's purpose was to lay the foundation for an argument that the *jury* should decide this matter. Hamilton knew that DeLancey would not accept this position, but he had skillfully maneuvered so that he could make the argument in an open courtroom and in front of the jury.

Even as Hamilton's argument was ostensibly directed to the bench, it was made to and for the benefit of the jury: twelve men who would eventually have the opportunity to rule on Zenger's guilt or innocence. The remainder of the record reflects precisely that: Hamilton's plea to the jury to return a verdict of acquittal regardless of the law they would receive from Justice DeLancey. There is no question that Hamilton was appealing for the jury to disregard the law and do what he believed to be the right thing. This is perhaps the earliest recorded instance of a lawyer urging juror nullification on the American continent.

Hamilton's closing argument, interrupted only briefly by warnings from Bradley and DeLancey, encapsulates the basis of the current constitutional right to both freedom of speech and freedom of the press. Hamilton's overriding theme was that men should have the right to speak of government—even criticize government—in order to create and maintain a *better* government. Hamilton reasoned that the press must have the right to report on the government in a factual manner so that citizens have adequate information to facilitate the frank political dialogue necessary for a free state. What remained was an inspired oration delivered by the reigning rhetorical master of the period, and what it represents is the touchstone of American political thought on the subject of freedom of speech and freedom of the press.

> **MR. HAMILTON:** I thank Your Honor; I am glad to find the Court of this opinion. Then it follows that those twelve men must understand the words in the information to be scandalous, that is to say false; for I think it is not pretended they are of the ironical sort; and when they understand the words to be so, they will say we are guilty of publishing a false libel, and not otherwise.
>
> **MR. CHIEF JUSTICE:** No, Mr. Hamilton; the jury may find that Zenger printed and published those papers, and leave it to the Court to judge whether they are libelous; you know this is very common; it is in the nature of a special verdict where the jury leave the matter of law to the Court.
>
> **MR. HAMILTON:** I know, may it please Your Honor, the jury may do so; but I do likewise know, they may do otherwise. I know they have the right beyond all dispute, to determine both the law and the fact, and where they do not doubt of the law, they ought to do so. This leaving it to [the] judgment of the Court, whether the words are libelous or not, in effect renders juries useless, to say no worse, in many cases; but this I shall have occasion to speak to by and by; and I will with the Court's leave proceed to examine the inconveniences that must inevitably arise from the doctrines Mr. Attorney has laid down; and I observe, in support of this prosecution, he has frequently repeated the words, for though I own it to be base and unworthy, to scandalize any man, yet I think it is even villainous to scandalize a person of public character, and I will go so far into Mr. Attorney's doctrine as to

agree, that if the faults, mistakes, nay even the vices of such a person be private and personal, and don't affect the peace of the public, or the liberty or property of our neighbor, it is unmanly and unmannerly to expose them either by word or writing. But when a ruler of a people brings his personal failings, but much more his vices, into his administration, and the people find themselves affected by them, either in their liberties or properties, that will alter the case mightily; and all the high things that are said in favor of rulers, and of dignities, and upon the side of power, will not be able to stop peoples' mouths when they feel themselves oppressed. It is true in times past it was a crime to speak truth, and in that terrible Court of Star Chamber, many worthy and brave men suffered for so doing; and yet even in that court, and in those bad times, a great and good man durst say, what I hope will not be taken amiss of me to say in this place, to wit, the practice of informations for libels is a sword in the hands of a wicked king, and an arrant coward, to cut down and destroy the innocent; the one cannot, because of his high station, and the other dares not, because of his want of courage, revenge himself in another manner.

MR. BRADLEY: Pray, Mr. Hamilton, have a care what you say, don't go too far neither, I don't like those liberties.

MR. HAMILTON: Sure, Mr. Attorney, you won't make any applications; all men agree that we are governed by the best of kings, and I cannot see the meaning of Mr. Attorney's caution; my well-known principles, and the sense I have of the blessings we enjoy under his present majesty, makes it impossible for me to err, and I hope, even to be suspected, in that point of duty to my king. May it please Your Honor, I was saying, that notwithstanding all the duty and reverence claimed by Mr. Attorney to men in authority, they are not exempt from observing the rules of common justice, either in their private or public capacities; the laws of our mother country know no exemption. And has it not often been seen—I hope it will always be seen—that when the representatives of a free people are, by just representations or remonstrances, made sensible of the sufferings of their fellow subjects, by the abuse of power in the hands of a governor, they have declared that they were not obliged by any law to support a governor who goes about to destroy a province or colony, or their privileges, which by His Majesty he was appointed, and by the law he is bound to protect and encourage.

But I pray it may be considered, of what use is this mighty privilege if every man that suffers must be silent? And if a man must be taken up as a libeler for telling his sufferings to his neighbor? I know it may be answered, have you not a legislature? Have you not a house of representatives to whom you may complain? And to this I answer, we have. But what then? Is an assembly to be troubled with every injury done by a governor? Or are they to hear of nothing but what those in the administration will please to tell them? Or what sort of a trial must a man have? And how is he to be remedied; especially if the case were, as I have known it to happen in America in my time, that a governor who has places to bestow, and can or will keep the same assembly— after he has modeled them so as to get a majority of the house in his interest—for near twice seven years together? I pray, what redress is to be expected for an honest man, who makes his complaint against a governor, to an assembly who may properly enough be said to be made by the same governor against whom the complaint is made? The thing answers itself. No, it is natural, it is a privilege, I will go farther, it is a right which all free men claim, and are entitled to complain when they are hurt; they have a right publicly to remonstrate the abuses of power, in the strongest terms, to put their neighbors upon their guard, against the craft or open violence of men in authority, and to assert with courage the sense they have of the blessings of liberty, the value they put upon it, and their resolution at all hazards to preserve it, as one of the greatest blessings heaven can bestow.

And we all very well understand the true reason why gentlemen take so much pains and make such great interest to be appointed governors, so is the design of their appointment not less manifest. We know His Majesty's gracious intentions to his subjects; he desires no more than that his people in the plantations should be kept up to their duty and allegiance to the crown of Great Britain, that peace may be preserved amongst them, and justice impartially administered; that we may be governed so as to render us useful to our mother country, by encouraging us to make and raise such commodities as may be useful to Great Britain, but will anyone say that all or any of these good ends are to be effected, by a governor's setting his people together by the ears, and by the assistance of one part of the people to plague and plunder the other? The commission which governors bear, while they execute the powers given them, according to the intent of the royal grantor, expressed in their commissions, requires and deserves very great reverence and submission; but when a governor departs from the duty enjoined him by his sovereign, and acts as if he was less accountable than the royal hand that gave him all that power and honor that he is possessed of; this sets people upon examining and enquiring into the power, authority, and duty of such a magistrate, and to compare those with his conduct, and just as far as they find he exceeds the bounds of his authority, or falls short in doing impartial justice to the people under his administration, so far they very often, in return, come short in their duty to such a governor.

For power alone will not make a man beloved, and I have heard it observed that the man who was neither good nor wise before his being made a governor never mended upon his preferment, but has been generally observed to be worse: for men who are not endowed with wisdom and virtue, can only be kept in bounds by the law; and by how much the further they think themselves out of the reach of the law, by so much the more wicked and cruel men are. I wish there were no instances of the kind at this day. And wherever this happens to be the case of a governor, unhappy are the people under his administration, and in the end he will find himself so too; for the people will neither love him nor support him.

I know men's interests are very near to them, and they will do much rather than forgo the favor of a governor, and a livelihood at the same time; but I can with very just grounds hope, even from those men, whom I will suppose to be men of honor and conscience too, that when they see the liberty of their country is in danger, either by their concurrence, or even by their silence, they will like Englishmen, and like themselves, freely make a sacrifice of any preferment or favor rather than be accessory to destroying the liberties of their country, and entailing slavery upon their posterity.

There are indeed another set of men, of whom I have no hopes, I mean such who lay aside all other considerations, and are ready to join with power in any shapes, and with any man or sort of men, by whose means or interest they may be assisted to gratify their malice and envy against those whom they have been pleased to hate; and that for no other reason but because they are men of abilities and integrity, or at least are possessed of some valuable qualities, far superior to their own. But as envy is the sin of the devil, and therefore very hard, if at all, to be repented of, I will believe there are but few of this detestable and worthless sort of men, nor will their opinions or inclinations have any influence upon this trial.

But to proceed; I beg leave to insist that the right of complaining or remonstrating is natural; and the restraint upon this natural right is the law only, and that those restraints can only extend to what is false: for as it is truth alone which can excuse or justify any man for complaining of a bad administration, I as frankly agree that nothing ought to excuse a man who raises a false charge or accusation, even against a private person, and that no manner of allowance ought to be made to him, who does so against a public magistrate. Truth ought to govern the whole affair of libels, and yet the party accused runs bisque enough even then; for if he fails in proving every title of what he has wrote, and to the satisfaction of the Court and jury too, he may find to his cost that when the prosecution is set on foot by men in power, it seldom wants friends to favor it.

And from thence, it is said, has arisen the great diversity of opinions among judges about what words were or were not scandalous or libelous. I believe it will be granted that there is not greater uncertainty in any part of the law than about words of scandal; it would be misspending of the Court's time to mention the cases; they may be said to be numberless; and therefore the utmost care ought to be taken in following precedents; and the times when the judgments were given, which are quoted for authorities in the case of libels, are much to be regarded.

If then upon the whole there is so great an uncertainty among judges in matters of this kind; if power has had so great an influence on judges; how cautious ought we to be in determining by their judgments, especially in the plantations, and in the case of libels? There is heresy in law, as well as in religion, and both have changed very much; and we well know that it is not two centuries ago that a man would have been burnt as an heretic for owning such opinions in matters of religion as are publicly wrote and printed at this day. They were fallible men, it seems, and we take the liberty not only to differ from them in religious opinions, but to condemn them and their opinions too; and I must presume that in taking these freedoms in thinking and speaking about matters of faith or religion, we are in the right: for though it is said there are very great liberties of this kind taken in New

York, yet I have heard of no information preferred by Mr. Attorney for any offenses of this sort. From which I think it is pretty clear that in New York, a man may make very free with his God, but he must take special care what he says of his governor.

It is agreed upon by all men that this is a reign of liberty; and while men keep within the bounds of truth, I hope they may with safety both speak and write their sentiments of the conduct of men in power—I mean of that part of their conduct only which affects the liberty or property of the people under their administration; were this to be denied, then the next step may make them slaves: for what notions can be entertained of slavery, beyond that of suffering the greatest injuries and oppressions, without the liberty of complaining; or if they do, to be destroyed, body and estate, for so doing?

It is said and insisted on by Mr. Attorney that government is a sacred thing; that it is to be supported and reverenced; it is government that protects our persons and estates; that prevents treasons, murders, robberies, riots, and all the train of evils that overturns kingdoms and states, and ruins particular persons; and if those in the administration, especially the supreme magistrate, must have all their conduct censured by private men, government cannot subsist. This is called a licentiousness not to be tolerated. It is said that it brings the rulers of the people into contempt, and their authority not to be regarded, and so in the end the laws cannot be put in execution. These I say, and such as these, are the general topics insisted upon by men in power, and their advocates. But I wish it might be considered at the same time, how often it has happened that the abuse of power has been the primary cause of these evils, and that it was the injustice and oppression of these great men which has commonly brought them into contempt with the people. The craft and art of such men is great, and who, that is the least acquainted with history or law, can be ignorant of the specious pretenses which have often been made use of by men in power, to introduce arbitrary rule, and destroy the liberties of a free people.

The people of England saw clearly the danger of trusting their liberties and properties to be tried, even by the greatest men in the kingdom, without the judgment of a jury of their equals. They had felt the terrible effects of leaving it to the judgment of these great men to say what was scandalous and seditious, false or ironical. And if the Parliament of England thought this power of judging was too great to be trusted with men of the first rank in the kingdom, without the aid of a jury, how sacred so ever their characters might be, and therefore restored to the people their original right of trial by juries, I hope to be excused for insisting, that by the judgment of a Parliament, from whence an appeal lies, the jury are the proper judges, of what is false at least, if not of what is scandalous and seditious. This is an authority not to be denied, it is as plain as it is great, and to say that this act indeed did restore to the people trials by juries, which was not the practice of the Star Chamber, but that did not give the jurors any new authority, or any right to try matters of law, I say this objection will not avail; for I must insist that where matter of law is complicated with matter of fact, the jury have a right to determine both.

Gentlemen, the danger is great, in proportion to the mischief that may happen, through our too great credulity. A proper confidence in a court is commendable; but as the verdict, whatever it is, will be yours, you ought to refer no part of your duty to the discretion of other persons. If you should be of the opinion that there is no falsehood in Mr. Zenger's papers, you will, nay, pardon me for the expression, you ought to say so; because you don't know whether others—I mean the Court—may be of that opinion. It is your right to do so, and there is much depending upon your resolution, as well as upon your integrity.

The loss of liberty, to a generous mind, is worse than death; and yet we know there have been those in all ages, who for the sake of preferment, or some imaginary honor, have freely lent a helping hand to oppress, nay to destroy their country. This brings to my mind the saying of the immortal Brutus, when he looked upon the creatures of Caesar, who were very great men, but by no means good men. "You Romans," said Brutus, "if yet I may call you so, consider what you are doing; remember that you are assisting Caesar to forge those very chains which one the day he will make yourselves wear." This is what every fey man, that values freedom, ought to consider: he should act by judgment and not by affection or self-interest; for, where those prevail, no ties of either country or the kindred are regarded; as upon the other hand, the man who loves his country, prefers its liberty to all other considerations, well knowing that without liberty, life to you is a misery.

A famous instance of this you will find in the history here of another brave Roman of the same name, I mean Lucius par Junius Brutus, whose story is well-known, and therefore I shall mention no more of it, than only to shew the value may be put upon the freedom of his country. After this great man, with his fellow citizens whom he had in the cause, had banished Tarquin the Proud, the last king of Rome, from a throne which he ascended by inhuman murders and possessed by the most dreadful tyranny all proscriptions, and had by this means amassed incredible riches, even sufficient to bribe to his interest, aye, many of the young nobility of Rome, to assist him in that recovering the crown; but the plot being discovered, the principal conspirators were apprehended, among whom were two of the sons of Junius Brutus. It was absolutely necessary that some should be made examples of, to deter others from attempting the restoring of the Tarquin cause and destroying the liberty of Rome. And to effect this it was, that Lucius Junius Brutus, one of the consuls of law, in the presence of the Roman people, sat judge and condemned his own sons, as traitors to their country; and to give the last proof of his exalted virtue, and his love of liberty, he with a firmness of mind, only becoming so great a man, caused their heads to be struck off in his own presence; and when he observed that his rigid virtue occasioned a sort of horror among the people, it is observed he only said, "My fellow citizens, do not think that this proceeds from any want of natural affection: no, the death of the sons of Brutus can affect Brutus only; but the loss of liberty will affect my country."

Power may justly be compared to a great river; while kept within its due bounds, is both beautiful and useful; but when it overflows its banks, it is then too impetuous to be stemmed, it bears down all before it, and brings destruction and desolation wherever it comes. If then this is the nature of power, let us at least do our duty, and like wise men use our utmost care to support liberty, the only bulwark against lawless power, which in all ages has sacrificed to its wild lust and boundless ambition, the blood of the best men that ever lived.

I hope to be pardoned, sir, for my zeal upon this occasion; it is an old and wise caution: that when our neighbor's house is on fire, we ought to take care of our own. For though blessed be God, I live in a government where liberty is well understood, and freely enjoyed: yet experience has shewn us all that a bad precedent in one government is soon set up for an authority in another; and therefore I cannot but think it mine, and every honest man's duty, that we ought at the same time to be upon our guard against power, wherever we apprehend that it may affect ourselves or our fellow subjects.

I am truly very unequal to such an undertaking on many accounts. And you see I labor under the weight of many years, and am borne down with great infirmities of body; yet old and weak as I am, I should think it my duty if required, to go to the utmost part of the land, where my service could be of any use in assisting to quench the flame of prosecutions upon informations, set on foot by the government, to deprive a people of the right of remonstrating, of the arbitrary attempts of men in power. Men who injure and oppress the people under their administration provoke them to cry out and complain; and then make that very complaint the foundation for new oppressions and prosecutions. I wish I could say there were no instances of this kind.

But to conclude; the question before the Court and you gentlemen of the jury is not of small nor private concern, it is not the cause of the poor printer, nor of New York alone, which you are now trying: No! It may in its consequence affect every free man that lives under a British government on the main of America.

It is the best cause. It is the cause of liberty; and I make no doubt but your upright conduct, this day, will not only entitle you to the love and esteem of your fellow citizens; but every man who prefers freedom to a life of slavery will bless and honor. You, as to men who have baffled the attempt of tyranny; and by an impartial and uncorrupt verdict have laid a noble foundation for securing to ourselves, our posterity, and our neighbors, that, to which nature and the laws of our country have given us a right— the liberty—both of exposing and opposing arbitrary power by speaking and writing truth.

With this magnificent, inspired—and timeless—closing argument, Andrew Hamilton joined the ranks of legendary trial lawyers who, undeterred by conventional wisdom, hostile judges, and zealous prosecutors, change not only laws, but nations.

In the aftermath of Hamilton's tour de force, Chief Justice DeLancey attempted to reassert some control over the jury.

MR. CHIEF JUSTICE: Gentlemen of the jury. The great pains Mr. Hamilton has taken to shew how little regard juries are to pay to the opinion of the judges, and his insisting so much upon the conduct of some judges in trials of this kind, is done no doubt with a design that you should take but very little notice of what I might say upon this occasion. I shall therefore only observe to you that, as the facts or words in the information are confessed, the only thing that can come in question before you is, whether the words as set forth in the information make a libel. And that is a matter of law, no doubt, and which you may leave to the Court. But I shall trouble you no further with anything more of my own, but read to you the words of a learned and upright judge in a case of the like nature.

Justice DeLancey then read the instructions to the jury:

To say that corrupt officers are appointed to administer affairs is certainly a reflection on the government. If people should not be called to account for possessing the people with an ill opinion of the government, no government can subsist, for it is very necessary for all governments that the people should have a good opinion of it. And nothing can be worse to any government than to endeavor to procure animosities; as to the management of it, this has been always looked upon as a crime, and no government can be safe without it be punished.

Now you are to consider whether these words I have read to you do not tend to beget an ill opinion of the administration of the government? To tell us that those that are employed know nothing of the matter, and those that do know are not employed. Men are not adapted to offices, but offices to men, out of a particular regard to their interest, and not to their fitness for the places; this is the purport of these papers.

A Swift Decision

With that admonition the jury withdrew to deliberate on Zenger's fate, but quickly returned, delivering a resounding rejection to the governor and his men as they acquitted John Peter Zenger of printing and publishing libelous information. Twelve New Yorkers disregarded the law and the instructions given them by the judge and returned a verdict based on the law as they felt it *should* be. Not only was John Peter Zenger free, but every colonist critical of the English government found himself more free to speak and print the truth.

On the night of Zenger's acquittal, more than forty New Yorkers entertained Andrew Hamilton at the local Black Horse Tavern for a dinner in his honor. Supporters of Alexander and Zenger toasted the printer's courage and Hamilton's brilliance. Upon Hamilton's departure for Philadelphia, several ships in New York harbor fired their guns in a salute. In September 1735, the Common Council of New York presented Hamilton with a solid-gold snuffbox, engraved inside and out with Latin quotes from Cicero. Translated, they said, "Submerged laws, frightened liberty, shall be rescued sometime. It is acquired not with money but with character. May it so result to each one as he deserves of the state."

Any analysis of the exact effect of the Zenger verdict proves difficult. Legally, the case provided no precedent for future courts, nor did it alter the law of seditious libel. The verdict, rendered by a jury, was legally significant solely for the parties directly involved. Furthermore, Hamilton never made a direct attack on the concept of seditious libel. The eloquent Philadelphia attorney argued for a man's right to challenge a corrupt and incapable government with factual statements. He never argued for, nor did any of his writings suggest, that he supported the unfettered right to verbally attack public officials. All Hamilton advocated in his closing argument was the right to speak the truth in an open forum, so that the people might control government more effectively.

Hamilton argued for Zenger's acquittal in a case where the jury knew the facts before entering the courtroom. More than anything, the Zenger trial represented a political revolt against Governor Cosby's reign as the chief executive of the colony and served to undermine his effectiveness.

However, to say that the trial had no legally binding effect is not to argue that Hamilton's speech in that New York courtroom and Zenger's subsequent acquittal had no lasting effect in a historical sense. The *Zenger* case and the subsequent printed account of the trial and its outcome provided a ready-made argument for the public, laying out the merits of a free press, in the words of the continent's greatest orator.

The Revolutionary War took place some forty years later, but the Zenger trial played an important role in the debate leading up to the conflict, not only in New York, but throughout the thirteen colonies, as the account of Zenger's ordeal—reprinted numerous times and widely disseminated—encouraged open criticism of British rule. The effect of Zenger's acquittal was so profound that it led Gouverneur Morris to say, "The trial of Zenger in 1735 was the morning star of that liberty which subsequently revolutionized America."

The trial's long-term effect upon the legal traditions of both American and British common law cannot be overlooked. The once radical beliefs that truth should provide a defense to a libel charge, and that a jury should decide all the issues in a libel trial, eventually became the law in America.

Today, the law of civil libel is governed by an "actual malice" standard, set forth by the U.S. Supreme Court. Under this doctrine, a speaker may only be prosecuted for libel of a public figure if the statement in question is false *and* the speaker either knew that the statement was false at the time it was made or recklessly disregarded the truth in making the statement. Thus, not only is truth now a defense to civil libel—as Hamilton so vehemently argued—but actual knowledge of the falsity of a statement is required to subject a speaker to litigation.

Only a handful of states still maintain statutes threatening criminal prosecution for libel. These are rarely utilized and they are held to the same actual-malice standard as civil libel. The most recent Supreme Court decision regarding criminal libel, rendered in 1964, failed to outlaw criminal libel, but placed the concept very much in doubt.

As for John Peter Zenger, Governor Cosby released him the day after the verdict. In 1737, he became New York's public printer and in the following year took the same office in New Jersey. Zenger died on July 28, 1746, leaving his wife (Zenger had remarried) and six children. Zenger's wife and son published the *Journal* until 1751. The account of the trial, taken from Hamilton's and Alexander's notes, appeared in the *Journal* in 1736. In all, *A Brief Narrative of the Case and Trial of John Peter Zenger, Printer of the New York Weekly Journal* encompassed some forty pages and took several editions of the *Journal* to publish. Published four times in London in 1738, once in Boston, and once in Philadelphia, *A Brief Narrative* reappeared as recently as the World War II era in the United States.

Zenger, in his conduct during his imprisonment and trial, continues to serve as a role model for journalists; he refused to reveal the names and identities of the men responsible for writing and editing his paper, the men actually responsible for the attacks on Cosby. Today, journalists can still point to Zenger when they protect their sources.

And politicians can serve their constituents, kept honest by the freedom fought for and won by a German immigrant and his Scots lawyer, more than 250 years ago.

CHAPTER SIX

The Porn King and the Preacher

Larry Flynt Takes on the Moral Majority and Becomes an Unlikely Champion for Free Speech

If there is no struggle, there is no progress. Those who profess to favor freedom, and yet deprecate agitation . . . want crops without ploughing the ground. They want rain without thunder and lightning. They want the ocean without the awful roar of its waters.

—*Frederick Douglass, 1834*

History reveals that, as often as not, the great First Amendment battles have been fought by our cultural rejects and misfits, by our communist agitators, our civil rights activists, our Ku Klux Klanners, our Jehovah's Witnesses, our Larry Flynts.

—*Rodney Smolla, historian*

Sometimes important legal battles take place on the margins. If well-informed Americans of the early 1980s were asked what the next flash point in society and politics might be, and who might be in the vanguard of the battle, they'd probably take a moment and review what was happening in the world before answering.

Sandra Day O'Connor had just been appointed the first female justice on the Supreme Court, and Nancy Reagan made headlines when she appeared at a Washington, D.C., benefit dressed as a bag lady in protest of criticisms about her "expensive" outfits. Ideas about sex and promiscuity were hot topics; television stations banned ads featuring the adolescent Brooke Shields seductively whispering that "nothing" came between her and her Calvins. Researchers were puzzled by the first reports of homosexual men dying of a strange immunological disease.

No one would have expected pornography and freedom of speech to be the centerpiece of one of the key Supreme Court decisions of the 1980s, nor would Larry Flynt, the man who famously featured a shapely woman being fed into a meat grinder on the cover of *Hustler* magazine, fit anyone's description of constitutional absolutist and defender of freedom.

Magazines like Hugh Hefner's *Playboy* and Bob Guccione's *Penthouse* featured "mainstream" nudity at neighborhood newsstands. What had been shocking when Hefner's magazine debuted in the 1950s had become ho-hum, while Guccione's monthly offered a more "sophisticated" view of American sexuality and mores.

Playboy and *Penthouse* strove for the respectability of artistic expression, accentuating the glamour and romance of their photography with photo spreads that, while depicting full-frontal nudity, shied away from the kind of clinical images found in gynecological textbooks. The magazines' journalistic pretensions found expression in their celebrity interviews and short fiction, with the *Playboy* interview featuring some of the most prominent persons in science, industry, and politics. *Playboy* achieved such a level of respectability by 1976 that presidential candidate and former Georgia governor Jimmy Carter—a devout Christian—agreed to be interviewed.

A relative newcomer on the scene was "porn peddler" Larry Flynt and his magazine, *Hustler.* Flynt didn't bother with the pretext that his photos strived for artistry: *Hustler* wasn't about romance; sex was its purpose, its (e)mission. Flynt's magazine, while not hard-core (it did not depict explicit intercourse or penetration), pushed the envelope, believing more graphic photographs were what his "readers" really wanted.

Squaring off against Hefner, Guccione, and Flynt were Christian fundamentalists who were harnessing a religious revival to garner funds and support to combat any expression that they considered sexually suggestive or offensive. Staving off pornography, abortion, homosexuality, and communism were primary concerns of this religious movement.

The most powerful of these groups was Moral Majority, Inc. This corporate conglomerate eventually grew to more than half a million supporters nationwide, including Jimmy Swaggart, James Kennedy, Greg Dixon, Charles Stanley, and Tim LaHaye. Televangelists Billy Graham, Oral Roberts, and Jim Bakker, although not directly involved with the Moral Majority, nonetheless helped fan the flames of fundamentalism through their own distinctly conservative Christian campaigns. Although many popular ministers of the era were involved in the Moral Majority's success, the unquestioned leader of the movement and the president of Moral Majority was America's preeminent televangelist, the Reverend Jerry Falwell.

Falwell, a charismatic Southern preacher who prided himself on his blemish-free reputation and unflagging dedication to Christian ideals, denounced "smut peddlers" like Larry Flynt and called their magazines depraved and sinful. Falwell publicly condemned Flynt's activities and told his vast television congregation that participating in the things depicted in the pages of *Hustler*, and other magazines like it, was an abomination to God.

Flynt took note of Falwell's attacks and also the fact that Falwell's Moral Majority took in more money each year than either the Republican or Democratic Party. The preacher's income—millions of dollars offered up by his faithful flock—seemed incongruent with Falwell's supposedly simple, Christian life. Flynt attacked this perceived hypocrisy, publishing a scabrous parody-advertisement that portrayed Falwell as a drunken, incestuous reprobate. The infamous smut king was about to go head-to-head with America's most powerful televangelist in one of the twentieth century's most significant trials. The First Amendment was about to be invoked and redefined.

An Empire Built on Smut

Larry C. Flynt was born November 1, 1942, into a family of sharecroppers living deep in the Kentucky mountains. Flynt and his brother would feed the chickens on his grandmother's farm before heading off to school, but his academic career was short-lived; Flynt barely finished grade school before dropping out. He lied about his age when he was fourteen and enlisted in the army. Discharged within a year, he then enlisted in the navy. By the time he was twenty-three, Flynt had left the service, declared bankruptcy, and been married three times. While still in his early twenties, Flynt quit his job at a General Motors plant and opened up a business that would become his life's calling, a "Hustler" strip bar in Ohio called Hillbilly Haven.

Flynt made a decent profit on his first Hustler strip club, located in Dayton. The dancers worked mostly for tips and the customers bought a boatload of liquor from Flynt's eager-to-please bartenders. Flynt soon expanded his business, acquiring a string of Hustler Clubs, strip joints he advertised in pamphlets containing photographs of his dancers. The pamphlets proved popular, and Flynt, recognizing an opportunity, began selling them. *Hustler* was born. Soon, *Hustler* had reached major-league status, its circulation skyrocketing to more than 2 million subscribers in just four years. By 1980, the thirty-seven-year-old Flynt was a multimillionaire, with profits from *Hustler* alone topping $13 million annually.

Hustler catered to an audience distinctly different from that of *Playboy* and *Penthouse*. *Hustler* went far beyond the more acceptable airbrushed sex-as-art themes contained within Hefner's and Guccione's magazines, opting instead for more explicit layouts and models renowned for having breasts of "grotesque proportions." *Hustler* avoided any semblance of journalism, juxtaposing sexual images with cruel parodies. No topic was too sacred for *Hustler*'s pages; the magazine's "humor" included crass cartoons about Chief Justice Warren Burger's sex life and First Lady Betty Ford's breast cancer. Flynt used his magazine to attack his personal enemies through a column, "The Asshole of the Month," and he encouraged the frequent use of cartoon depictions of excrement, mutilation, bestiality, dismemberment, and bondage. Flynt prided himself on *Hustler*'s themes of sex, hate, and perversion, claiming, "There's more reality in *Hustler* than in anything you read."

Flynt's obsession with the perverse extended well beyond his business and into his personal life. After making his first few millions, he commissioned a statue depicting him losing his virginity—as an eight-year-old boy to a chicken on his grandmother's farm. He enjoyed an extremely open and promiscuous sex life; his employees were well aware of the rumors that he had slept with every dancer who went onstage at his strip clubs.

One person who encouraged Flynt's sexual exploits was his fourth wife, Althea. Hired as one of Flynt's go-go dancers when she was seventeen, Althea had a troubled past. When she was eight, her father had shot and killed her mother, her grandfather, and her mother's best friend, before committing suicide. Orphaned, with few friends, Althea led a hardscrabble existence, eventually finding her way to Flynt's Columbus, Ohio, strip club. Attracted to Flynt and his easy-go-lucky lifestyle, Althea married him. Marriage didn't cramp her husband's extramarital activities: the openly bisexual Althea enjoyed choosing lovers to satisfy her husband's sexual appetites. Flynt boasted that he had sex with, on average, fifteen women a week, most of them personally selected by his wife.

Flynt diversified, starting the Flynt Distributing Company. With this latest business, he could go "legit." He bought into respectable journalism, acquiring several weekly papers including the *Atlanta Gazette* and *Ohio Magazine*. The Flynt Distributing Company allowed him to branch out and profit from magazines on hundreds of topics ranging from knitting to motorcycling. At one point, Flynt's company even distributed the *New York Review of Books*.

By 1977, Flynt had established himself as a permanent player on the national scene. With this success came attention from those opposed to pornography and the lifestyle that Flynt epitomized. One woman who took note of Flynt's influence was President Jimmy Carter's sister, Ruth Carter Stapleton. Stapleton was a devout Christian, openly opposed to any activity that hinted at sexual misconduct. Stapleton soon set out to "cure" the incorrigible Larry Flynt.

Stapleton contacted Flynt and by the fall of 1977 convinced him to renounce his evil ways and accept Christ as his savior. The actual moment of Flynt's conversion took place aboard a chartered jet flying between Denver and Houston. According to Flynt, "There I was, representing the pits of what is wrong in our society, and it happened. I'm not ashamed that I cried for God." Althea, displeased with Flynt's newfound Christian faith, was skeptical of her husband's overnight conversion, warning, "The Lord may have entered your life, but twenty million dollars just walked out of it."

Flynt and Stapleton visited each other's homes and wrote to each other frequently. During this time, Flynt turned *Hustler* into a strange mixture of sex and religion, featuring pornographic photographs of women surrounded by crosses and other religious paraphernalia. "I'll be a hustler for the Lord," the publisher proclaimed.

Flynt's conversion proved short-lived. Only a few months after Flynt "cried for God," he was openly decrying religion and everything associated with it. Much to Althea's relief, *Hustler*'s profits, which had fallen with the odd combination of pornography and religion, bounced back immediately. *Hustler* returned to its usual themes of unadulterated porn and lewd humor. Flynt used his failed religious experience as fodder for a new line of mocking and crude cartoons featuring religious themes and manifesting a heightened hostility. In an interview with *Vanity Fair*, Flynt called the Bible "the biggest piece of shit ever written."

In 1978, just a few months after his rejection of religion, Flynt was on trial in Lawrenceville, Georgia. The county prosecutor had determined that the contents of *Hustler* violated the state's prohibition on the publication of obscenity. Although the violation was only a misdemeanor, Flynt appeared in court alongside his lawyers to defend himself against the charge.

Lawrenceville was a quiet, sleepy town, and Flynt's trial was largely ignored by the locals. On March 6, Flynt gave his bodyguard the day off and walked to lunch with one of his lawyers, Gene Reeves. The two men were strolling back to the courthouse after a leisurely lunch when gunfire rang out; Flynt and Reeves were riddled with bullets. When the shooting stopped, they lay on the ground, bleeding, Flynt shot in the abdomen and writhing on the ground facedown, begging for help, Reeves shot twice, in the stomach and arm.

To save Flynt's life, surgeons removed most of his intestines; a second operation removed his damaged spleen. After a transfer to Atlanta's

Emory Hospital, surgeons performed yet another operation to remove the remnants of the .44 magnum slug lodged near Flynt's spine.

While Flynt was drifting in and out of consciousness, Reeves was undergoing emergency surgery. The damage had left Reeves extremely weak and confined to a bed in intensive care, but he sustained no lasting injuries.

When Ruth Carter Stapleton heard about the shooting, she flew to Atlanta. Seated at Flynt's bedside, she thanked God that his life had been spared while Flynt listened in angry silence. Flynt said he felt only bitterness toward the God Stapleton prayed to, for despite the surgeons' best efforts, the severed nerves near Flynt's spine could not be repaired. Larry Flynt was permanently paralyzed from the waist down.

Rumors circulated that a hit had been put out on Flynt by the Mafia as a means of protecting their turf as America's leader of the sex-for-profit empire. Some said that the Ku Klux Klan had ordered the shooting in retaliation for Flynt's lasciviousness. Flynt believed the shooting was a result of questions he had posed in *Hustler* regarding the assassination of President Kennedy. The truth may have been less interesting. A white supremacist named Joseph P. Franklin said he shot Flynt because he was angered by photos in *Hustler* depicting black men having sex with white women. Despite his confession, the case against Franklin was not compelling and the local prosecutors did not file charges. However, he is on death row for murders committed later that year.

Although Flynt's legs were paralyzed, the damage to his nerves was not total, and he suffered from shooting pains through his legs. His doctors prescribed a powerful painkiller, Dilaudid, to keep the pain at bay. After years on this morphinelike drug, Flynt decided to undergo an additional operation to completely sever the nerves to his legs. The operation succeeded in alleviating Flynt's pain, but it also left him with no control over his bowels or bladder.

Confined to a wheelchair and panicked by frequent death threats, Flynt hid inside his Bel Air mansion, leaving to his wife the daily management of *Hustler,* which continued to thrive under her leadership. When Flynt did occasionally venture out, he was closely watched by his bodyguards.

Undeterred by his injuries, the porn king continued to come up with increasingly outlandish stunts. In 1983, Flynt mailed five copies of *Hustler* to every member of the U.S. Congress, claiming he wanted every congressman to be "well informed on social issues." Although the politicians complained and the Postal Service eventually filed suit, a federal court ruled that members of Congress are not mere citizens who could "shield themselves from undesirable mail in the same manner as an ordinary addressee." Vindicated, Flynt sent more copies of his magazine to the legislators.

Congress wasn't a big enough target, so Flynt set his sights on the White House. In 1984, he announced his intention to run for president, naming American Indian activist Russell Means as his running mate. Flynt's campaign slogan was "A Smut Peddler Who Cares," and his platform included sexual liberation and battling hypocrisy. In his campaign announcement, Flynt proudly proclaimed, "I am running as a Republican rather than as a Democrat, because I am wealthy, white, pornographic, and like the nuclear-mad cowboy, Ronnie Reagan, I have been shot for what I believe in."

Although Flynt had a fondness for high-profile publicity stunts, he did possess some serious convictions, foremost among them the guarantees of the First Amendment: "Congress shall make no law . . . abridging the freedom of speech, or of the press." When the United States invaded Grenada and the Defense Department refused to allow journalists to report on the invasion, a nationwide outcry from newspapers and television stations ensued. Despite heated protests from the networks and the *New York Times,* no one actually brought suit against the government until Larry Flynt argued that the government was making a mockery of the First Amendment. Flynt was not interested in sending his writers to Grenada to report on the invasion, but was instead outraged by the government's denial of access. He believed that it was a blatant violation of the First Amendment to prohibit a disinterested party from investigating an issue important to the American public. Flynt's lawsuit was eventually dismissed because the prohibition on travel to Grenada had been lifted before the suit could be brought before the court.

Flynt also believed that adults should be able to conduct their sex lives in any way that they saw fit—what went on in the bedrooms of consenting adults was private. And he railed at those who would question his convictions.

Given Flynt's beliefs, his ultimate nemesis would be a person who had the audacity to interfere with the sexual decisions of consenting adults by imposing his own standards of morality—the Reverend Jerry Falwell.

Falwell didn't limit his activism to combating pornography; he spoke out against anything that even hinted at being politically liberal. Flynt saw this as an attempt to censor the free exchange of ideas. Falwell openly admitted that he wanted to convert every American to Christianity. Flynt regarded Falwell's outreach programs and public broadcast of his sermons as a step toward religious demagoguery. Falwell labeled Flynt's lifestyle an abomination, using Flynt's name and calling his business "garbage."

Flynt was appalled. By what right did Falwell pass judgment on the private decisions and choices of Larry C. Flynt? Angry and disgusted by Falwell's ideology and his organization, Flynt was determined not to let the personal attacks against him go unanswered. Picking up the telephone, Flynt made ready his weapon of choice, *Hustler.*

Flynt's initial attacks on Falwell came in the form of snide remarks and distasteful comments on religion in general. When Falwell didn't respond to *Hustler's* initial jabs, Flynt ratcheted up the intensity of the attacks. Falwell was featured several times in *Hustler's* "Asshole of the Month" column, and Flynt began churning out cartoons featuring Falwell committing sexual acts. One cartoon featured Falwell and President Reagan participating in a pagan sex orgy; another depicted Supreme Court justice Warren Burger begging Falwell for oral sex. When Falwell didn't respond to *Hustler's* parodies, Flynt became absolutely determined to get the preacher's attention and force him to hear what the pornographer was saying about him. Finally, in November 1983, the Reverend Jerry Falwell heard, and he was *not* amused.

America's Preacher

Although Jerry Falwell would someday become a symbol of American Christianity, his childhood was surprisingly free of religious influence. Falwell and his "younger" twin brother, Gene, were born on August 11, 1933, in Lynchburg, Virginia, to Carey and Helen Falwell. The twins were an unexpected addition to the Falwell family, more than a decade younger than their older siblings, Lewis and Virginia. The United States was mired in the Great Depression, and Carey Falwell's recent bankruptcy seemed even worse with two additional children to feed and care for.

Nonetheless, Carey Falwell remained a respected businessman, a man who pulled the family out of their financial crisis through hard work. His long hours at the office gave him little time for entertainment and less patience for organized religion. A strict agnostic, he cautioned the future televangelist to avoid becoming a preacher, because "when a preacher walks into a room, people start acting funny." Falwell's mother, however, was a Baptist who routinely attended church and spent time volunteering at church events.

No straitlaced teacher's pet, when Falwell was in grade school, he locked his math instructor in a storage closet. In high school, he hid a live rat in his Latin teacher's desk. As a teenager, Falwell and his friends would have one of their smaller pals stand in the street and pick fights with passing college students. Just when they were ready to pound the obnoxious teen, Falwell and his friends would burst out of their hiding places and pummel the surprised college students. On Halloween night in 1949, Falwell and his buddies set fire to a large pile of railroad ties in the center of town; it burned so hot that it ignited the underlying asphalt street, spreading down the road and incinerating the nearby homes' white picket fences.

Neighbors wondered if Falwell's raucous behavior was a result of his father's drinking. Carey Falwell and his brother had been working on a lucrative business deal; when it fell apart, Carey's brother burst into the house and attacked him in a drunken rage. Carey, trying to defend himself, grabbed his gun and shot his brother, killing him. Carey began drinking heavily, and when Jerry and Gene Falwell were only fifteen, their father died of cirrhosis of the liver. Jerry's mother would be left to provide for her twin boys.

Despite his pranks and the loss of his father, Falwell earned straight A's in his high school classes. His "nearly photographic" memory allowed him to remember almost everything he read. Falwell wanted to attend Harvard or Notre Dame and become a journalist. In the meantime, he was the chief editor of his high school paper and the high school's star athlete. Tall and athletic, he played on the basketball and baseball teams, and he soon joined the football team as well.

Falwell was named class valedictorian, but was forbidden from giving the graduating address after an investigation revealed he was the mastermind behind a scheme allowing the school athletes to eat at the dining hall without paying for meal tickets.

Shortly after Falwell graduated from high school, he encountered his first—and perhaps greatest—religious experience. Falwell and his brother initially followed in their father's footsteps, taking no interest in religion, but the brothers began attending church services intermittently by the time they were twelve. Although Falwell went to church because "it was the thing to do," he made it through five years of Sunday services without ever having been "saved." He had little interest in this religious experience; what interested him was the church piano player, a girl about his own age named Macel Pate. With auburn hair and fair skin, Falwell thought Macel was the most beautiful girl he had ever seen.

On the Sundays that the boys did not attend church, their mother would tune the radio to a revival sermon given by Dr. Charles Fuller, hoping the preacher would touch the heart of her rowdy son. On January 20, 1952, he did. Falwell said he was sitting at home listening to Dr.

Fuller explain the life, death, and resurrection of Jesus when he felt a lump in his throat. Falwell said that all at once he realized that all people need a relationship with God and with Christ. Although he was already in his second year at Lynchburg College, Falwell abandoned his journalism studies, believing that God was calling him to the ministry.

Promptly withdrawing from Lynchburg College, Falwell enrolled at Baptist Bible College in Springfield, Missouri. He said he could sense God's leadership in his life, but he wasn't sure if he was going to end up a preacher, a youth minister, or serving God in some other way. Falwell worked hard at Baptist Bible College, giving up sports and studying into the night.

Perhaps Falwell's most noteworthy indiscretion involved his own roommate, who was to be married. Falwell was shocked to find that the engagement was to the piano player from Falwell's hometown church, Macel Pate. Despite her engagement, Falwell began writing her frequent love letters. Offering to drop off his roommate's mail at the post office while on his way to class, Falwell then tore up his roommate's letters and mailed only his own. It took several months, but Falwell eventually got Macel to return her engagement ring to her now heartbroken ex-fiancé. Moving quickly, Falwell asked Macel to marry him. She accepted.

During the remainder of his time at Baptist Bible College, Falwell began his religious work. He was first given a Sunday school class for eleven-year-old-boys, the problem being that only one boy was in the class. Falwell combed the streets for youngsters and soon attracted fifty-six kids. During his last year of college, Falwell began working as a youth pastor in Kansas City. During one of his long drives between college and K.C., Falwell realized that God wanted him to become a preacher.

Returning to his hometown of Lynchburg, Falwell began to preach part-time at his childhood church. Soon, a group of thirty-five adults approached him and asked him to be the preacher at a new church they wanted to start across town. Falwell explained the difficulties of beginning a new ministry, but the group remained undaunted. He agreed to take on the challenge and began looking for a suitable meeting place.

One of the members of the new congregation bought an abandoned cinder-block building on the outskirts of Lynchburg that had previously been owned by the Donald Duck Bottling Company. The congregation named the church after its address, the Thomas Road Baptist Church. For years afterward, children who remembered the church's origins would point and laugh, calling the building the Donald Duck Baptist Church. Falwell was pastor, as well as song leader, secretary, and janitor. The congregation slowly grew, starting with Falwell's mother, who became a charter member at the very first service. Falwell received $65 a week.

Falwell and Macel had been engaged for nearly five years, but now that Falwell had a steady income and a church that he could call home, he felt financially able to support his future wife. He and Macel were married in the new church, the tiny building filled to the rafters with family, friends, and church members. Macel, radiant in head-to-toe white, sobbed throughout the entire ceremony. Over the next few years, Falwell's family grew in size, as he and Macel had three children. Falwell had his family; his ministry was now poised to take off.

Because he had received Christ as the result of a radio broadcast sermon, Falwell held a deep-seated conviction that church sermons should be put out over the air. In 1956, just about the time the Thomas Road Baptist Church was formed, a local radio station, WBRG, made its debut. Looking for customers, it allowed Falwell's church to purchase a half-hour slot once a week for $70. Falwell's charm and down-to-earth examples of religion at work made him an instant radio success. He was the preacher you could understand; he had been through the same tough times that you had; he had fought with doubts and questioned his own faith before accepting Christ; he was the reverend who played touch football with the youth group; and he understood the trials and tribulations of parenthood. His listeners loved him.

Once WBRG realized the size of Falwell's listening audience and the potential draw of the popular reverend, they increased his airtime to a half-hour show every day. Soon, much of Virginia was tuning in to hear Falwell speak.

Radio, however, was not the end of Falwell's reach. New members flocked to his church, seeking his "knowledge on fire" approach to preaching. He brought new converts to the front of the church at the end of every sermon, offering them salvation through Christ. His strong, fearless voice echoed throughout the recently expanded auditorium, condemning sin through the Bible's words.

He mixed judgment with forgiveness, sin with perfection, and hope with salvation. People drove for hours to hear Falwell preach, his infectious energy and confident spirit spreading throughout the surrounding communities and bringing many first-time churchgoers out of their homes and into the Thomas Road Church.

Still not satisfied with his ministry, Falwell continued to expand it, reaching out through television to speak to those too far away to see him in person or hear his radio sermons. His *Old Time Gospel Hour* program soon became the most popular televised sermon in the country. Falwell spoke out on all kinds of religious and moral issues. His program swathed itself in the unmistakable images of Americanism, opening with a picture of a waving American flag and closing with the image of the ringing Liberty Bell. Falwell was compared to a saint, extolled as America's finest preacher, and rated by *Good Housekeeping* magazine as the most admired American behind President Ronald Reagan.

Some criticized Falwell, claiming that it was not possible for a single preacher to adequately care for such a large congregation. Falwell retorted that a large church brought people together under a set of common beliefs and served to let each member of the congregation know that he was not alone. In response to questions about his use of "secular" television and radio to reach his audience, Falwell said, "the twentieth-century church must use twentieth-century methods or she will be extinct."

And use those methods he did. By 1985, Falwell's half-hour daily program was being carried on more than 500 radio and 392 television stations. Falwell had written nearly a dozen books, and he was annually showing up as one of America's top twenty-five most influential individuals in the *U.S. News and World Report* poll. Falwell soon had so many commitments that he was traveling an average of four hundred thousand miles a year, had more than twelve hundred annual speaking engagements, and claimed to be working seven days a week from 5:45 A.M. until midnight or later. Despite this busy schedule, Falwell continued to serve as pastor of the Thomas Road Baptist Church. The tiny church had grown, earned national recognition, and at more than twenty-eight thousand members, become the second-largest congregation in the United States.

The Moral Majority

Although Falwell had a great number of commitments related to his ministry, perhaps no other obligation consumed more of his time than managing the Moral Majority. Established by Falwell in 1979, the Moral Majority intended to affect conduct nationwide. It was a conduit through which Falwell could sense the political pulse of the nation and use his influence for the benefit of political candidates whose values most closely matched his own. Falwell recognized the intimate connection between religion and politics, belief and practice, and if he could persuade churchgoers that they owed God a duty to vote for a particular political candidate, then Falwell could use this influence to install political candidates who would affirm his religious views through legislative action and public endorsement.

Falwell's Moral Majority had a platform that stood upon the basic religious tenets of Christian fundamentalism. Falwell explained that he had founded the Moral Majority to combat America's five major sins: abortion, homosexuality, pornography, humanism, and the fractured family. Although Falwell claimed that it supported the separation of church and state, the Moral Majority openly endorsed the teaching of creationism and the reinstatement of prayer in public schools. By purporting to offer listeners "biblical" support for these views, Falwell implied that all true Christians must agree with his views on these controversial issues and that they should evidence their devotedness to God by supporting the Moral Majority with their patronage and financial support.

Although Falwell repeatedly declared that the Moral Majority was not a political group and that it did not seek to endorse any political candidates, there was plenty of evidence to the contrary. One of Falwell's earliest concerns was the Moral Majority's tax classification by the federal government. As his organization took in more money annually than either the Democratic or Republican parties, Falwell had a great interest in maintaining the Moral Majority's classification as a tax-free religious charity.

The IRS, however, was not blind to the Moral Majority's support for 1980 presidential nominee Ronald Reagan and its open opposition to the reelection of President Jimmy Carter and Carter's support of the U.S.-Soviet SALT treaties. These activities were clearly political, and when the IRS informed Falwell of its plans to revoke the Moral Majority's tax-free status, Falwell split the organization into several entities. Some of the groups were devoted to religious activities, thus allowing Falwell to maintain their tax-free classification. Others were considered political in nature and were taxed. To add confusion to controversy, Falwell maintained the name Moral Majority for all of the entities, calling one a corporation, another a foundation, a third the legal defense fund, and a fourth the non-tax-exempt political action committee.

Supporters of the Moral Majority were asked to make donations to the organization, but few donors knew which branch of the Moral Majority their dollars were funding. Falwell's opponents accused him of putting all of the donations into tax-free Moral Majority entities and then secretly funneling those tax-free dollars into his political action branches. Falwell's opponents turned out to be correct when in 1987, and again in 1993, the IRS fined his organization heavily for illegally transferring millions intended for religious outreach into his political activities.

In the Moral Majority, Falwell forged an amalgam of religion and politics, going on nationwide crusades to get would-be voters registered in their districts. He toured the country urging pastors to mimic his voter registration efforts, declaring, "If there is one person in this room not registered, repent of it; it's a sin." His mantra was to "get them saved, baptized, and registered."

Falwell rallied support for the Moral Majority by lobbying for the political touchstones of Christian fundamentalism. Falwell labeled pornographers people who "poison[ed] the American spirit" while injecting "cesspools of obscenity and vulgarity in our nation's living rooms." He spoke out about abortion, calling it a "massive biological holocaust" and labeling the doctors and women who condoned it murderers. Falwell called homosexuals "brute beasts" who would "one day be utterly annihilated and there will be a celebration in heaven." Falwell labeled AIDS as one of America's seven deadly sins, a plague inflicted on the guilty as a punishment for violating God's law.

Through Falwell's well-funded and rapidly expanding congregation and his television audience, he could reach every town in America and influence the nation's choices through his religious-political sermons. At his peak, Falwell was labeled by the *Washington Star* the "second most watched TV personality in the country, surpassed only by Johnny Carson." The Moral Majority's leader was managing a political machine that had millions of voting supporters, and Falwell's influence over them would soon be felt in the 1980 presidential election.

Falwell understood influence well, and he claimed to have used this influence in 1976 to rally support for presidential nominee Jimmy Carter. President Carter was a born-again Christian who still taught his church's Sunday school class, and Falwell anticipated that, as president, Carter would bring fundamentalist values into politics. After Carter granted an innocuous interview to *Playboy* and took steps to soften the U.S. hard-line position regarding the Soviet Union and the Cold War, Falwell decided that President Carter was not conservative enough to represent true Christian fundamentalist values. Falwell quickly turned his influence against President Carter, labeling him a man who had turned away from God's word.

When Carter was asked about Falwell's criticisms of his presidency, the president responded that he was responsible to all of America's citizens and not merely to the Moral Majority. When Carter was pressed for his opinion of Jerry Falwell, Carter responded, "In a very Christian way, as far as I'm concerned, he can go to hell."

Although Falwell continued to insist that the Moral Majority was not interested in affecting the outcome of political elections, the *New York Times* stated the obvious, saying that the Moral Majority was "something very similar to a political party." Holding up his Bible, Falwell preached against President Carter: "If a man stands by this book, vote for him. If he doesn't, don't."

Falwell soon escalated his attacks on Carter, accusing him of being permissive about homosexuals remaining on his presidential staff. The voice of the Moral Majority's political machine had spoken, and in no small part due to the efforts of the Moral Majority, Carter was crushed by Ronald Reagan in the election of 1980. Following this Moral Majority victory, Falwell offered a foreboding warning to other elected officials, demanding that they "get in step or prepare to be unemployed."

The Reverend Jerry Falwell had emerged from his humble Lynchburg upbringing to become America's most powerful evangelist and one of its most powerful individuals. Controlling a network of financial, religious, and political contacts, Falwell took in hundreds of millions of dollars, funds he used in an attempt to affect the political destiny of a nation. Falwell's every opponent was quickly decried through his sprawling collection of radio, television, and magazine outlets.

Journalists were among the few who dared to criticize Falwell's expanding empire. John Jenkins, writing in *The Humanist,* said, "Jerry Falwell is emerging as the potential dictator of the New Christian Nation." Many times, Falwell was likened on the pages of braver publications to Senator Joseph McCarthy. A writer for the magazine *NARAL* predicted that if Jerry Falwell was left unchecked, he would "bring into existence a kind of Christian Nazism (with the Bible as *Mein Kampf*) whose manipulated multitudes goosestep mercilessly over the godless." Years later when Falwell was asked if he ever attempted to influence public opinion, he answered, "With every breath in my body."

Flynt Strikes His Vile Blow

From his wheelchair, Flynt watched the *Old Time Gospel Hour* television broadcast. Televangelist Jerry Falwell was once again soliciting funds to combat pornography and sexual perversion through the sprawling network of the Moral Majority. Falwell was so sure of himself, so utterly contemptuous of Flynt's lifestyle and his work. Flynt believed that Falwell represented the worst kind of hypocrisy, amassing donations from gullible viewers and using them to advance Falwell's personal goals.

Disgusted, Flynt decided that Falwell's pristine persona would not go unchallenged, and he would use *Hustler* to convey his own opinions to the public. Flynt was about to order the publication of one of his crudest parodies.

Larry Flynt knew that Falwell prided himself on his virtuous reputation. Falwell regularly preached against the evils of extramarital sex, degradation of family unity, and excessive indulgence in alcohol. Flynt decided to use these themes to portray Falwell as the worst of hypocrites through a fictitious ad for a brand of alcoholic mixer called Campari.

Flynt had been amused by Campari's ads, which featured interviews with celebrities talking about their first time drinking Campari liquor. By utilizing the double entendre *first time,* the celebrities in the Campari ads could also seem as if they were talking about their first sexual encounter.

Flynt latched on to this idea and created an ad parody featuring Falwell as the celebrity endorsing Campari liquor. Next to the picture of a smiling Falwell, Flynt featured a fictitious interview with the reverend talking about his "first time." Dissatisfied with merely portraying Falwell as a promiscuous drunk, Flynt took the parody much further. The ad parody described Falwell's first time as a drunken sex orgy between him and his mother in a fly-infested outhouse. Although the "ad" was designed to look exactly like Campari's legitimate ads, Flynt did include a few words of warning. At the bottom of the ad, in very small type, were the words "Ad parody—not to be taken seriously." Flynt snickered at his completed product and proudly published it in 1983's November issue of *Hustler.*

While the November issue of *Hustler* was disappearing from news-stands across the country, Falwell was in Washington, D.C., preparing to fly home. As Falwell was rushing to make his flight, a reporter brandished a copy of *Hustler* at the preacher and asked what he thought about Larry Flynt's latest parody. Falwell muttered that he didn't pay much attention to anything printed on the pages of *Hustler.*

Try as he might to concentrate on next week's sermon, Falwell's thoughts continued to drift back to the look of surprise on the reporter's face when he had brushed aside the question about *Hustler,* and he decided that he had better have an aide buy a copy. Falwell stopped cold when he saw the ad parody. It went far beyond anything Falwell had seen in *Hustler*'s pages before, when he had been featured in the "Asshole of the Month" column. Here Falwell saw his own mother depicted as a drunken slut; he saw his reputation as a preacher sullied in a national publication; and he saw his dignity as a person openly assaulted. Falwell was determined not to allow Flynt to get away with such outrageous conduct; he was going to have to answer for it in a court of law.

Falwell would later explain that he recognized that the freedoms of speech and press are guaranteed to all Americans under the First Amendment, but he believed these freedoms are not limitless. Just as a person should be forbidden from shouting "Fire!" in a crowded theater, people should also be prohibited from attacking each other in the manner that Flynt did. Falwell viewed Flynt's publication as an abuse of the freedom of speech, hence Falwell had little hesitation in bringing suit.

Falwell called on the ranks of the Moral Majority and the members of the Thomas Road Baptist Church to raise money for his upcoming legal fees. Falwell arranged a mailing to fifty thousand Moral Majority members in which he described Flynt's parody and asked for contributions to help "defend his mother's memory" in court. Shortly thereafter, Falwell arranged a second mailing to nearly twenty-seven thousand Moral Majority "major donors" accompanied by an actual copy of the "ad" with eight of the more offensive words blacked out. Falwell's letter to these major donors declared in part:

> Sane and moral Americans all across our nation are outraged by how much these pornographers are getting away with these days. And pornography is no longer a thing restricted to back-alley book-shops and sordid movie houses. Now pornography has thrust its ugly head into our everyday lives and is multiplying like a filthy plague. Flynt's magazine, for example, advertises pornographic tele-

phone services where, for a fee, men or women will engage in an obscene phone call with you!

> *. . . Cable pornography with its "X"-rated and triple "X"-rated films can bleed over into a regular cable system right into your own living room. . . .*

And there, in my opinion, is clear proof that the billion-dollar sex industry, of which Larry Flynt is a self-declared leader, is preying on innocent, impressionable children to feed the lusts of depraved adults. For those porno peddlers, it appears that lust and greed have replaced decency and morality. . . .

As you know, legal matters are time-consuming and expensive. There are lawyer's fees and courts costs to consider, not to mention the personal time and energy I must devote in these next trying weeks and months. . . .

Will you help me defend my family and myself against the smears and slander of this major pornographic magazine—will you send a gift of $500 so that we may take up this important legal battle?

Only three days later, Falwell sent out a third mailing to 750,000 people under the auspices of the *Old Time Gospel Hour.* In just the first thirty days following these mailings, Falwell's devoted supporters supplied nearly $750,000 to finance his legal campaign against Flynt.

While donations were pouring into Falwell's seemingly endless litigation coffers, he had begun searching for an attorney. He wanted a lawyer who could go toe-to-toe with Flynt and remain undaunted. Falwell wanted someone who was an expert in First Amendment issues, someone who could offer him some kind of special advantage over his adversary.

The Preacher's Champion

Norman Roy Grutman was the perfect fit for Falwell's needs. Grutman had shown his potential as a great advocate early on, winning Yale's highest forensic honor, the Gardner White Memorial Debate. In 1952, Grutman had graduated Phi Beta Kappa from Yale University and enrolled in law school at Columbia University. Once again, Grutman foreshadowed his future success, winning Columbia's prestigious Laurence S. Greenbaum prize for advocacy. After law school, Grutman worked his way to head of litigation in a large New York firm, before leaving to start his own firm, Grutman, Miller, Greenspoon, Hendler, and Levin.

Grutman had become a skilled trial lawyer, and his commanding presence and courtroom bravado had intimidated many opposing attorneys.

Born and raised in New York, Grutman had acquired a good deal of New York City grit and was not easily rattled. This innate toughness made Grutman a good opponent for the obstinate and incorrigible Flynt. Attorney Gerry Spence, familiar with Grutman's tactics, summed up his style: "Norman Roy Grutman . . . was cunning, crafty, and tough. He would do whatever was necessary to win. His style was to attack straight on—everybody and everything—relentlessly. He gave no quarter until his opponent was subdued, prostrate, and begging for mercy, and—having none—he gave none."

Also important for Falwell was Grutman's experience with First Amendment litigation. He had once served as attorney for Bob Guccione, the owner of *Penthouse,* representing him in numerous lawsuits over free speech issues. Falwell had seen Grutman's skill firsthand when he had once sued Guccione to prevent publication of an interview Falwell had given to freelance journalists. Falwell claimed that he didn't want his interview to cause the sale of even a single copy of *Penthouse.* Grutman mixed clever arguments about the First Amendment rights of celebrities with veiled insults directed at "Reverend Foulwell." At the end of the trial, the court explained that when a celebrity gives an interview with no strings attached, then the reporter is free to sell to the highest bidder. Falwell recognized that Grutman's experience with the other side of the pornography trade gave him a unique advantage.

Grutman's skill and courtroom demeanor were not the only virtues that Falwell would gain. Falwell wanted an attorney who could get to Flynt, someone who could penetrate his defenses. Grutman was the perfect lawyer to accomplish this, precisely because he had worked for Bob Guccione in the past. Flynt viewed *Penthouse* as one of his greatest competitors, and Grutman was nothing less than Guccione's hired gun. Flynt had declared his hatred for Grutman, even featuring him in *Hustler's* "Asshole of the Month" column.

Larry Flynt was livid when he received notice that he was being sued by Falwell. Flynt believed that this was an obvious attempt to strip him of his right to free speech. Flynt thought that if Falwell was allowed to give his Christian fundamentalist views on social issues and public figures, then he should have the same right. Falwell had achieved iconic status in conservative America, and as such, he held himself out as a public figure. The First Amendment was drafted to allow citizens to comment on the honesty and character of public figures who voluntarily put themselves in the spotlight of American critique. Generally, persons in positions of influence are loath to mention their failures and indiscretions. Thus, absent the open commentary provided by the First Amendment, Americans would never be able to unearth the truth about those in power. Flynt knew that his parody was insulting, inflammatory, and downright mean, but he believed it was protected by the First Amendment.

Flynt believed his position had support. In the late 1700s, one political cartoonist had depicted George Washington as an ass being led around by his aide David Humphreys. Despite protests by Washington's supporters, the cartoonist was not subjected to legal punishment. Thomas Jefferson, whose sexual exploits were a constant source of criticism, was shown as a "lecherous beast waiting in his shirttails outside his wife's bedroom." In another cartoon, Jefferson was depicted as a depraved taskmaster who kept a slave harem and auctioned off his mulatto offspring at slave sales.

Decades later columnists and cartoonists displayed James Garfield as an unwed mother wearing a dress and Ulysses S. Grant as a lecherous drunk. Other investigators exposed President Grover Cleveland as the father of an illegitimate child, writing a little ditty that cost Cleveland his reelection: "Ma, Ma, where's my pa? Gone to the White House! Ha! Ha! Ha!"

Throughout American history people have been free to criticize or even to mock those in power. Elected representatives, government officials, and public figures intentionally place themselves in the public eye with the knowledge that they will be subject to close scrutiny and that such scrutiny may be unflattering. Flynt reasoned that if Thomas Jefferson could be portrayed as a vicious, womanizing animal, then Falwell could be depicted as an incestuous drunk. Flynt believed that the First Amendment stood for an open society in which each American should be allowed to reach his own decision as to what the truth is. Flynt also believed that public figures and officials should have skin thick enough not to sue every time their feelings were hurt. Larry Flynt planned to defend these views in court, and he soon found an attorney who would prove to be a worthy of opponent for Grutman. His name was Alan Isaacman.

The Pornographer's Advocate

Isaacman was born in Harrisburg, Pennsylvania, in 1942. In 1967, after finishing his undergraduate work at Pennsylvania State University, he was accepted to and enrolled at Harvard Law School. Isaacman's potential was quickly noticed by federal district judge Harry Pregerson, who offered Isaacman a clerkship in Los Angeles once Isaacman finished at Harvard. Isaacman accepted and soon moved west.

After completing his clerkship, Isaacman began getting practical in-court experience as a deputy federal public defender in California and later in a number of smaller private-practice law firms in the Los Angeles area. His excellence as an advocate and his ability to adeptly handle both civil and criminal cases brought him to the attention of some of the area's most prestigious firms. Isaacman soon became the head of the litigation department at the Beverly Hills law firm of Cooper, Epstein, and Hurewitz.

Isaacman's area of expertise centered on entertainment issues and the First Amendment problems that often accompanied them. Isaacman represented Lionel Richie in copyright infringement cases, Jerry Lewis in an antitrust case, and Rock Hudson in a negligence suit. Despite Isaacman's growing list of celebrity clients, no single client could match the amount of business that Larry Flynt and *Hustler* provided. Isaacman would find himself crisscrossing the country for years after the battle against Falwell, defending Flynt in suit after suit.

Isaacman was an excellent choice of attorney for Larry Flynt. Isaacman had an informal, cool style that helped a jury relate to him. Even when tensions in the courtroom rose, Isaacman could frequently be caught smiling, as though something about it all were slightly ridiculous. Isaacman's regular-guy persona would help compensate for Flynt's unorthodox lifestyle. Isaacman had no vices to exploit in front of the jury; he didn't even subscribe to or read *Hustler.*

Isaacman met with Flynt to discuss the impending suit and Falwell's accusations. Falwell had alleged three tort causes of action: libel, invasion of privacy, and the intentional infliction of emotional distress. Isaacman would have to show that Flynt's parody did not meet the legal definitions of any of these claims. Isaacman and Flynt also realized they would have to do battle on Falwell's home turf. The suit had been filed in the Roanoke, Virginia, district court, only a short drive away from Falwell's hometown of Lynchburg. A jury from the Virginia area would probably have some ties to Falwell and the sprawling network of the Thomas Road Baptist Church.

Falwell's first cause of action, libel, is legally established when a defendant makes a written, false statement of fact about another that lowers that person's reputation in the community. If the statement is not written, if the statement is true, if the statement is merely an opinion, not a fact, or if the plaintiff's reputation is not damaged, then the definition of libel has not been met and the defendant cannot be found liable. An additional requirement barring recovery was introduced in 1964 through the Supreme Court's decision in *New York Times v. Sullivan.*

The Supreme Court understood that in any action for libel, there exists an intersection of two American values. On the one hand, the First Amendment guarantees the unimpeded freedom to speak and to publish. In conflict with this freedom is the Anglo-American tradition of protecting one's good name and reputation. Shakespeare wrote, "Who steals my purse steals trash . . . but he that filches from me my good name . . . makes me poor indeed."

The Supreme Court, in *New York Times v. Sullivan,* held that before a public official can recover on a libel claim, he must show that the defendant published the libelous statement with actual malice, defined as the knowing or reckless disregard for the truth. Only through this heightened protection can the freedom of speech truly be squared with the protection of one's reputation. In a later case, *Gertz v. Robert Welch, Inc.,* the Supreme Court extended this requirement to public figures, which certainly included Falwell.

Although Falwell had the burden of proof in his suit against Flynt, Isaacman knew that he must be prepared to show either that the parody was merely a statement of Flynt's opinion ("Falwell is a hypocrite, and I hate him"); that Falwell's reputation was not lowered in the eyes of the community; or that Flynt had published the parody without malice. Unless Isaacman could establish one of these three theories, Flynt would probably be found liable.

Falwell's second cause of action was the invasion of privacy. This action allows for the recovery of profits that the defendant made from the misappropriation of a celebrity's name or likeness. *Hustler*'s "ad" featured Falwell's picture, which Falwell alleged that Flynt was using to help turn a profit. Isaacman was less worried about this cause of action because for a plaintiff to recover he must show that readers would take the advertisement seriously. Because the "ad" was so preposterous, Grutman would have a difficult time proving that readers took it seriously, much less that it increased Flynt's profits.

The last cause of action brought by Falwell was the intentional infliction of emotional distress. To recover under this tort, a plaintiff must show that the defendant intended to inflict emotional distress through an act that is so outrageous as to deeply offend a reasonable person. The act being sued upon need not be factual. Even an outrageous opinion could serve as the basis for recovery. Historically, courts have been reluctant to permit lawsuits based solely on the infliction of emotional distress. Because emotional injury is not readily quantifiable and is difficult to objectively diagnose, courts have feared that allowing an action to be based solely on emotional injury may open the floodgates for frivolous and fake claims. Nonetheless, Grutman found this claim the most appealing because of its potential with a jury. A jury, freed of the technical requirements of the libel or misappropriation claims, could "punish" a defendant simply because they did not like him or his actions. In the suit against Flynt, Grutman felt that he was nearly guaranteed a recovery under this tort, and that left Isaacman holding his breath at what the jury's response would be once they got a good look at Larry C. Flynt.

The final portion of Falwell's complaint dealt with compensation for harm suffered at the hand of Flynt. And how much damages was Falwell seeking? No less than $45 million.

The legal battle between Flynt and Falwell was shaping up to be dramatic, and the trial would have all the window dressing and flair of a prizefight. Neither Grutman nor Isaacman seemed willing to concede any point, establish any common ground with the other side, or admit to any impropriety. The first order of business for Grutman was to take Flynt's deposition. Flynt, paralyzed since the shooting five years earlier, was wheeled into the deposition room handcuffed to a gurney. He had been serving time in a federal correctional institution in Butner, North Carolina, since January 1984 on contempt charges imposed by Manual Real, the chief U.S. district judge for the Central District of California. Judge Real had imposed the contempt charges after Flynt screamed a stream of epithets at the courthouse and wore a U.S. flag into the courthouse as a diaper. Grutman inhaled slowly when he saw Flynt's condition. The sight of Flynt, strapped to gurney, unkempt, and covered with bedsores, was enough to evoke sympathy from even the coldest observer.

Grutman's deposition of Flynt was videotaped and would later be shown to the jury. To make the deposition appear as neutral as possible, Isaacman arranged to have Flynt videotaped only from the waist up so that the jury would never see his handcuffs. Flynt wasted no time before launching into a characteristically bombastic tirade. His answers to Grutman's questions were belligerent and riddled with insults and profanity.

Unruffled, Grutman extracted two critical concessions from Flynt. First, Flynt admitted that he wanted the public to believe that the parody was a statement of fact and not merely a "comical" depiction. Flynt was even opposed to the inclusion of "Ad parody—not to be taken seriously" because he wanted readers to consider it true. Second, Flynt admitted that he published the parody to attack Falwell personally. These two concessions all but sealed Grutman's victory against Flynt on the libel claim. No longer could Isaacman claim that Flynt didn't have "actual malice" when printing the parody; no longer could Isaacman try to show that the parody was merely a statement of Flynt's opinion that was never intended to be taken factually. Larry Flynt was digging himself into a legal hole.

Flynt first claimed during the deposition that he had an affidavit signed by three different people who had witnessed Falwell having sex with his mother.

> **GRUTMAN:** Do these witnesses say that his mother had intercourse with him and they observed it?
>
> **FLYNT:** Yes.
>
> **GRUTMAN:** Where did they say that it occurred?
>
> **FLYNT:** I believe they said it occurred in Missouri, but I'm not sure. We'll have to check the document.
>
> **GRUTMAN:** Does the affidavit indicate how these boys who say this were able to have observed this incident taking place?
>
> **FLYNT:** Yeah, they were watching.
>
> **GRUTMAN:** Where were they watching from?
>
> **FLYNT:** Through the window of the house.
>
> **GRUTMAN:** And they could see into the outhouse?
>
> **FLYNT:** No, this happened—this—the first time was in the outhouse, okay, with the picture, you see. And he was only masturbating. The next time, he was little older, and it was in—it took place in the house.

Flynt's second concession was even more devastating to his case, because he admitted that he published the "ad" in a deliberate attempt to hurt Falwell personally rather than comment on his ability as a religious leader.

> **GRUTMAN:** Do you recognize that, in having published what you did in this ad, you were attempting to convey to the people who read it that Reverend Falwell was just as you characterized him, a liar?
>
> **FLYNT:** He's a glutton.
>
> **GRUTMAN:** How about a liar?
>
> **FLYNT:** How about a hypocrite?
>
> **GRUTMAN:** That's what you wanted to convey?
>
> **FLYNT:** Yeah.
>
> **GRUTMAN:** And it didn't occur to you that, if that wasn't true, you were attacking a man in his profession?
>
> **FLYNT:** Yes.
>
> **GRUTMAN:** And wasn't one of your objectives to destroy that integrity, or harm it, if you could?
>
> **FLYNT:** To assassinate it.

This would not be the only revelation during the proceedings that provided a glimpse into the personal nature of the struggle between Flynt and Falwell. Flynt claimed that he had gotten the information about Falwell's incestuous proclivities in 1978. Grutman asked him why had he waited until 1983 to publish the story.

FLYNT: I was waiting to settle a score.

GRUTMAN: Oh, to settle a score?

FLYNT: Uh-huh.

GRUTMAN: You mean you were trying to get even with Reverend Falwell?

FLYNT: Yeah.

GRUTMAN: Has Reverend Falwell, to your knowledge, Mr. Flynt, ever made any personal remarks about your mother?

FLYNT: Hmm, no, but he did about my father, and that's no difference.

GRUTMAN: Has he ever made any remarks about your personal sexual practices?

FLYNT: Yes.

GRUTMAN: What do you say Reverend Falwell has said about your personal, private life?

FLYNT: He says it's abominable.

GRUTMAN: What you personally do with Althea is abominable, he has said?

FLYNT: Hmm, my conduct is abominable, he says.

GRUTMAN: Okay, now you said a moment ago that you were waiting to even a—settle a score with him, is that correct?

FLYNT: Uh-huh.

GRUTMAN: When you use that phrase, does that mean you were trying to get even with him?

FLYNT: Yep.

From Flynt's belligerent, disjointed, and nonsensical ramblings, Isaacman fashioned a simple defense: "Can't you take a joke, Jerry?" Isaacman would maintain throughout the trial that the parody could not reasonably be believed to be a statement of fact because it was so outrageous. If the parody could not possibly be believed, then Falwell's reputation would have suffered no harm and Flynt could not be liable on the libel claim. Unfortunately for Flynt, no such readily available defense existed for the emotional distress claim.

Pretrial preparations had dragged on for nearly a year, and winter 1984 had come when all assembled in the Roanoke district courthouse. The trial would be played out in front of a packed house. The Honorable James Clinton Turk entered the room and called to order the trial of *Falwell v. Flynt, Hustler Magazine, and Flynt Publishing.*

In stark contrast to his appearance during his deposition, Flynt entered the courtroom immaculately groomed and wearing a tailored three-piece suit. Noticeably absent was every shred of his typical cantankerousness. Instead, Flynt carried himself with pride and a touch of decorum. Even his wheelchair had a whole new custom look; Flynt had it plated in twenty-four-karat gold and upholstered in plush crimson velvet.

Following opening statements, Falwell took the stand and Grutman led him through his distinguished and respectable life story. Falwell's testimony made it quite clear that he would do everything in his power to stamp out the influence of pornographers such as Larry Flynt. And to drive home Flynt's despicableness, Grutman introduced Exhibit 1, a blown-up copy of the *Hustler* ad parody. Falwell cringed as the jury's eyes focused on the object of his suit. Grutman helped Falwell to express his outrage at the parody:

> **GRUTMAN:** You say that it almost brought you to tears. In your whole life, Mr. Falwell, had you ever had a personal experience of such intensity that could compare with the feeling that you had when you saw this ad?
>
> **FALWELL:** Never had. Since I have been a Christian, I don't think I have ever intentionally hurt anybody. I certainly have never physically attacked anyone in my life. I really think that, at the moment, if Larry Flynt had been nearby, I might have physically reacted.
>
> **GRUTMAN:** Mr. Falwell, as a man active in public life and who has taken positions about subjects which may be considered controversial, have you been criticized or opposed in your ideas by various publications?
>
> **FALWELL:** Daily, almost.
>
> **GRUTMAN:** Have you ever had caricatures drawn of you by cartoonists?
>
> **FALWELL:** Again, almost daily.
>
> **GRUTMAN:** Have you ever felt badly about criticism that you read about yourself or responsible caricatures?
>
> **FALWELL:** I rather enjoy most of it.

GRUTMAN: But with respect to the materials that I have shown to you in this case, what is your reaction or response to it in terms of your feelings?

FALWELL: It is the most hurtful, damaging, despicable, low-type personal attack that I can imagine one human being can inflict upon another.

Falwell's somber testimony earned sympathetic looks from the jury. These looks of concern for Falwell were soon turned to looks of disgust at Flynt as Grutman played the videotape of Flynt's deposition. There was no question where the jury's sympathies lay at the conclusion of Falwell's case-in-chief.

During the defense's case, Isaacman tried to minimize the impact of the videotape by suggesting that Flynt was gravely ill at the time the deposition was taken. In response to Isaacman's questions about his physical condition, Flynt said, "I feel fine today, but at the time of the deposition I was in terrible pain. I had a terrible bedsore . . . and I'd been in solitary confinement for several months, handcuffed to my bed most of the time." Isaacman asked Flynt how he felt mentally at the time of the deposition. Flynt replied, "Something triggers something in me, and I really don't know what this is. I think, if people have certain mental and psychological problems, they're usually not aware of them. As I told you earlier, I sought treatment, you know. I feel, you know, that I'm fine today. . . . But my doctor said that I was in a manic phase at the time . . . that I was suffering from manic depression. . . . I've already explained my physical condition, and in walks this attorney who had, in the past, got two forty-million-dollar judgments against me, both of them thrown out on appeal, because they were frivolous lawsuits."

Grutman interrupted, "Now, Your Honor, this—"

"And I see another one coming at me," finished Flynt.

"Your Honor," said Grutman, "how he feels is not the question—"

Judge Turk cut Grutman off: "We've played the tape in its entirety, and I'm going to let him tell us how he feels."

Judge Turk was no stranger to Grutman's go-get-'em tactics. Turk had presided over the *Falwell v. Penthouse* trial, in which Grutman had served as *Penthouse*'s attorney. Judge Turk had successfully shepherded that suit to its conclusion, and he was determined to do no less here. He was adamant about making sure that both Falwell and Flynt had a scrupulously fair trial. Flynt latched on to the judge's temporary gag on Grutman to quickly attract as much sympathy from the jury as possible:

What I'm trying to establish is my frame of mind, you know: I had been shot, prosecuted, imprisoned, fined, you know, for my ideas, my beliefs on the First Amendment. I realize that I'm not in the majority, that I'm in the minority, but minority rights, I feel, are important. So, when someone files a lawsuit against you, you know, that has no merit and you know that it's going to be extremely expensive, things like this put you in a depressed state of mind.

Whether this testimony was sincere or not, the groundwork had been laid for the jury to take Flynt seriously. Isaacman then questioned Flynt about a number of milder *Hustler* parodies, attempting to acclimate the jury to Flynt's style of sarcasm. After warming the jury up to Flynt's humor, Isaacman got down to business and asked Flynt what he intended to convey through the ad parody at issue. Flynt's lengthy answer conveyed to the jury that he didn't really intend for the public to take the parody as truth:

Well, we wanted to poke fun at Campari for their advertisements, because the innuendos that they had in their ads made you sort of confused as to if the person was talking about their first time as far as a sexual encounter or whether they were talking about their first time as far as drinking Campari. Of course, another thing that you had to do is to have a person, you know, that is the complete opposite of what you would expect. . . . If somebody like Reverend Falwell is in there, it is very obvious that he wouldn't do any of these things; that they are not true; that it's not to be taken seriously. But where the irony and the humor is found in this, while it might not be funny to certain people and they may not see the satire in there, they have to consider how different people around the country perceived Falwell to be in terms of his political activities, his beliefs, how he wants people to perceive him as, you know, he would like to be loved, have recognition, acceptance by the people. There's nothing wrong with this, but when it happens, you know, ego comes into play. . . . And there is a great deal of people in this country, especially the ones that read *Hustler* magazine, that feel that there should be a separation between church and state. So, when something like this appears, it will give people a chuckle. They know that it was not intended to defame the Reverend Falwell, his mother, or any members of his family, because no one could take it seriously.

After several more questions, Isaacman asked Flynt if the ad was something to be treated seriously. Flynt gave the expected answer:

> Well, you know, as far as making it with his mother, I mean, that's so outrageous, I mean, that no one can find that believable. . . . The irreverence and the whole iconoclastic appeal about your mom . . . I mean, if this stuff was true, it would be extremely inflammatory and offensive, but the fact that you know it's not true, you know, I can't comprehend how anyone could take it seriously. I mean, someone may not like it, but that's not what we're here for today, is whether somebody likes it or not, but whether it's in violation of the law.

During cross-examination, Grutman's plan was to provoke the anger that he knew resided just beneath the surface of his adversary. Grutman came out swinging: "I notice that in your examination today, that in answering the questions put to you by your counsel, there was not a single obscenity, not a single vile word uttered by you. Is that Larry Flynt that we are seeing here in court today the real Larry Flynt, or is the real Larry Flynt the one we saw on the television screen in your June fifteenth deposition?"

"I'm under treatment," Flynt said politely, "but I'm more myself today than I was then. And the reason why I didn't use any obscenities is I see no need to offend this jury here."

Grutman followed up by quoting from several of Flynt's expletive-laced tirades directed at the Supreme Court, about some of their free speech decisions. Grutman constantly returned to Flynt's behavior during his deposition. Isaacman continually objected. The lawyers and Judge Turk engaged in a lengthy sidebar discussion concerning the scope of Grutman's cross-examination. Grutman persisted and was permitted to examine Flynt concerning a number of expletive-laced and emotionally charged interviews he had given in the past. Again, Isaacman strenuously objected, to no avail. Grutman finished his cross-examination by making a subtle but essential point. He wanted the jury to see that Flynt did not, in fact, distinguish between parody, satire, and reality. He quoted Flynt in an interview with a reporter from *Vanity Fair* magazine saying, "Parody has become so real that we're going to stop doing parody." Flynt claimed that he didn't recall saying this, but a point had been made. If Flynt didn't care what effect his publications had on people, he might actually have been more aware of the damage to Falwell's reputation by the ad parody than he let on.

It seemed clear by the close of the trial that Falwell and Grutman had the momentum. In his closing argument, Grutman stressed Flynt's malicious intent and personal animus toward Falwell, while Isaacman, for his part, played the First Amendment card on behalf of Flynt. Both closing arguments would prove to be but preludes to what seemed to many observers to be an inevitable clash before the nine justices of the U.S. Supreme Court.

Judge Turk, before giving the jury its final instructions, dismissed Falwell's claim for appropriation of name and likeness because the use of Falwell's picture next to the fake Campari ad was not for "purposes of trade." Judge Turk allowed only the libel and emotional distress claims to be deliberated by the jury. Grutman, Isaacman, and their high-profile clients remained in the courtroom, anxiously awaiting the jury's result.

After deliberating a mere five minutes, the jury returned with its verdict. The jury had found that Flynt had published the parody with the intent to inflict severe emotional distress on Falwell and awarded him $100,000 in compensatory damages and $100,000 in punitive damages. As to the libel claim, the jury found that no reasonable person could have believed that the statements in the parody were true. This result meant that Falwell's reputation was not damaged by the parody, and hence Flynt had no liability on that claim.

What the jury had done in this trial was to allow a public figure, who suffered no harm whatsoever to his reputation, to recover damages from a defendant who had published nonlibelous speech because the plaintiff had suffered emotional damage. Flynt believed that the First Amendment would not permit a jury to award damages to a public figure simply because his feelings were hurt, without first requiring that the speech be libelous.

Isaacman sat quietly as the jury read its verdict. He knew the sympathies of the jury, especially in Virginia, favored Falwell, and he had no real defense to the emotional distress claim. The skilled lawyer took his defeat calmly; he was already mentally preparing for the next phase. Larry Flynt had previously expressed his desire to appeal the verdict if he lost. The courts had not seen the end of Flynt's courtroom battle against Falwell.

Heading toward the Supreme Court

Flynt wasted no time having Isaacman file his appeal. And shortly thereafter, Grutman filed his response on behalf of Falwell. The decision of the three-judge panel of the U.S. Court of Appeals for the Fourth Circuit in *Falwell v. Flynt* was announced on August 5, 1986, nearly twenty-one months after the jury's verdict had imposed liability on Flynt. It was unanimous. Falwell prevailed once again. The appellate court held that Flynt had published the parody with an active ill will or mean spirit, which was sufficient for liability. This, despite the arguments by Isaacman on behalf of Flynt that the higher malice standard, one requiring that the publication be made with a "knowing or reckless disregard" for the truth, is required for liability.

Requiring only a dictionary definition of malice was the death knell for Flynt. That nobody believed the parody to be true made little difference to the Fourth Circuit. Flynt had acted knowingly or recklessly to inflict emotional distress on Falwell, and for the Fourth Circuit, that was sufficient to uphold the jury's damages award. The court pointed to one particular fact that seemed to seal their decision about Flynt's acting recklessly to inflict emotional distress. During deposition, Flynt had been asked if one of his objectives was to destroy Falwell's integrity. He had answered that his goal was "to assassinate it."

Flynt was livid. How could a celebrity possibly have the right to recover damages from a publisher merely because he experienced "emotional distress"? Flynt believed that the First Amendment could not possibly protect a celebrity's reputation to such a degree that it would effectively inhibit commentary about the celebrity. Frustrated by the Fourth Circuit's ruling, Flynt cried out, "Either we live in a free country or we don't."

On to the Court of Last Resort

The U.S. Supreme Court reviews only a small fraction of the cases decided by the lower courts each year. For the court to take notice of one case among the thousands wishing to be heard, a certain amount of public debate must take place on the disputed legal issue. *Falwell v. Flynt* was no exception.

After Isaacman petitioned the Supreme Court for a review of the case, prominent legal scholars and proponents of giving the media wide latitude were forced to make a decision. Should they get involved in what had turned out to be an ugly litigation? While siding with a person like Flynt and a magazine like *Hustler* presented public relations problems, press groups and First Amendment lawyers nonetheless saw the case as too important for them to remain neutral observers. They realized that if the Fourth Circuit's opinion was allowed to stand, it could cause irreparable injury to the First Amendment.

Newspaper owners, television producers, and civil rights groups banded together to submit briefs to the Supreme Court, urging it to grant certiorari and hear the case. The New York Times Company, the

Reporters Committee for Freedom of the Press, the American Civil Liberties Union, and even HBO submitted briefs arguing that the Fourth Circuit's decision had to be overturned. The message was potent: *Hustler* was not the first publication to mock a public figure.

On March 20, 1987, the Supreme Court agreed to hear the case.

As Isaacman and Grutman prepared for their arguments before the court, Flynt's thirty-three-year-old wife, Althea, died. Addicted to Dilaudid, the painkiller Flynt had taken for years following his paralysis, Althea overdosed and drowned in the bathtub at Flynt's mansion.

In their preparations for oral arguments, Isaacman and Grutman studied and analyzed those "speech" cases that had come before. Precedent was something to be overcome or relied upon, depending on one's perspective.

In the 1942 case of *Chaplinsky v. New Hampshire,* a religious zealot had stood on a crowded Rochester street and accused all non–Jehovah's Witnesses of being a part of a religious "racket." When an officer warned the speaker that the surrounding crowd was growing restless, the speaker shouted out, "You are a goddamned racketeer" and "a damned fascist, and the whole government of Rochester are fascists or agents of fascists." The speaker was arrested and later convicted for violating a state law that forbade using vulgar or derisive language to insult any person on a public street. The Supreme Court unanimously affirmed the conviction, finding that such language could incite violence on the street and that "resort to epithets or personal abuse is not in any proper sense communication of information or opinion safeguarded by the Constitution." Such "fighting words" were not protected as speech under the First Amendment.

Ten years later in *Beauharnais v. Illinois,* Beauharnais, a white supremacist, wrote and circulated a pamphlet declaring, "If persuasion and the need to prevent the white race from becoming mongrelized by the Negro will not unite us, then the aggressions . . . rape, robberies, knives, guns, and marijuana of the Negro, surely will." He was arrested and convicted under a state law that forbade any publication that portrayed "depravity, criminality, unchastity, or lack of virtue of a class of citizens." The Supreme Court affirmed the conviction, finding that hate speech about an entire culture or race was of such grave moral repugnance that it carried no First Amendment protection.

Grutman would try to analogize *Hustler*'s ad parody to these types of unprotected speech. Grutman would claim that the parody was so offensive as to incite a reasonable person to violence and therefore constituted "fighting words," not protected under the First Amendment. Grutman would also claim that the parody was of such utter moral repugnance that it had no redeeming social value and should therefore not be protected speech.

Isaacman had a different philosophical bent. He would rely on the logic of Justice Oliver Wendell Holmes. Holmes understood the dangers of silencing speech that the community believed offensive:

> Every year, if not every day, we have to wager our salvation upon some prophecy based upon imperfect knowledge. While that experiment is part of our system, I think that we should be eternally vigilant against attempts to check the expression of opinions that we loathe and believe to be fraught with death, unless they so imminently threaten immediate interference with the lawful and pressing purposes of the law that an immediate check is required to save the country.

In 1969, the Supreme Court in *Brandenburg v. Ohio* reversed the conviction of a Ku Klux Klan member who was prosecuted under a state law that forbade the advocacy of force as a means to further political goals. Brandenburg had been the leader of a KKK meeting at which hooded figures carried rifles while Brandenburg shouted out, "If our President, our Congress, our Supreme Court, continues to suppress the white, Caucasian race, it's possible that there might have to be some revengeance [*sic*] taken." The court held that Brandenburg was not trying to incite immediate violence; rather he was saying that violence might ensue at some undefined future time. The court held that Brandenburg's point of view, although repugnant, still merited First Amendment protection because it did not pose an immediate threat to public order or personal safety.

In the 1968 case of *Cohen v. California,* Cohen was arrested after walking down a sidewalk outside the Los Angeles County municipal courthouse while wearing a jacket bearing the words "Fuck the draft." Women and children present were aghast at the profanity, and a police officer took him into custody for disturbing the peace. The Supreme Court reversed Cohen's conviction, explaining that although pure obscenity is not protected by the First Amendment, an expression of political opinion certainly is. Cohen's jacket may have used profanity to express his opinion, but the use of profanity in this manner presented no physical harm to anyone around him. Cohen was minding his own business, and the simple phrase on his jacket could not be said to incite a violent reaction in others. Further, the jacket did not merit a "captive audience" analysis. Onlookers were free to look the other way or to choose a different square of sidewalk to stand upon.

Isaacman would try to analogize Flynt's parodies to these cases. The parody was certainly offensive, but it didn't present an immediate threat of violence or threaten the personal safety of any individual. Further, the parody was contained in an adult magazine that did not have a "captive audience." If readers didn't like *Hustler,* then they were free to ignore it. Flynt admitted that *Hustler's* content was crass and not suitable for children, but he explained that even the nightly news may not be suitable for children. Isaacman would try to make the Supreme Court see that Flynt's parody, while clearly disgusting, did not pose a threat to safety and should therefore be protected under the First Amendment, just as speech had been in the past.

The battle between Flynt's and Falwell's interpretations of free speech had evolved throughout their courtroom confrontations. A lawsuit—begun as a complaint about defamation or libel—now focused on Flynt's liability for the intentional infliction of emotional distress. Falwell's efforts to recover damages on his defamation-based libel claim were thwarted by the jury in the trial court. The jury simply didn't find the constitutionally required level of "malice" needed to impose liability on Flynt. Seeing one door close, Falwell hoped that another would open in the form of liability for the infliction of emotional distress.

Flynt's appeal to the Supreme Court explained that a public figure should not be allowed to end-run the First Amendment's goals. The purpose of requiring a high level of malice in libel and defamation before allowing liability is to shield publishers and speakers from lawsuits. Publishers and speakers would prefer to remain silent rather than risk being sued for the articles or parodies they published. Flynt believed that if a public figure could avoid the requirement of "malice" by suing for infliction of emotional distress rather than for defamation, then the First Amendment's goal of protecting publishers and speakers would fail. In Flynt's view, a heightened malice standard must be required to prevent the liability of publishers and speakers; anything less would result in their silence. Flynt's and Falwell's vastly different rationales on this matter were based upon two very different interpretations of what the First Amendment intended.

Falwell viewed the First Amendment as a means of finding truth and furthering moral decision making. The Constitution speaks of self-governance, and to Falwell this meant the right to work for a better and more moral nation. In his view, only constructive speech was essential to self-governance.

If the First Amendment is intended to allow self-governance, and only constructive speech is essential to this goal, then, Falwell reasoned, the First Amendment will protect only constructive speech. If the court found Falwell's view convincing, then a public figure would be free to hold liable any person who offered parody or criticism in a nonconstructive way. Such a decision would nearly destroy the ability of commentators and publishers to speak out about public figures without fear of being sued.

In contrast to Falwell's view of the First Amendment, Flynt envisioned an entirely different model of constitutional self-governance. To Flynt, the Constitution did not speak to absolute morality or constructive behavior, but to absolute freedom and the ability to partake in even destructive speech. As long as destructive speech presents no harm to anyone, speech that is obscene, indecent, or disgusting is fully protected by the First Amendment. Flynt wanted Isaacman to explain that a trial jury had already found no harm to Falwell's reputation. No economic damage had been inflicted on Falwell's "empire." The only damage that Falwell had suffered was embarrassment, and this alone should not be enough to silence a speaker. If the court agreed with Flynt's view, then free speech would become increasingly robust, but the reputation of public figures would likely suffer under open assault from commentators and publishers in the form of parody.

Finally, December 2, 1987, arrived. The attorneys filed into the Washington, D.C., courthouse where the U.S. Supreme Court would hear arguments. It was still early, not yet 8:30 A.M., when the parties arrived. The capital was bitterly cold, an approaching storm ready to unleash its fury on the city. Isaacman had his usual smile and slight swagger. He nearly skipped up the steps, anxious to speak before the court. Briefcase in hand, Isaacman held the door open for his mother, siblings, and other family members. Just before taking his seat at the advocate's table, Isaacman's mother gave him a kiss for luck.

Grutman's entourage seemed more dour. His wife and a team of associates slowly climbed from their parked car and ascended the courthouse steps. Grutman seemed the very picture of an intense New York lawyer, no time for anything other than the issue at hand. His suit was flawlessly pressed and precisely tailored, the long lines of his trousers and fitted jacket giving him an elegant polish. As his party entered the courtroom, he seemed to glide away from them, his wife flashing him a smile before taking her place in the chairs reserved for spectators.

Falwell and Macel arrived with Falwell sporting a patriotic red-white-and-blue-striped tie; his face looked far from jubilant. Grutman wondered if his client had eaten breakfast that morning. Isaacman's mother introduced herself to the Falwells. After chatting with the couple for a few minutes, she returned to her seat; Falwell seemed more relaxed.

With all of seven minutes remaining before arguments began, Flynt made his entrance. Dressed in an impeccable business suit, he looked every inch the corporate magnate. His gold-plated wheelchair gleamed beneath the courthouse lights, and Flynt—having been in the Supreme Court once before—stifled a yawn while finding a place to watch the proceedings. Isaacman shot a worried glance in Flynt's direction. The attorney remembered Flynt's previous encounter with the Supreme Court in the 1983 case of *Keeton v. Hustler.* That suit had ended in disaster after Flynt was charged with contempt and physically dragged from the courthouse while screaming a streak of obscenities at the justices and insulting everyone in his wake. Reassured by Flynt's apparently calm demeanor, Isaacman could only hope that the justices had forgotten Flynt's tirade.

Arguments before the U.S. Supreme Court

At 10 A.M. sharp, the court marshal announced that the justices were prepared to begin: "All rise! Oyez, oyez, oyez. The honorable the chief justice, and the associate justices of the Supreme Court of the United States. All persons having business before this honorable Court are admonished to draw nigh and give their attention, for the Court is now sitting. God save the United States and this honorable Court."

CHIEF JUSTICE REHNQUIST: We'll hear argument first this morning in No. 86 1278, *Hustler* magazine and Larry C. Flynt versus Jerry Falwell. Mr. Isaacman, you may proceed whenever you're ready.

MR. ISAACMAN: Mr. Chief Justice and may it please the Court: The First Amendment protects all speech except for certain narrowly drawn categories. For example, the First Amendment does protect false statements of fact made with requisite fault. The First Amendment doesn't protect obscene speech. The First Amendment doesn't protect fighting words made in the presence of the person to whom the words are addressed and likely to incite violence.

This case raises as a general question the question of whether the Court should expand the areas left unprotected by the First Amendment and create another exception to protected speech. And in this situation, the new area that is sought to be protected is satiric or critical commentary of a public figure which does not contain any assertions of fact.

CHIEF JUSTICE REHNQUIST: Are you suggesting that would be a change in our constitutional jurisprudence to protect that?

MR. ISAACMAN: Yes, sir, I am. I am suggesting that.

In a specific way, the question becomes, is rhetorical hyperbole, satire, parody, or opinion protected by the First Amendment when it doesn't contain assertions of fact and when the subject of the rhetorical hyperbole is a public figure. Another way of putting this case is, can the First Amendment limitations which have been set out in *New York Times versus Sullivan* and its progeny be evaded by a public figure who instead of alleging libel or instead of alleging invasion of privacy, seeks recovery for an allegedly injurious falsehood by labeling his cause of action intentional infliction of emotional distress.

In judging the publication that's at issue here, I think it's important to look at the context in which it appeared. The speaker of course was *Hustler* magazine, and *Hustler* magazine is known by its readers as a magazine that contains sexually explicit pictures and contains irreverent humor. As an editorial policy, it takes on the sacred cows and the sanctimonious in our society. It focuses on three subject areas primarily. It focuses on sex, it focuses on politics, and it focuses on religion.

Hustler magazine has been the target of attacks and critical commentary by Jerry Falwell for years, and for years prior to this ad publication. *Hustler* magazine is at the other end of the political spectrum from Jerry Falwell. On the other hand, Jerry Falwell filling out the context of this speech is the quintessential public figure. It's hard to imagine a person in this country who doesn't hold political office who has more publicity associated with his name than Jerry Falwell.

Jerry Falwell is the head of the Moral Majority. The Moral Majority, he testified at the trial, numbers some six million people. It's a political organization. It was set up to advance certain political views. One of the foremost views is to attack what he considers to be pornography, and to attack "kings of porn," in his words. And foremost among those kings of porn in his mind is Larry Flynt. He includes in that group others as well, such as Bob Guccioni of *Penthouse* and such as Hugh Hefner of *Playboy*.

The Moral Majority and Jerry Falwell also attack sexual conduct that they don't consider appropriate. He has spoken on the subject of extramarital and premarital sex. He doesn't approve of heterosexuals living together outside of wedlock. He also doesn't approve of and condemns homosexuality. Now, these aren't private views he has kept to himself or just shared with his family. These are views that he's gone on the political stump and tried to convince other people about.

He has been known in his words, as he testified, by the *Good Housekeeping* magazine, which did a survey, as the second-most-admired man in the United States, next to the president.

JUSTICE O'CONNOR: Well, Mr. Isaacman, is the fact that you claim Mr. Falwell is a public figure in dispute in this case?

MR. ISAACMAN: It isn't in dispute at all.

JUSTICE O'CONNOR: Well, then, I guess we could move on to the arguments, because apparently your remarks are for the purpose of demonstrating he's a public figure. Is that right?

MR. ISAACMAN: Justice O'Connor, it's to fill out the political context and the fact that what we have here are people who are at opposite ends of the political spectrum, engaging in the uninhibited, robust, and wide-open debate as in *New York Times v. Sullivan.*

JUSTICE O'CONNOR: Does the state have an interest in protecting its citizens from emotional distress, do you suppose?

MR. ISAACMAN: Clearly, the state has an interest in protecting its citizens from emotional distress.

JUSTICE O'CONNOR: And perhaps that's an even greater interest than protecting reputation.

MR. ISAACMAN: I would submit that it is not a greater interest than protecting reputation, because in the area of reputational injury, libel as we know it, for example, when it's in written form, emotional distress is an element of recovery as well as damage to reputation, and reputation affects what other people think of you. It affects what goes on in the minds of other people as well, and not just the minds of one citizen. So reputation in a sense covers a lot more territory than emotional distress does.

And the point of what I'm trying to make is that we really have people who are engaging in political debate in a way that involves vehement caustic and sometimes unpleasantly sharp language, as in the *New York Times v. Sullivan.*

Now, this speech is protected as rhetorical hyperbole, it's protected as satire and parody and as the expression of opinion.

JUSTICE WHITE: Would this be a different case if the jury had found that the allegations could be considered factual?

MR. ISAACMAN: It certainly would be a different case. We think that even in that situation, this Court should find that these allegations could in no way be perceived as factual as a matter of law. I think the Court would have to do an independent review of the record to determine that constitutional fact, that is to say, that there was no actual malice in this case because this can't be perceived.

There's nothing in this ad parody that can be taken as a statement of fact. And we're in an unusual situation where the jury has made that determination for us. So we now know that even this jury should never have been allowed to consider this.

And we have ample lower court precedents on the subject, such as the *Pring* case, which was a *Penthouse* article about a Miss Wyoming which attributed certain sexual activities on her part, and she sued for libel, intentional infliction of emotional stress, and other causes of action. And the Tenth Circuit, after an adverse jury determination to *Penthouse,* reversed and dismissed that case, saying that that's rhetorical hyperbole. That article couldn't be perceived as describing actual facts about the plaintiff in that case, or actual events in which she participated. Same finding that the jury made in this case.

And the court then went on to say that since it's rhetorical hyperbole and protected by the First Amendment against a libel claim, it's also protected against an intentional infliction of emotional distress claim, which there was called outrage under Wyoming law because the same constitutional defenses apply.

JUSTICE SCALIA: Mr. Isaacman, what the *New York Times* rule provides is not an absolute protection, but what a knowing element, an element of specific intent to create a falsehood. It doesn't give an absolute privilege to state falsehood. It just says the falsehood is okay unless there's an intent. Now, here we have a state tort that is specifically an intentional tort. There must be an intent to create the emotional distress, so it really is not quite the same category of opening up that you're making it out to be. The issue is whether the intent element that is enough to provide a major exception from *New York Times* is also enough to make a major exception for purposes of this tort action. Isn't that right?

MR. ISAACMAN: Justice Scalia, we have a lot of cases that say it's not the intent to cause harm. It's not the hatred, it's not the ill will, it's not the spite that the First Amendment is directed at. It's intent to cause harm through knowing falsehood or reckless falsehood.

JUSTICE SCALIA: I understand you can draw the line there. But all

New York Times says is if you state falsehood with knowledge that it is false, the First Amendment does prevent it. All I'm asking you is why can't that principle be extended to say you can cause emotional harm to your heart's content, just as you can state falsity to your heart's content, but where you intend to create that emotional harm, we have a different situation. Isn't that a possible line?

MR. ISAACMAN: I don't think that any reasonable reader of any of the speech that has occurred in the cases including *New York Times v. Sullivan* and all the other cases that have come down could ever say that the speaker did not intend to cause harm. People intend the natural consequences of their actions. And they intend when they say something critical, they intend that that's going to cause some harm or some distress. And that speech has to be protected, or all we're going to have is a bland, milquetoast kind of speech in this country.

JUSTICE SCALIA: That may well be. My only point is *New York Times* doesn't speak to it. *New York Times* says intent is okay, is enough to get you out of it. What you're saying is, this kind of intent shouldn't be enough.

MR. ISAACMAN: That's correct. Knowing falsity may be enough.

JUSTICE WHITE: Well, even accepting what the jury found, that there was no reputational injury here because there was no believable fact asserted, for you to win, you have to say that opinion or parody is never actionable, even though it's done intentionally for the purpose of inflicting emotional distress. That's your proposition, isn't it?

MR. ISAACMAN: Well, Justice White, my proposition is—

JUSTICE WHITE: Is it or not?

MR. ISAACMAN: No. As you stated, Your Honor, no, it isn't.

JUSTICE WHITE: What is it, then?

MR. ISAACMAN: Because what that leaves out is opinion or parody that does not contain anything that can be reasonably understood as a statement of fact.

JUSTICE WHITE: All right. I agree with that, because that's what the jury found.

MR. ISAACMAN: The second thing that your hypothetical left out, your proposition left out, was that this is a public figure who is bringing this action, somebody who's supposed to have a thick skin.

JUSTICE WHITE: All right. Include that, and then you say, parody or opinion about a public figure is never actionable even though it's done intentionally for the purpose of causing emotional distress, that's your proposition.

MR. ISAACMAN: And even though it contains nothing that can be understood as a false statement of fact.

JUSTICE WHITE: Sure, sure.

MR. ISAACMAN: Including that, I agree, yes. That's my proposition.

JUSTICE WHITE: Would you say if there wasn't a public figure involved, that we could sustain this judgment?

MR. ISAACMAN: Fortunately, that's not my case. But I will answer that. I would say that if it does not contain a false statement of fact, or something that can be perceived as a false statement of fact, then even if it's a private figure, it's protected speech.

JUSTICE STEVENS: Assuming there's no public figure involved, and you've admitted there's a public interest in protecting the citizenry from emotional distress, what's the public interest in protecting speech that does nothing else?

MR. ISAACMAN: There is a public interest in allowing every citizen of this country to express his views. That's one of the most cherished interests that we have as a nation.

JUSTICE STEVENS: Well, what view was expressed by this?

MR. ISAACMAN: By this ad parody, or your example?

JUSTICE STEVENS: Well, either one, other than something that just upsets the target of the comment?

MR. ISAACMAN: The ad parody is really two views or more. In the first place, we have to understand that we're talking about one page out of one hundred and fifty pages in the magazine.

JUSTICE STEVENS: I understand.

MR. ISAACMAN: So it's not a treatise or a novel that's gone into a long development. It is a parody of a Campari ad, number one, if it does that.

JUSTICE STEVENS: I understand.

MR. ISAACMAN: And that's a legitimate view for it to express. And we all can understand how it parodied the ad. It is also a satire of Jerry Falwell, and he is in many respects the perfect candidate to put in this Campari ad because he's such a ridiculous figure to be in this ad. Somebody who has campaigned against alcohol, campaigned against sex and that kind of thing.

JUSTICE STEVENS: Well, is the public interest that you're describing, you're building up here that there's some interest in making him look ludicrous or is it just there's public interest in doing something that people might think is funny? What is the public interest?

MR. ISAACMAN: There are two public interests. There is a public interest in having *Hustler* express its view that what Jerry Falwell says as the rhetorical question at the end of the ad parody indicates is BS. And *Hustler* has every right to say that somebody who's out there campaigning against it saying don't read our magazine and we're poison on the minds of America and don't engage in sex outside of wedlock and don't drink alcohol—*Hustler* has every right to say that man is full of BS. And that's what this ad parody says. And the first part of the ad parody does put him in a ridiculous setting. Instead of Jerry Falwell speaking from the television with a beatific look on his face and the warmth that comes out of him, and the sincerity in his voice, and he's a terrific communicator, and he's standing on a pulpit, and he may have a Bible in his hand, instead of that situation, *Hustler* is saying, let's deflate this stuffed shirt, let's bring him down to our level, or at least to the level where you will listen to what we have to say.

(Laughter)

MR. ISAACMAN: I was told not to joke in the Supreme Court. I really didn't mean to do that.

JUSTICE STEVENS: That's the answer to the first half of my question. What's the public interest in the case involving a private figure?

MR. ISAACMAN: In the case of a private figure, the public interest is admittedly less.

JUSTICE STEVENS: Less? What is it?

MR. ISAACMAN: There is still interest in expressing your views, there's still an interest in people being able to express their views, apart from the fact that the public may not have any great interest in hearing those views.

JUSTICE SCALIA: Mr. Isaacman, to contradict Vince Lombardi, the First Amendment is not everything. It's a very important value, but it's not the only value in our society, certainly. You're giving us no help in trying to balance it, it seems to me, against another value which is that good people should be able to enter public life and public service. The rule you give us says that if you stand for public office, or become a public figure in any way, you cannot protect yourself, or indeed, your mother, against a parody of your committing incest with your mother in an outhouse. Now, is that not a value that ought to be protected? Do you think

George Washington would have stood for public office if that was the consequence? And there's no way to protect the values of the First Amendment and yet attract people into public service? Can't you give us some line that would balance the two?

MR. ISAACMAN: Well, one of the lines was suggested by a question earlier, and that is in the private-figure/public-figure area, if the Court really wants to balance. But somebody who's going into public life, George Washington as an example, there's a cartoon that has George Washington being led on a donkey and underneath there's a caption that so-and-so who's leading the donkey is leading this ass, or something to that effect.

JUSTICE SCALIA: I can handle that. I think George could handle that. But that's a far cry from committing incest with your mother in an outhouse. I mean, there's no line between the two?

MR. ISAACMAN: There's no line in terms of the meaning because *Hustler* wasn't saying that he was committing incest with his mother. Nobody could understand it to be saying that as a matter of fact. And what you're talking about, Justice Scalia, is a matter of taste. And as you said in *Pope v. Illinois,* just as it's useless to argue about taste, it's useless to litigate about it. And what we're talking about here is, well, is this tasteful or not tasteful. That's really what you're talking about because nobody believed that Jerry Falwell was being accused of committing incest. The question is, is this in good taste to put him in this, draw this image, paint a picture?

JUSTICE SCALIA: If it's against a public figure, it's okay?

MR. ISAACMAN: No.

JUSTICE SCALIA: No?

MR. ISAACMAN: If it's a knowing false statement of fact, if you're charging him with a crime and it's perceived that you're charging him with a crime, and you're doing it with knowledge that that's false, it's not okay against a public figure.

And in summing up, what I would like to do is say this is not just a dispute between *Hustler* and Jerry Falwell, and a rule that's applied in this case is not just that *Hustler* magazine can no longer perform what it does for its readers, and that is produce this type of irreverent humor or other types of irreverent humor. It affects everything that goes on in our national life. And we have a long tradition, as Judge Wilkinson said, of satiric commentary, and you can't pick up a newspaper in this country without seeing cartoons or editorials that have critical comments about people. And if Jerry Falwell can sue because he suffered emotional distress, anybody else who's in public life should be able to sue because they suffered emotional distress. And the standard that was used in this case, does it offend generally accepted standards of decency and morality, is no standard at all. All it does is allow the punishment of unpopular speech.

JUSTICE SCALIA: How often do you think you're going to be able to get a jury to find that it was done with the intent of creating emotional distress? I mean, there is that finding here.

MR. ISAACMAN: Almost every time that something critical is said about somebody, because how can any speaker come in and say I didn't intend to cause any emotional distress and be believed? If you say something critical about another person, and if it's very critical, it's going to cause emotional distress. We all know that. That's just common sense. So it's going to be an easy thing to show, intend to harm. That's why that's a meaningless standard.

CHIEF JUSTICE REHNQUIST: Thank you, Mr. Isaacman. We'll hear now from you, Mr. Grutman.

Alan Isaacman walked to his chair and sat down. He had finished, and the fate of *Falwell v. Flynt* was now out of his hands. Isaacman had argued that the First Amendment protects the right to criticize and comment on public figures; he had explained that this right would be diminished if a public figure could recover damages merely because the publisher had meant to offend him or his feelings. His argument had been the professional high point of his career, and he had clearly savored every moment of it. He would later say, "I didn't want to sit down, I really didn't—I could have stayed there another two hours, I was enjoying it so much."

If Norman Roy Grutman was nervous at the act he had to follow, he didn't show it. Slowly rising from his seat at the advocate's table, he approached the podium and began.

MR. GRUTMAN: Mr. Chief Justice, may it please the Court. Deliberate, malicious character assassination is not protected by the First Amendment to the Constitution. Deliberate, malicious character assassination is what was proven in this case. By the defendant's own explicit admission, the publication before this Court was the product of a deliberate plan to assassinate, to upset the character and integrity of the plaintiff, and to cause him severe emotional disturbance with total indifference then and now to the severity of the injury caused. When the publication was protested by the bringing of this lawsuit, the unregenerate defendant published it again. Justice Scalia, I'd like to answer a question that you raised with my adversary. How often are you going to be able to get proof like this. I dare say, very infrequently, and I dare say that the kind of behavior with which the Court is confronted is aberrational. This is not the responsible publisher. This is the wanton, reckless, deliberately malicious publisher who sets out for the sheer perverse joy of simply causing injury to abuse the power that he has as a publisher.

JUSTICE O'CONNOR: Mr. Grutman, I guess there are those who think that the conduct of certain newspapers in pursuing Mr. Hart [Senator Gary Hart, a presidential contender, was involved in a sex scandal at the time of these arguments] recently was of the same unwarranted character. Should that result in some kind of liability?

MR. GRUTMAN: I don't think so; in that case what was being done by the newspapers was reporting the truth, the truth about a public figure who was a candidate for public office. The context in which the publications about Gary Hart appeared cannot really be compared favorably with what was done here.

JUSTICE O'CONNOR: So you would limit the recovery for the tort of emotional distress to recovery for a falsehood?

MR. GRUTMAN: No.

JUSTICE O'CONNOR: No?

MR. GRUTMAN: Under the theory of the intentional infliction of emotional distress, even the truth can be used in such a way if it is used in some outrageous way, it must be something which is so repellent—

JUSTICE O'CONNOR: And what if the jury were to determine that what the newspapers did with regard to Mr. Hart fell in that category? Is that recoverable?

MR. GRUTMAN: If the jury were able to find from the evidence, Justice O'Connor, that the publication was outrageous—I would doubt that they would find that because it is not that kind of conduct—reporting the truth.

JUSTICE O'CONNOR: But you would say it's open to a jury determination?

MR. GRUTMAN: Only in a highly theoretical sense, if the animating purpose behind the publisher was simply to inflict intense and severe emotional distress upon Gary Hart. But I think that's really not the issue. The focus in this Court, which is not the

Court of libel, the focus is on the harm which is inflicted on the victim.

JUSTICE O'CONNOR: Well, do you think a vicious cartoon should subject the drawer of that cartoon to potential liability?

MR. GRUTMAN: Only in the event that the cartoon constitutes that kind of depiction which would be regarded by the average member of the community as so intolerable that no civilized person should have to bear it. That's the definition of the Court.

JUSTICE WHITE: Well, Mr. Grutman, you're certainly posing a much broader proposition than is necessary for you to win this case.

MR. GRUTMAN: Indeed, but I was answering the question of Justice O'Connor.

JUSTICE WHITE: Well, the way you put it from the very outset, you put it the same way. We're judging this case on the basis that the jury found that no one could reasonably have believed that this was a statement of fact. That's the way we judge this case.

MR. GRUTMAN: No. I'd like to address that point, Justice White, because I think a kind of semantic conundrum has been presented here when counsel says that there was no statement of fact. There was a statement of fact. Just as we argued in our brief, you could state gravity causes things to fly upward. That is a statement of fact. It's just a false statement of fact. And if one consults the record—

JUSTICE WHITE: What do you make out of the special verdict the jury returned?

MR. GRUTMAN: I make out of it the fact that the jury said that this was not describing actual facts about the plaintiff or actual events in which the plaintiff participated. That is a finding that what the statement was in the publication was false. Perhaps we should have appealed that. That's a finding of falsity, which is all that we needed to prove to sustain libel. But we did not appeal that, and that question is not before the Court. But in answer to your question, I find that the meaning of the answer to that question only goes to the issue of whether the jury thought that Reverend Falwell—

JUSTICE WHITE: I don't know why you insist on this because if there's anything factual about this statement, you certainly have to contend with *New York Times*. And if there's nothing factual about it, you don't have to contend with it at all. All you have to say is that using opinion or parody to inflict emotional distress is not protected by the First Amendment, which is a considerably different proposition than what you've been pushing.

MR. GRUTMAN: I agree that parody or so-called satire, whatever it calls itself, is not necessarily protected speech when the purpose of the publisher is to inflict severe emotional distress. And while the contention is made in the argument that you've heard this morning that this was a parody, I think that the jury could properly examine this and recognize it for what it is. A fig leaf isn't going to protect this kind of a publication from being recognized as the kind of behavior with which the tort of the intentional infliction of emotional distress is intended to deal.

CHIEF JUSTICE REHNQUIST: But you would subject the range of political cartoonists, for example, to that kind of jury inquiry, whether it was vicious enough to warrant recovery?

MR. GRUTMAN: No. Two things must conjoin. What you have to have is an irresponsible intention on the part of the defendant to inflict injury. That's only one-half of it. The other is that what the cartoonist, the writer, or the speaker does, constitutes in the mind of the community, an utterance of such enormity, such a heinous kind of utterance, usually false, that nobody should have to bear that if the purpose was to inflict severe emotional injury, and severe emotional injury results.

CHIEF JUSTICE REHNQUIST: What about a cartoonist who sits down at his easel, or whatever cartoonists sit down at, and thinks to himself, a candidate for the presidency as just a big windbag, a pompous turkey and I'm going to draw this cartoon showing him as such. You know, part of his intent, he enjoys cartooning and just likes to make people look less than they are, to show up the dark side of people. But he knows perfectly well that's going to create emotional distress in this particular person. Now, does that meet your test?

MR. GRUTMAN: No. It does not, unless what he depicts is something like showing the man committing incest with his mother when that's not true, or molesting children or running a bordello or selling narcotics.

CHIEF JUSTICE REHNQUIST: What about the state of mind required from the defendant?

MR. GRUTMAN: Well, the state of mind is precisely what we're concerned with.

CHIEF JUSTICE REHNQUIST: What about the state of mind I've hypothesized to you? Does that satisfy your test?

MR. GRUTMAN: No, it would not. If the man sets out with the purpose of simply making a legitimate aesthetic, political, or some other kind of comment about the person about whom he was writing or drawing, and that is not an outrageous comment, then there's no liability.

JUSTICE STEVENS: Even though he knows it will inflict emotional distress?

MR. GRUTMAN: Correct, because you cannot have emotional distress for mere slights, for the kinds of things which people in an imperfect world have got to put up with, calling somebody some of the epithets that were mentioned in the opposing argument, blackmailer, or some other conclusory and highly pejorative terms, an epithet, but when you say not that you are some foul conclusory term, but when you depict someone in the way in which Jerry Falwell was depicted with all of the hallmarks of reality including the pirated copyright and the pirated trademark so that the casual reader looking at it could think this is for real, that rises to the level of—

JUSTICE SCALIA: That's a different argument.

JUSTICE STEVENS: Yeah, that doesn't go to the question of intent. What about a case in which another magazine publisher today decided I think I could sell a lot of magazines by reprinting this very parody here because it's gotten so much publicity and some people may think it's funny and so forth, I don't care if it hurts Mr. Falwell, but it will cause precisely the same harm as this one. Is there recovery in that case or not?

MR. GRUTMAN: I do not think so, or it's a much harder case.

JUSTICE STEVENS: So it's free game now? Anybody can publish this other than Mr. Flynt?

MR. GRUTMAN: Justice Stevens, Mr. Flynt republished it for a third time after the jury verdict.

JUSTICE STEVENS: I understand. But what you're telling me under your test, anybody else may publish it without incurring liability?

MR. GRUTMAN: Liability requires an intent.

JUSTICE STEVENS: But you do agree with what I said?

MR. GRUTMAN: I do, I do, Mr. Justice Stevens. This is why this is such a rare tort. This is, as I've suggested, an interstitial tort.

JUSTICE SCALIA: Mr. Grutman, you're given us a lot of words to describe this: outrageous, heinous—

MR. GRUTMAN: Repulsive and loathsome.

JUSTICE SCALIA: Repulsive and loathsome. I don't know, maybe you haven't looked at the same political cartoons that I have, but some of them, and a long tradition of this, not just in this country but back into English history, I mean, politicians depicted as horrible-looking beasts, and you talk about portraying someone as committing some immoral act. I would be very surprised if there were not a number of cartoons depicting one or another political figure as at least the piano player in a bordello.

MR. GRUTMAN: Justice Scalia, we don't shoot the piano player. I understand that.

JUSTICE SCALIA: But can you give us something that the cartoonist or the political figure can adhere to, other than such general words as *heinous* and whatnot. I mean, does it depend on how ugly the beast is, or what?

MR. GRUTMAN: No, it's not the amount of hair the beast has or how long his claws may be. I believe that this is a matter of an evolving social sensibility. Between the 1700s and today, I would suggest, that people have become more acclimatized to the use of the kinds of language or the kinds of things that had they been depicted at an earlier age would have been regarded as socially unacceptable. And while that evolutionary change is taking place, and it's a salutary thing, there are certain kinds of things. It's difficult to describe them. This Court struggled for years to put a legal definition on obscenity, and Justice Stewart could say no more than "I know what it is when I see it." Well, this kind of rare aberrational and anomalous behavior, whatever it is, whatever the verbal formulation that the nine of you may come upon, clearly it can be condensed in the form of words that I used, which are not mine—they belong to the oracles of the restatement—who have tried to say that it is for the jury to decide whether or not what is being depicted is done in so offensive, so awful, and so horrible a way, that it constitutes the kind of behavior that nobody should have to put up with.

JUSTICE O'CONNOR: Well, Mr. Grutman, in today's world, people don't want to have to take these things to a jury. They want to have some kind of a rule to follow so that when they utter it or write it or draw it, they're comfortable in the knowledge that it isn't going to subject them to a suit.

MR. GRUTMAN: I frankly think that it isn't too much to expect, Justice O'Connor, that a responsible author, artist, or anyone would understand that attempting to falsely depict as a representational fact that someone is committing incest with his mother in an outhouse and saying that she's a whore, and that when the person involved is an abstemious Baptist minister, that he always gets drunk before he goes into the pulpit, it isn't too much to say that anybody who would do that ought to take the consequences for casting that into the stream.

JUSTICE WHITE: Well, the way you put it, we don't need any new law for that. *New York Times* wouldn't insulate any statement of fact like that.

MR. GRUTMAN: Justice White, I don't think this case is governed by the *New York Times* rule. This is not speech that matters. This is not the kind of speech that is to be protected. The *New York Times* rule is not a universal nostrum. It is a rule that you formulated to meet a constitutional crisis which is irrelevant here.

JUSTICE WHITE: Well, if these were factual statements like you mentioned, you could win under *New York Times* anytime.

MR. GRUTMAN: Yes, we could win under *New York Times*, but I'm suggesting that as a jurisprudential matter, the *New York Times* formulation of actual malice is inappropriate and irrelevant for this tort for the reason that when you're dealing with the tort of libel, the focus of inquiry, the gravamen, is on the issue of true or falsity in which facts become the measure of what is true or false, or something which has been dealt with recklessly. The gravamen of this, as I say, interstitial tort is on the harm that was inflicted on the victim, and the constitutional measure here is intentionality. It's what this Court said in the dissent of Chief Justice Rehnquist, we're really dealing with scienter or mens rea.

JUSTICE O'CONNOR: Well, Mr. Grutman, there's plenty of malice here all right. I mean, I don't think that's your problem. But the jury said this can't be reasonably viewed as making a factual allegation.

MR. GRUTMAN: I disagree, Justice O'Connor, that is not what they said. The question answered is, can this be understood as describing actual—meaning truth—actual facts about plaintiff or actual events in which plaintiff participated. And they said no. That to me means that they said this is not a true statement of fact, but it's nonetheless a statement of fact for the purposes of *New York Times* or for the purposes of this case.

JUSTICE SCALIA: Give me a statement that isn't a statement of fact.

MR. GRUTMAN: Pardon?

JUSTICE SCALIA: Give me a statement that isn't a statement of fact in your interpretation of what *statement of fact* means. I mean, when you say *statement of fact,* it means true fact, or it means nothing at all.

MR. GRUTMAN: No. That is the Aristotelian interpretation of a statement of fact as propounded by Professors Wexler and Michael in their famous monograph, but in the common parlance in which we speak, a statement of fact is an utterance about either an event or a thing or a person which can be proven either true or false. If it's true, then it's a true fact, but if it's false, like gravity causes things to float upward—that's a statement of fact, but it's manifestly false.

JUSTICE SCALIA: So there's no statement that is not a statement of fact is what you're saying.

MR. GRUTMAN: That's correct. However, there may be statements— that's an interesting philosophical question that we could explore endlessly, but—

JUSTICE SCALIA: Mr. Grutman, that's not the way the Fourth Circuit interpreted the finding in this case. They interpreted it, as I read their opinion, the majority, to mean that the jury understood it was not a statement of fact about him. They didn't admit that they thought the statement was false. So you're urging on us a meaning that's not been accepted by any of the courts that have had the case so far.

MR. GRUTMAN: Candidly, I must say that I do not think that the Fourth Circuit made the point which I first tried to make to Justice O'Connor, and which I am making to you: in retrospect, I believe we could have appealed this as a proper basis for libel with that finding.

JUSTICE STEVENS: You could, but you didn't.

MR. GRUTMAN: But I didn't and therefore it wasn't before the Fourth Circuit, and it's not before you now.

JUSTICE STEVENS: Not only that, but the purpose in the jury instruction was to ask that question as a predicate to the second question, which related to malice, which wouldn't have had any purpose to it unless it's interpreted the way—

MR. GRUTMAN: That is the way it looks in the cold light in the Supreme Court today. I remember that at the time that those jury instructions were being fought over in the pit of the trial, it really had to do with a certain contention that Judge Turk was flirting with.

JUSTICE STEVENS: Yes, but your second question all goes to whether the *New York Times* malice standard, and that just isn't even implicated unless it's a false statement of fact.

MR. GRUTMAN: In this case, subjective awareness of falsity or reckless disregard of truth are an appropriate way of examining actual malice when the gravamen of the tort is falsity as in libel. However, here with the intentional infliction of emotional distress, which has also been described as outrageous conduct, the harm done to the individual is the focus of this tort. It's not a new tort. It's been in existence for a hundred years.

CHIEF JUSTICE REHNQUIST: It's certainly a new tort when applied to the press.

MR. GRUTMAN: No, it is not a new tort, because there have been cases that have been decided in a number of states in which the press has been held libel for this tort, not only for the intentional infliction—

CHIEF JUSTICE REHNQUIST: What I said was it's only recently, isn't it, that the courts have been bringing activities of the press within this expanding tort of intentional infliction of emotional distress?

MR. GRUTMAN: To that extent, I agree with you, Mr. Chief Justice. And the reason for that is that the press, the press that clamors here for a universal exemption so that they should have license to do what these people have done, and that it should be condoned and considered just a trivial or trifling incident of being a public figure. In Mr. Justice Powell's decision in *Gertz,* he talked about protecting speech that mattered.

JUSTICE SCALIA: Mr. Grutman, I think it would be different if there were a Virginia statute saying, it's tortious to depict someone as committing incest, the cartoonist knows that he's up against. But just to say heinous and just leave it to the jury? You think, for example, it isn't only the incest that offends you, you think that portraying a Baptist minister as having taken a shot or two before he went onto the pulpit, that that would qualify in your notion as heinous?

MR. GRUTMAN: I think particularly it would satisfy.

JUSTICE SCALIA: You don't think that's debatable?

MR. GRUTMAN: All these questions are debatable. That's why they go to juries for determination. But I think it is highly unrealistic that a legislature should sit down and write a decalogue or a catalog of prohibitions to constitute guidelines for people exercising free speech. This is an established tort under the law of Virginia and under most of the states. And I believe as a constitutional rule, the protection of the individual's interest in his own sense of worth and dignity and to be free from this kind of gratuitous onslaught and damage to his feelings is something that ought properly to be left to the states. *Hustler* and Judge Wilkinson argued that there is some new kind of category that this Court ought to establish called the political public figure. That is a figure unknown in any other decision and certainly not in this Court, and I would surely argue against it. Because this Court has said that by becoming a public figure, a person does not abdicate his rights as a human being. And if libel will not protect someone who is subjected to this utterly worthless kind of verbal assault, then the tort of the intentional infliction of emotional distress which Virginia recognizes is a tort which deserves support and endorsement in this case and in this Court. This case is no threat to the media. It will be the rare case indeed where this kind of behavior will ever be replicated, but where it occurs, it deserves the condemnation which the jury gave it, which the Fourth Circuit found, and which I respectfully submit this Court should affirm. Thank you.

CHIEF JUSTICE REHNQUIST: Thank you, Mr. Grutman. The case is submitted.

Grutman sat down, exhausted. He had been at the podium only thirty minutes, but the argument had been the culmination of nearly four years of work on the case. Everyone in the courtroom stood as the justices filed out to begin their deliberations. Grutman and Isaacman had both held their own, and throughout the often contentious give-and-take of the argument, both had articulated and justified their respective positions.

Grutman had argued that free speech should not serve as a bastion for hatred or a shelter for perversion. Yes, free speech is a cherished right, but it is not limitless. From Falwell's perspective, free speech should be interpreted somewhat narrowly, protecting the core opinions and values that the founders of this nation clearly intended to include within the First Amendment's scope. Grutman argued that public figures should not be protected from all criticism, but they should have protection from the onslaughts of vicious opponents, whose sole goal was to humiliate and degrade.

Isaacman argued that free speech should be interpreted broadly, excluding speech only in a limited set of circumstances. When criticism of a public figure is published, regardless how distasteful, it too should be protected unless it causes actual harm to the public figure. In Falwell's suit, no person could possibly believe Flynt's ad parody claims, hence the only harm the preacher sustained was that of hurt feelings. According to Isaacman's argument, if America truly values the right to speak and publish freely, then mere anger cannot serve to silence the voice of a speaker.

The Court Rules

Christmas came and went. The New Year was ushered in with no word from the Supreme Court. Flynt tried to concentrate on business at *Hustler,* while Falwell continued to manage affairs for the Moral Majority. Isaacman and Grutman, after short reprieves to get some well-earned rest, returned to their law practices. The notoriety of *Falwell v. Flynt* increased the demand for the services of both attorneys.

Finally, on the morning of February 24, 1988, the four men got the news. The Supreme Court had issued a unanimous opinion, written by Chief Justice Rehnquist. "The candidate who vaunts his spotless record and sterling integrity," explained Rehnquist, "cannot cry 'Foul' when an opponent or an industrious reporter attempts to demonstrate the contrary." When speech about a public figure is given, it is not enough merely to show that the speaker or publisher has bad motives. A speaker may have malicious motives and still speak the truth, and if truth is spoken, then the First Amendment's goals of educating the public are met. Upon that rationale, the court explained that a public figure must show both that a statement was made with actual malice *and* that the statement was false before they could recover damages on an emotional distress claim.

Mere parody is not a statement that can be considered factual by reasonable readers, hence neither can it be considered a false statement of fact. The jury explicitly found that nobody could believe the parody was a representation of fact. Because *Hustler*'s ad was found to be a statement of opinion and a parody, Falwell could not show that any facts were involved, much less false ones. Absent this showing, the court found that the jury's award to Falwell based on the "outrageousness" of the *Hustler* parody could not be maintained.

Chief Justice Rehnquist explained that what is and what is not "outrageous" is too subjective a standard. What is and what is not "outrageous" is fluid, depending upon the area of the country, the time of the suit, and the composition of the jury. If the court allowed public figures to collect emotional distress damages solely based on the basis of an "outrageous" statement, then a jury could too easily penalize those defendants they did not like, and this would be an intolerable abatement of the First Amendment freedoms of speech and press.

While Falwell commented that "no sleaze merchant like Larry Flynt should be able to use the First Amendment as an excuse for maliciously attacking public figures," the Supreme Court's unanimous decision seemed to say otherwise. Once again, satirists and political commentators were free to publish their parodies and offer their opinions without fear of being sued over a celebrity's hurt feelings.

In the *Falwell v. Flynt* opinion, the court was careful to point out that not all speech is the same for purposes of First Amendment protection. Whereas celebrities and public figures voluntarily put themselves in America's spotlight, private individuals do not. Hence, the holding of *Falwell v. Flynt* would not necessarily apply to a private citizen who is lambasted on the pages of a local newspaper. In the case of a private citizen minding her own business, the line between free speech and personal reputation may be drawn to give much more protection to one's good name.

Flynt realized this, but his main concern was his commercial publication and the right to satirize freely on the pages of *Hustler.* Flynt touted his victory as a win for First Amendment supporters everywhere. He celebrated his role as a social outcast, confident that his contribution to First Amendment interpretation would memorialize him forever.

And he is likely right. Legal scholar and historian Rodney Smolla offers this thought: "History reveals that, as often as not, the great First Amendment battles have been fought by our cultural rejects and misfits, by our communist agitators, our civil rights activists, our Ku Klux Klanners, our Jehovah's Witnesses, our Larry Flynts."

Falwell v. Flynt, giving the First Amendment new life, was finally decided in 1988; coincidentally, it was also the bicentennial of the ratification of the U.S. Constitution.

Falwell's loss seemed to foreshadow a weakening in the Moral Majority network. In January of 1986, Falwell gave the Moral Majority a new name, the Liberty Federation. Despite his attempts to infuse power into this "new" organization, the network of grassroots support that had backed the Moral Majority had scattered in its leader's absence. Falwell's focus on the trial, and his subsequent loss in the Supreme Court, resulted in television and radio stations canceling his ministry shows. The Liberty Federation never regained the momentum it had had as the Moral Majority, and in June of 1989 it was officially dissolved.

Falwell claimed that the Moral Majority and the Liberty Federation were dismantled by choice. He explained, "The purpose of the Moral Majority was to activate the religious right. Our mission has been accomplished."

The reign of the Christian fundamentalists seemed over. Scandal erupted from within the televangelist community. Jim Bakker was accused of adultery, and fire-and-brimstone televangelist Jimmy Swaggart admitted to enjoying the company of prostitutes. "Gospelgate" seemed to strip Falwell of any further hopes of revitalizing his national fame.

Falwell took his losses in stride. Falwell had founded Liberty University in 1971 as a lasting stronghold for Christian fundamentalism. As his list of obligations and engagements shrank, Falwell found himself spending more and more time at his duties as chancellor. He continues to minister to the congregation at the Thomas Road Baptist Church and doggedly pursues the mobilization of America's conservative thinkers. His view of himself as a political-religious figure was demonstrated in a June 2003 interview with Fox News commentator Bill O'Reilly. Falwell claimed, "For twenty-five years, my self-appointed task has been to mobilize sixty to seventy million evangelicals in this country to the pro-family, pro-life candidates, which have been exclusively Republicans of late."

Falwell's attorney, Norman Roy Grutman, returned to New York following his arguments in the Supreme Court. The highly publicized trial generated a huge demand for the services of the law firm of Grutman, Miller, Greenspoon, Hendler, and Levin.

Larry Flynt, fueled by his victory in the Supreme Court, continues to speak out for the First Amendment, and he continues to test its boundaries through the pages of *Hustler.* Although *Hustler*'s popularity seems to have declined over the years, barely breaking half a million subscribers in 1997, Flynt's autobiography, *An Unseemly Man: My Life as a Pornographer, Pundit, and Social Outcast,* disappeared out of bookstores as fast as it was shelved, and the 1996 movie *The People vs. Larry Flynt* sold out in theaters across America.

Larry Flynt has been tested through his pursuit of the First Amendment, and he has paid a bitter price. When Flynt and Falwell appeared together in a January 1997 interview on *Larry King Live,* Flynt was asked how he felt about some people labeling him a hero. Looking down at his wheelchair, Flynt said, "I wouldn't give up my legs for anything or anyone, so I think that disqualifies me for hero status."

In the end, both Falwell and Flynt fought for deeply felt beliefs. Their attorneys' arguments relied upon no ruse, no pretense, nothing but an honest disagreement as to the First Amendment's limits. The U.S. Supreme Court struggles to make those difficult decisions in the most objective way possible. The justices have a disinterested view of cases, an impartiality the litigants lack, and it falls upon those nine justices to consider the greater good and the possible effects that today's decision may have on tomorrow's issues.

The court's decision in *Falwell v. Flynt* explicitly gave Americans the right to criticize celebrities and leaders. The First Amendment was intended to encourage robust and vigorous discussion among the people of this nation; mere humiliation, embarrassment, or anger cannot still that debate. The court recognized this and looked past Flynt's over-the-top, sophomoric antics to see the deeper meaning of the suit.

Philosophers, pundits, and pornographers share the same right of free speech; to muzzle one leads inevitably to the muzzling of all.

CHAPTER SEVEN

What Price Too High?

One Woman's Fight for Survival
against Cancer—and Her HMO

You are going to help decide whether we have treating doctors who
are experts in the field deciding what is the best medical procedure,
or we have nontreating vice presidents with incentives, deciding
what's going to be the best course of medicine, vice presidents with
incentives that interfere with the doctor-patient relationship.

—*Mark Hiepler on behalf of Nelene Fox*

Nelene Fox watched as her three daughters helped pack the family van
for the long drive from their California home to the North Dakota farm
where her parents grew up. It was June, and the warm weather was perfect for Nelene and her husband, Jim, to take their young daughters
camping and fishing on the way to their family reunion. In the midst of
the preparations, the phone rang. A nurse from Nelene's medical group
had news about a recent checkup: "Your mammogram appears to be
irregular." Not wanting to miss out on her aunt's sixtieth birthday party
celebration, Nelene scheduled a doctor's appointment in North Dakota
and the concerned family set out on their trek. That same week, a biopsy
confirmed the family's worst fears; Nelene had breast cancer.

She immediately scheduled surgery. First her right breast was
removed and, after more test results, the left breast. The mother of three
started chemotherapy treatments, but the surgery and chemotherapy
were too little, too late. The cancer had spread to her bone marrow.
Nelene had one year to live.

In view of Nelene's odds, her doctor suggested that she undergo a
bone marrow transplant. Such a transplant might offer her a chance of
recovery, or at least extend her life, allowing her more time with her
daughters and husband. The doctor warned Nelene and Jim that an
insurance company would likely be reluctant to authorize the transplant,
due to the procedure's expense. The desperate couple, clinging to any

hope, were relieved to read in their health insurance booklet that bone marrow transplants were a covered benefit, though another portion of the booklet explained that any investigational or experimental treatments were not covered. Their relief proved short-lived. The family's insurer, a health maintenance organization (HMO), denied the request. The HMO representative told Nelene that this particular type of bone marrow transplant was "investigational" and "experimental" and not covered under the family's insurance contract.

With no means to pay for the procedure, the family filed suit against their insurance company with the hope of forcing the HMO to cover the treatment that offered their only hope for Nelene's recovery, their only hope of buying a little more precious time together. While the family and their lawyer struggled to force the HMO to pay for the treatment, Nelene Fox died.

The fight waged by Nelene Fox and her family against Health Net, the second-largest HMO in their home state of California, culminated in a bittersweet victory for the Fox family. The decision represented the first major judgment against a managed health care organization for failure to authorize necessary treatment. The decision also unearthed the heartlessness of a health care system that was supposed to protect the safety of its patients. The legal battle between the Fox family and Health Net was the classic David-and-Goliath story: the individual patient versus the corporate HMO. With soaring health insurance costs and the rising demand for managed health, *Fox v. Health Net* sent shock waves through a health insurance industry that was struggling to limit the breadth of coverage in an effort to keep health care accessible and affordable—and profitable.

The Rise of Managed Health Care

The cost of medical care has soared over the last twenty-five years; from 1980 to 1985, increases averaged 14.6 percent per year, dropping slightly to 12.6 percent per year over the next five years. By 1989, health care expenditures in the United States accounted for more than 11 percent of the gross national product, climbing to 14 percent by 1994. In 1996 alone, Americans spent more than $1 trillion on health care.

As costs spiraled, more and more Americans found themselves unable to pay for medical services. Workers and many of their employers had opted for medical insurance coverage under the standard fee-for-service system, where the insurance provider contracted with a number of designated health care professionals for the predetermined costs of medical services. This group approach had worked well enough—but no longer.

The staggering increases in the cost of medical care have a number of causes. Some critics point to the traditional fee-for-service system, arguing that such an arrangement encouraged doctors and other health care providers to overutilize services, needlessly referring patients to specialists or ordering a battery of sophisticated tests. By allowing physicians to retain exclusive control over the diagnosis and treatment of patients, doctors were offered no incentives to keep the cost of treating each patient low. With each new series of tests, physicians and other health care professionals inadvertently caused the cost of health care to rise.

Other often-cited factors are the tremendous advances in medical technology. Under the fee-for-service system, patients could receive any and all treatments that promised *any* benefit, no matter how small. Extending this policy to the far-more-expensive procedures gaining acceptance in the 1980s and 1990s placed an unbearable financial burden on health care providers, who wasted little time passing the costs on to patients in the form of higher health insurance premiums.

Lawyers also came in for a portion of the blame: huge medical malpractice verdicts resulted in skyrocketing medical malpractice insurance rates, with the costs being passed on to patients.

"Managed care" was thought to be the solution to the health care crisis. Managed care is usually distinguished from traditional fee-for-service indemnity plans by the existence of a single entity that coordinates and integrates financing and delivery of medical services. When people join a managed care plan, they are not only buying insurance, but also access to a health care organization that has a contractual obligation to arrange and provide for medical services.

In the early 1990s, the most popular managed care systems were the independent practice associations (IPAs). These systems were generally based on contracts between the health plan and physician groups, specific hospitals, and other specified health care providers. A variation of this model is the preferred provider organizations (PPOs), which are usually a more expensive version of a managed care plan. In PPOs, a wider network of doctors contract to offer medical services on a fee-for-service basis, but at a discounted rate; nondiscounted rates are charged to patients who visit physicians outside the network. IPAs and PPOs helped curb the use and costs of medical services, because patients could no longer visit any provider of their choice and still receive full insurance coverage, as they had under fee-for-service plans.

Even under this "managed system," costs continued to soar for both individuals and employers. Staggered by double-digit premium increases, many looked for a more affordable way to contain health care costs. The answer seemed to be health maintenance organizations. Unlike other managed care systems, HMOs often directly employ salaried physicians, run their own hospitals, and have exclusive contracts with a smaller number of approved doctors and hospitals.

HMOs proved to be enormously popular. Between 1982 and 1992, HMO enrollment more than quadrupled. The number of Americans enrolled in HMOs rose from 36.5 million in 1990 to 50.2 million in 1995. By 1997, that number had jumped to 77 million HMO enrollees, fueled in large part by Medicare and Medicaid patients enrolling as a part of their federal health care coverage.

Efficient, cost-effective medical care served as the basis for all the various managed care systems, and as predicted, placing checks on physician-recommended procedures reduced the total amount of health care costs. The rise of managed care also initiated a mass exodus from the more expensive fee-for-service plans; from 1988 to 1998, employee enrollment in the plans dropped from 71 percent to 14 percent.

Managed care reduced costs by extracting discounts from physicians, many of whom cut their rates by 40 to 70 percent, and by reducing both hospital fees and the length of hospital stays. In essence, managed care plans promised savings by covering only certain care, excluding coverage for treatments not deemed medically necessary or proven effective. Dr. William McGiveny, vice president for clinical evaluation with Aetna's HMO, said the bottom line is that "we don't want to withhold good medical care from patients because of cost. But we don't want to pay for medical technologies that are not proven safe and effective."

Therein lies the rub: with reduced costs come reduced services. Insurance companies had struggled for years deciding which treatments and drugs to cover. With medical innovations on the rise, those choices were becoming more complex. The decisions were especially tough for HMOs; as insurers *and* providers, they had to make coverage decisions on a prospective basis.

In the fee-for-service system—and PPOs, as well—a physician treats a patient and then submits the bill to the insurer, who then issues a check if the treatment is part of a covered benefit. This is called retrospective review. Prospective review is more cost-effective because the HMO must first approve the treatment before it will authorize the doctor to treat the patient.

At first, managed care organizations, especially HMOs, seemed like the ideal way to control costs and still provide adequate medical care. But as analysts took a closer look, the quality of care under HMOs appeared to depend on the type of patient. While HMOs seemed to work well and provide quality care for younger, healthy enrollees, the elderly, poor, and chronically ill were at higher risk—a lesson Nelene Fox and her family would learn all too well.

Nelene Fox

Nelene (Hiepler) Fox was born in Pasco, Washington, to Orville and Florence Hiepler, one of four children. The family moved to California, and in 1973, Nelene, twenty-two, met Jim Fox. Nelene's father was a pastor, and Fox attended his church and played baseball after Sunday services. Nelene and Jim dated for three years and married in 1976. Both teachers—Jim in the L.A. Unified School District and Nelene at Lutheran High School—the couple had three daughters, Natalie, Nicole, and Jenna. They lived for several years in Hawthorne, near Los Angeles International Airport, before moving south to Temecula, a small town in Riverside County.

Jim began working at Temecula Middle School, where he enrolled his family in the second-largest HMO in California, Health Net. Nelene was a room mother for each of her daughters' school classes. Active in the community, Nelene was a member of the Christian Business Women's Association of America, Moms in Touch, and the PTA. An involved member of her church, Sunridge Community, she was also on the Little League board, launching a softball league for girls, and spent her afternoons and weekends helping Jim coach their girls' soccer teams.

A nondrinker and nonsmoker, Nelene was the picture of perfect health at thirty-nine. She had only been in the hospital three times—for the birth of each of her daughters.

In June 1991, many of Nelene's extended-family members went to her aunt's sixtieth birthday reunion, and they were all present when Nelene's biopsy confirmed that she had breast cancer. There had been no prior history of breast cancer in her family. The diagnosis came as a complete shock.

During her subsequent mastectomies, doctors found the cancer had spread to her lymph nodes, indicating a high probability of recurrence. After the surgery, Nelene began the difficult process of trying to control her disease, where the treatment's side effects often seemed worse than the cancer itself. She started on her first round of chemotherapy in September; Nelene did not lose her hair, but the treatment so weakened her that she could barely eat dinner before having to return to bed. Over the next few months, Nelene's oncologist, Dr. Camacho, noticed the effects that the chemotherapy was having on her body. The therapy was killing off Nelene's red blood cells, and without sufficient red blood cells to carry oxygen throughout her body, she became easily exhausted.

In December, concerned about Nelene's increasingly weakened condition, Camacho ordered a bone biopsy; the results were devastating. The biopsy showed the cancer had metastasized, spreading to Nelene's bone marrow. Dr. Camacho explained that when cells from a breast cancer tumor metastasize to other organs in the body, the patient has reached what is called stage IV—the most advanced stage of breast cancer. Camacho gave Nelene a devastating prognosis: her cancer was terminal, and it would likely take her life within the year, even with conventional chemotherapy.

In a follow-up meeting, the doctor told Nelene and Jim that a bone marrow transplant might be a possibility, although it was expensive.

Dr. Camacho first tried treating Nelene with another chemotherapy drug, Andriamycin. Nelene went in each Monday for the treatment, staying up as late as she could Sunday night because she knew she was going to be in bed for the next several days. The drug caused vomiting, dry heaves, and fatigue.

After spending the first few days of the week confined to her bed, Nelene could usually get up to eat dinner with her family on Thursday evenings. She would sit in the kitchen with them for as long as her strength allowed, the fear of ever-present nausea discouraging her from eating much of anything. On Friday, she might have enough strength to help get her daughters off to school. By Saturday, the drug had worn off enough to allow Nelene a few hours out of the house. Her enjoyment during the week was always short-lived; Sunday morning came, and Nelene knew she had to return to the doctor the next day. She would cry, dreading the Adriamycin, which made her so miserable and knowing she had to take it to survive. It only took two weeks for Nelene to lose all of her hair. She went through this brutal routine week after week for nearly three months.

In April 1992, Nelene started having chills and a high fever. Jim rushed her to the emergency room, and as Nelene sat shivering in the waiting room, Jim haggled with a Health Net representative on the phone before he could get approval to have her admitted. She was released the next day when the fever abated, but within days the fever and chills were back. Jim again struggled to get approval to admit Nelene to the hospital, calling Health Net three times before they gave the okay.

While Nelene was being treated for pneumonia at the Inland Valley Hospital, she met Dr. Schinke (Camacho did not have admitting privileges at this hospital). Schinke told the Foxes that Nelene could not stay on the Andriamycin indefinitely, because the medicine would damage her heart. On her current regimen, Nelene would be lucky if she lived five months. Schinke recommended that Nelene have a bone marrow transplant immediately. He also mentioned that Health Net had already covered another breast cancer patient's bone marrow transplant at the City of Hope Medical Center.

Jim was eager to follow up on Dr. Schinke's suggestion, and after a conversation with Dr. Camacho, all agreed that it was time to pursue a bone marrow transplant. Jim soon discovered that only a limited number of universities and cancer centers performed these transplants for breast cancer patients. The procedure, called high-dose chemotherapy with autologous bone marrow transplant (ABMT), involves harvesting healthy bone marrow from the patient and then administering high, near-lethal doses of chemotherapy to kill all the cancer cells in the body. The dose of chemotherapy may be one thousand times more potent than that of standard chemotherapy. The concentrated chemotherapy also destroys the bone marrow that produces white blood cells for the immune system, so the healthy bone marrow is transplanted back to the patient (called stem cell rescue) in hopes of regrowing healthy cells. The cost of the procedure ranges from $100,000 to $300,000.

The City of Hope Medical Center rejected Nelene as a candidate for their treatment program because they did not treat breast cancer patients whose cancer had spread to the bone marrow. Dr. Schinke then recommended the University of Southern California Norris Cancer Center. "If this were my wife," he told Jim, "I would get her in immediately."

Dr. Khan and Dr. Douer, oncologists with USC's Norris Center, began testing Nelene in late April 1992. As a stage IV breast cancer patient, Nelene had to endure extensive testing and additional chemotherapy treatment to determine whether her cancer would be responsive to high-dose treatment. Dr. Camacho helped administer some of the induction chemotherapy. Nelene also endured cardiac and pulmonary evaluations, to determine whether her heart and lungs were healthy enough to survive the procedure. Ultimately, Nelene qualified for the treatment at USC. Dr. Douer informed the Foxes that 25 to 28 percent of women with recurrent breast cancer who had the procedure were disease-free for two or more years after treatment. He added that there was even an outside chance of a complete cure.

Despite the risks, the Foxes now had hope. It was going to be tough on Nelene: after the chemo dose was administered, her immune system would be essentially nonfunctional, leaving her extremely vulnerable to infection and disease. They also learned that the risk of death from the procedure alone was 5 to 10 percent. After carefully considering the risks, they decided to go forward. Nelene was especially excited about the prospect of not having to endure additional chemotherapy and getting back some quality of life.

Dr. Camacho gave Jim a referral to the USC facility because Health Net's protocol required approval for the treatment before proceeding. The first indication that Health Net might not cover the procedure came when Jim received a letter from Teresa Cantrell at Rancho Canyon (a Health Net provider group) denying coverage because the treatment was deemed "experimental." Jim immediately challenged Cantrell, telling her, "My understanding is that the coverage decision is not final until it comes from Health Net. Is that correct?" Cantrell told Jim that he was correct about the approval process, adding, "It's all political." The Foxes, concerned by Cantrell's response, turned to Dr. Camacho, who explained that insurance companies often balk at the expense of bone marrow transplants and often use the term *experimental* to exclude treatment.

Jim was relieved that he and his wife still had Dr. Camacho's support for the transplant procedure. Dr. Camacho even offered to write letters to Health Net about Nelene's condition. He wrote two letters, one on June 6 and another on June 11, strongly supporting ABMT for Nelene.

Shortly after Dr. Camacho wrote the letters to Health Net, he asked Nelene and Jim to speak with him in his office before one of the chemotherapy appointments. During the meeting, Dr. Camacho informed the Foxes that he had some concerns about the transplant and told them that he did not think Nelene should go through with the procedure. The Foxes were shocked; wasn't this the doctor who had been so supportive of the transplant, even writing letters to the HMO only days before? When Jim asked Dr. Camacho why he had suddenly changed his opinion, the physician said he had just spoken with Dr. Ossorio, the medical reviewer at Health Net. Dr. Camacho told the Foxes that he believed Dr. Ossorio knew what he was talking about, and the concerns Dr. Ossorio had raised about the procedure seemed valid.

Jim, shocked, said, "You've already discussed the risks with us." Dr. Camacho looked at the couple and replied, "I know." He said that Health Net, through Dr. Ossorio, offered to have Nelene evaluated at the City of Hope. If the City of Hope approved Nelene for the treatment, Health Net would pay for the procedure at the UCLA Medical Center even though she had already been approved at USC. Jim, who realized that the City of Hope had already disqualified his wife as a candidate, asked, "Why would they send us back to someplace where we had already been denied?" Dr. Camacho sat with his palms up and his mouth open, silent. Eventually he looked at Jim and said, "I don't know." Dr. Camacho reluctantly agreed with Jim that an evaluation at City of Hope was a waste of time, saying, "It's ludicrous."

Jim and Nelene were suspicious of Dr. Camacho's changed behavior and felt that Health Net was giving them the runaround with their City of Hope/UCLA offer. The clock was ticking; Nelene needed to move as quickly as possible to obtain the treatment before her cancer worsened and she no longer qualified for ABMT. The Foxes heard about another breast cancer patient whose insurance company had delayed the procedure, and the woman's disease had progressed and she was eliminated from the ABMT program. The Foxes were determined not to let that happen to Nelene, and they refused to go through with the City of Hope evaluation.

On June 12, 1992, just a day after Dr. Camacho's letter, Health Net denied the marrow transplant, saying, "Based on our review, it is determined that the request for high-dose chemotherapy and autologous bone marrow transplant is considered investigational for the diagnosis of metastatic breast cancer," and not covered by the insurance contract.

Health Net did not have a formal appeals process, so Nelene's brother, Mark Hiepler, a lawyer not long out of law school, faxed a letter to Health Net requesting the denial be reconsidered and asking Health Net to provide coverage for the treatment, saying, "You marketed this coverage to her when she was well. Please provide it now that she is ill." On June 15, Health Net sent the Foxes another letter saying they had rereviewed Nelene's medical records and still believed that the transplant she sought was investigational. Health Net also reiterated its City of Hope/UCLA offer, but the Foxes, believing the offer was a ruse, viewed the letter as the final denial. Hope for a cure existed, but their HMO denied them the means to attain it.

Fund-Raising

Even before the HMO's refusal to approve the treatment, the Foxes had decided to look into privately funding the procedure. The Fox family clung to the hope that Health Net would ultimately give its approval, but they felt that they needed a backup "just in case." Initial estimates pegged the cost of the treatment at nearly $150,000. A schoolteacher, Jim could not pay for the treatment. The bank refused to accept the Fox home as collateral for a loan because they lacked sufficient equity. As a last resort, the Foxes turned to their friends and neighbors for help. Mark Hiepler and his wife initiated a letter-writing campaign, and Nelene's two older sisters helped out.

Using flyers, concerts, radio broadcasts, television interviews, and even an appearance on the NBC morning news, the Foxes spread the word that Nelene needed money for the transplant—money that could possibly save her life, money that her health insurance refused to provide.

In an overwhelming show of support, the community rallied round the family, launching an extensive campaign to raise funds for Nelene's transplant. The initial response amazed the Fox and Hiepler families. Fund-raisers named the campaign Join the Fight. The middle school where Jim taught held a jogathon, and neighborhood teenagers organized car washes, where townspeople paid with checks as large as $1,000. The coaches and board members Jim worked with put on a softball marathon, and community members even baked pies for one event. Children with proceeds from lemonade stands walked to the Fox home to donate their money. The Sizzler Restaurant designated one night each week to donate 20 percent of its proceeds toward Nelene's transplant, and a local yogurt shop dedicated its Monday-night receipts for the procedure.

Multiple accounts were set up through a fund at the Foxes' local church, and an accountant kept track of the donations. If Health Net ultimately paid, the Foxes planned to repay each donor, or if the donor agreed, donate the money to breast cancer research. Despite her husband's urging her to rest up for the procedure, Nelene felt that she had to attend as many events as possible. When worry and stress kept her up at night, she passed the hours writing thank-you notes; they mailed fifteen hundred handwritten letters to the donors.

Jim constantly ran into donors, many asking when and whether Health Net would pay the money back. One father reminded Jim that his daughter had donated money from her college fund and would soon need it back when she left for college. Jim avoided taking his daughters to the local ice cream parlor, so he would not have to confront people who asked about when they would get their money back. The stress affected Jim physically; the family doctor treated him for stomach problems related to his emotional distress.

On June 19, shortly after Health Net denied Nelene the transplant procedure, supporters staged a protest at the HMO's headquarters in Woodland Hills, California. Nelene's friends cheered as speakers demanded that Health Net "live up to its obligation to provide coverage paid for" and "save this dear woman's life." Supporters also announced that 1,006 people had donated $125,000—well within reach of the $150,000 required to begin the procedure at the Norris Center. The family reiterated the promise that if Health Net paid for the treatment, "every dollar will be returned to the donors."

Health Net issued a statement: "If you knew all the facts in this case, you would appreciate that Health Net and the Medical Group have sought to act in the best interest of Mrs. Fox." At the rally, Nelene cried as she spoke to a group of supporters and said later, "I kind of lost hope." However, she said the success of the fund-raising "gives me renewed hope of having a life with my husband and our three daughters."

That same day, the Foxes filed a lawsuit against Health Net, seeking to force them to pay for the bone marrow transplant. After unsuccessful attempts to retain a more experienced attorney, Mark Hiepler, who had graduated from law school only four years earlier, volunteered to represent his sister.

Eventually, more than twenty-five hundred relatives, friends, and strangers from across the nation contributed $220,000. Much of the family's support came from the Foxes' church, Sunridge Community, with 25 percent raised right in their own neighborhood.

In late August 1992, months after Dr. Camacho first suggested a bone marrow transplant, Nelene began her treatment. The procedure, lasting just under a month, brought about an immediate and dramatic improvement in her quality of life. When a patient undergoes high-dose chemotherapy with ABMT, doctors look for what they call a complete response. This term is used to indicate that there is no clinical evidence of any cancer in the patient. Initially, the doctors proclaimed "a complete response."

Nelene returned to her a normal way of life, no longer enduring brutal chemotherapy sessions. She had hope. She was able to return to her PTA activities at her daughters' school and began helping out at the American Red Cross. The Foxes even went on a family vacation. Nelene was soon able to walk three miles a day, and she spent time with her kids, ages four, nine, and eleven.

"We had a wonderful Christmas" that year, Jim Fox recalled. Nelene also began setting up speaking engagements at women's groups, discussing how her strong Christian faith helped her battle cancer and face fear, pain, and imminent death. But in March of the following year, the cancer returned—this time, doctors found it in her brain. She quickly declined, and on April 22, 1993, Nelene passed away at her home. She was only forty years old.

Hiepler's Story

Although Nelene had lost her battle with breast cancer, the battle against the HMO that had refused to pay for her treatment was far from over. Her brother, Mark Hiepler, led the way. Although Nelene was nine years his senior, the two were extremely close growing up and would remain so throughout Nelene's life.

Hiepler had long thought his future lay in politics, explaining he wanted to make a difference with his life. Law school, he felt, was a necessary step in that journey. Hiepler said, "I went to law school because I saw that people who changed things in the world always had a law degree." He graduated from Pepperdine School of Law in 1988, but not before meeting his wife, Michelle, a former Miss Colorado, during his last semester of law school. They married in November 1990.

After Hiepler got married he worked at a law office in downtown Los Angeles. Although his job seemed mundane, he explained to his sister that he needed the experience before he could pursue his loftier objectives.

The Hieplers moved to Ventura County and Mark accepted a position at Lowthorp, Richards, McMillan, Miller, Conway, & Templeman, in Oxnard. Hiepler started at his new job in January 1992, just around the time Nelene's physicians first recommended the bone marrow transplant.

When Nelene received Rancho Canyon's denial letter from Teresa Cantrell, she called her brother. "They're calling my transplant 'experimental,'" she said. Hiepler tried to reassure his panicked sister that insurance companies initially give some sort of an excuse, because they don't want to pay for expensive procedures. He told her not to worry; they'd have to cover it because the treatment was covered in the contract language. Despite his assurances, Hiepler said, "Let's start the fund-raising." They wanted to get an initial base of funds before they kicked off any major fund-raising campaign so that the goal didn't seem like such a long shot to potential donors. When Health Net denied the transplant request on June 12, Hiepler reassured Nelene, saying, "We'll write some letters. Don't worry." In his letter to Health Net, Hiepler explained, "We'll go anywhere, we'll do anything to get this procedure, but we don't want a lawsuit."

Preparing for Trial

Hiepler soon realized that his letter wouldn't be enough. "We were really naive," he said. "We thought they'd agree and that would be the end of it." Health Net wasn't so easily persuaded. Hiepler organized the June 19 rally in front of Health Net's headquarters, and fortunately for the Foxes, the rally turned into a media event, which widened the donor base.

Hiepler filed Nelene's lawsuit against Health Net, alleging breach of contract for denying coverage, bad faith in that denial of coverage, and intentional infliction of emotional distress on Jim and Nelene. Both

Nelene and Jim were reluctant to initiate a lawsuit. Nelene, who was focused on battling her disease, felt badly that she was bothering anybody. The Foxes did not want to go through a legal battle, but they acknowledged that as a last resort, they might have to, to pressure Health Net to pay. It was, they reasoned, a means to an end.

Mark and Michelle Hiepler began calling other attorneys, "bad faith gurus" who specialized in suing insurance companies for denial of coverage. From one attorney to the next, each refused to take Nelene's case. The front-office people at some law firms prevented them from getting through to the right people, and attorneys failed to return their calls.

When it became clear that Health Net would not budge, Hiepler and his wife knew they would have to push forward on their own. While their primary goal was to resolve the dispute informally, once they threatened a suit over the matter, Hiepler believed that they simply had to proceed.

Hiepler began deposing Health Net employees—potential witnesses— less than a month after filing the complaint. While Jim and Nelene spent their summer fund-raising, Hiepler labored through depositions and dug through corporate records. Remarkably, it was the first time "outsiders" would get an in-depth look at the inner workings of an HMO.

Hiepler uncovered troubling details about how many HMOs controlled medical care expenses, revealing much about HMO cost-control mechanisms—information largely unknown to the public prior to this case—exposing HMOs to substantial liability risks. First, HMOs, as providers and insurers, sell packages that limit access to specialists and hospitals, impose certain conditions on coverage, and limit other types of care. Disputes over coverage arise in situations where an HMO's denial of appropriate care leads to patient injury. Nelene and Jim Fox's decision to file suit was, in part, based upon the allegation that Health Net's refusal to fund Nelene's bone marrow transplant caused a delay in treatment, which may ultimately have led to her death.

Second, HMOs select a restricted group of health care professionals to provide services to the program's participants. If the HMO selects and retains incompetent and high-risk physicians to keep costs low, then patients may pay the ultimate price through injury or misdiagnosis.

Third, HMOs use primary care physicians as "gatekeepers" to control access to specialists and hospitals in an attempt to contain costs. By permitting access to specialists only when an HMO agent has determined that there is a medical "necessity," HMOs can effectively reduce the number of visits to specialists. Some HMO plans even reward primary care physicians who limit referrals to specialists. The rewards typically work in one of two ways: the HMO will either hold some of the physician's income in escrow, returning a portion of it at the end of the year only if specialist referral targets are met, or the HMO may offer primary care physicians an annual bonus based on the number of specialist referrals. These incentives provide primary care physicians with a clear conflict of interest: quality health care for their patients or extra cash from the HMO.

Fourth, HMO physicians are subject to plan rules and incentives to provide cost-effective care and keep the HMO plan within its budget. Incentives and cost-control methods may push physicians toward risky levels of undertreatment. Many HMOs pay for services through a "capitation program." Under capitation, an HMO, like Health Net, is paid a fee by the insured patient, who relinquishes control over treatment and choice of physician. The primary care physician, in turn, receives a capitation fee from the HMO based on the number of enrollees, and the physicians must accept certain controls over their practice in return for receiving these patients from the HMO. Capitation fees are the fixed amount paid to physicians for each patient, regardless of how much medical care is rendered.

In some contracts, if the capitation payments are exhausted for a particularly ill patient, the physicians are partly responsible for the cost of continued care—often up to $5,000 extra before the HMO will step in and assume the rest of the payments. Through this method, capitation is supposed to discourage physicians' overuse of services to increase their income, because any care not provided for the patient translates to profit for the doctor and for the plan. Intuitively, though, capitation provides an incentive to provide as little care as possible to enrollees. Physicians still receive the capitation payments even if no services are rendered.

Another method of cost containment is a shared-risk program, or risk pool. A portion of the physician's monthly payment is withheld and put into a risk pool, and the money is then used to pay for referrals to specialists and hospitalization expenses. Physicians receive a share of the pool, the equivalent of a year-end bonus, if referrals and the use of high-technology health services are kept to a minimum. On the other hand, if the HMO feels a physician is providing too much care, the physician risks banishment from the HMO rosters for "overtreatment."

Utilization review, a plan's oversight mechanism on doctors and patients, is another major method that managed care uses to prevent cost escalations from overuse of medical services by plan members. Utilization review departments within the HMOs evaluate the needs and condition of a patient to determine whether to approve the physician's procedures and to weed out extra days of hospitalization and unnecessary specialist referrals and diagnostic tests. The boards are staffed with in-house nurses and physicians and, in some cases, are independently employed. Under managed care's prospective review, utilization review boards must approve a treatment prior to administration. Conflict often arises between the physician's prescribed course of treatment and the reviewer's recommendation. In the past, physicians could order tests, referrals, and hospitalizations without much resistance from the insurers who ultimately paid the bill.

In Nelene Fox's case, Health Net's incentive programs for its in-house doctor responsible for denying her transplant request formed a basis for the Foxes' claims against the HMO. When physicians recommend a certain procedure, such as Nelene's oncologists' recommendation of a bone marrow transplant, HMO utilization review boards essentially serve to second-guess those physicians in order to limit health care costs. Health Net's utilization review of Nelene's condition led it to deny coverage for her bone marrow transplant, despite her treating oncologists' belief that it was the best course of treatment for her.

The Foxes were not the first to challenge an HMO. As many dissatisfied patients began to question their doctors' motivation when necessary treatment was not provided, some patients turned to the courts for redress. Two such cases helped pave the way for *Fox v. Health Net*.

In 1986, Lois Wickline sued California's Medicaid program, Medi-Cal, because its prospective utilization review board denied her additional days in the hospital, eventually leading to an infection and the loss of a leg. While the court held that the physician who released her was ultimately responsible, it recognized the need to hold HMOs liable for negligent decisions made during utilization review. The court noted that prospective utilization review posed a much greater risk to patients than traditional retrospective review.

In 1990, the parents of Howard Wilson brought suit against their managed care organization. Wilson, a depressed and anorexic teenager, committed suicide after being released from the hospital when a utilization review board refused to grant his physician's request for extra time in the hospital. The court held the private insurer liable for its negligent decision, opening the door for injured plaintiffs to sue their managed care organizations if denial of benefits is a substantial factor in the patient's injury.

The stage was set. Poised to expose Health Net's unsettling "insider tactics" and get his sister's transplant covered, Hiepler moved forward with a vigorous discovery process. As he pushed for more information to determine why his sister's transplant was denied, Health Net responded by greatly restricting the materials it turned over. During one deposition, Hiepler learned that Health Net had ordered a consultant's report on the status of ABMT. When Hiepler requested it, Health Net refused to turn it over. He suspected that the report might contain information damaging to Health Net's case. But Health Net stonewalled, and Hiepler threatened to compel disclosure. The HMO turned over the report, the Technology Assessment, which became a key piece of evidence at trial. The consultant study predicted that ABMT would be considered standard treatment for breast cancer by 1991—not experimental, as Health Net had told Nelene.

Hiepler did not ask his firm whether he could take on Nelene's case; he simply moved forward, with Michelle sharing the load. Hiepler would often bounce questions and ideas off his trial-tested colleagues, who otherwise remained uninvolved in the case. "No one ever felt we were actually going to trial," he said.

Health Net never offered to settle the case; the decision makers at the HMO remained confident. As the prospect of a full-blown trial loomed closer, Hiepler flew around the country searching for the best expert witness on breast cancer and ABMT. He had difficulty retaining an expert from California, because most physicians were afraid to testify against such a large HMO. Eventually, Hiepler retained Dr. Roy B. Jones from the University of Colorado.

In September of 1992, Hiepler received a call that would fundamentally alter the suit. Stephen Bosworth, a complete stranger, told Hiepler, "You're going to want to talk to my wife." Janice Bosworth, a former breast cancer patient and Health Net employee, had struggled to get coverage for a bone marrow transplant under her Health Net insurance contract. But rather than denying the authorization as they did with Nelene, Health Net paid for Bosworth's ABMT, just months before Nelene requested hers. Bosworth had read about Nelene's story in the *Los Angeles Times,* and she volunteered to testify against her employer because she had thought Health Net had "learned its lesson" in her case until she found out about Nelene.

Hiepler then found Evelyn Moulton, who had also received coverage for ABMT for her breast cancer from Health Net only two years before. Janice Bosworth and Evelyn Moulton would prove vitally important in the coming trial.

Hiepler was convinced that the two-and-a-half-month delay in receiving the treatment, along with Nelene's tireless efforts raising money when she should have been resting, had a significant, negative impact on her chances of a successful recovery. However, he believed that her recovery after the surgery was a victory—even though it only lasted seven months.

The Fox family avoided discussing the lawsuit as much as possible. Nelene always deferred to her brother: "I'll do whatever you want," she told him. She stayed focused on battling her disease, telling people, "I just want to live to see my kids graduate." Ever the protective "big sister," Nelene worried about her little brother, concerned that he poured so many hours into the lawsuit on her behalf.

Hiepler was in the middle of the deposition of Dr. Ossorio, the Health Net doctor who had denied Nelene's treatment, when Hiepler was interrupted by a call from his secretary. Nelene had collapsed suddenly— she didn't have long. He left immediately to be with his sister and was holding her hand when she passed away two days later.

The deposition of Health Net's expert witness, Dr. Van Scoy-Mosher, had been scheduled for what turned out to be the night after Nelene's funeral. Hiepler's voice was almost inaudible when he arrived, distraught after his sister's death and funeral. "After Nelene died, I think they expected me to just melt away," Hiepler said. But he was ready to at least give the appearance that he was not giving up. The primary goal was to pay back the donors who had given so much to help Nelene survive those last months with her family. Health Net and the Foxes stipulated that if Health Net lost on breach of contract at trial, the damage amount for that claim alone would be the full $212,000. Hiepler said that if Health Net had offered to cover the cost of the procedure, he would have settled.

Hiepler amended the complaint against Health Net to make Jim Fox and Nelene's estate (with Jim and the children as beneficiaries) the plaintiffs. By that point, Hiepler had amassed quite an arsenal of damaging evidence against Health Net, including interoffice e-mails, internal documents, company memos, and deposition testimony. The trial date was originally set for May 1993, but Health Net requested an extension. As the trial date was pushed further and further back, Hiepler became concerned—two of his key witnesses were breast cancer patients who could die before they ever had a chance to testify. The trial date could not be pushed back any further, he told the judge. The parties were set to appear before the Riverside County Superior Court in late November 1993.

The Trial

Judge Richard Van Frank, a former district attorney, presided over the case. Local attorneys referred to the judge as a "straight shooter," fair, and smart. Alan Templeman, a partner at Lowthorp, Richards, the Oxnard firm where Hiepler worked, served as Hiepler's cocounsel. Health Net was represented by Lyle Swallow and Steven Meadville of Vogt, Meadville & Swallow.

On Friday, December 3, 1993, Hiepler approached the jury of seven men and five women and began his opening statement. He told Nelene's story. From the time she learned of the lump in her breast through Health Net's denial of the transplant and the enormous fund-raising efforts, Hiepler painted the picture of every woman who wanted the one medical treatment that her doctors told her could save her life.

Lyle Swallow gave the opening statement for Health Net. He emphasized that while the circumstances of the case were sad, the jurors could not decide the case based on emotions and sympathy. Swallow called the case "a controversy about a controversy." The first controversy was over Nelene's requested transplant—Health Net would show that the treatment was not proven safe and effective within the medical community and was controversial among oncologists and therefore investigative. The second controversy concerned the circumstances leading to Health Net's decision to deny Nelene's treatment. The evidence would show, Swallow maintained, that Health Net's conduct was entirely reasonable and proper.

Through three full weeks of testimony, the pieces of the puzzle began to fall into place as each party made its case. Hiepler's first witness was cancer survivor Janice Bosworth, the wife and mother of a young son in her early thirties and a former top sales executive at Health Net. As Hiepler began his direct examination, Bosworth was clearly nervous and emotional, knowing that many of her friends and coworkers felt she should not be testifying against her former employer. After just a few questions, she started to break down. "I notice that you're trembling," Judge Van Frank interrupted. "What's your fear right now?" Bosworth answered through her tears, "It's just a very emotional thing for me, and you know, I know Nelene passed on and you know—you've had a very serious illness and all these thoughts are flooding back and it brings it all to the surface." Judge Van Frank dismissed the jury until she could regain her composure.

Bosworth testified that after being evaluated at Duke University and City of Hope, Health Net stalled for nearly a month on whether they would cover the bone marrow transplant that her doctor had recommended. In fact, the transplant was approved only after Bosworth had filed suit against Health Net. Health Net contended that it paid for Bosworth's transplant as a gift to a valued employee. To support his claim of bad faith, Hiepler attempted to establish that Health Net had a pattern of delaying decisions and coercing physicians to change their recommendations.

HIEPLER: Can you tell us the circumstances of how you met Dr. Ossorio?

BOSWORTH: Yes. One of my girlfriends had—I was explaining to her that I'd like to meet him, because he was going to be working on my case very closely. I had not met him. He was new to the company. So that he would look at me as a person and not just a stat on a piece of paper. . . . My girlfriend said, "I'll introduce you." And I thought that was great: "Good. I want to go meet him." And we went upstairs. And he was on the phone talking, so we waited outside his office for a few minutes. . . .

HIEPLER: What did Dr. Ossorio say?

BOSWORTH: I thought I was going to faint. I focused on what he was saying on the telephone. And all I could hear was, in not a happy tone, very angry, "How did she find out about Duke? I'm going to them." And he said, "Maybe Gary [Gary Davison, Bosworth's treating physician] told her. I'm going to have to call him." And about that point I looked at my girlfriend and said, I was just shaking, I was so upset, I was shaking and it's very unnerving to have someone talk about you.

In January of 1992, City of Hope approved Bosworth as a suitable candidate for a transplant, but Dr. Ossorio continued to deny coverage, believing she was not a good candidate. Although Health Net maintained the transplant was given to Bosworth as an employee gift, Bosworth testified, "I don't think you call it a gift when they make you go through the normal procedure and the normal fight that I didn't realize that everyone goes through."

Alan Templeman, Hiepler's cocounsel, next called Jim Fox to the stand. Hiepler asked Templeman to conduct Jim's direct examination, because Hiepler felt that he could not emotionally handle questioning his brother-in-law about Nelene. Templeman took Fox through the details of Nelene's cancer and how they came to battle Health Net for a bone marrow transplant, establishing that pressure from Health Net had caused Dr. Camacho to withdraw his support for Nelene's bone marrow transplant.

TEMPLEMAN: And at this point in time after [Dr. Camacho] had written a letter in support, what did he tell you?

FOX: We went to this meeting and we sat down with Dr. Camacho and he said that he had been contacted by Dr. Ossorio from

Health Net, and that he, Dr. Camacho, now had some concerns about—he had some concerns about the transplant, and that he didn't think we should go through with it. . . . He said that Dr. Ossorio from Health Net really sounded like he knew what he was talking about, and he had some concerns about the risks. And I said to Dr. Camacho, "You've already discussed risks with us." And he looked at me and said, "I know."

TEMPLEMAN: What else did he say?

FOX: He said at that time, that Health Net was going to offer another opinion at the City of Hope. . . .

TEMPLEMAN: Did you ask him, "Why should we get another opinion at City of Hope?"

FOX: My question to Dr. Camacho was, "Why would they send us back to someplace where we had already been denied?"

Witness after witness took the stand. The direct examinations by Hiepler and Templeman began to shape a story of corporate efforts aimed at lowering costs while gambling with lives. Templeman called Dr. Leonard Knapp, Health Net's medical director. Dr. Knapp had been in charge of hiring Dr. Ossorio, and Templeman wanted Dr. Knapp to explain the financial incentives that Nelene's lawyers contended had influenced Dr. Ossorio's decision to deny Nelene's treatment. The first incentive in his employment contract provided Dr. Ossorio with a bonus equal to 20 percent of his salary, based on the financial condition of Health Net at the end of the year. The other incentive plan provided bonuses to Dr. Ossorio based upon the results of his individual efforts to lower medical costs.

TEMPLEMAN: Was one of the reasons you hired Dr. Ossorio because he was able to modify physician behavior in directions that you would like?

KNAPP: Yes, sir.

TEMPLEMAN: Were there any bonuses or incentive plans that were offered to Dr. Ossorio?

KNAPP: I think there's a standard corporate bonus that was offered him.

TEMPLEMAN: Do you believe that Dr. Ossorio, under the plan that was set up for him, would benefit if services were denied by Health Net?

KNAPP: No.

TEMPLEMAN: Do you believe by refusing requests for bone marrow transplant, Dr. Ossorio would benefit in any way by the bonus plan?

KNAPP: No.

TEMPLEMAN: Reading from Dr. Knapp's deposition; "Question: 'Do you believe by refusing requests for bone marrow transplant Dr. Ossorio would benefit in any way by this plan?' Answer: 'Given the structure, yes, the incentive is there to deny services. Given the individual and the fact that he has a long-term view which says such practices cost you a tremendous amount down the line, I'm convinced that would never happen.'"

Later in Templeman's examination of Knapp, he asked, "Is it Health Net's philosophy to follow the Golden Rule?"

KNAPP: I have never heard that.

TEMPLEMAN: Did you have a golden rule?

KNAPP: No.

TEMPLEMAN: Do you recall at your deposition telling me your golden rule was "Them that got the gold makes the rules"?

KNAPP: I remember discussing that with you. I did not say that was my golden rule.

Hiepler called Dr. Aziz Khan of the USC Norris Cancer Center. He first established Dr. Khan's credentials as a qualified oncologist and bone marrow transplant doctor. Dr. Khan related how he had fully explained the risks to Nelene and guided her through all of her preliminary testing before she ultimately obtained her transplant.

Hiepler also questioned Dr. Khan about his opinion on the status of ABMT for breast cancer patients. At the heart of the breach-of-contract claim, the Foxes alleged that Health Net should have paid for the procedure under its Evidence of Coverage (EOC) clause. The EOC essentially defined an "experimental" procedure as one that had only progressed to limited use on humans and was still being tested on laboratory mice. The EOC defined "investigative" as a service that had not been widely accepted in the organized medical community as proven safe and effective. Health Net maintained that the ABMT was investigative.

HIEPLER: Now, I want you to look at this definition and tell me, because you're the one that has the expertise in transplantation. . . . Do you believe or have an opinion as to whether the procedure that you provided Mrs. Fox was investigative?

KHAN: Was not. . . . If it was not recognized as an effective procedure, community oncologists/hematologists would not be sending their patients to us. These are patients who are being sent to
us, not as a last-resort therapy. These are patients who have
shown that they've got metastatic disease, which is responsive to
the chemotherapy that they're getting and now are being sent to
us for something better. . . . A lot of—almost every hospital that
has a transplant facility is transplanting women with breast cancer, and I would not call that limited use on humans. . . . And the
fact that we are being referred patients by the treating physicians
means that the medical community out there recognizes this is
an effective treatment modality.

During cross-examination, Swallow sought to demonstrate that Dr.
Khan was unjustifiably optimistic in recommending the transplant for
Nelene. Dr. Khan had sent Dr. Camacho a report identifying the benefits
of the procedure.

SWALLOW: Do you agree that the use of high-dose chemotherapy
for patients with metastatic breast cancer in April of '92 was one
of the controversial areas of medicine?
KHAN: It was—it was a topic where there was a lot of discussion in
literature. There were a lot of trials, a lot of—there was a lot of
information out there.
SWALLOW: Doctor, with respect to the treatment that you provided
Mrs. Fox, is it your opinion that the success rate of that treatment
is not known?
KHAN: I've already told you the success rate of the treatment that I
provided.
SWALLOW (reading from Khan's deposition): "Question: 'Your success rate is not known?' Answer: 'The success rate with this kind
of therapy is not known.'"

Hiepler next called Evelyn Moulton, the breast cancer patient in her
early forties who had been given a bone marrow transplant with Health
Net's approval. Hiepler demonstrated that Moulton was similarly situated to Nelene and attempted to show that Health Net also stalled before
approving Moulton's transplant.

HIEPLER: Going back to your original diagnosis. . . . Did you
undergo any other treatment?

MOULTON: Well, at that time, it was recommended that I have a bone marrow transplant. So I needed to get permission from my insurance company for that.

HIEPLER: Then what happened next?

MOULTON: They denied the bone marrow transplant.

HIEPLER: Then what happened?

MOULTON: I went on hormonal treatment and paid out of pocket myself to have my bone marrow harvested, because I was afraid if I waited too long, it might mean I wouldn't be a good candidate, and it would be useless to me while I appealed the decision.

HIEPLER: And then were you approved after you had your harvest?

MOULTON: Not for another year.

HIEPLER: What happened in that year that you were waiting?

MOULTON: I was on hormonal treatments, which failed, and my disease progressed to liver metastasis.

HIEPLER: And then sometime thereafter, once the disease had spread further, did you get this letter from Health Net?

MOULTON: I did. Actually, that occurred almost simultaneously to the discovery of the liver metastasis.

Evelyn Moulton's testimony, along with Janice Bosworth's, proved to be powerful evidence supporting the claim for breach of contract and bad faith. Within four years of the trial, both Bosworth and Moulton succumbed to cancer, but they had each enjoyed several years of good health with their families while in remission.

Hiepler then called his chief expert witness, Dr. Roy B. Jones. As head of the bone marrow transplant program at the University of Colorado, Jones was a nationally recognized expert in the procedure and had written several medical journal articles about it. He testified that Dr. Khan and USC had done everything appropriate in treating Nelene. He also believed that Health Net's offer for Nelene to be evaluated at City of Hope was useless, because Nelene had already been given several recommendations and it was not optimal to get an opinion from a center for a treatment that they did not provide. Moreover, Health Net's delays could have harmed Nelene's chances of a successful recovery.

Hiepler had Dr. Jones explain the effect on his patients who were denied coverage for bone marrow transplants:

JONES: Well, you've alluded to the reality that tumors will grow while treatment is delayed, and that's a natural process of cancer. The other reality is that when one is essentially fighting for one's life, and at the same time fighting for a practical thing like insurance approval, which will allow one to have the option to fight for one's life, the stressors are enormous. . . .

HIEPLER: Have you seen any of them just give up?

JONES: Oh, yes.

HIEPLER: And what do you interpret that to mean, "give up"?

JONES: What I mean by giving up, they say this is, "I can fight one battle for my life and undertake the risks that you've described to me about the procedure, but I cannot fight a second battle at the same time. It's more than I can take emotionally and physically and have elected to discontinue attempts to get access to the procedure."

Health Net's lawyers called Sharyn Katz, manager of legal affairs at Health Net. The purpose of her testimony was to establish that Health Net granted Bosworth's transplant strictly as a gift to a Health Net employee. During cross-examination, Hiepler got Katz to admit that Bosworth's transplant was paid out of the transplant claims pool—just like all other Health Net subscribers.

Just days before Christmas, 1993, both sides had concluded their testimony. All that remained were closing arguments. Hiepler, as plaintiff's counsel, was to argue first, followed by defense counsel Swallow.

Mark Hiepler's Closing Argument on Behalf of Nelene and Jim Fox

Eighteen days ago, I think it was December third, I stood before you, and I gave you an opening statement. And I told you about what I believed were despicable acts committed against Jim Fox and his wife, Nelene, by their insurance carrier, Health Net. I told you that the reason they purchased insurance was for peace of mind, peace of mind that should a medical catastrophe ever strike their otherwise healthy family, that Health Net would be there for them.

Eighteen days ago, I couldn't tell you everything. I didn't tell you everything. I wanted you to hear it from the witnesses. I didn't tell you at opening statement about the fact that Mrs. Bosworth sat outside of Dr. Ossorio's office when she had metastatic breast cancer and overheard him saying something to the effect of "How did she find out about this treatment? Who told her about Duke University?" I didn't tell you about that. Mrs. Bosworth did. Remember, Mrs. Moulton, she walked up here, a metastatic breast cancer patient. Remember what she told you? That, as a result of Health

Net's denial, it moved to her liver, her cancer spread. She had a much more difficult battle because of the delays. And I didn't tell you about Dr. Knapp, medical director of Health Net, and about his interpretation of the golden rule: "He who has the gold makes the rules."

Now, I'm going to paraphrase some of the law. And the judge is going to tell you all of the law, specifically that an insurance contract is to be interpreted in a way that the ordinary reasonable person can understand them, not the way an insurance company wants you to understand them, not the way lawyers interpret them, and not the way doctors interpret them. And you heard the defense trying to ask multiple doctors about the different definitions, what this contract means. But what's at issue is what Jim Fox reasonably believed it to mean. The judge is going to tell you that you must interpret contract clauses broadly. Why? Because insurance companies write these things, they have staffs of attorneys and people, carefully selecting each and every word in there. And all Jim Fox has is that to rely on. Jim relied on it.

Nowhere in that contract does it say, "Bone marrow transplants are excluded." Common sense tells you that Jim was reasonable in believing what it said. Especially, when Health Net Drs. Schinke and Camacho told him about the treatment. And even more so, remember what Schinke told Jim? There's a woman, Mrs. Bosworth, her cancer treatment was paid for by Health Net. Remember what Dr. Schinke said? He said, "Yeah, they figured there was a precedent. And now, these are going to be paid for." And the law says, if something is written in an ambiguous fashion, because health insurance is so important, we need to interpret it in favor of whom coverage is for, the patient, for Mrs. Fox, for Jim.

And while we believe that this is clear from the contract, that it's a covered benefit, if you believe that these investigative clauses, which aren't referenced there, have anything to do with it, they at least make the contract ambiguous. You remember Dr. Jones. I showed him the actual definition and even asked him about that part. He said this treatment for Mrs. Fox was appropriate and not experimental and not investigational. All you need to find is that if it's ambiguous, you favor coverage for Mr. Fox.

Remember Dr. Jones, when he talked about dealing with women on a daily basis? Remember, he treated patients and he said that there are many people that he sees that he could help with metastatic breast cancer, just like Nelene. And, although the vast majority of the people he sees have an insurance company that pays for this, the ones that don't are already fighting the greatest battle for their lives, and they can't fight a financial catastrophe as well, so what do they do? And that's the tragedy. They go home and they die.

Now, what does that mean for an insurance company? An insurance company probably doesn't make much money on people with cancer, but they save a lot if they die. If you are an insurance company, why would you leave that language there for years? For marketing reasons it's wonderful, because you can appear from the defendant's standpoint to be everything, to everybody, just as good as any other. If all you have is a cold or the flu, sure, they will take good care of you. But when you get breast cancer, what happens? Out comes "investigative." Out comes "experimental."

So you intentionally leave it ambiguous, so that when everybody is well, you do it all; when they come to you and need that, you have both options. You find that little clause and say that "Well, we consider this investigative." But let's leave it ambiguous. A lot of people don't have twenty-five hundred people that will rally around like the Foxes did. A lot of people give up.

Now, there's a jury instruction that says part of your job is to evaluate the credibility of the individuals that walk up here, people who we called, people who are employed by Health Net, Jim Fox, himself. And that's to help you make your determination. Remember, these gentlemen at Health Net, each of them answered my question "Are you treating physicians?" What was their answer? "No, we do not practice medicine." They do other things at Health Net. I'm going to walk you through what some of these gentlemen at Health Net had to say.

Dr. Ossorio, remember him? Remember him sitting here? Well, Dr. Ossorio claimed that this was experimental based on the laboratory-rats type of definition. He denies that the bonuses or incentives that he receives, in any way, impact his judgment. He admitted that he never wrote an article on bone marrow transplant, never did a bone marrow transplant. And, of course, that he doesn't practice medicine. He admitted that within the last ten years the only article he's written was for a book entitled *The Business of Medicine*. That was one of their "experts."

The second one, you remember who else they designated? Good old Dr. Camacho, Nelene's initial treating physician. Dr. Camacho admitted that he's not an expert in this procedure, but he is a practicing physician at least. Dr. Camacho admitted that he never published any articles on the procedure, never done the procedure. He admitted that an evaluation of Mrs. Fox at City of Hope was a complete waste of time. Then, after he saw the letter from Health Net suggesting that "You go here for an opinion and there for an opinion," when time was of the essence, said, he thought it was a good idea.

And then—was it yesterday?—we saw Dr. Mosher [Health Net's chief expert witness], and he admitted, he's not an expert, never done a bone marrow transplant, never wrote an article about one. He admitted that he makes at least fifty thousand dollars a year testifying as an expert for insurance companies and other attorneys. He admits he is a former partner of Dr. Ossorio. Remember the end of his testimony after he said that this treatment is no good, even though he's not an expert, never written a publication about it? He never heard of Janice Bosworth. He never heard of Evelyn Moulton. Perhaps it would have helped him to have seen those two women walk up here and testify. While he admitted he wasn't an expert, he admitted that Dr. Jones was, and if I seemed a little frustrated with him yesterday, it's partly because this man designated by Health Net as an expert with regard to this procedure spends more time testifying for insurance companies and attorneys than he's ever spent doing the procedure at issue or writing about the procedure at issue.

And as I stand here today, Health Net still hasn't brought an expert up to help you to understand the procedure. And I submit, because they can't. Because all the experts in doing this procedure, who actually treat patients, know that it has moved beyond any labeled definition as "experimental" or "investigative."

What did you hear from Nelene's treating physician Dr. Schinke? Remember when I asked Dr. Schinke, "Do you have any financial incentives to send patients to get this type of treatment?" What did he say? He said, "No, if anything, it would work the other way. But if it's in the best interest of my patient, I'll do that." He sat there and explained what he knew of the procedure and said, "I don't do the procedure, but I had some training in bone marrow transplant." And he also said, "I told Jim and Nelene in April, if Nelene was my wife, I'd get her in there for bone marrow process, at least, start the process." What did Dr. Camacho say about that? All for it, jumped right along. In fact, Camacho helped him. Camacho did the tests, wrote the letters. He was all for it.

The second witness, Dr. Khan of USC, he told you all the grueling details and procedures, all of the hoops that Mrs. Fox had to jump through before they would treat her. And he also told you that USC eliminates, perhaps, fifty percent of the people that come there. They're very careful as to who gets this procedure. They only treat those with the best potential to be helped.

Quite a contrast between the different doctors. Dr. Khan's been treating patients with bone marrow transplant for five years. He said that she was a good candidate. He has no incentive to transplant people. He tries—if anything—to exclude them, if it's too much for them. Dr. Khan told you that this definition of rats and monkeys—experimental and investigative—just doesn't fit.

And who else came to town? Dr. Jones. Dr. Jones who's published fifty-two peer review journal articles on this procedure. He talked about the fourteen—I had to drag it out of him—talked about the fourteen textbook articles that he's written on this procedure. He told you he was head of the bone marrow transplant unit, treats patients, also a professor at Duke. And he also told you one thing that you've heard the other side throwing up in the air a lot, that based upon his experiences of actually treating patients and seeing these women, persons with bone marrow involvement do fifteen percent better than any other cases, including liver.

Remember the last statement I asked Dr. Jones about? We'd been talking about these incentives and talking about motivation. "What motivates you?" He said the hundred and eighty thousand women a year that get breast cancer motivate him. He says having to look into the eyes of these people that have no hope on conventional chemotherapy motivates him. He said that this procedure is not perfect. He said it's not a cure-all for everyone, but he told you that he daily sees women like Evelyn Moulton walk into his office, who, if they'd been treated by Dr. Mosher or on standard chemotherapy, most likely would never have been here. He sees patients like Janice Bosworth, who even—do you remember, "Whatever it takes, even against your own employer, to get this transplant." He said that's what motivates him. He says that's why he's going to continue.

Let's talk about two people that personally know this procedure works. Remember Janice Bosworth. She loved her company. Remember that letter from Dr. Ossorio that "Health Net will provide coverage for this procedure, in accordance with the benefits of Mrs. Bosworth's Health Net contract." Nowhere does it say, "It is a gift to you, a valued employee," or "It was an administrative decision." Nowhere. Nowhere does it make any exception because "we believe it's investigational." Nowhere.

Mrs. Bosworth had liver and spine metastasis. February would be her anniversary, two-year anniversary of this procedure. She talked about the employer that she loved, that took good care of her until, like the Foxes, she had breast cancer. And she told you about all the hoops and the conversations and calls and this pattern of despicable behavior that happened to her. And this was her employer. And [the defense] tell[s] you, God, they were so nice to her, helped her out, and it was an administrative decision to cover her. But, on cross-examination, she told you that she had to file a lawsuit.

Then you saw Evelyn Moulton. I never met Mrs. Moulton before the day she walked in here. She had liver involvement. Even Dr. Mosher thought that liver involvement was much worse. Then, Mrs. Moulton got a letter pursuant to her insurance benefits that said, "Health Net has conducted a reevaluation and authorized this treatment." The exact treatment that Mrs. Bosworth received and Nelene was denied. Mrs. Moulton, a similarly situated woman with metastatic breast cancer in her liver and they're paying for her. You've heard an explanation as to why Mrs. Moulton got covered. But she only got covered after some delays. Remember when she told you about that? And her condition went from, I think, she said seventy percent chance to thirty percent, because she was delayed, and it moved into her liver. Who was her insurer? The defendant. Thankfully, they finally made the right decision. She is living proof.

The denial letter hit the Foxes' home on June twelfth, 1992. Shattered them. Remember the denial letter? "We determined that this is experimental and investigative. Good-bye." Remember the other letter that they brought up? The June twelfth letter that I wrote. The last part of the letter said, "We would be pleased to meet you or speak with you with regard to this matter, to find a mutually agreeable solution, firstly, to save the life of your insured, Nelene Fox, and secondly, eliminate the need for aggressive litigation and all that this includes."

Jim wrote letters. The doctors wrote letters. And what happened? They got the runaround. Remember the fifteenth, Dr. Camacho had already told Jim and Nelene that Nelene couldn't be treated at City of Hope. Time is of the essence. It's a waste of time. They got a letter that "If you go to City of Hope"—now this is about the fourth or fifth opinion—"if they consider you an acceptable candidate, then we'll send you to UCLA. If you meet their standards, you're in." An impossible set of circumstances, outrageous, unreasonable behavior, given the circumstances Nelene was faced with, and Dr. Camacho couldn't tell them why.

The plaintiff, Jim Fox, Estate of Nelene Fox, Natalie, Nicole, and Jenna, have met the burden of proof, which is a little more than fifty percent, way beyond that. Let me just write a couple of things to summarize the breach-of-contract action, the same contract issue we went over earlier. Remember, plain language coverage. Ambiguities are interpreted in favor of Jim and Nelene Fox. Were Jim and Nelene reasonable in expecting that a bone marrow transplant would be covered when Nelene had this tragic disease? Yes, because of the plain language. They had supported Mrs. Bosworth and another similarly situated person.

It is not investigational. Even if Health Net had a good definition, it's not investigational. An HMO can't cover everything, but can't we expect it to, at least, honor the words that they choose and put in their contracts? Is that asking too much? Peace of mind, that's what they thought they purchased. They were faced with a medical catastrophe, and a financial one. There was no peace of mind.

The second part, the second cause of action that we described for you early on, was bad faith. What does that mean? We talked about the implied covenant of fair dealing in this insurance contract. It involves people's lives. And it says that insurance companies are to act reasonably in their conduct toward the Foxes in approving or denying. And it's unique to insurance contracts, because Jim didn't enter into this contract to make a profit. He entered it to have peace of mind so that he and Nelene and Natalie, Nicole, and Jenna could sleep well at night as they did in 1990, healthy, thinking, "Health Net will be there for us." Bargained-for peace of mind. The Foxes paid for that. It's not a gift. Health Net wrote the words.

I'm going to show you some examples of bad faith. The first is that a defendant insurance company cannot apply an unduly restrictive interpretation of a policy. Here is how it happened. Number one, the face of the policy provides for coverage. Health Net has been on notice that people reasonably believe that bone marrow transplants for breast cancer are covered.

Bad faith may also occur when a defendant's denial is based on unfounded standards. The Technology Assessment, this is Health Net's own consultant, remember, Ms. Smithey, who said, "I don't want to testify, because Health Net—we have a lot of business with Health

Net right now." She talked about preparing this report. It was a good report that she had done, a lot of work. She called hospitals. She got all the medical literature they provided to her. And you remember what she said on November twelfth of 1990? That this would be a prevailing practice by 1991. June twelfth, 1992, Health Net was on notice of this. Third, the golden rule. Remember, Ms. Smithey informed Dr. Knapp of this finding? Remember what Dr. Knapp told her? "I'm going to deny them anyway." The golden rule.

Fourth, unreasonable conduct. Besides the Technology Assessment, why is it unreasonable? Why is their conduct in bad faith? Because prevailing medical practices were different than their interpretation. They all came up here, and there were streams of these articles. And Dr. Mosher said, "I realize that Dr. Roy Jones and Dr. Peters wrote these articles, but I'm not sure if this is a good treatment yet." Remember when I asked him, when did those patients go through the treatment? He said it was '88. And, regardless of the doctor, they've all said this is an evolving process with these treatments. Health Net's doctors are relying on old articles. They said the textbooks are six and eight years old when they come up. They relied on medical practices that are eight years old. Something that is used to justify a clause that says investigative or experimental, when all these really mean is too expensive.

Number five. Unlawfully discriminating against similarly situated people. Now, if these contracts that Mrs. Moulton and Mrs. Bosworth had were different, I wouldn't be able to talk to you about it. But we heard it's the same contract. They were paid and I'm waiting for Health Net to tell you why.

Number six. Bad faith occurs if the defendant is engaged in deceptive practices. He's been helping. Remember that Dr. Camacho testified how he felt? He would do everything, do the tests, and encouraged the Foxes, wrote the two letters to Health Net. I'm just showing you the one of June sixth: "I strongly support this procedure." Then he testifies to the June fifteenth call from Dr. Ossorio. Remember what Dr. Knapp said about Dr. Ossorio, why he hired him? Remember that? "He's a very persuasive individual able to change doctors' behavior in a way that assists Health Net."

Number seven, the stall tactics. Dr. Jones explained certain places do certain procedures for certain cases. They can't all do everything. And the City of Hope said, "We don't do people with bone marrow involvement." Now, why would you send someone, after they've had numerous opinions, to the City of Hope when they already were approved someplace else and time is ticking away? Unreasonable, bad faith. Remember what Dr. Camacho told you about the process the Foxes went through just to become a candidate and all the hoops that they had to jump through. How come Dr. Ossorio wanted her to go to the City of Hope? Unreasonable. Time is of the essence.

The eighth one is keeping the Foxes from USC. Do you remember that Technology Assessment? USC seemed to be all for these transplants. Ninth, bad faith can occur if the defendant fails to ensure that claims are evaluated objectively and fairly. Is that too much to ask? Especially, expensive claims, claims that may mean the difference of someone's life. Objectively and fairly. Who was in charge of reviewing these claims? Dr. Ossorio. Do you remember a part of Dr. Ossorio's Health Net contract: "You'll be eligible to participate in an annual incentive plan, which is dependent on the company and individual performance." In summary: "You can earn some percentage of the target amount for substantially exceeding the agreed-upon goals." Do you remember, he told you he really wasn't sure about how much he made? The bonuses. His wife was concerned that he not take a big cut in pay when he left private practice. And he did take a cut in pay, and he told you how much he made. Is that more of a reason he needs a bonus? He needs to get that salary up.

What about the other bonus? Well, Dr. Knapp told us there was a new one based on limiting medical costs. He's one of the top guys, a vice president, the medical director. He's the one who hired Dr. Ossorio. When asked about this bonus situation, Dr. Knapp said, "There is an incentive to deny bone marrow transplant, but, of course, knowing Dr. Ossorio, it would never happen." Objective review. There were incentives to deny.

Tenth, bad faith also occurs if the defendant fails to properly investigate a claim. Remember when Mr. Templeman asked Dr. Khan if he'd ever been called by Dr. Ossorio. He said, "No." I think we asked Dr. Ossorio, "Did you ever call Dr. Khan?" "No." Dr. Ossorio knew his match. He knew that he could probably handle Camacho, but if he talked to an expert, someone who really knew about this procedure, unlike the people Health Net brought in, his persuasion might not work. Never called him and denied the treatment.

Now, I've just described for you what we believe are ten separate acts of bad faith. Again, this is not in a normal course of business. This is when Mrs. Fox had breast cancer. Time is ticking away. Ten separate acts. And you only need one act to find for bad faith. Where was the peace of mind?

Now, this is the difficult part. Based on bad faith, I've got to talk to you about damages. We've already talked about contractual damages. But I have to talk to you and give you some suggestions as to how to approximate damages based on ten acts of bad faith. Remember, you only need one act to find bad faith. And the suggestions I'm going to give to you could be more, could be less. Mr. Fox, with his own money, his own efforts, and the efforts of all these people over months, and with Nelene in that condition, going to all of these fund-raisers, and everybody joining in the fight, had to raise about $212,000. And they did, because people were so outraged in the general community, outraged by this behavior.

I'm going to suggest to you that for every act of bad faith you find, and remember, you need only find one, that you award damages. Consider what they had to go through, what they had to pay—these are the damages that Health Net has stipulated to. And you multiply that amount by the number of bad faith incidents, and that's the award you should give for the emotional distress. That's just a suggestion.

The last is entitled, "Intentional Infliction of Emotional Distress." Now, the judge will instruct you that you don't have to find that Health Net sat down and calculated to make the Foxes emotionally distressed. You don't have to find that. But what you can find is the defendant engaged in extreme and outrageous conduct with a reckless disregard for the probability of causing emotional distress.

Now, Dr. Ossorio, of all people, at least when he practiced, dealt with cancer patients. Do you think he had any clue as to the impact a denial of coverage might have on these people? He testified that, I think, he heard about the fund-raising efforts even before the denial. As if Jim is just supposed to sit there and not do anything. He knew what was going to have to happen. Reckless disregard.

Because we've all heard this concept "emotional distress," we all wonder what it means. I'm going to tell you what the instruction tells you about emotional distress. What are the factors? And there's ten that you're going to hear about.

The first one is fright. Jim testified that Dr. Robinson, his general doctor, talked about the fright that Jim had concerning this whole situation. Mrs. Endresen at the fund-raising efforts said that Jim was so afraid that this might not be helpful for her, but they had no other choice than work night and day on this campaign, unlike, even a politician who's running for office. Fright.

The second one is nervousness. Now, remember he wasn't an uninsured person. He had insurance. Nervousness. There's a timer on. Time is ticking. We all get a little bit nervous when, you know, you've got to be—something is going to happen, much less when life is on the line.

The third is grief. You heard Jim's assistant football coach and coaches: Jim sits around and feels sorry, many nights crying, and still does. Health Net didn't cause Mrs. Fox's cancer, but they abandoned the Foxes when she was fighting for her life.

The fourth, anxiety.

Number five, worry. Talk about the sleeplessness, they couldn't sleep so they'd write thank-you notes to try to help the mortification. They were so outraged, mortified by the fact that this doctor [Camacho] who had assisted them, that they trusted for about a year, who had written these letters, suddenly switched. Now, of course, do you think we're ever going to get him to admit that? That's why you can look at direct or indirect evidence. And I showed you what he did. Jim told you what he did. And he changed on Jim the last minute. Nothing had changed. Her condition hadn't changed. The status of the procedure hadn't changed. USC hadn't changed. But what we all know happened was, there was a phone call by a very persuasive individual.

Shock. I don't have to go into the details of that. Jim told you.

Humiliation. Happens to him daily still, because he has to face all these people. He is grateful for their help, but he doesn't want to feel indebted to anybody. That's why he had insurance and peace of mind that he thought he purchased, which was never there. Not only during the fund-raising events, but now as people who he doesn't know remind him of that and ask, "Are we going to get our money back?"

Humiliation. Indignity. I don't need to explain any of these. These explain themselves. Begging. Having to see Nelene's poster at every store. Dr. Robinson told you about his stomach problems, told you about emotional problems, told you about Jim's feelings like this insurance company was treating his wife like a dog. Reckless disregard. Ten of these.

They had to work hard to raise all of that money, some of their own, a lot of it from all of these people that were outraged. We would say that if you find that those elements are met in that cause of action, that each one of those factors be multiplied by the money that Health Net forced them into the streets to beg for, the money that Jim is constantly reminded of every day as he teaches out in Temecula.

"Extreme and outrageous." The definition definitely causes the average member of the community to act in outrage. Well, it wasn't just his community, all through California, all through the United States, numbers greater than twenty-five hundred acted in outrage. They didn't just act outraged. They gave money. A lot of people gave from a sacrificial standpoint, because they wanted to help. And they knew that time was ticking, time that, at least, Dr. Ossorio wanted her to go marching around to other facilities.

The defendant acted with a conscious disregard toward the patient, toward Nelene, toward Jim, toward the whole family.

The last thing I need to discuss with you is also very serious. And it's damages in the form of punitive damages. Punitive damages send messages to businesses, large and small, to individuals, large and small, who don't play fairly, who you really can't touch unless you touch them in their pocketbooks. Dr. Knapp talked about how to incentivize physicians. I think he did a good job. The structural mechanism that Health Net has, if you feel that should be changed, you're going to be asked to send a message to Health Net, and to determine what it's going to take to change their behavior.

Evelyn Moulton mentioned she might have thought that after going through this, it would be done. No. It continued. But then Nelene Fox got denied. No change in behavior. She was shocked. Mrs. Bosworth was to read about Nelene, because her employer hadn't learned the lesson and was continuing in this behavior. Jim may have to read in his local paper about another family, about another woman, whether she's single, married, young or old, it doesn't matter, but he may have to unless Health Net gets the message that this behavior cannot be tolerated, and that the doctor-patient relationship is something that's to be guarded, that insurance people who don't practice medicine should not be involving themselves. They may need to make coverage decisions, that's fine, but why are they involved in trying to change behavior of doctors? It's not their role.

If you find that the defendant is guilty of fraud, oppression, or malice, then you determine a money amount that it will take to punish Health Net. No conspiracy is necessary. No big plan to just go after Mrs. Fox is necessary, but there's structural incentivizing of people to deny services that they promised to provide. To paraphrase, a definition of *oppressive* is despicable conduct, which subjects a person to cruel and unusual hardship. Now, if what Jim Fox went through isn't that, I don't know what is. *Malice,* conscious disregard for the rights and safety of others. *Fraud,* misrepresentation and a conscious disregard for the rights of another.

How did the defendant act with fraud, oppression, or malice or all of them? We've already been through that. On notice since 1989, they don't change the contract language. They can have the appearance of doing everything but in reality doing nothing for metastatic breast cancer patients. Good marketing saved a lot of money. They know that a certain amount of people, like the women that see Dr. Jones, are going to go away and they aren't up to the second fight. They don't have the friends that the Foxes had. They don't have the ability to keep fighting when someone is suffering from breast cancer, serious breast cancer, and fighting for their lives. They ignored the consultant's report. They paid for that. It isn't a report I asked for. Remember, it's their own consultant. A manipulation of Camacho, overemphasizing the risks, calling the Foxes in when they're doing everything, and nothing has changed. Stall tactics. Evelyn Moulton. Evelyn's lucky, disease-free two years later. The bonus plan, unhealthy conflict of interest, refusal to consult with Dr. Khan.

You'll be allowed to consider, if you find, based on all the facts and all the evidence, grounds for punitive damage. You can look at the books and see, actually, what they make. For example, you might determine it's going to take fifteeen to ten percent, after they pay their taxes, to punish them.

A couple of years ago, there was a study that said the average salary of working America is eighteen thousand dollars. And it said that the fine for littering highways was five hundred dollars, and that's about a third of what an eighteen-thousand-dollar-a-year person monthly earns. Now, the statistics were real clear that in prior years when the fine for littering was twenty-five dollars, highways were filled with litter. And when the fine had to be five hundred dollars, it made a difference. It had an impact.

Punitive damages are a very, very serious thing. And what it seeks to do is stop arrogant corporate behavior. Arrogant behavior that says, "We deal according to the golden rule; he who has the gold, makes the rules." Defendant's outrageous action is part of a very profitable course of conduct, firmly grounded in established corporate policy. And, again, we're not asking the HMO to pay for everything, just that for which it says it will do. And its promise to the Foxes, in which the Foxes believe was the bottom line for peace of mind, peace of mind they never got. The defendant chose deliberately and consciously to ignore its own precedent. They chose to ignore the words they selected. They chose to ignore the USC doctors. They chose to ignore Nelene's battle to live. And they chose to ignore the Foxes. They sent them into a campaign in the streets, in the mornings, noon and night, all around the clock

There are corporate boardrooms throughout the United States waiting to see what you decide, what kind of message you're going to send. Because insurance companies are wondering if Health Net can get away with this, what's been exposed before you, in Department Eight, of Riverside Superior Court. You are going to help decide whether we have treating doctors who are experts in the field deciding what is the best medical procedure or we have nontreating vice presidents with incentives, deciding what's going to be the best course of medicine, vice presidents with incentives that interfere with the doctor-patient relationship.

And we all vote, sometimes, even though we wonder if our vote makes any difference. Your vote has a chance to make a big difference. I was telling you about the corporate boardrooms of every insurance company in every HMO in California and the United States, they're watching. They're listening. They're wondering what kind of message you're going to send.

And the legitimate companies that pay for something, that write words and act upon their words, they're watching you. They have to compete with people who show the appearance of doing everything and in reality do nothing, which saves money. That's very lucrative, but it doesn't help the people that have the contract. Your vote counts in this one. Your vote will make a difference.

It's your vote that's going to count. You can send a message that will go a long way beyond the county of Riverside. You can send a message that, even if you don't have political power, and even if you're working as a junior high school teacher, the fact that there's a promise to you, a promise means something. You can send a message that may help the other million people that may still be insured by the defendant, those same million who right now may be sleeping well at night believing Health Net will be there for them. The other people who might not right now have breast cancer, but eventually will be one of those statistics, those one in nine women.

One last thing, the thing that shocked me so much, is that when I asked Dr. Ossorio, "Do you know how many women get breast cancer?" He said, "No." Then they send in a vice president, happens to be a female, to talk about Mrs. Bosworth and the transplant pool. I asked her, and she didn't know how many women get breast cancer. There was another one I asked. I can't remember which one right now, that didn't know. Well, hopefully, if nothing else, they now know how many people get breast cancer, one hundred and eighty thousand. "Do you know how many people will die, out of one hundred and eighty thousand, not a perfect cure, but can be helped by the thing they say they covered?" "No."

Thank you for your time, and during the holiday season, coming in here every day. And I ask that on all causes of action, you find for the Foxes. And that you send a message and make a difference for all those other people that may come down the line after Nelene and after Jim. Thanks.

Nelene would have been proud. Her brother, a young and inexperienced trial lawyer, had struck a passionate, thorough, and heartfelt blow on behalf of her and her family. Hiepler and Templeman had overturned every corporate rock and brought into clear view a series of unseemly corporate practices and procedures. Speaking from the emotional perspective of a brother who had lost a dear sister, Hiepler's closing argument, while maintaining that prickly edge of a family violated, had never succumbed to emotional bathos. He had meticulously made the case for breach of contract, bad faith, and emotional distress before turning to punitive damages. His simple "littering" analogy told the jurors all they needed to know about punitive damages.

Swallow's Closing Argument for the Defense

Lyle Swallow had watched the jury during Hiepler's close, and the tears in the eyes of jurors foreshadowed an imposing challenge. Undaunted, he rose and began to explain the defense's theme:

At the start of this trial I told you that, in my view, this was a controversy about a controversy. I think that's become very apparent. This trial is the first controversy. And the evidence has been compelling that the controversy decided here is the status of high-dose chemotherapy for patients with metastatic breast cancer. Every physician who has testified, every single one of them, states the treatment is controversial in one way, shape, or form, they admitted it was controversial. I'd also like to reiterate, briefly, something I said in opening statement, and something His Honor said early on in the matter. There are a lot of emotional overtones to this case. And again, we all can be and are very sympathetic with the Foxes and what transpired here. But the decision in this case can't be decided on emotions. Health Net can't cure cancer. Health Net doesn't give people cancer. We believe the evidence shows that high-dose chemotherapy doesn't cure breast cancer.

Swallow then worked through what he characterized to be "red herrings" in the case. The first concerned any financial incentive by Dr. Ossorio to deny coverage:

What were Dr. Ossorio's goals on which he's developed to participate in the corporate bonus program? Not denying claims, not reducing medical costs, but things like setting up systems to evaluate outcomes of medical treatment. The implication is that somehow having a corporate bonus or incentive is inherently wrong. I would submit to you that is a very common practice, one of the things used by companies to attract and maintain good employees.

GM has an employee stock option plan. Does that mean there's an incentive to leave parts off of cars? Dr. Ossorio testified he doesn't consider costs and it was not part of his bonus program.

Swallow next attempted to rebut Hiepler's argument that since two other women had received the bone marrow treatment, it was unfair and discriminatory to deny Nelene Fox that treatment:

More red herrings. Payment by Health Net for the bone marrow transplants for Janice Bosworth and for Evelyn Moulton. Plaintiffs are arguing this was unfair. This was discriminating treatment or differential treatment under the same contract, that it wasn't fair to pay for Mrs. Bosworth and not for Mrs. Fox. What was the evidence? The evidence was that all three of those patients were treated exactly the same way under that contract.

Looking at Mrs. Bosworth, what did she do? She went to her employer. There is sort of an oddity here, with respect to Mrs. Bosworth, in that Health Net wears two hats, with respect to Mrs. Bosworth. They just, also, happen to be putting on another hat, they provided her health plan.

Health Net made the decision, as her employer, and despite the determination by Dr. Ossorio that this was investigational, that if City of Hope concluded this [the bone marrow transplant] was medically appropriate treatment, and she was an appropriate candidate, they would approve treatment for Mrs. Bosworth at City of Hope. That testimony was one hundred percent consistent. Any employer could agree to do that. Any employer could agree to do this. Health Net was acting as her employer. Any employer who has an employee that they value can give them something they're not obligated to give. That's the decision that was made.

Evelyn Moulton. Again, she testified that her request for this treatment was denied on the grounds that it was investigational. And upon reviewing documents, admitted that she was told by a physician at UCSF that it was investigational. That occurred in 1990. I would submit to you that in light of the emphasis put by plaintiffs on the Technology Assessment, that was an entirely correct decision.

What was the Technology Assessment in 1990? That it wasn't the standard of care. What did Mrs. Moulton do? She wasn't a Health Net employee, she couldn't make another appeal to them. She retained an attorney. She retained an attorney who contacted Health Net. Almost a year later what happened was Health Net made a business decision to provide the coverage for Mrs. Moulton.

There's no testimony that this was a change in their decision. The correspondence you heard doesn't say that Health Net decided not to enforce its right under the contract not to pay for this. Health Net doesn't have to explain it any further. Companies make business decisions all the time. The issue is whether or not she was, she and Mrs. Fox, were treated differently, looked at differently under the contract. They weren't. Under the contract, all three women were treated identically.

Swallow next turned to evidence that he believed established that the bone marrow transplant procedure was "investigative" and "experimental" and therefore not covered in the contract:

His Honor will instruct you that you read the contract provision as a whole, as a lay person, not as an attorney, not as an expert, would read it. That's the audience you're writing to. The language in that exclusion, I can quote it almost verbatim in that definition: "Investigative services or procedures are those which have progressed to limited use on humans, but which are not widely accepted as proven and effective in the organized medical community."

Dr. Jones and Dr. Schinke and a number of other witnesses talked about the limited use of this treatment. They testified regarding the statistics of the percentage of patients with Stage IV metastatic breast cancer in 1992 that underwent high-dose chemotherapy [Nelene Fox was diagnosed Stage IV]. One of the witnesses says five percent or less. And one said one percent. They talked about the number of centers offering this treatment compared to the number of centers that offer standard chemotherapy. The numbers were dramatically different.

Dr. Schinke testified that it was his opinion in November of '92 that this treatment shouldn't be being done in the community by oncologists. He testified it was his opinion that this treatment should be limited to the centers with the most experience, primary university research centers. And he testified that he thought it should be provided under strict protocols. What about "widely accepted as proven and effective"?

If we take the Technology Assessment done in 1990, as counsel would like to have us do, then in 1990 the treatment was not standard treatment. It wasn't proven and effective. The question then, what evidence has come along since 1990 to change that? Several of the witnesses testified about a survey that was done by the American Medical Association and published in late 1991, either October or November, I can't remember the month. And I believe, in that case, quoting Dr. Van Scoy-Mosher as saying that "the conclusion reached regarding this treatment for patients with metastatic breast cancer was that it was investigative at best."

Dr. Jones was a little more careful. He disagreed. He thought it was conservative. Dr. Jones testified that he published articles on this treatment in order to, quote, "keep the medical community advised of advancements."

The suggestion has been made by the time peer review journals are published, that the data is six years old and the conclusions are meaningless. If that's the case, then one must wonder why Dr. Jones is publishing fifty-five articles in peer review articles and who he's trying to convince. The reality is, for example, with the '93 article, as Dr. Van Scoy-Mosher testified, that patient treatment began in 1988. The data was completed very recently. The article was published in 1993, and the authors made their comments about the result and their opinions. Their comments aren't six years old; the comments are current.

Dr. Jones testified that, in his opinion, the technique is promising. Dr. Schinke testified that the data that came out of the phase one and phase two trials on this treatment he characterized as hopeful. Counsel seemed to be implying that "proven and effective" meant that it was guaranteed. Counsel has made an argument that there doesn't have to be a guarantee in anything. I would agree with him. There's no guarantee in any medical procedures. There are risks with any of them.

However, it is not disputed that the patients with appendicitis, those undergoing appendectomies, do better than those that don't. It's been proven to be effective. There is no doubt the patients that are insulin dependent, diabetics who live, will do better there than those that don't take the insulin. It's proven and effective.

The bottom line is that from the testimony of the witnesses here, there's no data, there's no documentation to show that the treatment is widely accepted as proven and effective. There is no data to show that the patients live longer. There is no claim by anyone that this treatment cures breast cancer. It does, however, carry risks associated with it, but a substantially higher risk than those with standard chemotherapy.

At best, there's a controversy about this treatment and its relative efficacy. At best, all of the physicians, again, said it was controversial. There are differences in patient selection criteria versus little or no agreement, also, to who are the candidates to have good results. The distinction between Mrs. Fox with her bone marrow and bone metastasis and Mrs. Bosworth with her liver—I mean, there was a real difference of opinion about that.

The overwhelming evidence is that it's still investigative as that's defined. It's in limited use, not widely accepted as proven and effective in the organized medical community.

Swallow then focused on Hiepler's claim that Health Net engaged in stall tactics:

The first time that Health Net is contacted is June fifth. They asked for the records to review. While they think it's investigational, the policy is to review all records, makes sense, evaluating new treatments. The records come in on June tenth. Dr. Ossorio reviews the records on the eleventh, and he testified that in consultation with the other doctors at Health Net, he concluded that the treatment was investigative for her condition.

So Dr. Ossorio makes the determination that this is not widely accepted as proven and effective. Dr. Ossorio also had serious concerns about Mrs. Fox's undergoing this treatment. This is an HMO. It doesn't pay bills. It arranges for care to be provided. Dr. Ossorio's duties don't stop at making the claims decision. He's involved in doing health outcomes, analysis involved in quality assurance programs.

In light of those concerns and his obligations, he is real concerned. What are his concerns? His concerns are that from his reading and his speaking with people, this type of patient does particularly poorly under high-dose chemotherapy. He expressed a concern, also, about the materials that were in writing about this, the letters, and, in particular, the consult from Dr. Khan, which would have been the consult from April twenty-third. His concern was that it didn't seem to be presenting a balanced view of the risks and benefits of this treatment for this particular patient, and was quoting data from Duke University that he did not believe applied to this patient.

So, what did Dr. Ossorio do? He called Duke University. He testified he did it because he was seeing statistics that were being quoted that he did not believe applied to Nelene Fox. And he wanted to get their opinion. And he was told that she was not an appropriate candidate.

He also called Dr. Camacho. There was no dispute about that. He called Dr. Camacho to discusses his concerns about the patient, to see what Dr. Camacho's concerns were and, also, discuss his concern about whether or not the risks and benefits had been adequately explained to her and that the data really applied to this patient.

Dr. Camacho testified very honestly about that conversation. He testified that Dr. Ossorio appeared to be well educated, well informed, had done his homework here, knew what he was talking about. He testified that it was a pleasant, straightforward, honest conversation. He characterized it as "good."

He said that Dr. Ossorio did not say anything during the conversation that he believed was inappropriate and did nothing he interpreted as trying to coerce him in any way. They agreed that they had concerns. Dr. Camacho agreed with Dr. Ossorio that this was a high-risk patient for this treatment. And he also agreed to communicate an offer from Health Net to have her independently evaluated. Dr. Camacho testified he didn't believe that any of those requests were inappropriate, didn't have any problems doing it, and thought they might be a good idea.

Then Dr. Camacho at a meeting on June fifteenth with Mr. and

Mrs. Fox explained that "I'd been called by Dr. Ossorio." Then he goes on to say, "Dr. Ossorio's feeling was since the tumor was metastasized to bone and bone marrow and has not had a complete response with chemotherapy, the patient was at a very high risk for undergoing high-dose chemotherapy with stem cell rescue. I told Ossorio that I agreed with him completely." Consistent with Dr. Camacho and Dr. Ossorio's testimony about what went on. "I also explained to Dr. Ossorio that these risks had been explained to the patient and the patient is willing to accept those risks."

There was no testimony that Dr. Ossorio was trying to somehow prohibit Mrs. Fox from having this procedure. His concern was that she make an informed choice, and that arose out of the records he saw from Norris (USC) that raised concerns about whether or not the risks had been explained to them.

I think that the evidence is plain and clear and undisputed that Dr. Camacho did not change his mind about Mrs. Fox undergoing this procedure after he spoke with Dr. Ossorio. The plaintiffs have pointed to the two letters written by Dr. Camacho, the purported letters of support, as an indication of support and then pointing to this meeting as some change in his position was a hundred-eighty-degree turn.

Dr. Camacho explained what the letters were about. He was honest and straightforward in that explanation, saying that he wrote those letters for the singular purpose of helping Mrs. Fox get the insurance company to pay for the treatment. He admitted that they were inaccurate and incomplete in certain ways. And his point was to assist the patient in getting insurance coverage. He admitted the letters did not contain any reference to his concerns about the treatment or whether she was a high-risk patient. But if his point was to get insurance coverage, why would he be including those? What he was doing was admittedly putting a positive spin on the situation to try to get the insurance company to pay.

And I would also suggest that Drs. Khan and Douer were doing the exact same thing in the letters they were writing in an attempt to put a positive spin on this. Dr. Khan admitted that the letters didn't set forth all of the risks. Beyond that testimony, Dr. Camacho didn't change his mind and that testimony is entirely consistent with other evidence that's in this case.

Look at the evidence, that's all you have to do. Beyond asking Dr. Camacho to explain the risks, what else did Health Net do? Dr.

Ossorio testified about his concerns about this patient, because of her extensive bone marrow metastasis, which has sort of been lost in the discussion here, but the metastasis was a very big concern of his. Dr. Camacho agreed with him about the concerns of her being a high risk, which heightened when he spoke to Duke University about this. What did they do?

Because of those concerns, they offered Mrs. Fox the opportunity to have an evaluation at City of Hope. And the offer of the evaluation at City of Hope was "We'll have this done and if they agree that you're a candidate, if it is medically appropriate treatment for you, we'll pay to have it done at UCLA."

Dr. Camacho testified that was perfectly reasonable and fine. He did testify that he did feel it was a waste of time to refer her to City of Hope, because everybody knew she wouldn't fit this protocol, but that wasn't the purpose of the referral. The purpose of the referral was for an evaluation. None of the physician witnesses, in this case, have testified that City of Hope physicians were not qualified, completely qualified to conduct that evaluation on Mrs. Fox. In fact, Dr. Camacho admitted that "in my opinion, it would be ludicrous." Simply, this particular patient doesn't fit their protocols. But they are eminently qualified to evaluate the patient, explain the risks and benefits to her, and make a determination as to whether or not, in their opinion, this is appropriate treatment for her.

Despite Health Net's determination that this was investigative and not covered under the health plan, they made that offer to Mrs. Fox. "If City of Hope says this is medically appropriate, we'll pay for it at UCLA." The question is, then, why UCLA and not Norris? There has been a great deal of testimony about the fact that Health Net had selected certain transplant centers throughout the state of California, and they made that selection based on a group of criteria that were developed for them by oncologists and transplanters throughout the state of California.

The testimony was that they did that review and made that selection for one purpose only, and that was to make certain they are the highest-quality centers for transplant procedures to be performed for Health Net members. And testimony was that Norris was not selected as one of the preferred transplant centers. They didn't meet the criteria. This isn't to bash Norris, certainly not. We wouldn't deny the great reputation of Norris. They have a reputation as a very fine cancer treatment center, designated by the NCI as a cancer center in Southern California. But the question is not their reputation, in general. The decision was made based on their experience with respect to performing bone marrow transplants for breast cancer patients. So that's the reason for UCLA.

The testimony is there. There's been argument that this offer by Health Net was somehow a delay tactic, but there isn't any evidence that going through this evaluation at City of Hope would have caused any delay, whatsoever, in the treatment of Mrs. Fox. There's no evidence as to how long it would have taken to have gotten the evaluation at City of Hope. I would suggest to you, in light of the efforts and the speed in which Health Net was responding to this matter, in a very short period, it's reasonable to expect they would have made every effort to have that procedure done as soon as it could possibly have been done.

There's been discussion about the many hoops Mrs. Fox had to go through at Norris and the suggestion that she had to start from the beginning, if she went to UCLA. I remind you that the testimony was that many of those hoops involved doing tests to restage her disease, to find out what her current status and other issues regarding her health were. And there's been no evidence that would have to be redone.

No one has testified that Mrs. Fox stop the treatment and evaluation that was going on at Norris in order to have the evaluation at City of Hope. This offer was made on June fifteenth. The testimony has been that Mrs. Fox didn't actually have the transplant at Norris until late August, early September. So the delay issue isn't there. It's an argument with no facts. Health Net made the offer trying to resolve the matter, and the offer was rejected. Now, plaintiffs want to penalize Health Net for making the offer.

Swallow argued that even if Health Net was wrong in denying coverage and breached the contract, that alone was insufficient to establish bad faith. This was a difficult argument for the defense to make. Simply by rebutting Hiepler's bad-faith argument, Swallow might be viewed by some of the jurors as implicitly conceding that Health Net was liable. On the other hand, if the defense failed to answer Hiepler's accusations of bad faith, the jurors would be left with only the plaintiffs' view.

Plaintiffs contend that this is a case about money. Experimental and investigational equals expensive. Let's look at that. The testimony was clear that Health Net covers high-dose chemotherapy and bone marrow transplant for other conditions, conditions under which the treatment would not have been investigative. The testimony was that the treatment for some of those conditions, actually, costs more than it does for this treatment for breast cancer patients. The testimony was that if the patient didn't have high-dose chemotherapy, she would have continued on chemotherapy. Dr. Ossorio expressed an estimate that the cost would have been somewhere over half the cost of the high-dose chemotherapy.

Health Net did not want Mrs. Fox to go away, as has been suggested. If she had continued on conventional chemotherapy, Health Net would have provided coverage for her. Plaintiffs have contended that Health Net wasn't there for Mrs. Fox when she got breast cancer. That simply isn't true. The evidence is that Mrs. Fox had treatment through her Health Net plan for her surgeries, her hospitalization, her chemotherapy. From the time that she was diagnosed through and until June of '92 when the issue of the high-dose chemotherapy came up, Health Net was there for Mrs. Fox. The only dispute is their request for coverage of the high-dose chemotherapy.

If you conclude that the decision was wrong, Health Net should have covered under the plan, that's not enough to prove a bad-faith claim. In addition to having an incorrect decision, you have to find that Health Net acted unreasonably in making that decision.

Look at the circumstances here. I know, I've said it a lot, but it's very clear from the evidence, this is very controversial treatment. Oncologists don't agree on the potential benefits for patients with metastatic breast cancer. There is no requirement, as the plaintiffs' counsel has pointed out, that Health Net pay every claim that comes in the door. There can be good-faith disputes. We know that. And this is an issue that's fairly debatable. If there isn't agreement among the oncologists about the treatment, how could the decision have been unreasonable? They point to some conduct here they contend is unreasonable. One is the referral to City of Hope as being unreasonable. In light of the circumstances and what we previously discussed, we would submit it was an entirely reasonable offer.

They point to Dr. Ossorio coercing Dr. Camacho. That didn't happen. There's no evidence of it. They pointed to Janice Bosworth and Evelyn Moulton, discriminatory treatment of the people under the plan. As we discussed, all three of them were treated exactly the same.

They pointed to the fact Dr. Ossorio didn't call Dr. Douer or Dr.

Khan at Norris. My question is, for what purpose? Dr. Ossorio's testimony was that he had all of the information he needed in his possession at the time that he made the decision. He talked to the treating oncologist, Dr. Camacho. He made a call to Duke. He had the documents from Norris, which he contended were not entirely accurate, with respect to their evaluation of her. Can anyone here believe that a call from Dr. Ossorio to Norris would have made any difference in the outcome of this matter? Again, if you find that the treatment should have been covered, that's not enough for a bad-faith claim. You have to find that Health Net acted unreasonably or without proper cause. We contend there's no evidence they did anything unreasonable.

With respect to the emotional distress. For you to find there was an intentional infliction of emotional distress, which we believe you can't, you can award Mr. Fox damages for emotional distress, but you can only award him damages once. And it's got to be Mr. Fox's emotional distress, not for Mrs. Fox, not for the children. They aren't parties here. And you can only award him damages for emotional distress relating to this, not with his emotional distress over his wife's health or her death.

Counsel made a measure of damages that you should award. You're going to get an instruction as to what the appropriate measure of damages will be, but you're to fairly compensate Mr. Fox, if you conclude he's entitled. There isn't anything in that instruction that is an implication that this award is to be, in any way, punitive. It's a fair compensation award.

Looking at Mr. Fox's emotional distress itself. Mr. Fox had emotional distress. There's no doubt about that. But what was that emotional distress? With Dr. Robinson on the stand, we went through his records of visits and his counseling sessions. He was a little testy. We had records of seventeen visits, in which there was counseling. Five of those visits, there were documented references to matters relating to the dispute or the lawsuit in some way, shape, or form, also, reference to other things going on. And in not one of those records was there any mention anywhere of any emotional distress or any problems being caused to Mr. Fox by the fund-raising. Those records show a man who's had a great deal of distress relating to his wife's illness or possible death and his dealing with it.

We're not contending he didn't have emotional distress. We're simply questioning what the cause of that was and suggesting you should look at the testimony and the records to make that determination. If, as Mr. Hiepler contends, the fund-raising and the ongoing contact with Mr. Fox about it up to today is, as they claim, was "eating him alive," I would submit to you that we should find some reference to that in those records, and it's not there. The records simply don't bear out that claim.

Finally, the issue of punitive damages. We would submit that you're never going to get to that stage in that claim, but despite that, I need to make a few comments. Again, you're going to get jury instructions about that particular claim. And there's a different burden of proof with respect to that claim than there is with the rest of the case. You're going to be told "clear and convincing evidence of conduct constituting oppression, fraud, or malice," and the instructions will give you definitions of those words, you'll hear about terms like *despicable conduct* and *conscious disregard of rights* and *intentional* conduct.

I'd like to point out that clear and convincing evidence is "evidence that is so clear as to leave no substantial doubt sufficiently strong to command the unhesitating assent of every reasonable mind." That's the burden of proof. If the evidence doesn't support that level of proof, then no award of punitive damages can be given.

Where is that conduct here? Where is there evidence of despicable conduct, a conscious disregard, intentional conduct, here at all? Where is there clear and convincing evidence or any evidence of that?

This is a case about decisions. It's a case about people making decisions. And we all make decisions every day in our jobs, no matter what the job is. It doesn't matter whether we're attorneys or doctors or schoolteachers, whatever. We make decisions every single day. And we make the best decisions we all can under the circumstances. That's what we do when we're doing our job as jurors. You're going to be making decisions, the best decisions you can with the evidence and resources available to you.

In this case, the people at Health Net made decisions. They did them in the course of doing their job. You saw them. You heard them testify. I would submit to you that what you saw were intelligent, articulate, caring, honest people with nothing to hide. They made the best decisions they could under the circumstances. They didn't act in any malicious way or with any intention to harm Mr. or Mrs. Fox.

When Swallow finished, Alan Templeman gave a rebuttal argument for the plaintiffs, concluding the closing arguments on the afternoon of Wednesday, December 22, 1993. Judge Van Frank instructed the jury on the law, explaining they would answer numerous questions on a special verdict form, and asked the jury to apply the law to the facts as they found them to be.

Verdict

At nine thirty in the morning of the second day of deliberations, jurors sent a note to the judge: "We recall a statement during instructions allowing us access to Health Net's financial status. How do we decide punitive damages? Or do we?" Hiepler was at the hotel with his wife when Judge Van Frank called him in to discuss the note. The implications of the question sank in; Hiepler knew, because the jury was considering punitive damages, that his sister had won, and he told Michelle, "Oh, man, this thing might have really made a difference!"

Later that afternoon, jury foreman Robley Bowen handed the completed verdict form to the judge, who called the attorneys to his chambers, where he read the verdict: "$87,128,153.10. That's the total amount of damages that they find." The judge, taken aback, added, "Clearly that amount is not sustained by the damages." The jurors were subsequently polled—questioned by the court; they had jumped to the punitive-damages stage too soon. The jurors were instructed to first decide the issue of compensatory damages, and if and when they found for the Foxes, then move on to the question of punitive damages.

The jurors resumed their deliberations and, an hour later, returned to the courtroom with a unanimous $12.1 million compensatory-damages verdict—the largest ever in a Riverside County civil trial and the largest bad-faith verdict ever in California. The jurors found for the Foxes on every cause of action.

The court declared a recess for the Christmas holiday, and an exhausted Hiepler visited his sister's grave. He knelt, looked at Nelene's smiling picture, and read the inscription from Philippians 4:13 on the headstone: "I can do all things through Christ who strengthens me."

As Hiepler prepared for the final phase of the trial that weekend, the *Wall Street Journal* reported the jury's possible $87 million award for punitive damages. The size of the potential verdict attracted the attention of the national media to the Riverside County courthouse.

The jury returned on Tuesday, December 28, to hear testimony about the punitive damages. As the litigants arrived at the courthouse, news crews from around the nation swarmed outside, cramming into the crowded courtroom and spilling out into the hallway. Supporters of the Fox family lined up next to worried insurance executives, all trying to get a view of the action. Health Net's CEO testified about the HMO's financial condition, and the jurors retired to deliberate. After only two hours, the jury returned an astonishing $77 million punitive-damages award.

Stunned by the size of the award—despite the jury's having tipped its hand earlier—Hiepler hugged his brother-in-law and nieces, crying. When he left the courthouse, Hiepler saw media vans everywhere. A reporter from a national newsmagazine approached and asked for his picture; Hiepler thought, "No one ever wanted to take *my* picture!" The attorney spent ten hours giving interviews throughout that first night, telling reporters that his sister's case was the first in the country to go to trial for refusing a bone marrow transplant to a breast cancer patient. "It was the first [lawsuit] in the nation against an HMO to ever expose" a plan to victimize customers by reneging on contract coverage. "We're exposing the secrets of managed care—that the man who makes the decision on whether you get a procedure gets a bonus on how well the company does financially," he said.

The jury's staggering $89.1 million award was the largest in California since a $128 million verdict for burn victims in the 1978 *Grimshaw v. Ford Motor Co.* and ranked among the highest awards in the nation. Hiepler commented on the enormous size of the verdict, telling family members and reporters that he'd gladly forfeit the huge award to have his sister back.

The trial now over, the jury was free to talk to the press. Bowen, the foreman, said he had gone to great lengths to keep sympathy for the Foxes and other emotions out of the deliberations and to make an objective decision based on the facts. He said the most damaging conclusion reached by the jurors was that Health Net's denial was less a reasoned medical decision than a calculated, strategic delay of treatment in hopes that Nelene's condition would worsen to the point that doctors would no longer recommend the transplant.

Health Net's attorneys attacked the verdict, calling the $77 million punitive award "outrageous, inconsistent, and rendered solely on the basis of emotion." While Health Net was filing its appeal, activists, commentators, and interest groups weighed in on the jury's decision. Women's health advocates praised the award, claiming patients with little hope of recovery might take hope from the decision. University of Southern California ethicist Alexander M. Capron viewed the verdict with skepticism, saying treatment based upon doing everything theoretically possible would bankrupt the health care system.

In the end, the Foxes and Health Net settled for an undisclosed amount on April 5, 1994. The settlement did not include an agreement that Health Net would start covering ABMT for breast cancer patients. Hiepler explained that they settled with Health Net because "we didn't want it to be tied up in appellate court for several years." As the money came in, Jim Fox and the Hieplers spent time writing checks to supporters who had given money for Nelene's treatment. From $5,000 to all $5 donations, the settlement money was used to pay them back with interest. Any money that could not be returned was donated to breast cancer research.

Fox donated some of the settlement money to build a lighted football stadium and softball fields at the Linfield School, a private Christian school where he coached, in memory of Nelene, who had been active in youth sports. He also gave money to install lights above the sports fields at Temecula Middle School, where he continued to teach English.

Fox and his three daughters entered counseling. "We're working through a situation where we're comfortable talking about Mom," he said. Fox took refuge in his classroom—a place he had sought out even while Nelene was dying. Inside the classroom, he had control, while outside he had none. Despite his desire for privacy, Fox does what he can to educate others on the ordeal that he and his family endured, anxious to spare everyone else the pain of such an unbearable loss.

Hiepler took advantage of his sudden celebrity and opened his own law office, Hiepler & Hiepler, with his wife, Michelle, as a partner in August 1994. Denial-of-coverage cases came flooding in, and Hiepler went up against other managed care organizations, committing himself to a crusade that began with Nelene's case. "It's a great buzz that you get," Hiepler said of his new cause. "But it's so closely related to the worst thing that I've ever been through that I don't get too excited about it."

Aftermath

Just as managed health care seemed to be putting the brakes on medical spending and things started to look promising for the industry, *Fox v. Health Net* exploded, unleashing an outpouring of national media coverage on HMO problems and consumer complaints about delays and denials of coverage. It also sparked an increase in managed care litigation. Americans, many of whom believed that even the most expensive and obscure treatments could and should be available to all, got a rare and shocking look into the workings of a managed care company.

Nelene Fox's story raised troubling questions: What if my HMO won't pay for a costly procedure that my doctor recommends? Will my health insurance be there for me when I need it most? Does my doctor have a financial incentive to withhold certain treatments? Are the insurance executives more concerned about salary bonuses when coverage for expensive patient care is denied?

However, many who sought to bring managed care complaints to court found their claims were limited as a result of a far-reaching federal law. In 1974, the federal government had enacted the Employee Retirement Income Security Act (ERISA). ERISA gave the government authority over the most common form of health insurance: employee health benefits. Many HMOs, IPAs, and PPOs that administer job-related health plans qualify as ERISA plans. Roughly 75 percent of people who get health insurance through their employer are covered by ERISA.

ERISA preempts state laws that "relate to any employee benefit plan" covered by ERISA. State laws enacted to protect consumers from potentially harmful managed care methods often do not apply to ERISA-covered plans. Not all managed care plans are preempted by ERISA. Managed care members who are public employees, church employees, or those who directly contract with their health organization are the most common exceptions to ERISA restrictions.

As a general rule, ERISA governs employee benefits issues if the plaintiff receives those benefits from a private employer. Accordingly, the plaintiff must bring his suit in federal court. Persons injured through the administration of an ERISA plan do not have the same remedies available that plaintiffs like the Foxes had because ERISA excludes damages for bad faith, emotional distress, and punitive damages. An ERISA plaintiff may only recover benefits due him under the plan—usually the cost of a particular procedure or treatment that was denied.

Ironically, ERISA was intended to shield employee pension funds from legal action, but in effect it has shielded managed care organizations from liability. Some critics characterize ERISA as antiquated legislation, often harmful to the very people it was intended to protect. Not only does ERISA produce inequitable outcomes, with a select few plaintiffs recovering large damage awards, but medical organizations complain that ERISA unfairly exposes physicians to liability risks, because injured patients who cannot sue their health plan go after their doctors instead.

For example, in *Ching v. Gaines,* a young woman's treating physician failed to promptly diagnose her colon cancer after she complained of abdominal pains. Mark Hiepler, who represented Ching in her suit against her physician, argued that the doctor ignored unambiguous symptoms pointing to cancer and turned down repeated requests to have her sent to a specialist. By the time Ching finally received the referral, it was too late to save her. Ching's physician received a capitation fee from her HMO, but would have had to pay the equivalent of a $5,000 deductible if he had referred her to a specialist at the beginning of her treatment. Although Ching's husband eventually won a $2.9 million medical-malpractice verdict, he was left to raise their young son alone.

Ching v. Gaines revealed formerly hidden physician incentives imposed by HMOs, even though the HMO itself was not sued; the jurors in *Ching* said they were amazed to find out about the incentive plans.

In a 1995 poll by *California Physicians,* 20 percent of the 1,122 physicians polled admitted that capitation issues "frequently" influenced their medical decisions. Dr. Rex Green, a California oncologist, told CBS's *60 Minutes,* "We're getting pushed. We're getting pushed closer and closer to that margin where we have to think consciously about cost rather than quality each time we're making a decision about taking care of a patient." In the same report, internist Dr. Robert Plancey agreed, "There's certainly that pressure. And there are fines which can be levied if [the HMOs] second-guess, look back in retrospect, and say, 'Gee, this patient could have left the hospital a day earlier, and therefore, Doctor, we're fining you so many dollars for an unnecessary bed day.' " Despite the concerns expressed by doctors and patients, HMOs insist that financial incentives do not lessen the quality of patient care.

The federal government and many state legislatures responded to the conflict of interest resulting from capitation schemes by passing legislation—due in part to *Fox v. Health Net.* In March 1996, the federal Health Care Financing Administration (HCFA), the agency in charge of Medicaid and Medicare administration, issued regulations that required HMOs to disclose the specific terms of physicians' financial incentives to HCFA or state agencies administering Medicaid programs. While the information is not disclosed directly to the patients, at least it may leak out to the public. The states have followed, many passing similar laws requiring disclosure of incentives to patients.

By 1997, eleven states had passed legislation requiring health insurers to offer or cover high-dose chemotherapy with autologous bone marrow transplant (HDCT-ABMT) for breast cancer patients, regardless of "experimental" or "investigational" provisions in insurance contracts. Although the details vary from state to state, the possibility of obtaining treatment quickly without objection based on "experimental treatment" has provided hope for thousands of breast cancer patients. While recent legislative trends indicate progress, the debate over HDCT-ABMT and experimental-therapy coverage in general is far from over. Physicians are divided over the efficacy of HDCT-ABMT for breast cancer patients, and the National Cancer Institute reports that, due to a lack of conclusive studies, researchers are still conducting clinical trials on the treatment.

Faced with spiraling costs, some HMOs resorted to internal intimidation. Linda Peeno, a former HMO medical director, told *U.S. News and World Report* about the pressures she faced as the final person to approve or deny requests for care. In one case, an HMO nurse brought her a letter from a doctor requesting a voice machine for a young woman who was paralyzed after a stroke. "The letter is layered with colored Post-it notes. One bright blue square says, 'Approve this and it will be your last!' I had started this new career full of enthusiasm. But what I found was that the pressure was always there: deny as much care as possible in order to cut costs. I couldn't overcome the pressures to manipulate medical guidelines and contract language, and to push physicians toward some practices that endangered patient care." Peeno approved the voice machine and left her job soon thereafter.

Fox v. Health Net helped to expose the problems within the managed care system, and with exposure comes an understanding of the problem. The "managed care backlash," inspired in part by cases like Nelene Fox's, developed as physicians and patients bristled against its restrictions and hard bargaining policies. For a brief period during the HMO heydays of the mid-1990s, annual spending actually decreased, but the success of HMOs in controlling health care costs was short-lived.

The nation is currently in its seventh straight year of increased health care spending, due in part to more diagnostic tests, more prescriptions written— a result of increased drug advertising, greater use of new technology, more days spent in the hospital, and an aging baby-boomer population requiring more health care. In an effort to maintain their profit margins, many HMOs and other managed care organizations have simply increased their insurance premiums; health care spending hit $1.4 trillion in 2001.

How best to handle the crisis remains an exceedingly difficult problem for legislators and patients. Americans have a voracious appetite for new drugs and innovative treatments, but also a deep-seated resentment of any restraints on their health care choices. While politicians and health care experts struggle to come up with a comprehensive plan for cost containment and a solution to the national health care crisis, there appears to be no viable alternative to managed care. For now, individual families are left to make their own economic decisions on what health insurance, if any, they should get to supplement their work-related coverage. Meanwhile, society strives to find a balance between the availability of medical services and the cost of health care.

Reflecting years later on his sister's tragic death and the numerous managed care cases he has handled since, Hiepler said, "If I could turn back time and have an afternoon with my sister again—and get rid of the benefits that have come to us—I'd do it in a heartbeat. But I can't. So through the curse of Nelene's situation, we've been sought out by a lot of people. And I think we've helped a lot of them. That's her legacy. And if she could see us now, you know what? She'd love every minute of it."

CHAPTER EIGHT

Cleansing the Gene Pool

Carrie Buck's Forced Sterilization
and the Limits on Reproductive Freedom

> It is better for all the world, if instead of waiting to execute degen-
> erate offspring for crime, or to let them starve for their imbecility,
> society can prevent those who are manifestly unfit from continu-
> ing their kind. . . . Three generations of imbeciles are enough.
>
> *Supreme Court justice Oliver Wendell Holmes,*
> *upholding the forced sterilization of Carrie Buck*

Ask a stranger on any street in America, "What do you think about *Roe v. Wade*?" and you've issued an invitation to enter a heated debate. For more than thirty years, Americans who do not ordinarily express strong opinions about Supreme Court decisions have engaged in often acrimonious discussions—by the office watercooler or taking to the streets in mass demonstrations pro and con—to tell their fellow citizens exactly what they think about the issue of legalized abortion.

But the struggle of Carrie Buck in *Buck v. Bell* has never achieved the same prominence in the public debate over a woman's ability—her right—to control her body. In many ways as important as *Roe v. Wade* some five decades later, the 1927 Supreme Court decision legalizing forced sterilization had an impact spanning oceans and bolstered the Nazis' dream of purifying the gene pool using the gun and the gas chamber.

This story stands in stark contrast to the others included in this book. They set forth the remarkable arguments and accomplishments of lawyers who with passion, tenacity, and intellect fought for their clients, arguing to advance and protect their rights. Unfortunately, Carrie Buck had no equivalent to Paul Armstrong, pressing the system to allow Karen Ann Quinlan to die; to Andrew Hamilton, standing up for that coura-geous German immigrant; to former president Adams, arguing for the freedom of the *Amistad* survivors.

Her so-called advocate, Irving P. Whitehead, rather than being her champion, battling intolerance, prejudice, and fighting for the integrity of the human body, remained for the most part mute, offering only the most cursory of arguments. His collusion with the proponents of forced sterilization doomed not only his client, but thousands of others deemed undesirable, to the shock of the cold steel operating table and the cruelty of the scalpel.

We included this chapter not because there was a great closing argument—there wasn't—or because some lawyer battled for a noble principle; none did. It is here because it underscores the difference a lawyer, armed with his passion and intellect, and fighting for a just cause, can make. Without that courtroom champion, Carrie Buck and thousands of other Americans were deprived of an essential right. The story of Carrie Buck could have been—should have been—the story of Irving P. Whitehead, a lawyer who understood what lawyers must do; who understood that a lawyer's first obligation is to his client.

No lawyer presented Carrie's case, for although a lawyer appeared with her, no lawyer truly stood *with* Carrie Buck.

A Difficult Beginning

Carrie Buck was born July 2, 1906, in Charlottesville, Virginia, to Frank and Emma Buck. Her parents separated when Carrie was three or four—some accounts have Frank abandoning the family, tired of living in poverty, while others said he was killed in an accident.

Faced with the task of supporting three children (Carrie and half brother Roy and half sister Doris), Emma soon found herself living on the streets, accepting charity and relying upon the kindness of strangers. She turned to prostitution and lost her children; in 1920, she was committed to the Virginia Colony for Epileptics and Feeble-Minded.

Carrie was taken in by the Dobbs family and for almost fourteen years lived with them in their small stone house on Grove Street in Charlottesville. To the end of her life, Carrie recalled how "the endless work" and "the servants' chores" left her with the feeling that she was "never . . . a family member in the house."

She attended church, regularly sang in the choir, and "liked going to school," a surprising sentiment in a girl soon to be deemed "feeble-minded." During the years she attended school, from 1913 until 1918, Carrie performed as well as any of the other "normal" children, even receiving a commendation from her teacher, "very good—deportment and lessons." The teacher recommended that she be promoted to the sixth grade, but in the fall of 1918, the Dobbses withdrew her from classes "to help with chores at home," occasionally even sending her to do housework for other families in the neighborhood.

In the summer of 1923, Carrie's foster mother, Alice Dobbs, left for a time, reportedly due to an illness. While she was gone, Carrie was raped by Dobbs' nephew.

Carrie told her foster parents about the rape, but they refused to accept that a family member was capable of committing such a heinous crime. Making matters worse, it soon became apparent that Carrie was pregnant, and the Dobbs family began maneuvering, desperate to preserve their reputation and hide the "shameful" condition of their unwed foster child. After sharing their home with Carrie for fourteen years, they desperately wanted to be rid of her, and Constable J. T. Dobbs, a man who regularly dealt with vagrants and the "feebleminded," knew how to accomplish just that.

Playing upon the reputation of Carrie's mother as a woman of loose morals and unsound mind, her foster parents petitioned Justice Charles Shackelford of the Juvenile and Domestic Relations Court in Charlottesville for a hearing, so that Carrie might be examined and institutionalized as feebleminded.

The Dobbses were so anxious to be rid of their pregnant ward they didn't bother to get their stories straight. The Dobbses originally said that Carrie's alleged feeblemindedness "did not develop until she was ten or eleven years of age."

At a deposition taken the same day as Carrie's hearing, they were asked, "At what age was any mental peculiarity first noticed?" They responded, "Since birth," in the first portion of their testimony, but later said her "epilepsy" (which they had earlier denied Carrie had suffered) had appeared "since childhood."

The Dobbses even testified that Carrie experienced "some hallucinations and some outbreaks of temper," that she was "delinquent," and that she was not "honest and truthful." They did not provide any examples to back up their accusations, despite the seeming conflict with their statements that Carrie had never been "confined in any reformatory, prison, or place of detention for incorrigibility," that she had never attempted acts of violence, that she could count, read, write, feed, and dress herself and "keep herself in a tidy condition," that she could recognize and distinguish objects, and that she was "capable of protecting [her]self against ordinary dangers without an attendant."

On January 23, 1924, the Dobbs family doctor, J. C. Coulter (appointed by the judge for the hearing), managed to reach the conclusion for which the Dobbses had been hoping, based only upon the inconsistent testimony of J. T. and Alice Dobbs, and no testimony by Carrie Buck:

> I, J. C. Coulter, citizen of Virginia, physician and practitioner in the city of Charlottesville, hereby certify that I have examined Carrie E. Buck and find that she is feebleminded within the meaning of the law, and is a suitable subject for an institution for the feebleminded. The patient's bodily health is good and she has no contagious disorder.

Dr. Coulter's "diagnosis" was also signed by J. F. Williams, the other court-appointed physician. The judge approved of the findings and ruled:

> Whereas, Carrie E. Buck, who is suspected of being feebleminded or epileptic, was this day brought before us, C. D. Shackleford, Justice of said county, and J. C. Coulter and J. F. Williams, two physicians . . . constituting a commission to inquire whether the said Carrie E. Buck be feebleminded or epileptic and a suitable subject for an institution for the care, training, and treatment of feebleminded and epileptic persons; and whereas the Justice has read the warrant and fully explained the nature of the proceedings to the said suspected person, and we, the said physicians, have in the presence (as far as practicable) of said Justice, by personal examination of said Carrie E. Buck . . . satisfied ourselves as to the mental condition of the said Carrie E. Buck, we do decide that the said Carrie E. Buck is feebleminded, or epileptic, and ought to be confined in an institution for the feebleminded, or epileptic.

The judge ordered Carrie delivered to the superintendent of the Colony for Epileptics and Feeble-Minded, the same order he had given for Carrie's mother only three years earlier.

Despite the judge's order, Carrie was not immediately delivered to the colony because, according to Superintendent Dr. Albert S. Priddy in a March 14, 1924, letter, it was "a rule to positively refuse admission of any expectant mothers to the Colony." Instead, Carrie remained with the Dobbses until she delivered her baby, Vivian Elaine.

What of the newborn infant? The superintendent wrote, "Should this child be ascertained to be feebleminded we will receive it here. However, the law puts a limit of eight years in feebleminded cases and we could not take it until it is eight years of age." The Dobbses agreed to keep and care for Vivian upon Carrie's departure (perhaps a tacit admission of their nephew's role in fathering the child), but Caroline Wilhelm, a social worker assigned to handle Carrie's case, noted in a letter to the superintendent of the colony that it was only "with the understanding that it will be committed later on if it is found to be feebleminded also."

Thus, almost immediately after delivering her daughter, Carrie was stripped of her baby and shipped off to the institution, arriving June 4, 1924.

The Case for Eugenics

The State Colony for Epileptics and Feeble-Minded was founded in 1910, when state senator Aubrey Strode led a movement to build an institution to care for Virginia's epileptics and was granted a charter by the state of Virginia. This charter appointed a Special Board of Directors to govern the colony, one of whom was Irving P. Whitehead, a man who had been friends with Strode since they grew up on neighboring farms. The Special Board of Directors then selected Dr. Albert S. Priddy to act as the colony's superintendent.

Priddy began to issue official reports indicating concern over Virginia's continued ability to pay for the care of the colony's growing number of "defective" citizens, stating, "Of the known causes which contribute to the development and growth of epilepsy . . . bad heredity is the most potent, and with the unrestricted marriage and intermarriage of the insane, mentally defective, and epileptic, its increase is but natural and is thus to be reasonably accounted for."

Only a year later, Priddy reported, "It is reasonable to anticipate a rapid increase in epileptics and mental defectives, out of proportion to the normal increment of population, and to infer that the State of Virginia is rapidly accumulating a greater population of these defectives and dependents than her resources will permit the comfortable care and support of."

The solution, Priddy suggested, was "to give thought to the practicability of a law permitting the sterilization of inmates of our eleemosynary and penal institutions," and even more to the point, "it seems not importune to call the attention of our lawmakers to the consideration of legalized eugenics."

Priddy pressured the state government to take action, participating in studies with the Virginia Board of Charities and Corrections, reporting to the General Assembly and writing regular reports to the governor in which he drew connections between hereditary mental defects, prostitution, drunkenness, and various crimes and other problems caused by what he referred to as "nonproducing and shiftless persons, living on public and private charity."

It seems strange to the sensibilities of the modern reader, but eugenics as an organizing principle of society became increasingly popular in the early part of the twentieth century. Eugenics was the study of human heredity and genetic principles, primarily for the purpose of "improving" the human race by limiting the proliferation of the "defective" gene pools. In the first quarter of the twentieth century, there was a marked difference in eugenics schools of thought, typically divided between British and American eugenicists. British eugenicists (who coined the term for the "science," meaning "wellborn") believed in more "positive" measures to encourage people to improve family genetic makeup, while the explosion of American eugenicists focused on what is called the "negative" approach—promotion, advocacy, and creation of legislation to sterilize the "unfit."

Pennsylvania saw the first real attempt to create a law allowing the eugenic sterilization of "unfit" persons in 1905, but the law was vetoed by the governor, and not until 1907 did Indiana enact the first such statute. By the time Harry H. Laughlin published his *Model Eugenical Sterilization Law* for the Eugenics Records Office in 1914, proposing sterilization of "socially inadequate" people (the "feebleminded, insane, criminalistic, epileptic, inebriate, diseased, blind, deaf, deformed, and dependent"—including "orphans, ne'er-do-wells, tramps, the homeless, and paupers"), twelve states had sterilization laws in effect, and by 1930, twenty-seven states had started sterilization campaigns supported by statute.

Virginia was to become the laboratory for testing the legality of involuntary (eugenic) sterilization, Dr. Priddy would be the determined "scientist," and the unfortunate Carrie Buck was to be the hapless guinea pig.

Priddy was not alone in his quest for legally sanctioned eugenics. Aubrey Strode fought on Priddy's behalf in the state legislature. Strode recalled:

> Dr. A. S. Priddy, then superintendent of the Virginia State Colony for Epileptics and Feeble-Minded . . . came to me as counsel for the colony to convey the request of the State Hospital Board upon the prospect of having the legislature legally enact that inmates of State Institutions for the Epileptic, Feeble-Minded, and Insane might, after proper proceedings, be sterilized for eugenical purposes.
>
> In the several states in which the legality of similar enactments had been drawn in question in the courts, in every case that I could find, the acts had been declared unconstitutional on grounds as being class legislation, if confined in operation to patients in state institutions, as not affording due process of law, if the sterilizing was done without

proper previous notice and reasonable opportunity to defend against its need, and as depriving a person of the natural rights of procreation beyond the power of the state legally to take away.

So, reporting to the board, I added that several years before that I recalled when I was a member of the State Senate, Dr. Carrington, surgeon to the State Penitentiary, had come before the Committee on Public Institutions to suggest the advisability of legislation to allow the sterilization of selected prisoners, but got no favorable response in light of public sentiment on the subject.

Strode introduced five separate bills dealing with the treatment of the "feebleminded" in the 1916 session. One bill amended the earlier 1910 charter establishing the colony, allowing the superintendent and the board to "see that such moral, medical, and surgical treatment as they deem proper be given to colony patients in order to promote the objects for which the institution is provided." The change was worded carefully to allow eugenics-based treatment, as one of the charter's primary reasons for the establishment of the colony was for "the protection of society."

Though not as prominent as Priddy and Strode, Irving P. Whitehead was no less involved in advancing the implementation of eugenic sterilization. A member of the Special Board of Directors of the colony, Whitehead also served for several years with Priddy on the General Board of State Hospitals. Whitehead was particularly encouraged by the amendment secured by Strode to the colony's charter.

With a budget crisis to deal with, Virginia governor E. Lee Trinkle, working hand in hand with the General Board of State Hospitals, agreed it was time for legislators "to legalize under proper safeguards, the sterilization of insane, epileptic, and feebleminded persons . . . to relieve the institutions of their crowded conditions and in order that patients could leave the institutions, become producers, and not propagate their kind."

Priddy, as an outspoken member of the General Board of State Hospitals in favor of eugenics, was appointed by the governor to work with Strode—his longtime friend—to draft a bill.

Strode structured his proposed legislation for the Virginia General Assembly around Laughlin's *Model Eugenical Sterilization Law,* and the bill was signed into law as "an act to provide for sexual sterilization of inmates of state institutions in certain cases" in March of 1924.

The law affirmed that "heredity plays an important part in the transmission of insanity, idiocy, imbecility, epilepsy, and crime." Only two "no" votes were cast in the Assembly; the idea of eugenic sterilization was apparently repugnant to only a tiny minority.

The Test Case

All that remained was to test whether Strode had been able to craft a law that could successfully navigate treacherous legal waters without foundering upon the rocks and shoals of due process and equal protection. Previous attempts at similar laws had been found unconstitutional and were thus struck down for one of two reasons.

First, the right to have children was considered to be a fundamental right, falling under the general constitutional category of the individual's right to life and property. Because the sterilization laws were to impact upon, and even nullify, that right, previous laws had been stricken because they failed to provide for sufficient due-process protection. The people subject to those laws had no means—or right—to fight a sterilization decision, or to appeal that decision once it had been reached.

Second, earlier attempts at sterilization legislation were overturned because they were viewed as "class" legislation, laws that unfairly affected only a particular class or group of people and thus violated those individuals' constitutional rights to equal protection under the Fourteenth Amendment.

Strode was unconcerned about the due process issue; he was certain that the carefully crafted, multitiered hearing, review, and appeal process built into the Virginia act would satisfy any court. However, Strode was not nearly as certain that the act met the equal protection standard.

Strode told the colony's Board of Directors that, because the Virginia act specifically targeted institutionalized "feebleminded" persons, it could still be found to be unconstitutional. Because it did not require the sterilization of *all* persons found to be feebleminded, it could be argued that it violated the equal protection requirement. Strode recommended that although the act had been passed, the colony not perform any sterilizations until the law was reviewed, at least up to the level of the Virginia Court of Appeals, "and possibly the Supreme Court of the United States." He pointed out to the board that, were they to perform sterilizations only to have the Virginia act overturned as unconstitutional, Dr. Priddy, or any physician who performed the sterilizations, and the colony might be found liable.

The board, mindful of Strode's warning, agreed that it would be best to test the law. "I was instructed to take to court a test case," Strode said. "With the very active and with the helpful cooperation of . . . Priddy . . . this was done, having as the subject of the litigation Carrie Buck, a typical nineteen-year-old, feebleminded patient of the colony."

Carrie lived and worked in Ward FB9 of the colony. She had been given kitchen duty; she was responsible for preparing food, serving, and cleaning up after the majority of the other inmates in her ward. Typically, no sooner had one meal been served and consumed than it was time to clean up and prepare for the next meal.

Despite her backbreaking and near constant work in the kitchen, Carrie still managed to find time to locate and reconnect with her mother, who had lived in the colony since her commitment in 1920 (and where she would live until her death in 1944), and to dream, as she later put it, of "being free." Ironically, Carrie would instead lose even more of her freedom.

She had been legally designated "feebleminded." She had borne an illegitimate child who was also to be classified "feebleminded." Her mother was institutionalized and legally "feebleminded." Most importantly, she was under the control of the colony. Carrie Buck was the ideal test case, with a "provable" family history of feeblemindedness and a "proclivity" for childbearing, and the board, Priddy, and Strode saw in her the perfect opportunity.

Six months after Carrie's placement in the colony, Priddy appeared in front of the colony's Special Board of Directors, R. G. Shelton (who had been appointed as Carrie's guardian), Aubrey Strode, who was present as the attorney for the board, and Carrie herself. Priddy presented his opinion of Carrie Buck's condition:

> I have had Carrie Buck under observation and care in the colony since the date of her admission, June 4, 1924, and from psychological examination and the Stanford revision of the Binet-Simon mental test, I have ascertained that she is feebleminded of the lowest grade Moron class. Her mental age is nine years or of the average normal child at nine years, and her chronological age is eighteen years her last birthday. The sworn history of her case as shown in the depositions constituting a part of the commitment papers is that she is of unknown paternity, her mother, Emma Buck, is and has been for several years a feebleminded patient in the colony of low mental grade. According to the depositions Carrie Buck has had one illegitimate mentally defective child; she is a moral delinquent, but physically capable of earning her own living if protected against childbearing by sterilization. Otherwise she would have to remain under custody in an institution for mental defectives during the period of her childbearing potentiality covering thirty years. The history of all such cases in which mental defectiveness, insanity, and epilepsy develop in two generations of feebleminded persons is that the baneful effects of heredity will be shown in descendants of all future generations.

Priddy requested that he be allowed to eugenically sterilize Carrie. He claimed that he wanted to perform upon her "the simple and comparatively harmless operation of salpingectomy," the cutting and tying off of her fallopian tubes, so she "could leave the institution, enjoy her liberty and life, and become self-sustaining."

In response to questioning by Strode, Priddy insisted that it would be better both for Carrie and for society in general if she was rendered incapable of childbearing, citing "the teaching and experience of all authorities on mental defectiveness, sterpicultura, and heredity."

Carrie's appointed guardian, R. G. Shelton, conducted only a brief cross-examination of Priddy. He asked how Priddy could provide assurance that the operation would not be dangerous. Priddy responded that he had a great deal of experience operating on female patients and inmates of the institution for pelvic disease and that "the operation . . . is as harmless as any surgical operation can be."

Shelton asked if Carrie Buck could not be "restored to society" through some course of training at the colony. Priddy replied, "This would be an impossibility, as in her mental defectiveness, self-control, and moral conception are organically lacking and cannot be supplied by teaching or training, she being congenitally and incurably defective."

The remainder of Shelton's questioning merely reinforced Priddy's report, giving the doctor the opportunity to restate his opinion that Carrie could not be returned to society in any condition other than sterilized, and that unless she was sterilized, she would have to remain in the colony during the entire time she was capable of childbearing.

After Priddy concluded his testimony, only one other question was asked. Aubrey Strode stood, looked at Carrie Buck, who had remained silent throughout the proceeding, and asked, "Do you care to say anything about having this operation performed on you?"

Carrie sat quietly for a few minutes, then, deferring to those people she thought were looking out for her, said, "No, sir, I have not, it is up to my people."

It did not take the board long to issue a carefully worded decision on Carrie's fate, crafted to satisfy the new Virginia sterilization law:

This Special Board of Directors finds that the said Carrie Buck is a feebleminded inmate of this institution and by the laws of heredity is the probable parent of socially inadequate offspring, likewise afflicted, that she may be sexually sterilized without detriment to her general health, and that the welfare of the said Carrie Buck and of society will be promoted by such sterilization:

UPON CONSIDERATION WHEREOF, this said Special Board of Directors of the State Colony for Epileptics and Feeble-Minded hereby orders that the said petitioner, A. S. Priddy, superintendent of this institution, perform or have performed by Dr. J. H. Bell, a competent and capable physician, after not less than thirty days from the date of this order, the operation of salpingectomy upon the said Carrie Buck.

In short, Carrie Buck was to have her fallopian tubes cut and tied off, thereby preventing her from ever conceiving another child.

This order of the Special Board of Directors was not to be carried out, for Carrie was, after all, their test case. Special care had to be taken to ensure that she was afforded the substantial due process that Strode had earlier noted was lacking in previous sterilization laws enacted.

The Trial

Their plan required Carrie Buck to file an appeal, and for this, Carrie Buck needed a lawyer. Strode, who usually served as legal counsel for the colony and had drafted the law in the first place, was already representing Priddy, the board, and the colony, so he was not available. Carrie's guardian, R. G. Shelton, hired by the colony, was directed to choose "some competent lawyer" to represent her in her appeal.

Shelton chose Irving P. Whitehead, the same Irving P. Whitehead who served with Priddy on the General Board of State Hospitals; the same Irving P. Whitehead who served on the colony's Board of Directors, who had completely supported and authorized, and even attempted to persuade other board members to agree to, the use of eugenic sterilization in the colony; the same Irving P. Whitehead who was not only a professional associate of Priddy's, but was also a childhood friend and associate of Aubrey Strode's; the same Irving P. Whitehead who had helped Strode get a commission as a major in the JAG corps during World War I; the same Irving P. Whitehead who, only two months before Carrie Buck's institutionalization at the colony, dedicated a new building at the colony named in his honor; the same Irving Whitehead who, days before Carrie Buck's trial, would be recommended by Strode for a government post.

Whitehead's motivations for agreeing to "represent" Carrie Buck will most likely forever be lost in history. His representation may well have been choreographed so as to simply expedite the "test case" along its way. The one definite aspect of Whitehead's "efforts" on behalf of Carrie was his complete disregard of the hallowed duty a lawyer owes his client.

Carrie's appeal of the sterilization order, titled *Buck v. Priddy*, was heard in the Circuit Court of Amherst County, Virginia. Carrie Buck was present, along with her attorney, Irving Whitehead; Aubrey Strode appeared on behalf of Priddy and the colony.

Judge Bennett Gordon knew both Whitehead and Strode as local boys and as young lawyers practicing in Amherst. The judge first recognized Whitehead, whose grave request was merely that the presence of all parties, particularly of Carrie's guardian, Shelton, be noted on the record, which was done. Afterward, Whitehead yielded to Strode, who made two requests: that he be allowed to call his witnesses in an "order that would not be done normally," and that all the witnesses be excluded from the courtroom when not testifying, with the exception of Dr. DeJarnette, the superintendent of the Western State Hospital at Staunton, Virginia.

With those formalities completed, Carrie's case began. There were no opening statements; the trial went directly into testimony from witnesses. It was the morning of November 18, 1924.

The first witness to take the stand was Mrs. Anne Harris, a nurse from Charlottesville. Strode sought to elicit testimony that would paint a picture of the Buck family as poverty-stricken, sexually promiscuous, and generally feebleminded; Mrs. Harris complied. She testified that Emma Buck, Carrie's mother, was "absolutely irresponsible" and "on the charity list for a number of years . . . that she was living in the worst neighborhoods, and that she was not able to, or would not, work and support her children."

Prompted by Strode, Harris also claimed that Emma continued to have children—though no longer living with her husband—and that there was "no question of them being her husband's." Finally, Strode suggested that the family might be called "feebleminded." Harris readily agreed, claiming she believed Emma Buck to have "the mentality of a child of twelve" and "the children less than that."

After Strode finished, Whitehead stood to begin his cross-examination. However, his questions seemed less like a cross-examination and more like a continuation, clarification, and embellishment of Strode's direct examination.

Whitehead clarified that Harris believed Carrie was illegitimate. He elicited from Harris the admission that she had not observed Carrie Buck at all during the many years since Carrie was placed with the Dobbses, but he then allowed her to tell a story about Carrie passing notes in school to boys, something Harris said showed Carrie should have been sent off to a stricter private school or institution where she could not engage in such activities.

WHITEHEAD: So far as you know, you know nothing about her after the Dobbses took her?

HARRIS: Except one time when she was in school, in the grammar grade. The superintendent called me and said she was having trouble with Carrie. She told me that Carrie was writing notes, and that sort of thing, and asked what she could do about it.

WHITEHEAD: Writing notes to boys, I suppose?

HARRIS: Yes, sir.

WHITEHEAD: Is writing notes to boys in school, nine or ten years old, considered antisocial?

HARRIS: It depends on the character of the note.

WHITEHEAD: Did you see the notes?

HARRIS: Yes, sir.

WHITEHEAD: Well, if the note is not altogether proper, is it evidence of antisocial—

HARRIS: [Interrupting] For a child ten years old to write the notes she was writing, I should say so.

WHITEHEAD: Suppose the child had been sixteen years old, would it have been regarded as antisocial for writing that class of notes?

HARRIS: I should say so, assuredly.

WHITEHEAD: Well, then, there is nothing in the age of the child—I mean the actual age—I ask you, if the child had been sixteen years old, would it still have been antisocial?

HARRIS: Well, if a girl of sixteen had written that kind of note, she ought to have been sent to Parnell—Isle of Hope.

Strode next called a series of three schoolteachers to emphasize the "feebleminded" aspect of his classification of the Bucks. None of the teachers called, however, had any firsthand knowledge of Carrie.

He first called Eula Wood, who testified about Doris Buck, Carrie's half sister. Wood testified that she actually knew little about Doris, having had her for only six weeks in her class. At Strode's prompting, however, Wood testified she had "heard right much" about Doris—namely, that she had been held back in school—and that she wouldn't call Doris a bright child, but instead "would call [Doris] dull in her books."

Whitehead did not cross-examine the witness, although he said he might "later, if [he] so desired."

The next teacher, Virginia Beard, testified about Roy Smith, Carrie's half brother. She claimed that "he tried to be funny" and that his schoolwork was "below the grade of other boys of his age in school." She concluded by saying she didn't know if she could consider him "weak-minded."

Whitehead stood up to begin his cross-examination, then repeated many of Strode's questions.

The last teacher to testify, Virginia Landis, was questioned regarding George Dudley, a cousin of Carrie Buck's. Landis immediately responded that she didn't know anything about Carrie Buck (not even that George was Carrie's cousin). However, she described George as "a dull child" and "below the average." Whitehead's cross was only one question, the answer to which remained the same: "I don't know Carrie Buck at all."

Strode next called Albemarle County Home superintendent John Hopkins, for information on Carrie's half bother, Roy. Hopkins described Roy as "rather an unusual boy," "right peculiar," "mentally defective," and "foolish."

Whitehead, supposedly representing Carrie Buck's interests, failed to note that Hopkins's opinion that Roy was mentally defective was based upon one incidental encounter on the street; failed to point out that Hopkins didn't know Carrie or Emma Buck; and didn't note for the record that every person Strode asked Hopkins to describe was "right peculiar."

Strode next called Samuel Dudley to the witness stand. Dudley, a neighbor of various Buck family members, was asked to comment on Carrie's grandfather Richard Harlow; unlike most of the witnesses called by Strode, Dudley didn't stick with the "Bucks are feebleminded" line.

When asked by Strode for his opinion of Richard Harlow's intelligence, Dudley described him as having "just as good ordinary sense as the generality of people." Under pressure from Strode, he admitted that he had told one of the expert witnesses that Richard Harlow "had these peculiar ways." However, Dudley refused to back down from his original statement that Richard Harlow had not been "a thorough [*sic*] educated man" and that "he had some little joking ways sometimes, but outside of that he was all right." In a surprising turn of events, Whitehead's brief cross-examination revealed that Dudley was Carrie's great-uncle. The only thing Dudley had to say as to his great-niece was that he knew "they got her in with a family by the name of Dobbs." Other than that, he "never saw the child before."

Caroline Wilhelm, a social worker, was to prove the most damaging witness thus far. Her involvement began with the Dobbses' commitment of Carrie to the colony and Wilhelm's observation and opinion of Carrie and her child, Vivian.

Wilhelm carried many of the same prejudices against Carrie as the Dobbses, and these carried over into her testimony at the trial. She described Carrie as "a distinct liability" to society. After all, she felt that "[Carrie's] mother had three illegitimate children," and she believed "that Carrie would be very likely to have illegitimate children" as well. From her dealings with Carrie for the "few weeks between the time when the commission [for Carrie's commitment] was held" and when Carrie was sent to the colony, Wilhelm had decided that Carrie was "obviously feebleminded."

Wilhelm took a decisive stand on the intelligence of Carrie's baby, despite that Vivian was not quite eight months old at the time. Regarding Vivian, Wilhelm testified that "there is a look about it that is not quite normal," though she couldn't tell exactly what it was that was abnormal. Years later, it would prove to be untrue; school records show Vivian earned a place on the honor roll.

Whitehead's cross-examination of Wilhelm, while uncharacteristically long, further damaged Carrie's cause. He highlighted that Carrie had had an illegitimate child, and that Wilhelm had personally judged Carrie to be "feebleminded" because of that child and because "as a social worker [she] knew girls of that type." He also elicited testimony from Wilhelm that suggested Carrie was able to perform the type of work typical for a woman her age, but only under supervision. Finally, Whitehead summarized Wilhelm's testimony, simply asking for her agreement:

"Your idea is, while she would never become an asset, she would become less of a liability by sterilization, and your idea is that she could be turned over to somebody and under careful supervision be made self-supporting? Is that your idea?"

Wilhelm replied, "I think so, yes, sir."

Strode next called Mary Duke, another social worker from Charlottesville, who described Carrie's mother as "a charity case." She also testified that she had heard that Carrie was feebleminded, but admitted that she "never had any dealings with her." Somehow, despite never having had any dealings with Carrie, Duke had formed the opinion that Carrie "didn't seem to be a bright girl."

Whitehead lodged no objections with the court and chose not to cross-examine the witness.

Having presented the court with a detailed picture of the Buck family and their "defective" nature, Strode turned to sterilization, presenting it as the most effective and efficient means to maintain and control these "defectives." Strode intended to prove this with the testimony of Dr. J. S. DeJarnette, the superintendent of the Western State Hospital at

Staunton; Arthur H. Estabrook, one of the eminent American eugenicists of the day; and Dr. Priddy, the superintendent of the Virginia Colony.

Strode called DeJarnette to the stand first, intent on showing DeJarnette to be an experienced professional in the business of treating "defective" members of society. DeJarnette testified he had been connected with the hospital in Staunton, the largest in the state, for thirty-six years, and that he had served as superintendent of that hospital since 1906. Strode also established that DeJarnette was a physician "specializing in insanity."

When Strode asked DeJarnette how many "mental defectives" he had treated, he was not disappointed with the answer: the doctor had "treated a little over eleven thousand patients." Strode asked DeJarnette's opinion of the effect of sterilization upon the welfare of the individual and upon society in general. DeJarnette dutifully answered that it was the best thing that could be done for them, "for the patient and for society." DeJarnette asserted that "feeblemindedness runs in families," and by allowing the sterilization of "mental defectives," society would benefit when "the standard of general intelligence would be lifted" and "it would lower the number of our criminals."

Finally, having heard the evidence that Carrie Buck, her mother, and her illegitimate child were all feebleminded, DeJarnette affirmed Strode's statement that Carrie was "the probable parent of socially inadequate offspring by the laws of heredity." Whitehead's cross-examination again seemed designed more to help Strode rather Carrie. He asked DeJarnette why those people the institutions sought to sterilize and release were not just kept in the institutions. DeJarnette answered:

It benefits society by not taking care of them, and by the work they do. They are hewers of wood and drawers of water, and there is not very much more likelihood that they would spread venereal disease if sterilized than if they were not. And then it is only for one generation, and the state is not able to pay for segregating them, and by having an in-and-out method, that is to take these feebleminded, put them in for a month or two, sterilize them and turn them out, you can get most of them sterilized, whereas the state would keep them all in.

Carrie's lawyer commented on the record that he agreed with DeJarnette, "that society would be benefited to that extent."

Strode successfully presented DeJarnette's testimony as scientific evidence of Carrie Buck's hereditary "defectiveness," but his next witness, the eminent eugenicist Arthur H. Estabrook, was just as crucial, as Strode hoped Estabrook's testimony would provide scientific validation of the necessity of sterilizing Carrie and "her kind."

As he had with DeJarnette, Strode began his examination of Estabrook with questions intended to demonstrate Estabrook's scientific experience and the validity of his testimony. Estabrook informed the court that he was a member of the Carnegie Institute of Washington, "a private organization conducting research along scientific lines." In particular, Estabrook was a member of a department "studying heredity in humans, animals, and plants," a position he had held since 1910, during which time he had carried on studies discovering "definite laws . . . covering inheritance of feeblemindedness."

Estabrook did not testify, however, that he was also an experienced fieldworker on behalf of the Eugenics Records Office (ERO). The Eugenics Records Office served a rather unusual purpose—besides recruiting members (such as Harry Laughlin, author of the *Model Sterilization Law*) who were vocal proponents of eugenics, and particularly of eugenic sterilization. It kept active fieldworkers who conducted research throughout the country and served as an unusual sort of library, with enormous listings of detailed information on family lineages, physical and personality traits, and mental and behavioral traits (among which the ERO included alcoholism and epilepsy), all researched and cataloged by those fieldworkers.

This library was accessible not only to American eugenicists and proponents, but also served as a consulting service for young couples on suitable marriage partners and other matters of family planning.

Estabrook was an important member of the ERO's research team, authoring seminal eugenics studies of two family lineages and the connection of those families to crime, "degeneracy," and "defectiveness": *The Jukes in 1915* (about a family in New York that he had studied due to the article of another eugenicist of the period, Robert Dugdale, entitled *The Jukes: A Study in Crime, Pauperism, Disease, and Heredity* and published in 1910) and *The Tribe of Ismael* (about a family in Indiana in 1923).

Estabrook testified much as though he were documenting another family lineage for the Eugenics Records Office catalog. He described his "field study" of Carrie's family. He explained that he had visited the colony and seen Carrie and her mother there and made a "brief study of the two," and that he had traveled to Albemarle County, where Carrie and her mother had lived years ago and "visited as many members of her family as possible." As a result of his "studies," Estabrook concluded:

The evidence points to the fact that Emma Buck is a feeble-minded woman. That she has had three feebleminded children by unknown fathers. The evidence further points, as gathered from my investigation in Albemarle County, that on the mother's side there are a sufficient number of cases of defective makeup, mentally, to lead me to conclude that the Dudley germ plasm, of which Emma Buck is a member, carries a defective strain in it.

As had DeJarnette, Estabrook stated that he believed "that by the laws of heredity" Carrie was feebleminded and "the probable parent of socially inadequate offspring likewise afflicted."

Whitehead's cross-examination, as with his examination of DeJarnette, appeared more a continuation of Strode's questioning than zealous questioning on behalf of Carrie. He asked if Carrie would be capable of earning a living if sterilized and returned to society. Estabrook answered that he believed she could "in the proper kind of home where somebody would be looking after her." Whitehead also prompted Estabrook to state that society would benefit "in that a feebleminded person, sterilized . . . would be able to maintain herself in a comparatively sufficient condition."

Strode saved perhaps his best, certainly his most passionate, witness for last. Although Dr. Priddy had become increasingly sick throughout the preparation for and the proceeding of the trial, he was dedicated to ensuring the sterilization bill he had originally asked Strode to draft became accepted law through this test case. The final day of testimony in the trial, Priddy came to court, but he was forced to walk slowly, capable of standing only with the assistance of a cane. His infirmity did not prevent Priddy from being the perfect witness for Strode. Priddy testified, much as he had before the Special Board of Directors of the colony, that Carrie Buck "was a highly proper case for the benefit of the Sterilization Act by study of her family history, personal examination of Carrie Buck, and subsequent observation since admission to the hospital." Referring to a notebook he had brought with him to the trial, Priddy reminded the court:

[Carrie] was eighteen years old on the second of last July, and according to the natural expectancy, if the purpose of the act chartering this institution are to be observed and carried out, that is to keep her under custody during her period of childbearing, she would have some thirty years of strict custody and care, under which she would receive only her board and clothes, would be denied all of the blessings of outdoor life and liberty, and be a burden on the state of

Virginia of about two hundred dollars a year for thirty years. Whereas if by the operation of sterilization, with the training she has got, she could go out, get a good home under supervision, earn good wages, and probably marry some man of her own level.

Priddy said this solution would enable her to be a "producer" and lead a happy and useful life. He also agreed with DeJarnette and Estabrook that Emma Buck, Carrie Buck, and Vivian Buck all were "feebleminded," and that if Carrie were to have any more children, the "laws of heredity" would guarantee the children would be "defective."

Priddy "absolutely" reaffirmed the guarantee that he had made at the sterilization petition hearing, that Carrie could be sterilized without detriment to her general health, and that such a sterilization would promote her welfare, would allow her to escape the custodial care of an institution, and would promote the welfare of society by removing "one potential source of an incalculable number of descendants who would be feebleminded."

Once again Whitehead's "cross-examination" effectively reinforced Priddy's point that if Carrie was sterilized, she would be capable of returning to society to work and care for herself, and Whitehead clarified the scope and procedure of the sterilizing operation itself.

After concluding the testimony of Dr. Priddy, Strode read into the record the deposition of Harry H. Laughlin, the eugenicist who had published the *Model Eugenical Sterilization Law* in 1914, which had served as Strode's model for his Virginia sterilization act. The deposition had been taken in New York, on November 6, 1924, less than two weeks before the trial began.

There is no evidence that Laughlin ever met Carrie Buck. Regardless, Laughlin's lengthy deposition supported the assertions that had been made by the other experts, doctors, and eugenicists. Laughlin testified that Carrie had a history of "social and economic inadequacy" and "a record during her life of immorality, prostitution, and untruthfulness." In language that was becoming all too familiar and had undoubtedly been provided by Dr. Priddy (who had requested by letter that Laughlin provide the deposition for the case), Laughlin agreed with DeJarnette, Estabrook, and Priddy that Carrie was "a potential parent of socially inadequate or defective offspring."

Strode called a total of eleven witnesses who alleged mental "defects" attributable to Carrie, her mother, her half brother and half sister, her child, and other family members. Two of the witnesses were doctors, superintendents of two of the four major mental institutions in Virginia, who provided cost-benefit analyses of sterilizing Carrie Buck, as well as their professional opinions on the "mental defectiveness" present in her family. Strode read into the record a deposition by another famed eugenicist that supported every diagnosis and benefit promised by the doctors in their testimony, sometimes using the exact same language.

Irving Whitehead, in his "defense" of Carrie Buck, called no witnesses. He did not argue with any of the glaring contradictions to be found in Carrie's commitment record. He did not argue that the Virginia sterilization law violated either the Virginia or the U.S. Constitution, though other states had struck down as unconstitutional similar sterilization laws.

Whitehead made no mention of *Williams v. Smith,* an Indiana case that had struck down a sterilization law similar to the Virginia act as unconstitutional because it was deemed not to provide adequate due process rights to the individual scheduled to be sterilized. Furthermore, Whitehead did not bring to the court's attention the precedent set in *Smith v. Board of Examiners of Feeble-Minded, Epileptics, etc.* that declared a New Jersey sterilization law unconstitutional because is applied only to feebleminded inmates of state institutions, an application that the court found to be in violation of the rights to equal protection under the law—the very precedent and argument about which Strode had been concerned! Although Whitehead indicated that he might object to the testimony of several witnesses, his objections, with the exception of an objection to the Laughlin deposition, which was overruled, never materialized.

Within weeks of the trial, the judge presiding over the case decided in favor of Virginia's sterilization law and affirmed the decision to sterilize Carrie Buck.

Priddy never had the opportunity to see his dream of legalized eugenic sterilization come to fruition; he died of Hodgkin's disease just weeks before the judge handed down his decision.

Priddy's assistant, Dr. J. H. Bell, took over as superintendent of the colony, and when the judge issued his decision a month after Priddy's death, it was to Bell that Strode directed his letter:

My dear Dr. Bell,

   Judge Gordon has delivered his opinion this week in the court at Amherst in the case of . . . *Buck v. A. S. Priddy, Superintendent,* sustaining the validity of the Virginia sterilization law and affirming the order of the board in that case.

   While I regret that Judge Gordon did not deliver a written opinion, nevertheless, of course, the result reached by him was satisfactory

374

and, by the appeal which will now be pressed, the constitutionality of the statute will be further tested.

In view of the death of Dr. Priddy, it will be necessary to substitute someone in his place as a party to the suit, and it seems to me that the case should now be carried on in your name as acting superintendent in the place and stead of Dr. A. S. Priddy. Please advise me whether this course is agreeable to you . . .

Bell answered, "If you are of the opinion that this case should . . . be carried on in my name, it is agreeable with me as I am in entire sympathy with the effort being made to reach a final conclusion as to the legality of this sterilization procedure."

With that, *Buck v. Priddy* became *Buck v. Bell.*

The First Appeal

The same month the judge in Amherst County announced his decision, Irving Whitehead, Carrie's attorney, appeared before the General Board of State Hospitals. The minutes note that Whitehead told the board that the county court had upheld the constitutionality of the Virginia law but promised that the matter would eventually be brought to the U.S. Supreme Court. In keeping with that promise, Whitehead submitted a petition to appeal the verdict of the Amherst County court in June of 1925.

Whitehead's petition raised the two constitutional issues that, much earlier, had been noted by Strode as potential weak points for eugenic sterilization laws—the deprivation of due process and the denial of equal protection, they being restricted to persons who were institutionalized as "epileptics" or "feebleminded." Whitehead also made the further point that the Virginia law legalizing eugenic sterilizations was unconstitutional because it violated the Eighth Amendment; that is, it inflicted a "cruel and unusual punishment."

Two of the three points Whitehead made in his petition, however, never appeared in the final brief he filed with the Virginia Supreme Court of Appeals in September 1925. Whitehead's brief focused entirely on the issue of due process of law. Furthermore, Whitehead's brief was a mere five pages long. He mentioned only two cases and cited only one as precedent, *Munn v. Illinois,* which he used only to provide a definition for "deprivation of life." He argued that the Virginia law created a system that unfairly required a person to submit to a surgical operation (which rendered that individual sterile) because the tribunal system for ordering the operation was nevertheless "made legal evidence by the statute" and was used as the mistaken and unfair basis for finding that society would benefit from carrying out Carrie's sterilization. Whitehead's brief ended with more of an accusation than a conclusion, when he claimed that if the Virginia law was found constitutional, "judicial trials are a farce and the courts have become mere executives to carry into effect the legislative sentence."

Strode's brief to the Virginia Supreme Court of Appeals was as different from Whitehead's brief as night is to day. First of all, Strode's appeal was forty-four pages long. Whitehead's introduction, discussion, and conclusion focused entirely on due process and an issue of hearsay at Carrie's trial; Strode's brief introduced the issues brought about by the trial, presented the facts regarding the procedure up to that point (from Carrie's commitment at the colony, through Priddy's sterilization petition, through both the board decision and the circuit court decision), and summarized the testimony of the expert witnesses, using extensive quotes. Where Whitehead's brief cited one case as a precedent, Strode's cited six cases in a section entitled "Court Decisions upon Similar Enactments" and countless other cases in his argument sections. Where Whitehead briefly addressed the due process issue, Strode presented first the argument that the Virginia law did not impose cruel and unusual punishment, second that the law did afford due process of law, and third that the act was a valid exercise of the police power granted to the states, focusing in particular on the right of the states to enact legislation to protect the public health and safety. With this intent in mind, Strode argued, the law did not deny anyone its equal protection. Whereas Whitehead railed against the "farcical" nature of the judicial trial, Strode noted simply that "with the policy, expediency, and wisdom of the act the courts have nothing to do," and that the court "should not serve to block the path of progress in the light of scientific advance toward a better day both for the afflicted and for society whose wards they are."

Not surprisingly, in November 1925, the Virginia Supreme Court of Appeals found Strode's arguments more convincing. Justice John West wrote the Virginia Supreme Court of Appeals opinion:

Carrie Buck complains of a judgment of the Circuit Court of Amherst County by which Dr. J. H. Bell, Superintendent of the State Colony for Epileptics and Feeble-Minded, was ordered to perform on her the operation of salpingectomy, for the purpose of rendering her sexually sterile.

On the 23rd day of January, 1924, Carrie Buck was adjudged to be feebleminded within the meaning of the Virginia statute, and committed to the State Colony for Epileptics and Feeble-Minded. On September 10, 1924, A. S. Priddy, then superintendent of the colony, presented to the Special Board of Directors his petition praying for an order that Carrie Buck be sexually sterilized by the surgical operation known as salpingectomy. The hearing was conducted strictly in accordance with the provisions of the statute, and, upon the evidence introduced before them, the board entered the order prayed for. From this order an appeal was taken by Carrie Buck and R. G. Shelton, her guardian and next friend, to the Circuit Court of Amherst County. Upon the record and evidence introduced at the trial in the circuit court, the judgment complained of was entered, from which this appeal was allowed.

These facts, among others, appear from the evidence:

The operation of salpingectomy is the cutting of the fallopian tubes between the ovaries and the womb, and the tying of the ends next to the womb. The ovaries are left intact and continue to function. The operation of vasectomy consists of cutting down of a small tube which runs from the testicle, without interference with the testicle. These operations do not impair the general health, or affect the mental or moral status of the patient, or interfere with his, or her, sexual desires or enjoyment. They simply prevent reproduction. In the hands of a skilled surgeon, they are 100 percent successful in results.

At the time Carrie Buck was committed to the State Colony for Epileptics and Feeble-Minded, she was seventeen years old and the mother of an illegitimate child of defective mentality. She had the mind of a child nine years old, and her mother had theretofore been committed to the same colony as a feebleminded person. Carrie Buck, by the laws of heredity, is the probable potential parent of socially inadequate offspring, likewise affected as she is. Unless sterilized by surgical operation, she must be kept in the custodial care of the colony for thirty years, until she is sterilized by nature, during which time she will be a charge upon the state. If sterilized under the law, she could be given her liberty and secure a good home, under supervision, without injury to society. Her welfare and that of society would be promoted by such sterilization.

The appellant contends that the judgment is void because the Virginia sterilization act is repugnant to the provisions of the state and federal Constitution in that—

(a) It does not provide due process of law

(b) It imposes a cruel and unusual punishment; and

(c) It denies the appellant and other inmates of the state colony the equal protection of the law.

1. An adjudication by an impartial tribunal vested with lawful

jurisdiction to hear and determine the questions involved, after reasonable notice to the parties interested and an opportunity for them to be heard, fulfills all the requirements of due process of law.

There is no controversy as to the legality or regularity of the proceedings by which appellant was adjudged to be feeble-minded and committed to the state colony.

The statute under review clearly vests the Special Board of Directors of the State Colony for Epileptics and Feeble-Minded, after notice according to law, with jurisdiction to hear and determine the prayer of any petition filed by the superintendent of the colony for the sexual sterilization of an inmate thereof.

In the instant case, the proceeding was strictly in conformity with the statute. The superintendent of the colony, having first served a copy of the petition and a notice of the time and place it would be presented on the inmate, her guardian, and her mother, her father being dead, presented to the Special Board of Directors of the colony his petition, stating the facts of the case and the grounds of his opinion, verified by his affidavit and praying that an order be entered by the board requiring him, or some other competent physician, to perform upon Carrie Buck the operation of salpingectomy. Upon a later day, fixed by the board, the board proceeded in the presence of the inmate, her guardian, and her attorney, to hear and consider the petition and evidence offered in support of and against the petition, and entered its final order, from which the inmate appealed to the circuit court and subsequently to this court.

The act complies with the requirements of due process of law.

2. The contention that the statute imposes cruel and unusual punishment cannot be sustained.

The act is not a penal statute. The purpose of the legislature was not to punish but to protect the class of socially inadequate citizens named therein from themselves, and to promote the welfare of society by mitigating race degeneracy and raising the average standard of intelligence of the people of the state.

The evidence shows that the operation, practically speaking, is harmless and 100 percent safe, and in most cases relieves the patient from further confinement in the colony.

In *State v. Feilin*, which was a criminal case, the court held that the operation of vasectomy was not a cruel punishment.

The constitutional prohibition against cruel and unusual punishment, Virginia Bill of Rights, section 9, has reference to such bodily punishments as involve torture and are inhumane and barbarous, and has no application to the case at bar.

3. Does the statute deny to appellant and other inmates of the state colony the equal protection of the law? This question must be answered in the negative.

It is not controverted that the state may, in proper cases, by due process of law, take into custody and deprive the insane, the feebleminded, and other defective citizens of the liberty which is otherwise guaranteed them by the Constitution.

The right to enact such laws rests in the police power, which the states did not surrender when they entered the federal union, and the exercise of that power the Virginia Constitution provides shall never be abridged.

Where the police power conflicts with the Constitution, the latter is supreme, but the courts will not restrain the exercise of such power, except where the conflict is clear and plain.

In *Jacobson v. Massachusetts,* the court, in sustaining a compulsory vaccination statute, said: "According to settled principles, the police power of a state must be held to embrace, at least, such reasonable regulations established and directed by legislative enactment as will protect the public health and the public safety. The defendant insists that his liberty is invaded when the state subjects him to fine or imprisonment for neglecting or refusing to submit to vaccination; that a compulsory vaccination law is unreasonable, arbitrary, and oppressive, and therefore hostile to the inherent right of every freeman to care for his own body and health in such way as to him seems best; and that the execution of such a law against one who objects to vaccination, no matter for what reason, is nothing short of an assault upon his person. But the liberty secured by the Constitution of the United States to every person within its jurisdiction does not import an absolute right in each person to be, at all times and in all circumstances, wholly freed from restraint. There are manifold restraints to which every person is necessarily subject for the common good."

In *Hayes v. Missouri,* Mr. Justice Field, speaking for the Court, said: "The Fourteenth Amendment to the Constitution of the United States does not prohibit legislation which is limited whether in the object to which it is directed, or by the territory within which it is to operate. It merely requires that all persons subjected to such legislation shall be treated alike, under like circumstances and conditions, both in the privileges conferred and in the liabilities imposed."

Disregarding other classes of mental defectives, upon whom the statute operates, the purpose of the act is to promote the welfare and prevent procreation by those who have been, or may hereafter be, judicially ascertained to be feebleminded and are inmates of the State Colony for Epileptics and Feeble-Minded. The status of a feebleminded person, who comes under the operation of the sterilization act, is not fixed until such patient, after judicial commitment to the colony, shall have undergone expert observation for at least two months and been subjected to the Binet Simon measuring scale of intelligence, or some other approved test of mentality, and found to be feebleminded.

Code, section 1078, designates those who have not been adjudged to be feebleminded as persons "supposed to be feeble-minded." The sterilization act has no reference to the latter class except in so far as they may be legally ascertained to belong to the former and are committed to the colony. It cannot be said, as contended, that the act divides a natural class of persons into two and arbitrarily provides different rules for the government of each. The two classes existed before the passage of the sterilization act. The female inmate, unlike the woman on the outside, was already deprived of the power of procreation by segregation, and must remain so confined until sterilized by nature, unless it is ascertained that her welfare and the welfare of society will be promoted by her sterilization under the act. There can be no discrimination against the inmates of the colony, since the woman on the outside, if in fact feebleminded, can, by the process of commitment and afterwards a sterilization hearing, be sterilized under the act.

Appellants rely upon *Smith v. Board of Examiners of Feeble-Minded, Epileptics, etc.* The New Jersey act provided for the sterilization of epileptics who were "inmates confined in the several charitable institutions in the counties and state." The Court held the act unconstitutional because the statute arbitrarily created two classes and applied the statutory remedy to that one of the classes to which it had the least application, and therefore denied Smith, who was an inmate of a charitable institution, the equal protection of the laws. The right to sterilize did not, as in Virginia, depend upon whether the welfare of the patient would be promoted by the operation. For the reasons given in discussion of the Virginia act, we decline to follow the New Jersey case.

We have found no case involving similar statutes where the Court has held that the state is without power to enact such laws, provided it be exercised through a statute which affords due process of law and equal protection of the laws to those affected by it.

For the foregoing reasons, we are of the opinion that the Virginia sterilization act is based upon a reasonable classification and is a valid enactment under the state and federal Constitutions.

Affirmed.

The "test case" was nearly complete, and the woman, whose freedom to conceive children hung in the balance, was nearly out of options. On December 7, 1925, less than a month after the Virginia Supreme Court of Appeals rendered its decision, the Special Board of the Colony met. Just as he had appeared before to report on the case after the trial court result, Whitehead appeared before the board, this time with Strode to accompany him to make a report on the status of the Carrie Buck case. The minutes of that Board meeting describe the report Whitehead and Strode gave:

Colonel Aubrey E. Strode and Mr. I. P. Whitehead appeared before the board and outlined the present status of the sterilization test case and presented conclusive argument for its prosecution through the Supreme Court of the United States, their advice being that this particular case was in admirable shape to go to the court of last resort, and that we could not hope to have a more favorable situation than this one.

Certain that the Virginia sterilization law would be upheld, Whitehead and Strode prepared for the final step of their "test case," an appearance before the U.S. Supreme Court. Whitehead filed the petition for certiorari, which the court accepted in 1926, and both Whitehead and Strode filed their briefs later that same year.

The U.S. Supreme Court Weighs In

Strode's performance echoed the thorough nature of his previous brief, though most of his argument, precedent, and form was repeated from that earlier effort. Whitehead's written motion, amazingly, increased more than three times in size to a "massive" eighteen pages. Whitehead again argued that Carrie had been denied substantive due process throughout the preliminaries authorizing her sterilization, but he also changed his approach, including another argument he had first mentioned in his original petition to be heard at the Virginia Supreme Court of Appeals but had never argued. Whitehead changed the main focus of his argument from the due process issue to the question of the individual's right to equal protection—the issue about which Strode had expressed concern to the colony years earlier.

In this argument, Whitehead maintained that a person's "full bodily integrity" was guaranteed under the Fourteenth Amendment, and that surgically preventing a person from exercising that integrity by removing the capability to have children was an unconstitutional intrusion upon that right. Unlike in his previous brief, Whitehead actually addressed Strode's argument directly, claiming that although the state should have the police power to protect the public health and safety, this power could not abridge or overwhelm personal liberties.

Whitehead's effort, although an improvement on his earlier performances, was too little, much too late. After the case was argued before the court in April of 1927, the Supreme Court of the United States returned its verdict on May 2. Justice Oliver Wendell Holmes wrote the opinion:

> This is a writ of error to review a judgment of the Supreme Court of Appeals of the State of Virginia, affirming a judgment of the Circuit Court of Amherst County, by which the defendant in error, the superintendent of the State Colony for Epileptics and Feeble-Minded, was ordered to perform the operation of salpingectomy upon Carrie Buck, the plaintiff in error, for the purpose of making her sterile. The case comes here upon the contention that the statute authorizing the judgment is void under the Fourteenth Amendment as denying to the plaintiff in error due process of law and the equal protection of the laws.
>
> Carrie Buck is a feebleminded white woman who was committed to the State Colony above mentioned in due form. She is the daughter of a feebleminded mother in the same institution, and the mother of an illegitimate feebleminded child. She was eighteen years old at the

time of the trial of her case in the circuit court in the latter part of 1924. An act of Virginia approved March 20, 1924, recites that the health of the patient and the welfare of society may be promoted in certain cases by the sterilization of mental defectives, under careful safeguard, etc.; that the sterilization may be effected in males by vasectomy and in females by salpingectomy, without serious pain or substantial danger to life; that the Commonwealth is supporting in various institutions many defective persons who if now discharged would become a menace but if incapable of procreating might be discharged with safety and become self-supporting with benefit to themselves and society; and that experience has shown that heredity plays an important part in the transmission of insanity, imbecility, etc. The statute that enacts that whatever the superintendent of certain institution including the abovenamed [*sic*] State Colony shall be of opinion that it is for the best interest of the patients and of society that an inmate under his care should be sexually sterilized, he may have the operation performed upon any patient afflicted with hereditary forms of insanity, imbecility, etc., on complying with the very careful provisions by which the act protects the patients from possible abuse.

The attack is not upon the procedure but upon the substantive law. It seems to be contended that in no circumstances could such an order have been justified. It certainly is contended that the order cannot be justified upon the existing grounds. The judgment finds the facts have been recited and that Carrie Buck "is the probable potential parent of socially inadequate offspring, likewise afflicted, that she may be sexually sterilized without detriment to her general health and that her welfare and that of society will be promoted by her sterilization," and thereupon makes the order. In view of the general declarations of the legislature and the specific findings of the Court obviously we cannot say as matter of law that the grounds do not exist, and if they exist they justify the result. We have seen more than once that the public welfare may call upon the best citizens for their lives. It would be strange if it could not call upon those who already sap the strength of the state for these lesser sacrifices, often not felt to be seen by those concerned, in order to prevent our being swamped with incompetence. It is better for all the world, if instead of waiting to execute degenerate offspring for crime, or to let them starve for their imbecility, society can prevent those who are manifestly unfit from continuing their kind. The principle that sustains compulsory vaccination is broad enough to cover cutting the fallopian tubes. Three generations of imbeciles are enough.

But, it is said, however it might be if this reasoning were applied generally, it fails when it is confined to the small number who are in the institutions named and is not applied to the multitudes outside. It is the usual last resort of constitutional arguments to point out shortcomings of this sort. But the answer is that the law does all that is needed when it does all that it can, indicates a policy, applies it to all within the lines, and seeks to bring within the lines all similarly situated so far and so fast as its means allow. Of course so far as the operations enable those who otherwise must be kept confined to be returned to the world, and thus open the asylum to others, the equality aimed at will be more nearly reached.

Judgment affirmed.

"Three generations of imbeciles are enough." With that infamous line, and by an eight to one vote of the Supreme Court, eugenic sterilization, embodied and legalized in state statute, was found constitutional. Justice Pierce Butler, the only Supreme Court justice to vote against the finding of constitutionality, did not even write a dissent to explain his vote.

Whitehead filed a petition with the Supreme Court for a rehearing, giving Carrie Buck a short reprieve from her inevitable sterilization order. The court reconvened in October 1927 and received the petition; the request was denied—not surprising considering the near unanimous verdict from only six months earlier—and Carrie's borrowed time ran out.

The Sterilization

Carrie Buck had served her purpose as the "test case," but there was little notice nationwide that the test was complete. A small article ran in the *New York Times,* and the local paper provided modest coverage. An unsigned postcard in Carrie's file at the colony, postmarked Madison Square Garden in New York City, May 4, 1927, was addressed to Dr. Bell. The anonymous sender wrote, "May God protect Miss Carrie Buck from Feeble-Minded justice." The words "from Feeble-Minded justice" were scratched through and "from injustice" added.

The appeals exhausted and Carrie's "purpose" served, the order that had been given by the Special Board of the Colony three years earlier was carried out. Carrie Buck was sterilized by Dr. Bell in the infirmary of the colony on October 19, 1927. Her medical record, annotated by Dr. Bell, indicated that she had an "uneventful recovery. No infection" and that she was "allowed up" again on November 3.

Carrie's sterilization went unnoticed beyond the walls of the colony; her Supreme Court decision, however, had an impact far beyond the Virginia border. States that had enacted sterilization laws prior to Virginia's began sterilizing people in ever-increasing numbers. Other states passed laws modeled on the Virginia law legitimized by *Buck v. Bell.* Eugenic sterilization in the United States continued for decades; by the late 1950s, nearly sixty thousand involuntary sterilizations had been reported nationwide. Virginia, the original testing ground of the laws, continued the practice until 1972 and is reported to have sterilized approximately eight thousand people, with more than half of those sterilizations performed at the colony from which Carrie so desperately wanted to be free.

The ripples felt in the United States as a result of the *Buck v. Bell* decision, while appalling, are dwarfed by their impact overseas—a tidal wave of legally supported and sanctioned involuntary eugenic sterilizations. On July 14, 1933, Germany passed a law based on the model sterilization law of Harry Laughlin—the same Harry Laughlin whose deposition testimony helped deprive Carrie of her right to have children; the same model sterilization law upon which Strode based his draft of the Virginia bill authorizing involuntary eugenic sterilization. The German law established government-appointed courts, eerily reminiscent of the tribunal that had institutionalized Carrie Buck in 1923; each was composed of two doctors and a judge. By the end of the first year of the new German law, more than fifty-six thousand people were involuntarily sterilized. Worst of all, *Buck v. Bell* was cited by the defendants at the Nuremberg war trials as the precedent for Nazi sterilization programs, programs under which an estimated two million people were classified as "defective" and sterilized in merely twelve years. From forced sterilization of "defectives," it was a short journey down the slippery slope to the crematoriums of the death camps, where hundreds of thousands of so-called mental defectives were murdered by the Nazis.

Shockingly, despite the unfairness of Carrie Buck's ordeal, despite the thousands of Americans who suffered as a result of the decision, despite the crimes committed by the Nazis citing the Supreme Court decision, *Buck v. Bell* has never been overturned.

The Supreme Court did strike down a law allowing the involuntary sterilization of criminals in *Skinner v. Oklahoma* in 1942. *Skinner,* much like the case involving Carrie Buck, was intended primarily as a test case for a 1935 Oklahoma law prescribing involuntary sexual sterilization for repeat criminals. Jack Skinner was a three-time felon, found guilty of stealing chickens while still in his teens and later convicted twice for armed robbery.

The opinion that struck down the Oklahoma criminal sterilization law focused on the unfairness of the categories to which that particular law applied. It observed that while a three-time thief might be sterilized, a person found guilty of embezzling three times could not. Because the court felt that there was no evidence that "the inheritability of criminal traits follows the neat legal distinctions which the law has marked between those two offenses," the law denied equal protection, an argument that had been made but dismissed in Carrie Buck's Supreme Court case, and was therefore unconstitutional.

Nevertheless, this decision had no effect upon the decision the Supreme Court had handed down previously in *Buck v. Bell*. The Supreme Court has never overturned or reversed its precedent allowing eugenic sterilization that focused not on criminals, but instead on the allegedly "feebleminded."

Freedom, Obscurity, and an Apology

Carrie, classified as "feebleminded" and involuntarily sterilized, was almost forgotten. Despite the promise in Dr. Priddy's testimony at Carrie's appeal before the Amherst County Circuit Court that she would be free to leave the colony following her sterilization, she was not. Instead, Carrie was "paroled" from the colony by Dr. Bell to the homes of families where she was to be a domestic servant. The families were asked to provide money to cover her travel by rail to their home, and they were required by Dr. Bell to pay her a minimal salary. They could, however, report on Carrie's "progress" and return her if they encountered any "problems."

Carrie remained with the first family to which she was assigned, the Colemans, for only a couple months, but her assignment to the Newberrys of Bland, Virginia, lasted several years. In her regular letters to Bell, Mrs. Newberry described Carrie as a hard worker and said she was "getting on well." However, after meeting Carrie, Mrs. Newberry did wonder why Carrie had been institutionalized at the colony in the first place. Bell's answer was deceptively simple: "[She] was committed here on account of being feebleminded."

Strangely, Carrie, the supposedly feebleminded young woman, also corresponded regularly with Bell. She wrote primarily to ask about her mother, to tell how she was faring, and to inquire as to her permanent discharge from the colony. Finally, by the spring of 1933, Carrie's letters show that she was freeing herself from the colony's hold. She wrote Bell that she had married William Eagle on May 14. Her marriage guaranteed her discharge from the colony—at long last, her escape from "probation."

Dearest Dr. Bell,

Will answer your letter which I received yesterday, will send you a negative of my husband and myself. When you finish with it, I would like for it to be sent back to me as it is the only one I have of him and myself. I am thinking about having it enlarged and some more taken from it to send my mother and Dorris [*sic*], so please return it if possible.

I am getting along just fine.

My husband and I both joined the Methodist Church last Saturday and going to Sunday school and preaching both every Sunday unless we are both sick. We sure are having some windy weather here. We have made some garden, have onions and lettuce planted. We have cabbage, tomatoes and pepper seed planted and they are up and believe me, I will be glad when summer comes and I can caned [*sic*] a few things to eat and have plenty. Tell mother when my garden comes in [I] will send her some things to eat and also a few clothes.

With best wishes to you and Mrs. Bell.

She signed the letter, "A friend, Carrie."

Carrie Buck, now Carrie Eagle, lived with her husband in Bland, Virginia, until 1941. Although he was many years her senior when they married (Carrie was twenty-six, William a sixty-three-year-old widower), they lived a quiet and apparently happy life, even through the difficult years of the Depression. William Eagle was well thought of in the community, and he held a number of municipal employments throughout that time, including jailer, game warden, constable, and town sergeant, though when times were tight for their family, he frequently took carpentry work where he could get it. Carrie tended to the house and their garden. Carrie and William, as she indicated in her letters, attended church regularly, and Carrie once again sang in the choir, just as she had as a young girl. Carrie wrote several more times to Bell (and his successor, Dr. J. B. Arnold), usually to inquire as to the health of her mother. Unfortunately, William Eagle died in 1941, and Carrie moved, once again alone, to Front Royal, Virginia.

In Front Royal, the happier life Carrie had ironically found in Bland slowly gave way over a number of years of difficult labor. Carrie worked a number of different jobs, from "keeping house" for others (reminiscent of her domestic duties at first the Dobbses', then the colony, then during her "probation") to washing dishes in restaurants to, as she reported to a social worker one year, "migrant worker."

Despite the difficulty of her life in Front Royal, Carrie met an orchard worker, Charles Albert Detamore, and they were married on April 25, 1965; Carrie was fifty-eight, Charles was sixty-one.

By 1970, Carrie's health had begun to deteriorate. She and her husband moved to Charlottesville, to return to the town Carrie considered home. Carrie and Charles lived in a single-room cinder-block shed without plumbing, provided to them rent-free by the owner. The Detamores lived in abject poverty for ten years until, in 1980, Carrie was finally hospitalized for exposure and malnutrition. After her hospitalization, Carrie made a partial recovery, and she and her husband were taken to the state-operated District Home in Waynesboro, Virginia. Carrie lived in the home for only three years. She died on January 28, 1983, at the age of seventy-six. Her body, which had never been entirely her own, was returned to Charlottesville, where she was buried in the same graveyard, but on the opposite side of a hill, as the daughter she never had the chance to know. Vivian, Carrie's only offspring, had died of measles in 1933; she was only eight.

What, then, is the legacy of Carrie Buck? Through no fault or choice of her own, Carrie had no family to remember her. Her name is attached not to successive generations of people carrying her genes within them, but instead to a terrible precedent still awaiting reversal. Carrie seemed to realize this late in life when she remarked to two visiting reporters only three years before she died, "They done me wrong. They done us all wrong."

Only recently has Virginia realized and admitted the harm done to Carrie and to the thousands like her who were involuntarily sterilized. In January 2002, the Virginia General Assembly—the political body that in 1924 passed the sterilization law in Virginia—passed a resolution expressing "its profound regret" over its involvement in the development of the legalization of eugenic sterilization laws.

The joint house resolution read:

Honoring the Memory of Carrie Buck.

WHEREAS, in 1924 Virginia passed two eugenics-related laws, the second of which permitted involuntary sterilization, the most egregious outcome of the lamentable eugenics movement in the Commonwealth; and

WHEREAS, under this act, those labeled "feebleminded," including the "insane, idiotic, imbecile, feebleminded, or epileptic" could be involuntarily sterilized, so that they would not produce similarly disabled offspring; and

WHEREAS, May 2, 2002, is the seventy-fifth anniversary of the United States Supreme Court decision in the case of *Buck v. Bell,* in which Virginia's 1924 Eugenical Sterilization Act was allowed to stand; and

WHEREAS, following the *Buck* decision, an estimated sixty thousand Americans, including about eight thousand in Virginia, were sterilized under similar state laws, and the decision was applauded by German eugenicists who supported comparable legislation early in the Nazi regime; and

WHEREAS, in 1927 Carrie Buck, a poor and unwed teenage mother from Charlottesville, was the first person sterilized under the provision of the 1924 law; and

WHEREAS, subsequent scholarship has demonstrated that the Sterilization Act was based on the now-discredited and false science of eugenics; and

WHEREAS, legal and historical scholarship analyzing the *Buck* decision has condemned it as an embodiment of bigotry against the disabled and an example of the use of faulty science in support of public policy; and

WHEREAS, that scholarship has also pointed out the fallacies contained in the *Buck* opinion, noting, among other points, that Carrie Buck's daughter, Vivian, the supposed third-generation "imbecile," later won a place on her school's honor roll; and

WHEREAS, the General Assembly in 2001 expressed its "profound regret" over the Commonwealth's role in the eugenics movement in this country and over the damage done in the name of eugenics; now, therefore, be it

RESOLVED by the House of Delegates, the Senate concurring, That the General Assembly honor the memory of Carrie Buck on the occasion of the seventy-fifth anniversary of the *Buck v. Bell* Supreme Court decision.

On May 2, 2002, the seventy-fifth anniversary of the decision in *Buck v. Bell,* the governor of Virginia issued a statement offering "the Commonwealth's sincere apology for Virginia's participation in eugenics." The statement was read at a ceremony dedicating the erection of a new highway marker in Charlottesville, Virginia, honoring Carrie Buck. The text of the marker, unfortunately, reads more like an explanation than an apology:

In 1924, Virginia, like a majority of states then, enacted eugenic sterilization laws. Virginia's law allowed state institutions to operate on individuals to prevent the conception of what were believed to be "genetically inferior" children. Charlottesville native Carrie Buck (1906–1983), involuntarily committed to a state facility near Lynchburg, was chosen as the first person to be sterilized under the new law. The U.S. Supreme Court, in *Buck v. Bell,* 2 May 1927, affirmed the Virginia law. After Buck, more than 8,000 other Virginians were sterilized before the most relevant parts of the act were repealed in 1974. Later evidence eventually showed that Buck and many others had no "hereditary defects." She is buried south of here.

Carrie, however, would probably have appreciated the gesture, or at the very least not have minded its dry, dispassionate tone had she lived to see it. Trusting, seeing the best in the intentions of others, and forgiving came naturally to Carrie Buck, who, although recognizing that she had been "done wrong," and admitting that she had thought about the sterilization forced upon her and would have liked to have had more children, told reporters only three years before her death that she was not bitter. Trying to understand, the reporters asked her to explain.

In her answer, it was possible to hear echoes from fifty years past, of the young woman who answered trustingly, "it is up to my people," not knowing nobody was watching out for her; of the Carrie who had sat quietly through her commitment hearing and her appeals, trusting, believing that things would come out for the best; of the former inmate who had written to the man who had sterilized her and signed her letters, "A friend."

Carrie told the reporters, "I tried helping everybody all my life, and I tried to be good to everybody. It just don't do no good to hold grudges."

Index